Computational Bayesian Statistics

An Introduction

Meaningful use of advanced Bayesian methods requires a good understanding of the fundamentals. This engaging book explains the ideas that underpin the construction and analysis of Bayesian models, with particular focus on computational methods and schemes. The unique features of the text are the extensive discussion of available software packages combined with a brief but complete and mathematically rigorous introduction to Bayesian inference. The text introduces Monte Carlo methods, Markov chain Monte Carlo methods, and Bayesian software, with additional material on model validation and comparison, transdimensional MCMC, and conditionally Gaussian models. The inclusion of problems makes the book suitable as a textbook for a first graduate-level course in Bayesian computation with a focus on Monte Carlo methods. The extensive discussion of Bayesian software – R/R-INLA, OpenBUGS, JAGS, STAN, and BayesX – makes it useful also for researchers and graduate students from beyond statistics.

MARIA ANTÓNIA AMARAL TURKMAN was, until 2013, a full professor in the Department of Statistics and Operations Research, Faculty of Sciences, University of Lisbon. Though retired from the university, she is still a member of its Centre of Statistics and Applications, where she held the position of scientific coordinator until 2017. Her research interests are Bayesian statistics, medical and environmental statistics, and spatiotemporal modeling, with recent publications on computational methods in Bayesian statistics, with an emphasis on applications in health and forest fires. She has served as vice president of the Portuguese Statistical Society. She has taught courses on Bayesian statistics and computational statistics, among many others.

CARLOS DANIEL PAULINO is a senior academic researcher in the Center of Statistics and Applications and was an associate professor with habilitation in the Department of Mathematics of the Instituto Superior Técnico, both at the University of Lisbon. He has published frequently on Bayesian statistics and categorical data, with emphasis on applications in biostatistics. He has served as president of the Portuguese Statistical Society. He has taught many undergraduate and graduate-level courses, notably in mathematical statistics and Bayesian statistics.

PETER MÜLLER is a professor in the Department of Mathematics and the Department of Statistics & Data Science at the University of Texas at Austin. He has published widely on computational methods in Bayesian statistics, nonparametric Bayesian statistics, and decision problems, with emphasis on applications in biostatistics and bioinformatics. He has served as president of the International Society for Bayesian Analysis and as chair for the Section on Bayesian Statistics of the American Statistical Association. Besides many graduate-level courses, he has taught short courses on Bayesian biostatistics, Bayesian clinical trial design, nonparametric Bayesian inference, medical decision-making, and more.

INSTITUTE OF MATHEMATICAL STATISTICS
TEXTBOOKS

IMS Textbooks give introductory accounts of topics of current concern suitable for advanced courses at master's level, for doctoral students and for individual study. They are typically shorter than a fully developed textbook, often arising from material created for a topical course. Lengths of 100–290 pages are envisaged. The books typically contain exercises.

In collaboration with the International Society for Bayesian Analysis (ISBA), selected volumes in the IMS Textbooks series carry the "with ISBA" designation at the recommendation of the ISBA editorial representative.

Other Books in the Series (*with ISBA)

Computational Bayesian Statistics

An Introduction

Maria Antónia Amaral Turkman
University of Lisbon

Carlos Daniel Paulino
University of Lisbon

Peter Müller
University of Texas, Austin

CAMBRIDGE
UNIVERSITY PRESS

University Printing House, Cambridge CB2 8BS, United Kingdom

One Liberty Plaza, 20th Floor, New York, NY 10006, USA

477 Williamstown Road, Port Melbourne, VIC 3207, Australia

314–321, 3rd Floor, Plot 3, Splendor Forum, Jasola District Centre,
New Delhi – 110025, India

79 Anson Road, #06-04/06, Singapore 079906

Cambridge University Press is part of the University of Cambridge.

It furthers the University's mission by disseminating knowledge in the pursuit of
education, learning, and research at the highest international
levels of excellence.

www.cambridge.org
Information on this title: www.cambridge.org/9781108481038
DOI: 10.1017/9781108646185

First published 2019

Printed and bound in Great Britain by Clays Ltd, Elcograf S.p.A.

A catalogue record for this publication is available from the British Library .

ISBN 978-1-108-48103-8 Hardback
ISBN 978-1-108-70374-1 Paperback

Additional resources for this publication at www.cambridge.org/9781108481038

Contents

Preface to the English Version

This book is based on lecture notes for a short course that was given at the *XXII Congresso da Sociedade Portuguesa de Estatística*. In the translation from the original Portuguese text we have added some additional material on sequential Monte Carlo, Hamiltonian Monte Carlo, transdimensional Markov chain Monte Carlo (MCMC), and variational Bayes, and we have introduced problem sets. The inclusion of problems makes the book suitable as a textbook for a first graduate-level class in Bayesian computation with a focus on Monte Carlo methods. The extensive discussion of Bayesian software makes it useful also for researchers and graduate students from beyond statistics.

The core of the text lies in Chapters 4, 6, and 9 on Monte Carlo methods, MCMC methods, and Bayesian software. Chapters 5, 7, and 8 include additional material on model validation and comparison, transdimensional MCMC, and conditionally Gaussian models. Chapters 1 through 3 introduce the basics of Bayesian inference, and could be covered fairly quickly by way of introduction; these chapters are intended primarily for review and to introduce notation and terminology. For a more in-depth introduction we recommend the textbooks by Carlin and Louis (2009), Christensen et al (2011), Gelman et al (2014a) or Hoff (2009).

Preface

In 1975, Dennis Lindley wrote an article in *Advances in Applied Probability* titled "The future of statistics: a Bayesian 21st century," predicting for the twenty-first century the predominance of the Bayesian approach to inference in statistics. Today one can certainly say that Dennis Lindley was right in his prediction, but not exactly in the reasons he gave. He did not foresee that the critical ingredient would be great advances in computational Bayesian statistics made in the last decade of the twentieth century. The "Bayesian solution" for inference problems is highly attractive, especially with respect to interpretability of the inference results. However, in practice, the derivation of such solutions involves in particular the evaluation of integrals, in most cases multi-dimensional, that are difficult or impossible to tackle without simulation. The development of more or less sophisticated computational methods has completely changed the outlook. Today, Bayesian methods are used to solve problems in practically all areas of science, especially when the processes being modeled are extremely complex. However, Bayesian methods can not be applied blindly. Despite the existence of many software packages for Bayesian analysis, it is critical that investigators understand what these programs output and why.

The aim of this text, associated with a minicourse given at the *XXII Congresso da Sociedade Portuguesa de Estatística*, is to present the fundamental ideas that underlie the construction and analysis of Bayesian models, with particular focus on computational methods and schemes.

We start in Chapter 1 with a brief summary of the foundations of Bayesian inference with an emphasis on the principal differences between the classical and Bayesian paradigms. One of the main pillars of Bayesian inference, the specification of prior information, is unfortunately often ignored in applications. We review its essential aspects in Chapter 2. In Chapter 3, analytically solveable examples are used to illustrate the Bayesian solution to statistical inference problems. The "great idea" behind the development of computational Bayesian statistics is the recognition that Bayesian infer-

ix

ence can be implemented by way of simulation from the posterior distribution. Classical Monte Carlo methods are presented in Chapter 4 as a first solution for computational problems. Model validation is a very important question, with its own set of concepts and issues in the Bayesian context. The most widely used methods to assess, select, and compare models are briefly reviewed in Chapter 5.

Problems that are more complex than the basic ones in Chapter 4 require the use of more sophisticated simulation methods, in particular Markov chain Monte Carlo (MCMC) methods. These are introduced in Chapter 6, starting as simply as possible. Another alternative to simulation is the use of posterior approximations, which is reviewed in Chapter 8. The chapter describes, in a generic fashion, the use of integrated nested Laplace approximation (INLA), which allows for substantial improvements in both computation times (by several factors), and in the precision of the reported inference summaries. Although applicable in a large class of problems, the method is more restrictive than stochastic simulation. Finally, Chapter 9 is dedicated to Bayesian software. The possibility of resorting to MCMC methods for posterior simulation underpins the development of the software BUGS, which allows the use of Bayesian inference in a large variety of problems across many areas of science. Rapid advances in technology in general have changed the paradigm of statistics, with the increasing need to deal with massive data sets ("Big Data"), often of spatial and temporal types. As a consequence, posterior simulation in problems with complex and high-dimensional data has become a new challenge, which gives rise to new and better computational methods and the development of software that can overcome the earlier limitations of BUGS and its successors, Win-BUGS and OpenBUGS. In Chapter 9 we review other statistics packages that implement MCMC methods and variations, such as JAGS, Stan, and BayesX. This chapter also includes a brief description of the R package R-INLA, which implements INLA.

For the compilation of this text we heavily relied on the book *Estatística Bayesiana* by Paulino, A. Turkman, and Murteira, published by Fundação Calouste Gulbenkian in 2003. As all copies of this book were sold a long while ago, we also extensively used preliminary work for an upcoming second edition, as well as material that we published in the October 2013 edition of the bulletin of the Sociedade Portuguesa de Estatística (SPE).

This text would not have been completed in its current form without the valuable and unfailing support of our dear friend and colleague Giovani Silva. We owe him sincere thanks. We are also thankful to the Sociedade Portuguesa de Estatística for having proposed the wider theme of Bayesian statistics and for the opportunity to give a minicourse at the 22nd conference of the society. We also acknowledge the institutional support from the Universidade de Lisboa through the Centro de Estatística e Aplicações (PEst-OE/MAT/UI0006/2014, UID/MAT/00006/2013), in the Department of Statistics and Operations Research in the Faculdade de Ciências and of the Department of Mathematics in the Instituto Superior Técnico. We would like to acknowledge that the partial support by the Funda cão para a Ciência e Tecnologia through various projects over many years enabled us to build up this expertise in Bayesian statistics.

Finally, we would like to dedicate this book to Professor Bento Murteira to whom the development of Bayesian statistics in Portugal owes a lot. In fact, Chapter 1 in this book reflects in many ways the flavor of his writings.

1

Bayesian Inference

Before discussing Bayesian inference, we recall the fundamental problem of statistics: "The fundamental problem towards which the study of Statistics is addressed is that of inference. Some data are observed and we wish to make statements, inferences, about one or more unknown features of the physical system which gave rise to these data" (O'Hagan, 2010). Upon more careful consideration of the foundations of statistics we find many different schools of thought. Even leaving aside those that are collectively known as classical statistics, this leaves several choices: objective and subjective Bayes, fiducialist inference, likelihood based methods, and more.[1]

This diversity is not unexpected! Deriving the desired inference on parameters and models from the data is a problem of induction, which is one of the most controversial problems in philosophy. Each school of thought follows its own principles and methods to lead to statistical inference. Berger (1984) describes this as: "Statistics needs a: 'foundation', by which I mean a framework of analysis within which any statistical investigation can theoretically be planned, performed, and meaningfully evaluated. The words 'any' and 'theoretically' are key, in that the framework should apply to any situation but may only theoretically be implementable. Practical difficulties or time limitations may prevent complete (or even partial) utilisation of such framework, but the direction in which 'truth' could be found would at least be known". The foundations of Bayesian inference are better understood when seen in contrast to those of its mainstream competitor, classical inference.

[1] Subjective Bayes is essentially the subject of this volume. In addition to these schools of thought, there are even half-Bayesians who accept the use of a priori information but believe that probability calculus is inadequate to combine prior information with data, which should instead be replaced by a notion of causal inference.

1.1 The Classical Paradigm

Classical statistics seeks to make inference about a population starting from a sample. Let x (or $x = (x_1, x_2, \ldots, x_n)$, where n is a sample size,) denote the data. The set $\mathcal{X}$ of possible samples x is known as the sample space, usually $\mathcal{X} \subseteq \mathbb{R}^n$. Underlying classical inference is the recognition of variability across samples, keeping in mind that the observed data are only one of many – possibly infinitely many – data sets that could have been observed. The interpretation of the data depends not only on the observed data, but also on the assumptions put forward about the process generating the observable data. As a consequence, the data are treated as a realization of a random variable or a random vector X with a distribution F_θ, which of course is not entirely known. However, there is usually some knowledge (theoretical considerations, experimental evidence, etc.) about the nature of the chance experiment under consideration that allow one to conjecture that F_θ is a member of a family of distributions $\mathcal{F}$. This family of distributions becomes the statistical model for X. The assumption of a model is also known as the *model specification* and is an essential part of developing the desired inference.

Assuming that X is a continuous random variable or random vector, it is common practice to represent the distributions $\mathcal{F}$ by their respective density functions. When the density functions are indexed by a parameter θ in a parameter space Θ, the model can be written as $\mathcal{F} = \{f(x \mid \theta), x \in \mathcal{X} : \theta \in \Theta\}$. In many cases, the n variables $(X_1, X_2, \ldots, X_n)$ are assumed independent conditional on θ and the statistical model can be written in terms of the marginal densities of X_i, $i = 1, 2, \ldots, n$:

$$\mathcal{F} = \{f(x \mid \theta) = \Pi_{i=1}^n f_i(x_i \mid \theta) : \theta \in \Theta\}, x \in \mathcal{X},$$

and $f_i(\cdot \mid \theta) = f(\cdot \mid \theta)$, $i = 1, 2, \ldots, n$, if additionally the variables X_i are assumed to be identically distributed. The latter is often referred to as random sampling.

Beyond the task of modeling and parametrization, classical inference includes many methods to extract conclusions about the characteristics of the model that best represents the population and tries to answer questions like the following: (1) Are the data x compatible with a family $\mathcal{F}$? (2) Assuming that the specification is correct and that the data are generated from a model in the family $\mathcal{F}$, what conclusions can be drawn about the parameter θ_0 that indexes the distribution F_θ that "appropriately" describes the phenomenon under study?

Classical methods – also known as frequentist methods – are evaluated under the principle of repeated sampling, that is, with respect to the performance under infinitely many hypothetical repetitions of the experiment carried out under identical conditions. One of the aspects of this principle is the use of frequencies as a measure of uncertainties, that is, a frequentist interpretation of probability. See , Paulino et al. (2018, section 1.2), for a review of this and other interpretations of probability.

In the case of parametric inference, in answer to question (2) above, we need to consider first the question of point estimation, which, *grosso modo*, is: Given a sample $X = (X_1, X_2, \ldots, X_n)$, how should one "guess," estimate, or approximate the true value θ, through an estimator $T(X_1, X_2, \ldots, X_n)$. The estimator should have the desired properties such as unbiasedness, consistency, sufficiency, efficiency, etc.

For example, with $\mathcal{X} \equiv \mathbb{R}^n$, the estimator $T(X_1, X_2, \ldots, X_n)$ based on a random sample is said to be centered or unbiased if

$$E\{T \mid \theta\} = \int_{\mathbb{R}^n} T(x_1, x_2, \ldots, x_n)\Pi_{i=1}^n f(x_i \mid \theta)\, dx_1 dx_2 \ldots dx_n = 0, \ \forall \theta \in \Theta.$$

This is a property related to the principle of repeated sampling, as can be seen by the fact that it includes integration over the sample space (in this case $\mathbb{R}^n$). Considering this entire space is only relevant if one imagines infinitely many repetitions of the sampling process or observations of the n random variables $(X_1, X_2, \ldots, X_n)$. The same applies when one considers other criteria for evaluation of estimators within the classical paradigm. In other words, implicit in the principle of repeated sampling is a consideration of what might happen in the entire sample space.

Parametric inference often takes the form of confidence intervals. Instead of proposing a single value for θ, one indicates an interval whose endpoints are a function of the sample,

$$(T^*(X_1, X_2, \ldots, X_n), T^{**}(X_1, X_2, \ldots, X_n)),$$

and which covers the true parameter value with a certain probability, preferably a high probability (typically referred to as the confidence level),

$$P\{T^*(X_1, X_2, \ldots, X_n) < \theta < T^{**}(X_1, X_2, \ldots, X_n) \mid \theta\} = 1 - \alpha,$$

$0 < \alpha < 1$. This expression pre-experimentally translates a probability of covering the unknown value θ to a random interval (T^*, T^{**}) whose lower and upper limits are functions of $(X_1, X_2, \ldots, X_n)$ and, therefore, random variables. However, once a specific sample is observed (i.e., post-experimentally) as n real values, $(x_1, x_2, \ldots, x_n)$, this becomes a specific interval on the real line (now with real numbers as lower and upper limits).

$$(T^*(x_1, x_2, \ldots, x_n), T^{**}(x_1, x_2, \ldots, x_n)),$$

and the probability

$$P\{^*T(x_1, x_2, \ldots, x_n) < \theta < T^{**}(x_1, x_2, \ldots, x_n) \mid \theta\} = 1 - \alpha,$$

$0 < \alpha < 1$, is no longer meaningful. In fact, once θ has an unknown, but fixed, value, this probability can only be 1 or 0, depending upon whether the true value of θ is or is not in the real interval

$$(T^*(x_1, x_2, \ldots, x_n), T^{**}(x_1, x_2, \ldots, x_n)).$$

Of course, since θ is unknown, the investigator does not know which situation applies. However, a classical statistician accepts the frequentist interpretation of probability and invokes the principle of repeated sampling in the following way: If one imagines a repetition of the sampling and inference process (each sample with n observations) a large number of times, then in $(1 - \alpha)$ 100% of the repetitions the numerical interval will include the value of θ.

Another instance of classical statistical inference is a parametric hypothesis test. In the course of scientific investigation one frequently encounters, in the context of a certain theory, the concept of a hypothesis about the value of one (or multiple) parameter(s), for example in the symbols

$$H_0 : \theta = \theta_0.$$

This raises the following fundamental question: Do the data $(x_1, x_2, \ldots, x_n)$ support or not support the proposed hypothesis? This hypothesis is traditionally referred to as the null hypothesis. Also here the classical solution is again based on the principle of repeated sampling if one follows the Neyman–Pearson theory. It aims to find a rejection region W (critical region) defined as a subset of the sample space, $W \subset X$, such that

$$(X_1, X_2, \ldots, X_n) \in W \implies \text{rejection of } H_0,$$

$$(X_1, X_2, \ldots, X_n) \notin W \implies \text{fail to reject } H_0.$$

The approach aims to control the probability of a type-I error,

$$P\{(X_1, X_2, \ldots, X_n) \in W \mid H_0 \text{ is true}\},$$

and minimize the probability of a type-II error,

$$P\{(X_1, X_2, \ldots, X_n) \notin W \mid H_0 \text{ is false}\}.$$

What does it mean that the critical region is associated with a type-I error, equal to, for example, 0.05? The investigator can not know whether a false or true hypothesis is being rejected when a particular observation falls into the critical region and the hypothesis is thus rejected. However, being a classical statistician the investigator is convinced that under a large number of repetitions and if the hypothesis were true, then only in 5% of the cases would the observation fall into the rejection region. What does it mean that the critical region is associated with a type-II error equal to, say 0.10? Similarly, when a particular observation is not in the rejection region and thus the hypothesis is not rejected, then the investigator cannot know whether a true or false hypothesis is being accepted. Being a classical statistician, the investigator can affirm that under a large number of repetitions of the entire process and if the hypothesis were in fact false, only in 10% of the cases would the observation not fall into the rejection region.

In the following discussion, it is assumed that the reader is familiar with at least the most elementary aspects of how classical inference approaches estimation and hypothesis testing, which is therefore not discussed here in further detail.

1.2 The Bayesian Paradigm

For Lindley, the substitution of the classical paradigm by the Bayesian paradigm represents a true scientific revolution in the sense of Kuhn (1962) The initial seed for the Bayesian approach to inference problems was planted by Richard Price when, in 1763, he posthumously published the work of Rev. Thomas Bayes titled *An Essay towards Solving a Problem in the Doctrine of Chances*. An interpretation of probability as a degree of belief – fundamental in the Bayesian philosophy – has a long history, including J. Bernoulli, in 1713, with his work *Ars Conjectandi*. One of the first authors to define probabilities as a degree of beliefs in the truth of a given proposition was De Morgan, in *Formal Logic*, in 1847, who stated: (1) probability is identified as a degree of belief; (2) the degrees of belief can be measured; and (3) these degrees of belief can be identified with a certain set of judgments. The idea of coherence of a system of degrees of belief seems to be due to Ramsey, for whom the behavior of an individual when betting on the truth of a given proposition is associated with the degree of belief that the individual attaches to it. If an individual states odds or possibilities (chances) – in favor of the truth or untruth – as $r : s$, then the degree of belief in the proposition is, for this individual, $r/(r+s)$. For Ramsey, no set of bets in given propositions is admissible for a coherent individual if it would

lead to certain loss. The strongest exponent of the concept of personal probabilities is, however, de Finetti. In discussing the Bayesian paradigm and its
application to statistics, one must also cite Harold Jeffreys, who, reacting
to the predominantly classical position in the middle of the century, besides
inviting disapproval, managed to resurrect Bayesianism, giving it a logical
basis and putting forward solutions to statistical inference problems in his
time. From there the number of Bayesians grew rapidly and it becomes
impossible to mention all but the most influential – perhaps Good, Savage,
and Lindley.

The well-known Bayes' theorem is a proposition about conditional probabilities. It is simply probability calculus and is thus not subject to any
doubts. Only the application to statistical inference problems is subject to
some controversy. It obviously plays a central role in Bayesian inference,
which is fundamentally different from classical inference. In the classical
model, the parameter θ, $\theta \in \Theta$, is an unknown but fixed quantity, i.e., it is a
particular value that indexes the sampling model or family of distributions
$\mathcal{F}$ that "appropriately" describes the process or physical system that generates the data. In the Bayesian model, the parameter θ, $\theta \in \Theta$, is treated as an
unobservable random variable. In the Bayesian view, any unknown quan-
tity – in this case, the parameter θ – is uncertain and all uncertainties are
described in terms of a probability model. Related to this view, Bayesians
would argue that initial information or *a priori* information – prior or external to the particular experiment, but too important to be ignored – must
be translated into a probability model for θ, say $h(\theta)$, and referred to as the
prior distribution. The elicitation and interpretation of prior distributions
are some of the most controversial aspects of Bayesian theory.

The family $\mathcal{F}$ is also part of the Bayesian model; that is, the sampling
model is a common part of the classical and the Bayesian paradigms, ex-
cept that in the latter the elements $f(x \mid \theta)$ of $\mathcal{F}$ are in general assumed to
also have a subjective interpretation, similar to $h(\theta)$.

The discussion of prior distributions illustrates some aspects of the dis-
agreement between Bayesian and classical statisticians. For the earlier,
Berger, for example, the subjective choice of the family $\mathcal{F}$ is often considered a more drastic use of prior information than the use of prior distributions. And some would add: In the process of modeling, a classical statistician uses prior information, albeit in a very informal manner.
Such informal use of prior information is seen critically under a Bayesian
paradigm, which would require that initial or prior information of an investigator needs to be formally stated as a probability distribution on the
random variable θ. Classical statisticians, for example, Lehmann, see an

important difference between the modeling of $\mathcal{F}$ and the specification of $h(\theta)$. In the earlier case one has a data set $x = (x_1, x_2, \ldots, x_n)$ that is generated by a member of $\mathcal{F}$ and can be used to test the assumed distribution.

To understand the Bayesian point of view, recall that for a classical statistician *all* problems that involve a binomial random variable X can be reduced to a Bernoulli model with an unknown parameter θ that represents a "success" probability. For Bayesians, each problem is *unique* and has its own real context where θ is an important quantity about which there is, in general, some level of knowledge that might vary from problem to problem and investigator to investigator. Thus, the probability model that captures this variability is based on *a priori* information and is specific to a given problem and a given investigator. In fact, *a priori* information includes personal judgements and experiences of most diverse types, resulting from in general not replicable situations, and can thus only be formalized in subjective terms. This formalism requires that the investigator comply with coherence or consistency conditions that permit the use of probability calculus. However, different investigators can in general use different prior distributions for the same parameter without violating coherence conditions.

Assume that we observe $X = x$ and are given some $f(x \mid \theta) \in \mathcal{F}$ and a prior distribution $h(\theta)$. Then Bayes' theorem implies[2]

$$h(\theta \mid x) = \frac{f(x \mid \theta)h(\theta)}{\int_\theta f(x \mid \theta)h(\theta)\, d\theta}, \quad \theta \in \Theta, \tag{1.1}$$

where $h(\theta \mid x)$ is the posterior distribution of θ after observing $X = x$. Here, the initial information of the investigator is characterized by $h(\theta)$, and modified with the observed data by being updated to $h(\theta \mid x)$. The denominator in (1.1), denoted $f(x)$, is the marginal (or prior predictive) distribution for X; that is, for an observation of X whatever the value of θ.

The concept of a likelihood function appears in the context of classical inference, and is not less important in the Bayesian context. Regarding its definition, it is convenient to distinguish between the discrete and continuous cases (Kempthorn and Folks, 1971), but both cases lead to the function of θ,

$$\begin{aligned} L(\theta \mid x) &= kf(x \mid \theta), \quad \theta \in \Theta \quad \text{or} \\ L(\theta \mid x_1, \ldots, x_n) &= k\Pi_i f(x_i \mid \theta), \quad \theta \in \Theta, \end{aligned} \tag{1.2}$$

which expresses for every $\theta \in \Theta$ its likelihood or plausibility when $X = x$ or $(X_1 = x_1, X_2 = x_2, \ldots, X_n = x_n)$ is observed. The symbol k represents a

---

[2] Easily adapted if x were a vector or if the parameter space were discrete.

factor that does not depend on θ. The likelihood function – it is not a probability, and therefore, for example, it is not meaningful to add likelihoods – plays an important role in Bayes' theorem as it is the factor through which the data, x, updates prior knowledge about θ; that is, the likelihood can be interpreted as quantifying the information about θ that is provided by the data x.

In summary, for a Bayesian the posterior distribution contains, by way of Bayes' theorem, all available information about a parameter:

prior information + information from the sample.

It follows that all Bayesian inference is based on $h(\theta \mid x)$ [or $h(\theta \mid x_1, x_2, \ldots, x_n)$].

When θ is a parameter vector, that is, $\theta = (\gamma, \phi) \in \Gamma \times \Phi$, it can be the case that the desired inference is restricted to a subvector of θ, say γ. In this case, in contrast to the classical paradigm, the elimination of the nuisance parameter ϕ under the Bayesian paradigm follows always the same principle, namely through the marginalization of the joint posterior distribution,

$$h(\gamma \mid x) = \int_{\Phi} h(\gamma, \phi \mid x)d\phi = \int_{\Phi} h(\gamma \mid \phi, x)h(\phi \mid x)d\phi. \tag{1.3}$$

Possible difficulties in the analytic evaluation of the marginal disappear when γ and ϕ are *a priori* independent and the likelihood function factors into $L(\theta \mid x) = L_1(\gamma \mid x) \times L_2(\phi \mid x)$, leading to $h(\gamma \mid x) \propto h(\gamma)L_1(\gamma \mid x)$.

1.3 Bayesian Inference

In the Bayesian approach, it is convenient to distinguish between two objectives: (1) inference about unknown parameters θ, and (2) inference about future data (prediction).

1.3.1 Parametric Inference

In the case of inference on parameters, we find a certain agreement – at least superficially – between classical and Bayesian objectives, although in the implementation the two approaches differ. On one side, classical inference is based on probabilities associated with different samples, x, that could be observed under some fixed but unknown value of θ. That is, inference is based on sampling distributions that "weigh" probabilistically the values that a variable X or statistic $T(X)$ can assume across the sample space. On the other hand, Bayesian inference is based on subjective probabilities or *a posteriori* credibilities associated with different values of the parameter θ and conditional on the particular observed x value. The main point is that x is fixed and known and θ is uncertain.

For example, once x is observed, a Bayesian being asked about the hypothesis $\{\theta \leq 0.5\}$ would directly address the question by calculating $P(\theta \leq 0.5 \mid x)$ based on $h(\theta \mid x)$, i.e., without leaving probability calculus. In contrast, a classical statistician would not directly answer the question. Stating, for example, that the hypothesis $H_0 : \theta \leq 0.5$ is rejected at significance level 5% does not mean that its probability is less than 0.05, but that if the hypothesis H_0 were true, (i.e., if in fact $\theta \leq 0.5$), then the probability of X falling into a given rejection region W would be $P(X \in W \mid \theta \leq 0.5) < 0.05$, and if in fact $x \in W$, then the hypothesis is rejected.

In O'Hagan's words (O'Hagan, 2010), while a Bayesian can state probabilities about the parameters, which are considered random variables, this is not possible for a classical statistician, who uses probabilities on data and not on parameters and needs to restate such probabilities such that they seem to say something about the parameter. The question is also related to a different view of the sample space. For a classical statistician, the concept of the sample space is fundamental, as repeated sampling would explore the entire space. A Bayesian would start by objecting to the reliance on repeated sampling and would assert that only the actually observed value x is of interest and not the space that x belongs to, which could be totally arbitrary, and which contains, besides x, observations that could have been observed, but were not.[3]

In estimation problems a classical statistician has several alternatives for functions of the data – estimators – whose sampling properties are investigated under different perspectives (consistency, unbiasedness, etc.). For a Bayesian there is only *one* estimator, which specifically is the posterior distribution $h(\theta \mid x)$. One can, of course, summarize this distribution in different ways, using mode, mean, median, or variance. But this is unrelated to the problem facing a classical statistician, who has to find a so-called *optimal estimator*. For a Bayesian such a problem only exists in the context of decision theory, an area in which the Bayesian view has a clear advantage over the classical view. Related to this, Savage claims that in past decades

---

[3] The irrelevance of the sample space also leads to the same issue about stopping rules, something which Mayo and Kruse (2001) note, recalling Armitage, could cause problems for Bayesians.

the central problem in the face of uncertainty is shifting from *which infer-ence one should report*, to *which decision should be taken*. As individual decisions have been considered outdated by some philosophers, we have also recently seen a resurgence of the Bayesian approach in the context of group decisions.

Under a Bayesian approach, confidence intervals are replaced by credi-ble intervals (or regions). Given x, and once a posterior distribution is deter-mined, one finds a credible interval for a parameter θ (assume, for the mo-ment, a scalar). The interval is formed by two values in θ, say $[\underline{\theta}(x), \bar{\theta}(x)]$, or simpler, $(\underline{\theta}, \bar{\theta})$, such that

$$P(\underline{\theta} < \theta < \bar{\theta} \mid x) = \int_{\underline{\theta}}^{\bar{\theta}} h(\theta \mid x)\, d\theta = 1 - \alpha, \qquad (1.4)$$

where $1 - \alpha$ (usually 0.90, 0.95, or 0.99) is the desired level of credibility. If $\Theta = (-\infty, +\infty)$, then one straightforward way of constructing a (in this case, central) credible interval is based on tails of the posterior distribution such that

$$\int_{-\infty}^{\underline{\theta}} h(\theta \mid x)\, d\theta = \int_{\bar{\theta}}^{+\infty} h(\theta \mid x)\, d\theta = \frac{\alpha}{2}. \qquad (1.5)$$

Equation (1.4) has an awkward implication: The interval $(\underline{\theta}, \bar{\theta})$ is not unique. It could even happen that the values θ in the reported interval have less credibility than values θ outside the same interval. Therefore, to pro-ceed with the choice of an interval that satisfies (1.4) and at the same time is of minimum size, Bayesians prefer to work with HPD (*highest posterior density*) credible sets $A = \{\theta : h(\theta \mid x_1, x_2, \ldots, x_n) \geq k(\alpha)\}$, where $k(\alpha)$ is the largest real number such that $P(A) \geq 1 - \alpha$. For a unimodal posterior, the set becomes a HPD credible interval.

Credible sets have a direct interpretation in terms of probability. The same is not true for confidence intervals, which are based on a probability not related to θ, but rather a probability related to the data; more specif-ically, they are random intervals based on a generic sample, and which after observing a particular sample become a *confidence* of covering the unknown value θ by the resulting numerical interval. In general, this can not be interpreted as a probability or credibility about θ. Besides other crit-ical aspects of the theory of confidence intervals (or regions), there are the ironical comments of Lindley (1990), who says to know various axioms of probability – for example, those due to Savage, de Finetti, or Kolmogorov – but no axiomatic definition of *confidence*.

For example, when a Bayesian investigates a composite hypothesis H_0 :

$\theta \in \Theta_0$ versus a composite alternative $H_1 : \theta \in \Theta_1$, with $\Theta_0 \cap \Theta_1 = \emptyset, \Theta_0 \cup \Theta_1 = \Theta$, she or he uses expressions in terms of probabilities on θ. When the investigator possesses a distribution $h(\theta)$, $\theta \in \Theta$, representing the initial credibility attributed to different parameter values, her or his prior probabilities of the competing hypotheses are determined by

$$P(\Theta_0) = \int_{\Theta_0} h(\theta)\, d\theta, \qquad P(\Theta_1) = \int_{\Theta_1} h(\theta)\, d\theta .$$

The ratio $P(\Theta_0)/P(\Theta_1)$ is known as the *prior odds* for H_0 versus H_1. After the experiment resulting in the observations x, and after determining $h(\theta \mid x)$, a Bayesian statistician calculates the corresponding posterior probabilities

$$P(\Theta_0 \mid x) = \int_{\Theta_0} h(\theta \mid x)\, d\theta, \qquad P(\Theta_1 \mid x) = \int_{\Theta_1} h(\theta \mid x)\, d\theta,$$

and usually also the posterior odds for H_0 versus H_1, that is, $P(\Theta_0 \mid x)/P(\Theta_1 \mid x)$. One can therefore say that in the Bayesian framework the inference outcome is not so much the acceptance or rejection of a the hypothesis H_0 – as is the case in the Neyman–Pearson framework – but rather the updating of the plausibility that is attributed to the competing hypotheses. Bayesian inference can be described as a comparison of posterior odds versus prior odds through

$$B(x) = \frac{P(\Theta_0 \mid x)/P(\Theta_1 \mid x)}{P(\Theta_0)/P(\Theta_1)}, \tag{1.6}$$

which is known as the Bayes factor in favor of H_0 (or Θ_0). The Bayes factor quantifies the evidence in the data x in favor of H_0. Of course, the larger the Bayes factor, the larger is the increase of the posterior odds relative to the prior odds and thus the support that the data give to the hypothesis H_0. In general, the Bayes factor depends on the prior distribution and can be expressed as a ratio of likelihoods weighted by the prior distributions conditional on the respective hypothesis on Θ_0 and Θ_1 (see also Paulino et al., 2003). In this sense one can not say that the Bayes factor is a measure of the support for H_0 based on *only* the data.

When the hypothesis about θ is specific to the point of being defined as $H_0 : \theta = \theta_0$, evaluation of a Bayes factor or of posterior odds requires that the prior distribution be consistent with this conjecture in the sense of avoiding zero probability for H_0, implying in general that the prior is a mixture model. This implication is considered natural by Bayesians such as Jeffreys, with the argument that a prior distribution needs to integrate probabilistic judgments that are inherent in the statement of competing hypotheses, which in this case attribute some importance to θ_0, as opposed to other values of θ.

Other Bayesians such as Lindley and Zellner advocate a different approach, with a certain formal analogy with classical significance tests, in a way in which the statement of point hypotheses does not interfere with the prior distribution. Their approach can be described as a quantification of relative plausibility under the posterior for the value θ_0, via the evaluation of $P = P(\theta \notin R_0(x) \mid x)$, where $R_0(x) = \{\theta \in \Theta : h(\theta \mid x) \geq h(\theta_0 \mid x)\}$ is the smallest HPD region that contains θ_0. Large (small) values of the posterior relative plausibility P for H_0 are evidence in favor of (against) this hypothesis.

The fundamental tool of the Bayesian approach and the way the joint model $M = \{f(x \mid \theta)h(\theta), x \in X, \theta \in \Theta\}$ is used in the implementation of inference already suggest that the question of evaluating the adequacy of a conjectured model in absolute terms might not have an answer in the sense of Popper (reject/not reject) of the type that is guaranteed by classical goodness-of-fit tests.

Bayes factors can be used if it is possible to extend the model M (or parts of it) to a larger family that contains the true model as an unknown quantity, and that allows comparing models within it. Otherwise, one can only define various measures of model adequacy for a relative analysis of a reference model in the context of a class of suitably defined competing models (see Chapter 5). The unsatisfactory nature of such options has lead some statisticians to defend a Bayesian approach only when the underlying model is not put into question, a condition which Gillies (2001) refers to as *fixity of the theoretical framework*.

1.3.2 Predictive Inference

Many Bayesians believe that inference should not be restricted to statements about unobservable parameters. They note that parametric inference is awkward in that actual values are rarely known for parameters and therefore such inference can rarely be compared with reality. For Bayesians like Lindley, the most fundamental problem is to start with a set of observations $(x_1, x_2, \ldots, x_n)$ (yesterday) and infer conclusions, in terms of (subjective) probability, about a set of future observations $(x_{n+1}, x_{n+2}, \ldots, x_{n+m})$ (tomorrow).

For easier exposition we assume $m = 1$ and that the $n + 1$ random variables $X_1, X_2, \ldots, X_n, X_{n+1}$ are independent and identically distributed, given

θ with probability density function $f(x \mid \theta)$. The problem is to predict the random variable X_{n+1} after observing $(X_1 = x_1, X_2 = x_2, \ldots, X_n = x_n)$. Trying to predict X_{n+1} with sampling model $f(x \mid \theta)$ we face two sources of randomness: (1) uncertainty that has to do with X_{n+1} being a random variable; (2) the impact of the uncertainty on θ. For example, if we estimate θ with the maximum likelihood estimator $\hat{\theta} = \hat{\theta}(x_1, x_2, \ldots, x_n)$ and write $P(a < X_{n+1} < b \mid x_1, x_2, \ldots, x_n) \cong \int_a^b f(x \mid \hat{\theta}) \, dx$, as estimate of the probability of the event $a < X_{n+1} < b$, then this expression ignores the randomness in the substitution of the parameter by its estimate. However, both types of randomness need to enter the prediction. The method of substituting an estimate for an unknown parameter in the sampling model (*plug-in procedure*) should thus be seen with some caveat.

Although the classical solution of the prediction problem involves much more than this (Amaral Turkman, 1980), it still could be said that the Bayesian solution is much cleaner. If one has only prior information, formalized as a prior distribution $h(\theta)$, the natural tool to use is the already discussed marginal or prior predictive distribution $f(x)$. The more interesting case is when one observes $x = (X_1 = x_1, X_2 = x_2, \ldots, X_n = x_n)$ and wishes to predict X_{n+1}, assuming that conditional on θ the latter is independent of the previous observations [the problem of predicting $(X_{n+1}, X_{n+2} \ldots, X_{n+m})$ is not very different]. Using a completely probabilistic argument we have $f(x_{n+1} \mid x) = \int_\theta f(x_{n+1} \mid \theta) h(\theta \mid x) \, d\theta$, where the posterior distribution takes the place of the prior, as representing the information given the sample. One can then report summaries of this predictive distribution, including probabilities of any region in the sample space for X_{n+1} or values, $a = a(x)$ and $b = b(x)$ for any pre-specified probability $P(a < X_{n+1} < b \mid x) = \int_a^b f(x_{n+1} \mid x) \, dx_{n+1}$, which then determine a prediction interval (of HPD type if desired).

1.4 Conclusion

In summary, from a Bayesian point of view:

- The classical approach to statistical inference proceeds by arguments of an inductive type, such as, the notion of confidence intervals, which do not have a direct interpretation as probabilities. The difficulty or impossibility of making inference with a direct probabilistic interpretation – as the parameter θ itself is not even considered as a random variable – is strongly criticized by Jaynes (2003).
- Under a Bayesian approach, all inference can be derived from a logical

application of probability calculus. Bayesian statistical inference does not rely on any results that could not be derived from the rules of probability calculus, in particular Bayes' theorem. As O'Hagan (2010) puts it: "Probability theory is a completely self-consistent system. Any question of probabilities has one and only one answer, although there may be many ways to derive it."

Short of taking an extremist position, it is convenient to recall statements like that of Dawid (1985), who, besides confessing a clear preference for Bayesian theory comments that no statistical theory, Bayesian or not, can ever be entirely satisfactory. A position that some statisticians would argue for today is not the *exclusively Bayesian* option of authors like Savage, but rather an eclectic position shared by Wasserman (2004) when he argues that, in summary, combining prior judgments with data is naturally done by Bayesian methods, but to construct methods that guarantee good results in the long run under repeated observations, one needs to resort to frequentist methods.

Problems

1.1 Suppose there are N cable cars in San Francisco, numbered 1 to N. You don't know the value of N, so this is the unknown parameter. Your prior distribution on N is a geometric distribution with mean 100; that is

$$h(N) = \frac{1}{100}\left(\frac{99}{100}\right)^{N-1},$$

$N = 1, 2, \ldots$. You see a cable car at random. It is numbered $x = 203$. Assume that $x =$number on a randomly picked car and has the probability distribution $f(x \mid N) = 1/N$ for $x = 1, \ldots, N$, and $f(x \mid N) = 0$ for $x > N$.

   a. Find the posterior distribution $h(N \mid x)$. Find the Bayes estimate of N, i.e., the posterior mean of N, and the posterior standard deviation of N (use results for a geometric series $\sum_{x=k}^{\infty} a^x$; or use a numerical approximation).
   b. Find a 95% HPD credible interval for N (you will not be able to exactly match the 95% – get as close as possible).

1.2 Recording the number of bacteria (y_i) found in $n = 6$ water samples (of the same volume), we find $y_i = 2, 3, 8, 6, 4$, and 1 (you might need $S = \sum y_i = 24$). It is thought reasonable to assume that y_i follows a Poisson distribution with mean θ, $i = 1, \ldots, n$.
   Also suppose that the prior $h(\theta) \propto 1/\sqrt{\theta}$ is used for the parameter θ (this is a so-called improper prior – see Chapter 2 for more discussion).

a. Find the posterior distribution $h(\theta \mid y)$, and show how you will obtain a 95% credible interval for θ.

b. Suppose that you are now told that only non-zero outcomes were recorded in the above experiment, and therefore the correct distribution for y_i, $i = 1, ..., 6$, is the truncated Poisson given by

$$f(y \mid \theta) = \frac{e^{-\theta}\theta^y}{y!(1 - e^{-\theta})}, \quad y = 1, 2, ...$$

(i) Write down the likelihood function, and the posterior (using the same prior as before) up to a constant.

(ii) Find a 95% credible interval using numerical integration (the previous posterior is no longer in a simple form that allows analytic evaluation of credible intervals).

1.3 Assume that the waiting time for a bus follows an exponential distribution with parameter θ. We have a single observation, $x = 3$. Assume that θ can only take one of 5 values, $\Theta = \{1, 2, 3, 4, 5\}$, with prior probabilities $h(\theta) \propto 1/\theta$, $\theta \in \Theta$.

a. Find the posterior mode (MAP), the posterior standard deviation $\text{SD}(\theta \mid x)$, and the (frequentist) standard error of the estimator, i.e., $\text{SD}(\text{MAP} \mid \theta)$.

b. Find a 60% HPD credible interval $A = (\theta_0, \theta_1)$, i.e., find the shortest interval A with $P(A \mid x) \geq 0.6$.

c. Find $h(\theta \mid x, \theta \geq 2)$, i.e., find the posterior distribution for θ when we know that $\theta \geq 2$.

d. Find the posterior mode MAP_0 conditional on $\theta \geq 2$, the conditional posterior standard deviation $\text{SD}(\theta \mid x, \theta \geq 2)$, and the (frequentist) standard error of the estimator, $\text{SD}(\text{MAP}_0 \mid \theta)$.

Compare with the answers under item (a) and comment.

e. How would you justify the choice of the prior distribution $h(\theta) \propto 1/\theta$?

1.4 Your friend always uses a certain coin to bet "heads or tails"[4] and you have doubts whether the coin is unbiased or not. Let θ denote the probability of a head. You want to test $H_1 : \theta < 0.5$ versus $H_2 : \theta = 0.5$ versus $H_3 : \theta > 0.5$. Assign a prior probability $1/2$ that the coin is unbiased and equal probability to the other two hypotheses. That is, $p(H_2) = 0.5$ and $p(H_1) = p(H_3) = 0.25$. The prior distribution for θ under H_1 and H_3 is uniform. That is, $h(\theta \mid H_1) = U(0, 0.5)$ and $h(\theta \mid H_3) = U(0.5, 1)$. Assume you observe $n = 1$ coin toss. Let $x_1 \in \{0, 1\}$ denote an indicator of "head."

a. Find the predictive distribution (i.e., the marginal distribution) for the first toss, under each of the three hypotheses, i.e., find $p(x_1 = 1 \mid H_1)$, $p(x_1 = 1 \mid H_2)$, and $p(x_1 = 1 \mid H_3)$.

b. Find the predictive distribution for the first toss, $p(x_1 = 1)$.

---

[4] The labels "head" and "tail" refer to the two sides of a 25 cent coin.

c. Still using the data x_1 from one coin toss, given $x_1 = 1$,

(i)   find the Bayes factors for H_1 versus H_2 and for H_3 versus H_2;

(ii)   find the posterior probability that the coin is unbiased.

(iii)   In general it is not meaningful to compute a Bayes factor with a non-informative uniform prior $h(\theta) \propto c$ (because the choice of c is arbitrary). Why is it okay here?

2

Representation of Prior Information

The mechanics of the inference process require that all basic ingredients be properly specified. The first one is a sampling model that can explain (with more or less accuracy) the data as they arise from some experiment or observational process and which we wish to analyze. This model encompasses a set of unknown aspects about which one could have prior information that should be included in the analysis, no matter how vague or significant this information is, and that need to be somehow represented and quantified.

The process of representing prior information is often complicated by the involvement of subjective elements that need to be elicited. We address this here for two cases:

- The first case is when no prior information is available, neither objective nor subjective (sometimes referred to as "*a priori* ignorance") or when prior knowledge is of little significance relative to the information from the sampling model ("vague" or "diffuse" prior information). We review some of the principal methods to derive prior distributions that are in some sense very little informative, and which commonly are referred to as **non-informative priors**.
- The second case assumes a convenient parametric family and then chooses a member of that family using carefully elicited summary measures for the desired distribution. An example of this elicitation process arises in the medical inference problem that is discussed by Paulino et al (2003). This is the context of so-called **natural conjugate priors**. Such priors can also be used to generate improper non-informative priors. In this sense it is closely related to the first case.

For more discussion about the problem of prior specification and other methods to generate vague priors or to elicit subjective priors, see O'Hagan (2010), Kass and Wasserman (1996), and Paulino et al (2018).

2.1 Non-Informative Priors

Non-informative priors were widely interpreted as formal representations of ignorance, but today the tendency (motivated by the lack of unique objective representations of ignorance) is to accept them as conventional default choices that can be used when insufficient prior information makes the elicitation of an adequate subjective prior difficult. Unrelated to interpretation, this type of distributions can still play a role as a reference, even in the presence of strong prior beliefs:

- to derive posterior beliefs for someone who starts with little knowledge, i.e., when the sample provides overwhelming information about the parameters, and it is difficult to subjectively determine a reasonable distribution;
- to allow the comparison with classical inference that "only" uses information from the sample (all or part of it);
- to evaluate the impact on inference of a subjective prior distribution that describes actually available information, by comparison with inference under a default prior.

We review some of the most widely used arguments to construct such prior distributions.

The Bayes–Laplace Method

Based on the "principle of insufficient reason," this method, in the absence of prior information, uses the idea of equiprobability. Depending on the cardinality of Θ, the argument leads to a discrete uniform or a continuous uniform prior.

In the case of a finite number of values for θ, e.g., $\Theta = \{\theta_1, \ldots, \theta_k\}$, the argument leads to a distribution $h(\theta) = 1/k$, $\theta \in \Theta$. However, the same is not true in other situations. If Θ is countably infinite, the resulting distribution is improper, and the same applies when Θ is an unbounded uncountable infinite set, which is inconvenient for investigators who do not like un-normalized measures (even if this does not necessarily prevent the use of Bayes' theorem, as the posterior distribution, the source of all inference, might often still be proper).

Another and perhaps more serious critique against the argument that the lack of information, which some refer to as ignorance, should be represented by a uniform distribution, is the fact that this is not invariant with respect to non-linear transformations, thus leading to contradictions. To illustrate, take the model $\{Ber(\theta),\ \theta \in (0,1)\}$ which is part of the exponential family with natural parameter $\psi = \ln[\theta/(1-\theta)] \in \mathbb{R}$. The use of uniform distributions for θ (proper) and ψ (improper) is probabilistically inconsistent. In fact, $\theta \sim U(0,1) \equiv Be(1,1)$ is equivalent to the reduced logistic distribution for ψ, with density $h(\psi) = \frac{e^{\psi}}{(1+e^{\psi})^2}$, $\psi \in \mathbb{R}$.

In general, letting $\psi = \psi(\theta)$ denote a one-to-one transformation of a real-valued parameter θ with prior density $h(\theta)$, the implied prior on ψ is

$$h(\psi) = h\left[\theta(\psi)\right]\left|\frac{d\theta}{d\psi}\right|. \tag{2.1}$$

The latter is not uniform when $h(\theta)$ is uniform and the Jacobian depends on ψ, as is the case for non-linear transformations, as in the previous example.

Jeffreys' Prior

One of the approaches that ensure invariance under one-to-one transformations is the one proposed by Jeffreys. Jeffreys' prior is based on Fisher information for $\theta \in \mathbb{R}$, defined as

$$I(\theta) = E\left[\left(\frac{\partial \ln f(X \mid \theta)}{\partial \theta}\right)^2 \Big| \theta\right].$$

For the univariate case Jeffreys' prior is defined by $h(\theta) \propto [I(\theta)]^{\frac{1}{2}}$. The fact that for any real-valued one-to-one transformation ψ of $\theta \in \mathbb{R}$,

$$I(\psi) = I(\theta(\psi))\left(\frac{d\theta}{d\psi}\right)^2,$$

shows that Jeffreys' prior for the univariate case has the desired invariance property and thus, ensures invariance of inference under arbitrary transformations of the parameter space (that is, under reparametrization).

To understand the non-informative nature of Jeffreys' prior, note that $I(\theta)$ grows with the square of the change (in expectation over the sample space) with respect to θ of $\ln f(X \mid \theta)$. Also note that the better the model can differentiate θ from $\theta + d\theta$, the larger $I(\theta)$, that is, the sample information on θ. Therefore, considering values of θ with larger (smaller) $I(\theta)$ to be *a priori* more (less) plausible maximally reduces the impact of prior information. This explains the non-informative nature of Jeffreys' prior. And it can be claimed to be objective as it is derived in an automatic fashion from the assumed generative model for the data.

Example 2.1 *Consider a sampling model with likelihood function*

$$L(\theta \mid x, n) = k\,\theta^x(1 - \theta)^{n-x}, \quad \theta \in (0, 1),$$

where k does not depend on θ. *If n is fixed and* $k = C_x^n$, *the model reduces to a binomial model,* $X \mid n, \theta \sim Bi(n, \theta)$, *with mean* $n\theta$ *and* $I(\theta) \propto \theta^{-1}(1 - \theta)^{-1}$, *and thus Jeffreys' prior*

$$h(\theta) \propto \theta^{-1/2}(1 - \theta)^{-1/2}, \quad \theta \in (0, 1) \text{ i.e., } \theta \sim Be(1/2, 1/2),$$

which by the earlier transformation argument corresponds to a uniform distribution $U(0, 2\pi)$ *for* $\psi = arc\ sin\ \sqrt{\theta}$.

If, alternatively, x is fixed and $k = C_{x-1}^{n-1}$ *we get the negative binomial model* $N-x \mid x, \theta \sim NBin(x, \theta)$, *with mean* $x(1-\theta)/\theta$ *and* $I(\theta) \propto \theta^{-2}(1-\theta)^{-1}$, *implying Jeffreys' prior*

$$h(\theta) \propto \theta^{-1}(1 - \theta)^{-1/2}, \quad \theta \in (0, 1),$$

which corresponds to an improper prior distribution that we shall denote as "Be(0, 1/2)," which is consistent with a "uniform" distribution for

$$\psi = \ln \frac{1 - \sqrt{1 - \theta}}{1 + \sqrt{1 - \theta}}.$$

∎

Example 2.1 highlights that Jeffreys' prior, by definition, entirely depends on the sampling model and not only on the kernel. This dependence on the sample space motivates some to be vehemently critical of Jeffreys' prior, especially because this can lead to different posterior inferences, with respect to the same parameter, depending on the type of the observed experiment; for example, direct binomial or inverse binomial sampling in Example 2.1. However, differences might be quite minor for moderate sample sizes, as the example illustrates. Others argue that such dependence is legitimate because of the vague prior information, which Jeffreys' prior aims to represent – that is, the dependence should be seen as a function of the information that is associated with different types of sampling plans, and not in absolute terms.

The application of Jeffreys' rule for univariate location parameters, $\{f(x \mid \theta) = g(x - \theta), \theta \in \Theta \subseteq \mathbb{R}\}$ (e.g., a normal model with known variance), leads to a continuous uniform distribution, which is invariant under linear transformation (that is, under shifts) and improper if Θ is unbounded. If it is applied for univariate scale parameters, $\{f(x \mid \theta) = \frac{1}{\theta}g(x/\theta), \theta \in \Theta \subseteq \mathbb{R}_+\}$ (e.g., a normal model with known mean), it leads to an improper distribution $h(\theta) \propto \theta^{-1}I_{(0,+\infty)}(\theta)$, which is invariant under power transformations (i.e., under rescaling). Here, invariance refers to the fact that the implied prior for any $\psi = \theta^r$ is of the same type, $h(\psi) \propto \psi^{-1}$, $\psi > 0$.

In multiparameter models, Jeffreys' rule is based on the square root of the determinant of the Fisher information matrix. However, due to undesirable implications on the posterior distribution, the rule tends to be replaced, as even suggested by Jeffreys himself, by an assumption of *a priori* independence between parameters (especially when they are of a different nature) and the use of univariate Jeffreys' rules for the marginal prior distributions. For example, in the model $\{N(\mu, \sigma^2) : \mu \in \mathbb{R}, \sigma^2 \in \mathbb{R}_+\}$, Jeffreys' prior is

$$h(\mu, \sigma^2) \propto \sigma^{-m}, \ \mu \in \mathbb{R}, \ \sigma^2 > 0,$$

with $m = 3$ when the bivariate rule is used and $m = 2$ when the mentioned factorization of the joint prior for location, μ, and scale, σ^2 is used.

Maximum entropy methods

The notion of entropy is borrowed from physics, where it is associated with a measure of uncertainty, and was proposed by Jaynes (2003) as a way to arrive at prior distributions that could represent a state of relative ignorance. Such a distribution would have to correspond to a maximum entropy.

Defining the entropy $\mathcal{E}$ of a distribution $h(\theta)$, $\theta \in \Theta$, as the expected value $\mathcal{E}(h(\theta)) = E_h[-\ln h(\theta)]$, it is easy to show that in the finite case when $\Theta = \{\theta_1, \ldots, \theta_k\}$ the maximum entropy distribution (that is, with maximum uncertainty) is the discrete uniform $h(\theta_i) = 1/k$, $i = 1, \ldots, k$, which has entropy $\ln k$. It suffices to maximize the Lagrange function defined by $\mathcal{E}(h(\theta))$ and the added term $\lambda \left(\sum_{i=1}^{k} h(\theta_i) - 1 \right)$, where λ is the Lagrange factor for the restriction to a probability function.

Next, consider maximizing entropy subject to information that is represented as pre-specified values for moments or quantiles, e.g., of the form $E(g_j(\theta)) = u_j$, $j = 1, \ldots, m$. The same procedure can be used (Lagrange multipliers method), introducing the additional restrictions to get the expression

$$h(\theta_i) = \frac{\exp\{\sum_{j=1}^{m} \lambda_j g_j(\theta_i)\}}{\sum_{l=1}^{k} \exp\{\sum_{j=1}^{m} \lambda_j g_j(\theta_l)\}},$$

where the m coefficients λ_j arise from the corresponding restrictions.

Example 2.2 *In the context of a discrete distribution, assume that* $\Theta =$

$\{1, \ldots, k\}$, *and that the median is fixed at one of the possible values, say q.* *Thus, we have a restriction imposed with $u_1 = q$ and $g_1(\theta)$ being an indicator for $\theta \leq q$, that is, given by $\sum_{i=1}^{q} h(i) = 1/2$. By the earlier expression*

$$h(i) = \begin{cases} \frac{e^{\lambda_1}}{e^{\lambda_1} q + (k-q)}, & \text{if } i \leq q \\ \frac{1}{e^{\lambda_1} q + (k-q)}, & \text{if } q < i \leq k \end{cases},$$

where $e^{\lambda_1} = (k-q)/q$ by the restriction on the median. We get then

$$h(i) = \begin{cases} \frac{1}{2q}, & \text{if } i \leq q \\ \frac{1}{2(k-q)}, & \text{if } q < i \leq k \end{cases},$$

that is, a piecewise uniform distribution. ∎

In the case of Θ being a bounded interval on the real line, variational calculus shows that the maximum entropy distribution is the continuous uniform distribution which, as we already know, is not invariant under all injective transformations, which creates problems when using entropy $\mathcal{E}(h(\theta))$ as an absolute measure of uncertainty.

Based on the relationship between entropy and the Kullback–Leibler measure of information in the discrete case, Jaynes (1968) redefined entropy in the continuous case with respect to a non-informative reference distribution $h_0(\theta)$ as $\mathcal{E}(h(\theta)) = E_h\left[-\ln\frac{h(\theta)}{h_0(\theta)}\right]$.

If we assume again initial information represented by restrictions as before, then variational calculus leads to a solution of the maximization problem which can then be expressed as

$$h(\theta) \propto h_0(\theta) \exp\left\{\sum_{j=1}^{m} \lambda_j\, g_j(\theta)\right\},$$

where the multipliers λ_j are obtained from the introduced restrictions.

Example 2.3 *Assume that θ is a location parameter that is known to be positive, that is, $\Theta = (0, +\infty)$, and to have mean u. Using as the non-informative, translation invariant prior distribution the "uniform" distribution on Θ, we get $h(\theta) \propto \exp(\lambda_1\,\theta)$, $\theta > 0$, which implies*

$$h(\theta) = -\lambda_1 \exp(\lambda_1\,\theta)\, I_{(0,+\infty)}(\theta),$$

with $\lambda_1 < 0$, that is, an exponential distribution. Keeping in mind that the fixed mean is $-1/\lambda_1 = u$, we find the maximum entropy distribution $\theta \sim Exp(1/u)$. ∎

Example 2.4 *Again, let θ be a location parameter, with Θ = ℝ and assume that $E(\theta) = u_1$ and $Var(\theta) = u_2$. Using the same (improper) reference distribution as before, we get $h(\theta) \propto \exp\{\lambda_1\theta + \lambda_2(\theta - u_1)^2\}$, $\theta \in \mathbb{R}$. Simple algebra gives*

$$\lambda_1\theta + \lambda_2(\theta - u_1)^2 = \lambda_2\left[\theta - \left(u_1 - \frac{\lambda_1}{2\lambda_2}\right)\right]^2 + \left[\lambda_1 u_1 - \frac{\lambda_1^2}{4\lambda_2}\right].$$

Thus,

$$h(\theta) \propto \exp\left\{\lambda_2\left[\theta - \left(u_1 - \frac{\lambda_1}{2\lambda_2}\right)\right]^2\right\},$$

which is the kernel of a normal distribution with mean $u_1 - \lambda_1/(2\lambda_2)$ and variance $-1/(2\lambda_2)$, with $\lambda_2 < 0$. Checking the two pre-specified moments, we find that $\lambda_1 = 0$ and $\lambda_2 = -1/(2u_2)$ and recognize the maximum entropy prior as $\theta \sim N(u_1, u_2)$. ∎

2.2 Natural Conjugate Priors

A parametric family, where one selects a member of the family in keeping with elicited summaries, should ideally satisfy the following requirements:

- flexibility to accommodate the largest number of possible prior beliefs;
- interpretability that facilitates the process of summarizing its members;
- simplicity in analytical derivation of posterior and predictive distributions.

Bayesian updating becomes straightforward if we use a family of prior distributions, $\mathcal{H} = \{h_a(\theta) : a \in \mathcal{A}\}$, where $\mathcal{A}$ is a set of values for the hyperparameters, and $\mathcal{H}$ is **closed under sampling** from (any element of) $\mathcal{F} = \{f(x \mid \theta) : \theta \in \Theta\}$, that is, if

$$h_a(\theta) \in \mathcal{H} \Rightarrow h(\theta \mid x) \propto h_a(\theta)f(x \mid \theta) \in \mathcal{H}.$$

Under these conditions, we call $\mathcal{H}$ a **natural conjugate family** for $\mathcal{F}$. In other words, the family $\mathcal{H}$ is said to be the natural conjugate of $\mathcal{F}$ if $L(\theta \mid x) \equiv f(x \mid \theta)$, for any x, is proportional to a member of $\mathcal{H}$ and $\mathcal{H}$ is closed with respect to products, i.e., for any a_0, $a_1 \in \mathcal{A}$, there is $a_2 \in \mathcal{A}$ such that

$$h_{a_0}(\theta)h_{a_1}(\theta) \propto h_{a_2}(\theta).$$

Example 2.5 *Let* $x = (x_i, i = 1, \ldots, n)$ *be an observation of a random sample from a Bernoulli model Ber(θ), that is,*

$$f(x_1, \ldots, x_n \mid \theta) = \theta^{\sum_i x_i}(1 - \theta)^{n - \sum_i x_i},$$

which is proportional to the kernel of a Be($\sum_i x_i + 1, n - \sum_i x_i + 1$) distribution in θ, which is closed under products. The natural conjugate model for a Bernoulli sampling model is therefore a family of beta distributions, with well-known versatility. In summary,

$$\theta \sim Be(a, b) \Rightarrow \theta \mid x \sim Be(A, B), \quad A = a + \sum_i x_i, B = b + n - \sum_i x_i,$$

which shows how sampling information enters the easily computed posterior distribution, through the number of successes and failures (that is, the minimum sufficient statistic), additively with respect to the prior hyperparameters (a, b).

Since $a, b > 0$, prior information vanishes (relative to the information in the likelihood) when $a, b \to 0$. Thus a non-informative (or vague) prior obtained from the natural conjugate family is the improper Haldane prior, "Be(0, 0)," defined as $h(\theta) \propto \theta^{-1}(1 - \theta)^{-1}$, $\theta \in (0, 1)$, which corresponds to the "uniform" prior for $\psi = \ln[\theta/(1 - \theta)] \in \mathbb{R}$. Consequently, the prior distribution Be(a, b) can be interpreted as a posterior distribution resulting from updating a non-informative prior based on a hypothetical sample of size $a + b$ with a successes. ∎

In conjugate families, the process of Bayesian updating, that is, the combination of prior and sample information by Bayes' theorem, is carried out entirely within them. This allows us to symbolically represent the updating by a transformation in the space $\mathcal{A}$ of hyperparameters, e.g.,

$$a \in \mathcal{A} \xrightarrow{\mathcal{F}} A = a + (A - a) \in \mathcal{A}.$$

in Example 2.5. The transformation shows the relative weights of the two types of information and highlights the interpretative and analytical simplicity of the Bayesian mechanism in the context of a natural conjugate family. In the above form, $A - a$ represents the role of the sample information in the updating of prior information, represented as a. This is illustrated in Example 2.5.

Example 2.6 *In Example 2.5, assuming a random sample from a Geo(θ) sampling model with density function $f(x_i \mid \theta) = \theta(1 - \theta)^{x_i}$, $x_i \in \mathbb{N}_0$, would still lead to the same natural conjugate family and the same non-informative distribution. However, we would have $\theta \mid x \sim Be(A, B)$, $A =$*

$a + n$, $B = b + \sum_i x_i$ *for a* $Be(a, b)$ *prior distribution, which in turn could be interpreted as the posterior resulting from updating* "$Be(0, 0)$" *prior with a hypothetical sample following a geometric sampling distribution with size a and b successes.* ∎

Example 2.7 *Let* $x = (x_i, \ i = 1, \ldots, n)$ *denote the realization of a random sample from an Erlang model, that is,* $Ga(m, \lambda)$, *where* $m \in \mathbb{N}$ *is assumed known. The sampling density function is* $f(x_1, \ldots, x_n \mid \lambda) \propto \lambda^{mn} e^{-\lambda \sum_i x_i}$. *This is a* $Ga(mn + 1, \sum_i x_i)$ *kernel in* λ, *which is closed under products. Thus, the gamma family is the natural conjugate under the Erlang sampling model, implying the posterior distribution* $\lambda \mid x \sim Ga(A, B)$, *with* $A = a + mn$, $B = b + \sum_i x_i$, *corresponding to a* $Ga(a, b)$, $a, b > 0$, *prior. This prior can thus be interpreted as a posterior resulting from a vague* "$Ga(0, 0)$" *prior, defined as* $h(\lambda) \propto \lambda^{-1}$, $\lambda > 0$, *and a hypothetical Erlang sample of size* a/m *and with sample mean* mb/a. ∎

Example 2.8 *Consider now a random sample from a normal distribution with mean* μ *and known precision* $1/\sigma^2$. *The kernel of the corresponding density function for a realization* $x = (x_i, \ i = 1, \ldots, n)$ *of this sample can be written as*

$$f(x_1, \ldots, x_n \mid \mu) \propto e^{-\frac{n}{2\sigma^2}(\mu - \bar{x})^2},$$

which is proportional to the kernel of a normal distribution for μ *with mean* $\bar{x}$ *and variance* σ^2/n. *The product of the two kernels is again a kernel of the same type* [1].

Thus the natural conjugate family is Gaussian, with $\mu \sim N(a, b^2) \Rightarrow \mu \mid x \sim N(A, B^2)$, *where by the mentioned identity*

$$A = B^2 \left(\frac{1}{b^2} a + \frac{n}{\sigma^2} \bar{x} \right), \quad 1/B^2 = \frac{1}{b^2} + \frac{n}{\sigma^2}$$

Letting $b \to +\infty$ *we get the "uniform" in* $\mathbb{R}$ *as a vague distribution, which in turn implies a posterior distribution* $\mu \mid x \sim N(\bar{x}, \sigma^2/n)$. *In summary, the prior distribution* $\mu \sim N(a, b^2)$ *can be seen as the outcome of posterior updating of this vague prior with a hypothetical normal sample of size m, with empirical mean a and (known) variance* mb^2. ∎

The illustrative examples in this chapter were all with univariate parameters. However, the argument to identify the natural conjugate family for

---

[1] Note the algebraic identity $d_1(z - c_1)^2 + d_2(z - c_2)^2 = (d_1 + d_2)(z - c)^2 + \frac{d_1 d_2}{d_1 + d_2}(c_1 - c_2)^2$, where $c = \frac{d_1 c_1 + d_2 c_2}{d_1 + d_2}$.

models with multivariate parameters, if it exists, proceeds entirely in the same way as in the described examples. Illustrations with multiparameter models can be found in Chapter 3.

The big difference is the incomparably bigger difficulty of eliciting a larger number of summaries that are needed to identify the natural conjugate distribution for a multivariate parameter. Unfortunately, there is no similarly rich set of distributional forms as in the univariate case. Strategies that try to overcome these limitations in the choice of prior distributions include the specification of independence across subsets of parameters and the use of continuous or finite mixtures of natural conjugate distributions.

There are also other methods for prior construction, specifically for models with multivariate parameters. A specific example is the method of reference objective priors of Berger and Bernardo, which is described in detail by Bernardo and Smith (2000). However, the method does not always work, due to the sometimes analytical intractability of the required results, especially in complex parametric models.

Problems

2.1　Consider a Poisson sampling model $f(n \mid \lambda) = \text{Poi}(\lambda)$. Find Jeffreys' prior for λ.

2.2　In order to diagnose the cause of a certain symptom, a patient's physician analyzes the tetrahydrocortisone content (THE) in the urine of the patient over 24 hours. The laboratory returns a result of THE = 13 mg/24 h. There are two possible causes, adenoma ($z = 1$) and carcinoma ($z = 2$). It is known that the distribution of, $y = \ln(\text{THE})$, i.e., the logarithms of the amount of THE in the urine has approximately a normal distribution. We assume

$$M_1 : \quad y \quad \sim \quad N(\mu_1, \sigma_1^2)$$
$$M_2 : \quad y \quad \sim \quad N(\mu_2, \sigma_2^2)$$

for adenoma (M_1) and carcinoma (M_2), respectively. A data bank of THE measures is available with information about six patients with adenoma and five patients with carcinoma as follows (in mg/24 h):

| adenoma | 3.1, 3.0, 1.9, 3.8, 4.1, 1.9 |
| carcinoma | 10.2, 9.2, 9.6, 53.8, 15.8 |

a.　First, we use the data to determine the parameters in the sampling model. That is, use the data to estimate μ_j and σ_j, $j = 1, 2$.

　　　Fix the parameters, and determine the posterior probability of this patient having carcinoma, i.e., $p(z = 2 \mid y)$, if the initial opinion of the physicians team, based on the patient's history, is that the patient has a carcinoma with probability 0.7.

b. Alternatively, let x_{ji}, $i = 1,\ldots,6$, denote the historical data and assume $x_{ji} \sim N(\mu_j, \sigma_j^2)$. Using a vague prior, find the posterior distribution $h(\mu, \sigma^2 \mid x)$ and use it as a prior probability model for the new patient. Again, find the posterior probability of the new patient having carcinoma.

c. Discuss more variations of the approach in part (b). What does the model in part (b) assume about the historical patients and the current patient? What does the model assume about cortisol measurements under the two conditions? There is no need for more calculations, discuss the problems only in words.

2.3 For fixed n and r, consider the following two experiments:

E1: $X \sim \text{Bi}(n, \theta)$ and

E2: $Y \sim \text{NBin}(r, \theta)$,

using a negative binomial with $f(y \mid \theta) = C_y^{y+n-1} \theta^n (1 - \theta)^y$ where C_k^n is the binomial coefficient and θ is a Bernoulli success probability.

a. Find Jeffreys' prior $h(\theta)$ in both experiments.
   Hint: $E(Y) = r(1 - \theta)/\theta$ for the negative binomial distribution in E2 (in contrast to the parametrization used in Appendix A).

b. Use $n = 2$, $r = 1$. Using the priors found in part (a), compute $p(\theta > 0.5 \mid X = 1)$ in E1; and $p(\theta > 0.5 \mid Y = 1)$ in E2.

c. The two probabilities computed in part (b) will differ. Based on parts (a) and (b), argue that inference based on Jeffreys' prior can violate the Likelihood Principle (stated below for reference).

   Likelihood Principle: Consider any two experiements with observed data x_1 and x_2 such that $f(x_1 \mid \theta) = c(x_1, x_2) f(x_2 \mid \theta)$, i.e., the likelihood functions are proportional as a function of θ. The two experiments bring the same information about θ and must lead to identical inference (Robert, 1994, ch. 1).[2]

2.4 Suppose that the lifetimes $x_1,\ldots,x_n$ of n bulbs are exponentially distributed with mean θ.

a. Obtain Jeffreys' prior $h(\theta)$ for θ and show that it is improper.

b. Let $y = \sum_i I(x_i < t)$ denote the number of failures at a fixed time t. Obtain the likelihood function $f(y \mid \theta)$.

c. Show that if no bulbs fail before a pre-specified time, $t > 0$, then the posterior distribution is also improper.

---

[2] Bayesian inference satisfies the likelihood principle since it is entirely based on the posterior distribution which in turn depends on the data only through the likelihood $f(x \mid \theta)$.

3

Bayesian Inference in Basic Problems

Having understood the fundamental ideas of the Bayesian approach to statistical inference and the main methods to represent prior information, it is now time to continue with some illustrations. The basic Bayesian paradigm is best illustrated in problems in which inference can be represented as exactly as possible, preferably analytically or at least by simulation from well-known posterior distributions.

This is done in this chapter by discussing the analysis of eight Bayesian models which, together with Examples 2.5 – 2.8 and some of the exercises in this chapter, cover the majority of textbook problems in a basic statistics course. Since a Bayesian model is defined by a joint distribution of a vector (X) of observations and of parameters (θ), the statement of each model includes a sampling model $\{f(x \mid \theta)\}$ (the model of classical statistics) and a prior distribution $h(\theta)$, which we will indicate by notation like $f(x \mid \theta) \wedge h(\theta)$. See Appendix A for a statement of all the parametric families that are used in the following discussion.

3.1 The Binomial $\wedge$ Beta Model

Let $x = (x_i, \ i = 1, \ldots, n)$ be a realization of conditionally independent binomial random variables $X_i \mid m_i, \theta \sim Bi(m_i, \theta)$, $i = 1, \ldots, n$, with known m_i and unknown parameter θ, equipped with a $Be(a, b)$ prior distribution with fixed hyperparameters. Let $C_k^n = k!(n-k)!/n!$ denote binomial coefficients. The posterior density for θ has the kernel

$$h(\theta \mid x) \propto \Pi_{i=1}^n \left\{ C_{x_i}^{m_i} \theta^{x_i}(1 - \theta)^{m_i - x_i} \right\} h(\theta \mid a, b)$$

$$\propto \theta^{a + \Sigma_i x_i - 1}(1 - \theta)^{b + \Sigma_i(m_i - x_i) - 1},$$

implying that $\theta \mid x \sim Be(A, B)$, with $A = a + \sum_i x_i$ and $B = b + \sum_i(m_i - x_i)$.

This posterior distribution corresponds to using other types of distributions for some transformations of θ that are of interest in certain applications, such as Fisher's F and Z distributions,

$$\frac{B}{A}\frac{\theta}{1-\theta} \mid x \sim F_{(2A,2B)}$$

$$\left[\frac{1}{2}\ln\left(\frac{B}{A}\right) + \frac{1}{2}\ln\left(\frac{\theta}{1-\theta}\right)\right] \mid x \sim Z_{(2A,2B)}.$$

Let $B(a,b) = \Gamma(a)\Gamma(b)/\Gamma(a+b)$ denote the beta function. Mixed moments of the posterior for θ are easily found as

$$E\left[\theta^{r_1}(1-\theta)^{r_2} \mid x\right] = \frac{B(A+r_1, B+r_2)}{B(A,B)},$$

which allow evaluation of various summaries of the distribution, such as the mean $E(\theta \mid x) = A/(A+B)$ and the posterior variance. Another relevant point estimate, the posterior mode, is well defined if $A, B > 1$, as $m_0 = \frac{A-1}{A+B-2}$. Posterior quantiles and probabilities of θ can be evaluated by incomplete beta functions (there is no explicit form), or in the case of integer a, b, as binomial distribution functions using

$$F_{\text{Be}(A,B)}(\theta_0) = 1 - F_{\text{Bi}(A+B-1,\theta_0)}(A-1).$$

Regarding predictive calculation, consider new responses $Y_j \equiv X_{n+j}, j = 1, \ldots, k$ of the same model and assume that they are independent of the observed ones as $Y_j \mid \theta \sim \text{Bi}(m_{n+j}, \theta)$, $j = 1, \ldots, k$, independently. By definition the posterior predictive distribution for $Y = (Y_1, \ldots, Y_k)$ is a mixture of the sampling model (product of binomials) with respect to the posterior distribution (beta) on θ. We find the predictive probability function

$$p(y_1, \ldots, y_k \mid x) = \left[\Pi_{j=1}^{k} C_{y_j}^{m_{n+j}}\right] \frac{B(A+y., B+m_{n+.} - y.)}{B(A,B)},$$

where $y. = \sum_{j=1}^{k} y_j$, and $m_{n+.} = \sum_j m_{n+j}$. It is useful to write it as a product of two probability functions, a multivariate hypergeometric distribution conditional on $y.$ and the beta-binomial marginal posterior predictive distribution for $y.$,

$$p(y_1, \ldots, y_k \mid x) = p_{\text{HpG}(\{m_{n+j}\}, y.)}(y_1, \ldots, y_k \mid y.) \times p_{\text{BeBin}(m_{n+.}, A, B)}(y. \mid x).$$

In fact, this expression highlights the type of dependence that exists in the multivariate predictive distribution, as well as its univariate nature as $\text{BeBin}(m_{n+1}, A, B)$ for $k = 1$, with mean $E(Y_1 \mid x) = m_{n+1}\frac{A}{A+B}$ and variance $\text{Var}(Y_1 \mid x) = m_{n+1}\frac{AB}{(A+B)(A+B+1)}(1 + \frac{m_{n+1}}{A+B})$.

3.2 The Poisson ∧ Gamma Model

Assume now that $x = (x_i, \ i = 1, \ldots, n)$ is a realization of a random sample from a $Poi(\theta)$ model, with corresponding sampling probability function $f(x_1, \ldots, x_n \mid \theta) \propto e^{-n\theta}\theta^{x.}$. Since this is proportional to the kernel of a $Ga(x_. + 1, n)$ for θ, which in turn is closed under products, we see that the natural conjugate family is the gamma family, that is:

$$\theta \sim Ga(a, b) \ \Rightarrow \ \theta \mid x \sim Ga(A, B), \ A = a + x_., B = b + n,$$

with $h(\theta) \propto \theta^{-1}I_{(0,+\infty)}(\theta)$ being the corresponding diffuse improper prior distribution. The posterior $h(\theta \mid x)$ can alternatively be written as $\alpha = 2B\theta \sim \chi^2_{2A}$. Posterior probabilities of pre-selected events in $\Theta = \mathbb{R}_+$ or relative posterior plausibility for point hypotheses on θ can be evaluated as incomplete gamma functions or as chi-square distribution functions.

Posterior moments are given by

$$E(\theta^r \mid x) = \frac{\Gamma(A + r)}{\Gamma(A)} \frac{B^A}{B^{A+r}}.$$

For predictive inference, let $Y_j \equiv X_{n+j} \overset{iid}{\sim} Poi(\theta)$, $j = 1, \ldots, k$, denote future observations, independent of the observed random sample. The posterior predictive distribution for $Y = (Y_1, \ldots, Y_k)$ is a mixture of the sampling model (product of Poisson) with respect to the $Ga(A, B)$ posterior distribution on θ. Integrating out θ, the posterior predictive probability function becomes

$$p(y_1, \ldots, y_k \mid x) = \frac{\Gamma(A + y_.)}{\Gamma(A)\Pi_j y_j!} \left(\frac{B}{B + k}\right)^A \left(\frac{1}{B + k}\right)^{y.}.$$

Since the sampling distribution of $y_. = \sum_j Y_j$ is $Poi(k\theta)$, an argument analogous to the previous discussion shows that the posterior predictive distribution for $y_.$ is a Poi–Ga mixture, with probability function

$$p(y_. \mid x) = \frac{\Gamma(A + y_.)}{\Gamma(A)y_.!} \left(\frac{B}{B + k}\right)^A \left(\frac{k}{B + k}\right)^{y.},$$

better known as the generalized negative binomial with parameters (A, $B/(B + k)$). The two parameters can be interpreted as the fixed number of "successes" and the probability of each of them. Compared with the previous expression, we can rewrite it as $p(y_1, \ldots, y_k \mid x) \, \Pi_j y_j! (k^{y.})/y_.!$, and therefore

$$p(y_1, \ldots, y_k \mid x) = p_{M_{k-1}(y_., \frac{1}{k}\mathbf{1}_k)}(y_1, \ldots, y_k \mid y_.) \times p_{BiN(A, B/(B+k))}(y_. \mid x).$$

That is, similar to the binomial $\wedge$ beta case, the posterior predictive probability function can be written as a product of a homogeneous multinomial probability function and a Poi–Ga marginal probability function. This representation highlights the nature of the dependence in the posterior predictive distribution, which reduces to a negative binomial when $k = 1$.

3.3 Normal (Known μ) $\wedge$ Inverse Gamma Model

Let $x = (x_i, \ i = 1,\ldots,n)$ be a random sample of $X_i \mid \sigma^2 \sim N(\mu_0, \sigma^2)$, $i = 1,\ldots,n$, i.i.d., with known μ_0. The corresponding density function,

$$f(x_1,\ldots,x_n \mid \sigma^2) \propto (\sigma^2)^{-n/2} e^{-\frac{\sum_i (x_i - \mu_0)^2}{2\sigma^2}},$$

as a function of σ^2 is proportional to the kernel of an inverse gamma distribution, $IGa(\frac{n}{2} - 1, \frac{1}{2}\sum_i (x_i - \mu_0)^2)$, which in turn is closed under products. Therefore, the IGa family is a natural conjugate prior for this sampling model, with $\sigma^2 \sim IGa(a,b) \Leftrightarrow 1/\sigma^2 \sim Ga(a,b)$ implying that $\sigma^2 \mid x \sim IGa(A,B)$ with $A = a + \frac{n}{2}$, $B = b + \frac{1}{2}\sum_i (x_i - \mu_0)^2$. The $IGa(a,b)$ prior distribution can therefore be interpreted as an updated vague "$Ga(0,0)$" prior based on a hypothetical sample of size $2a$ from the corresponding normal model with mean zero and sum of squares $2b$.

Parametric inference about the scale or precision can readily be obtained from the IGa or Ga (or related) posterior distributions. Predictive inference for a future observation Y from the same sampling model, independent of X_i, $i = 1,\ldots,n$, is obtained as a scale mixture of $N(\mu_0, \sigma^2)$ with respect to the posterior distribution $\sigma^2 \mid x \sim IGa(A,B)$. This defines a Student-t distribution with $2A$ degrees of freedom, location parameter μ_0 and scale parameter $\sqrt{B/A}$, written as $t_{(2A)}(\mu_0, B/A)$, with predictive density function

$$p(y \mid x) = \frac{B^A}{\sqrt{2\pi}\,\Gamma(A)} \int_0^{+\infty} (\sigma^2)^{-(A+3/2)} e^{-(1/\sigma^2)\left[B + \frac{(y-\mu_0)^2}{2}\right]} d\sigma^2$$

$$= \left[B\left(\frac{2A}{2}, \frac{1}{2}\right) \right]^{-1} (\sqrt{2AB/A})^{-1} \left[1 + \frac{(y - \mu_0)^2}{2AB/A} \right]^{-\frac{2A+1}{2}}$$

3.4 Normal (Unknown μ, σ^2) $\wedge$ Jeffreys' Prior

Assume that $x = (x_i, \ i = 1,\ldots,n)$ is an observed random sample from a $N(\mu, \sigma^2)$ model with likelihood function

$$f(x_1,\ldots,x_n \mid \mu, \sigma^2) \propto (\sigma^2)^{-n/2} \exp\left\{ -\frac{n}{2\sigma^2}(\mu - \bar{x})^2 - \frac{ks^2}{2\sigma^2} \right\},$$

where $k = n - 1$ and $ks^2 = \sum_i (x_i - \bar{x})^2$. This is the kernel of a joint normal-inverse gamma distribution for (μ, σ^2), defined as a normal for μ given σ^2 and an inverse gamma for σ^2. The family of normal-inverse gamma distributions is closed under products. The natural conjugate family is therefore defined by density functions of the type $h(\mu, \sigma^2 \mid a, v, c, d) = h_{N(a, \sigma^2/v)}(\mu \mid \sigma^2) \, h_{IGa(c,d)}(\sigma^2)$.

Jeffreys' prior under prior independence of μ and σ^2, $h(\mu, \sigma^2) \propto \sigma^{-2}$, is a limiting case of an improper NIGa. Bayesian updating with the given likelihood function yields the posterior distribution

$$h(\mu, \sigma^2 \mid x) \propto (\sigma^2)^{-1/2} e^{-\frac{n}{2\sigma^2}(\mu - \bar{x})^2} \times (\sigma^2)^{-\left(\frac{n-1}{2}+1\right)} e^{-\frac{ks^2}{2\sigma^2}}$$

implying $\mu \mid \sigma^2, x \sim N(\bar{x}, \sigma^2/n)$ and $\sigma^2 \mid x \sim IGa(\frac{k}{2}, \frac{ks^2}{2}) \Leftrightarrow \frac{ks^2}{2\sigma^2} \mid x \sim \chi^2_{(k)}$.

The marginal posterior distribution for μ is therefore a mixture of normals with respect to an IGa, which we already know to be a Student t type distribution. In fact, integrating σ^2 with respect to the IGa density function, we get

$$h(\mu \mid x) = \left[B\left(\frac{k}{2}, \frac{1}{2}\right) \right]^{-1} \left(\sqrt{ks^2/n} \right)^{-1} \left[1 + \frac{(\mu - \bar{x})^2}{ks^2/n} \right]^{-\frac{k+1}{2}},$$

that is, $\mu \mid x \sim t_{(k)}(\bar{x}, s^2/n) \Leftrightarrow \frac{\mu - \bar{x}}{s/\sqrt{n}} \mid x \sim t_{(k)}(0, 1) \Leftrightarrow \frac{(\mu - \bar{x})^2}{s^2/n} \mid x \sim F_{(1,k)}$, where $t_{(k)}(0, 1)$ is the Student t distribution, well known in classical statistics. Therefore, $E(\mu \mid x) = \bar{x}$ (if $k > 1$) and $\mathrm{Var}(\mu \mid x) = \frac{k}{k-2}\frac{s^2}{n}$ (if $k > 2$). The conditional posterior distribution for σ^2, given μ, can also be found as $\sigma^2 \mid \mu, x \sim IGa(\frac{k+1}{2}, \frac{ks^2 + n(\mu - \bar{x})^2}{2})$.

Inferences about the location and scale parameters in the sampling model are easily obtained from the Student t and inverse gamma distributions (or χ^2 after appropriate transformation). In terms of prediction, consider, for example, a future random sample of size m from the same model, and assume that we wish to predict its mean $\bar{Y}$. The posterior predictive distribution for $\bar{Y}$ is a mixture of $\bar{Y} \mid \mu, \sigma^2 \sim N(\mu, \sigma^2/m)$ with respect to the joint posterior $h(\mu, \sigma^2 \mid x) = h(\mu \mid \sigma^2, x) h(\sigma^2 \mid x)$. Using an algebraic identity for the linear combination of the quadratic forms, $\frac{1}{\sigma^2}\left[m(\mu - \bar{y})^2 + n(\mu - \bar{x})^2 \right]$, we see that this distribution takes the form of a Student t,

$$\bar{Y} \mid x \sim t_{(k)}\left(\bar{x}, \frac{m+n}{mn} s^2 \right),$$

from which one can easily find point and interval estimates.

3.5 Two Independent Normal Models ∧ Marginal Jeffreys' Priors

Let $x_j = (x_{ji}, i = 1, \ldots, n_j)$, $j = 1, 2$, denote the realizations of two independent random samples from the models $N(\mu_j, \sigma_j^2)$, and complete the model with the usually assumed Jeffreys' priors for the four parameters, $h(\mu_1, \mu_2, \sigma_1^2, \sigma_2^2) \propto (\sigma_1^2 \sigma_2^2)^{-1}$ over the standard joint parameter space.

Comparison of Means

Following an analogous argument as in the previous section, we easily find that (μ_1, σ_1^2) and (μ_2, σ_2^2) are *a posteriori* again independent with univariate marginal distributions:

$$\mu_j \mid x_j \sim t_{(k_j)}(\bar{x}_j, s_j^2/n_j) \Leftrightarrow v_j = \frac{\mu_j - \bar{x}_j}{s_j/\sqrt{n_j}} \mid x_j \sim t_{(k_j)}$$

$$\sigma_j^2 \mid x_j \sim \mathrm{IGa}(\frac{k_j}{2}, \frac{k_j s_j^2}{2}),$$

where $k_j = n_j - 1$ and $k_j s_j^2 = \sum_{i=1}^{n_j} (x_{ji} - \bar{x}_j)^2$.

The standardized difference $\lambda = \mu_1 - \mu_2$, written as

$$\tau = \frac{\lambda - (\bar{x}_1 - \bar{x}_2)}{\sqrt{\frac{s_1^2}{n_1} + \frac{s_2^2}{n_2}}} \equiv v_1 \sin u + v_2 \cos u,$$

where $u = \arctan(\frac{s_1}{\sqrt{n_1}} / \frac{s_2}{\sqrt{n_2}})$, is *a posteriori* distributed as a linear combination of independent Student t distributions, known as the Behrens–Fisher distribution, and parametrized by k_1, k_2, and u[1]. Its density function, which is symmetric but not of closed form, is usually evaluated by a Student t approximation (Patil, 1964), $\tau \mid x_1, x_2 \sim BF(k_1, k_2, u) \overset{\text{approx}}{\sim} t_{(b)}(0, a)$, where

$$b = 4 + c_1^2/c_2, \quad a = \sqrt{c_1(b-2)/b}, \text{ with}$$

$$c_1 = \frac{k_1}{k_1 - 2} \sin^2 u + \frac{k_2}{k_2 - 2} \cos^2 u, \text{ and}$$

$$c_2 = \frac{k_1^2}{(k_1 - 2)^2(k_1 - 4)} \sin^4 u + \frac{k_2^2}{(k_2 - 2)^2(k_2 - 4)} \cos^4 u.$$

As an alternative to the use of Patil's approximation, one could by computer simulation generate a Monte Carlo sample from the posterior distribution

---

[1] Note that the dependence on u implies that there is no duality between the posterior and sampling distributions for τ, and thus, no numerical identity of Bayesian and classical inference on the difference of means. This is in contrast to what happens in other situations under non-informative priors.

of τ by simulating from the posterior distributions for v_1 and v_2. Based on this sample, one could then empirically evaluate point and interval estimates and test point hypotheses about the difference of means.

Comparing Variances

Assume now that the parameter of interest is $\psi = \frac{\sigma_1^2}{\sigma_2^2}$. Based on the independent gamma posteriors for $\{1/\sigma_j^2\}$ we find that $\psi \mid x_1, x_2 \overset{d}{\equiv} \frac{s_1^2}{s_2^2} F_{(k_2, k_1)}$, which allows easy implementation of inferences about ψ.

Comparing Means of Homoscedastic Populations

Assume $\sigma_1^2 = \sigma_2^2 \equiv \sigma^2$ and use Jeffreys' prior $h(\mu_1, \mu_2, \sigma^2) \propto \sigma^{-2}$, $\mu_1, \mu_2 \in \mathbb{R}$, $\sigma^2 > 0$. From the results in the previous section we quickly find:

$$\lambda = \mu_1 - \mu_2 \mid \sigma^2, x_1, x_2 \sim N\left(\bar{x}_1 - \bar{x}_2, \sigma^2(\tfrac{1}{n_1} + \tfrac{1}{n_2})\right);$$
$$\sigma^2 \mid x_1, x_2 \sim \mathrm{IGa}(\tfrac{k}{2}, \tfrac{ks^2}{2}),$$

where $k = n_1 + n_2 - 2$ and $s^2 = k^{-1} \sum_j (n_j - 1)s_j^2$ is the pooled empirical variance. This implies, in particular for $\lambda = \mu_1 - \mu_2$:

$$\lambda \mid x_1, x_2 \sim t_{(k)}\left(\bar{x}_1 - \bar{x}_2, s^2(\tfrac{1}{n_1} + \tfrac{1}{n_2})\right) \Leftrightarrow \frac{\lambda - (\bar{x}_1 - \bar{x}_2)}{s\sqrt{\tfrac{1}{n_1} + \tfrac{1}{n_2}}} \mid x_1, x_2 \sim t_{(k)},$$

which is then the basic inference result for the comparison of two normal populations under homoskedasticity.

3.6 Two Independent Binomials $\wedge$ Beta Distributions

Let t_j denote observed counts for $T_j \mid \theta_j \overset{\mathrm{ind}}{\sim} Bi(m_j, \theta_j)$, with known $\{m_j\}$, $j = 1, 2$. Complete the model with a prior $\theta_j \sim Be(a_j, b_j)$, $j = 1, 2$, independently. Using the results for the Bi $\wedge$ Be model, we find

$$\theta_j \mid t_j \sim Be(A_j, B_j), \ A_j = a_j + t_j, \ \text{and} \ B_j = b_j + m_j - t_j$$
$$\Leftrightarrow \frac{B_j}{A_j} \frac{\theta_j}{1 - \theta_j} \mid t_j, \sim F_{(2A_j, 2B_j)}$$
$$\Leftrightarrow \left[\frac{1}{2} \ln \frac{B_j}{A_j} + \frac{1}{2} \ln \frac{\theta_j}{1 - \theta_j}\right] \mid t_j \sim Z_{(2A_j, 2B_j)},$$

$j = 1, 2$, independently. We will use these distributional results in the next two inference problems.

Exact One-Sided Test for Two Proportions

Consider testing $H_0 : \theta_1 \leq \theta_2$ versus $H_1 : \theta_1 > \theta_2$. The evaluation of posterior odds and the Bayes factor requires the quantities

$$P(H_0 \mid t_1, t_2) = \int_0^1 h(\theta_1 \mid t_1) \left[\int_{\theta_1}^1 h(\theta_2 \mid t_2) d\theta_2 \right] d\theta_1,$$

and a similar expression for prior probabilities. In the case of integer a_2 and b_2, the integrals can be evaluated using the result $F_{Be(A_2, B_2)}(\theta_1) = 1 - F_{Bi(A_2 + B_2 - 1, \theta_1)}(A_2 - 1)$ for beta and binomial distribution functions. We get

$$P(H_0 \mid t_1, t_2) = \frac{1}{B(A_1, B_1)} \sum_{u=0}^{A_2-1} C_u^{A_2+B_2-1} B(A_1 + u, B_1 + A_2 + B_2 - 1 - u).$$

If a_1 and b_1 are also integers, the beta functions can be evaluated in terms of factorials.

Testing Homogeneity $H_0 : \theta_1 = \theta_2$ versus $H_1 : \theta_1 \neq \theta_2$

Consider first $H_0 : \pi = 0 \Leftrightarrow \ln \Delta = 0$ using the transformations $\pi = \theta_1 - \theta_2$ and $\Delta = \frac{\theta_1/(1-\theta_1)}{\theta_2/(1-\theta_2)}$. First, simulate from the $Be(A_j, B_j)$ posterior distributions on θ_j. Transform to posterior samples for π or Δ (or $\ln \Delta$), which then allow good Monte Carlo approximations of the level of relative posterior plausibility of H_0 or HPD intervals. Of course the same approach can be used for one-sided hypotheses by way of calculating the appropriate proportions based on the simulated samples.

In the case of large numbers of observed successes and failures, one can use asymptotic approximations of Fisher's Z distribution; for example:

$$Z_{(\nu_1, \nu_2)} \overset{approx}{\sim} N\left[\frac{1}{2} \ln \frac{\nu_1^{-1} - 1}{\nu_2^{-1} - 1}, \frac{1}{2}(\nu_1^{-1} + \nu_2^{-1}) \right].$$

This, together with the distributional result for $(1/2) \ln[\theta_j/(1-\theta_j)]$ that was stated at the beginning of this subsection, give the approximate posterior distribution

$$\ln \Delta \mid t_1, t_2 \overset{approx}{\sim} N\left[\ln \frac{(A_1 - 1/2)/(B_1 - 1/2)}{(A_2 - 1/2)/(B_2 - 1/2)}, \sum_{j=1,2} (A_j^{-1} + B_j^{-1}) \right].$$

This can be used to construct one-sided or two-sided Bayesian tests for the comparison of proportions.

3.7 Multinomial ∧ Dirichlet Model

This Bayesian model is a multivariate version of the binomial ∧ beta model, but much less used than the latter. We first review the main properties of the model relevant to inference.

Let $X = (X_1, \ldots, X_c)$ and $\theta = (\theta_1, \ldots, \theta_c)$ be random vectors taking values in the subspaces $\mathcal{X} = \{x = (x_1, \ldots, x_c) : x_i \in \mathbb{N}_0, x_. = \sum_{i=1}^{c} x_i \leq N\}$, with known N, and $\Theta = \{(\theta_1, \ldots, \theta_c) : \theta_i \in (0, 1), \theta_. = \sum_{i=1}^{c} \theta_i < 1\}$, respectively. The space Θ is also known as the c-dimensional simplex $\mathcal{S}_c$.

A (c-Dimensional) Multinomial Model for X

The probability function for $X \mid \theta \sim M_c(N, \theta)$ is

$$f(x \mid \theta) = \frac{N!}{\prod_{i=1}^{c+1} x_i!} \Pi_{i=1}^{c+1} \theta_i^{x_i}, \quad x \in \mathcal{X},$$

with $x_{c+1} = N - x_.$ and $\theta_{c+1} = 1 - \sum \theta_i$. The first two moments are defined as (using, e.g., the moment-generating function):

$$\mu = E(X \mid \theta) = N\theta; \quad \Sigma = \text{Var}(X \mid \theta) = N(D_\theta - \theta\theta'),$$

where $D_\theta = \text{diag}(\theta_1, \ldots, \theta_c)$.

Next, we consider the implied distribution on aggregate counts over subsets. Let $C_k = \{j_{k-1} + 1, \ldots, j_k\}$, $k = 1, \ldots, s + 1$ denote the subsets of a partition of the set of indices $\{1, 2, \ldots, c, c + 1\}$ into $s + 1$ subsets with $\#C_k = d_k$, $j_0 = 0$, and $j_{s+1} = c + 1$. A corresponding segmentation of X is defined as

$$X^{(k)} = (X_i, i \in C_k); \quad M_k = \sum_{i \in C_k} X_i, \quad k = 1, \ldots, s + 1,$$

where the M_k stand for aggregate counts – of X_i – over subsets C_k.

Using the moment-generating function technique and the definition of a conditional distribution, we find

$$M = (M_1, \ldots, M_s) \mid \theta \sim M_s(N, \alpha), \quad \alpha = (\alpha_1, \ldots, \alpha_s), \quad \alpha_k = \sum_{i \in C_k} \theta_i$$
$$X^{(k)} \mid M, \theta, \ k = 1, \ldots, s + 1 \overset{\text{ind}}{\sim} M_{d_k-1}(M_k, \pi_k),$$

with $\pi_k = (\theta_i/\alpha_k, \ i \in C_k - j_k)$. These results show that the component-specific marginal and conditional distributions of a multinomial are also multinomial (binomial in the univariate case). This is clearly relevant in several contexts such as analysis of contingency tables. For example, if X represents the vector of frequencies in a two-dimensional contingency table, the marginal frequencies of the rows (or columns) are given by M

and the conditional frequencies of rows (or columns), conditional on the marginal totals, are the indicated products of multinomials.

A Dirichlet Model for θ

The Dirichlet model is defined by the density function $\theta \mid a \sim D_c(a)$: $h_a(\theta) = [B(a)]^{-1} \times \prod_{i=1}^{c+1} \theta_i^{a_i - 1}$, $\theta \in \Theta = S_c$ where $a = (a_1, \ldots, a_c, a_{c+1}) \in \mathbb{R}_+^c$, $\theta_{c+1} = 1 - \theta$, and $B(a) = \prod_{i=1}^{c+1} \Gamma(a_i)/\Gamma(a_.)$ is the multivariate beta function.

For theoretical and computational reasons it is better to define the Dirichlet distribution based on independent gamma distributions through the following transformation: $\theta_i = v_i / \sum_{j=1}^{c+1} v_j$, $i = 1, \ldots, c$, with random variables v_i, $i = 1, \ldots, c+1 \overset{\text{ind}}{\sim} Ga(a_i, 1)$.

By their definition, the mixed moments are given by $E\left[\prod_{i=1}^{c+1} \theta_i^{r_i} \mid a\right] = B(a+r)/B(a)$, where $r = (r_1, \ldots, r_c, r_{c+1})$, from which we find

$$E(\theta_i \mid a) \equiv E_i = \frac{a_i}{a_.}; \quad \mathrm{Var}(\theta_i \mid a) = \frac{E_i(1 - E_i)}{a_. + 1};$$

$$\mathrm{cov}(\theta_i, \theta_j \mid a) = -\frac{E_i E_j}{a_. + 1}, \ i \neq j.$$

Since $(\alpha, \pi_1, \ldots, \pi_{s+1})$ is a reparametrization of θ, one can find (from, e.g., the representation by gamma distributions):

$$\alpha \mid a \sim D_s(\sum_{i \in C_k} a_i, \ k = 1, \ldots, s+1)$$
$$\pi_k \mid a, \ k = 1, \ldots, s+1 \overset{\text{ind}}{\sim} D_{d_k - 1}(a_i, i \in C_k).$$

A Multinomial-Dirichlet Model for X

This distribution, also known as a Pólya distribution, arises as a mixture of a multinomial with respect to a Dirichlet, $X \mid a \sim \mathrm{MD}_c(N, a)$, with probability function

$$p(x \mid a) = \frac{N!}{\prod_{i=1}^{c+1} x_i!} \frac{B(a_1 + x_1, \ldots, a_{c+1} + x_{c+1})}{B(a_1, \ldots, a_{c+1})}, \ x \in \mathcal{X}.$$

The first two moments can be expressed as (using, e.g., the properties of conditional expectations):

$$E(X \mid a) = N \frac{a}{a_.}; \quad V(X \mid a) = \frac{a_. + N}{a_.(a_. + 1)} N \left(D_a - \frac{aa'}{a_.}\right).$$

Using a segmentation of X as before, one easily finds that

$$M = (M_1, \ldots, M_s) \mid a \sim \text{MD}_s(N; \sum_{i \in C_k} a_i, \, k = 1, \ldots, s + 1)$$
$$X^{(k)} \mid M, a, \, k = 1, \ldots, s + 1 \overset{\text{ind}}{\sim} \text{MD}_{d_k - 1}(M_k; a_i, i \in C_k).$$

Application to Inference

Assume $x = (x_1, \ldots, x_c)$ is a realization of a random vector $X \mid \theta \sim M_c(N, \theta)$. Since $f(x \mid \theta)$ is proportional to the kernel of a $D_c(x_i + 1, i = 1, \ldots, c + 1)$ distribution that is closed under products, we conclude that the Dirichlet family is the natural conjugate for a multinomial sampling model. Thus, if $\theta \mid a \sim D_c(a)$, then $\theta \mid a, x \sim D_c(A)$, $A = (A_i = a_i + x_i, \, i = 1, \ldots, c + 1)$.

Bayesian estimates of $(\theta_i, \, i = 1, \ldots, c + 1)$ can be derived in particular from the components of the posterior mode $(A - 1_{c+1})/A$. (if $A_i > 1, \forall i$), where 1_{c+1} is a $c + 1$ vector of all 1s, or the posterior mean A/A. Note how this is a weighted mean of the prior mean, a/a, and the vector of sample proportions $p = (x_i/N, \, i = 1, \ldots, c + 1)$.

In the analysis of contingency tables, inference of interest is often related to independent structures (or other log-linear models) in which parametric functions $\sum_i b_i \ln \theta_i$ with $\sum_i b_i = 0$ often play a critical role (see, e.g., Paulino and Singer, 2006). When the components of A are large, one can invoke approximate posterior normality of the posterior distribution and use the resulting χ^2 distribution for appropriate quadratic forms, allowing tests for such structures. For more detail see, e.g., (Paulino et al, 2018, ch. 6). In the special case of a 2×2 table the use of such an approach to the test of independence, which reduces simply to a test of homogeneity of two binomials, leads to the approach mentioned at the end of the previous section.

Assume now the aim is to predict a vector Y with $Y \mid m, \theta \sim M_c(m, \theta)$. The corresponding posterior predictive distribution is a multinomial-Dirichlet, $Y \mid m, x \sim \text{MD}_c(m, A)$, whose summary by the first two moments can be obtained by the formulas in Appendix A.

3.8 Inference in Finite Populations

Consider a finite population of known size N, partitioned into $c \leq N$ groups of unknown sizes $N_i, i = 1, \ldots, c$, with $\sum_{i=1}^{c} N_i = N$. Assume one selects randomly (without replacement) a sample S of $n \leq N$ units with the aim of drawing inference about the population sizes of the groups, $\theta = (N_1, \ldots, N_c)$. Let $n_i, i = 1, \ldots, c$, be the observed frequencies of the groups, with $\sum_{i=1}^c n_i = n$, and let $x = (n_1, \ldots, n_c)$ which, by assumption, is now an observation from the multivariate hypergeometric distribution $X \mid N, n, \theta \sim Hpg_{c-1}(\theta, n)$ (for convenience we use here and in the following redundant notation in the definition of random vectors such as X by explicitly stating all hyperparameters).

Denote by U_k a vector of group membership indicators for the k-th unit. The possible values of U_k are the standard basis of $\mathbb{R}^c$ (that is, binary $(c \times 1)$ vectors with exactly one "1"). The inference goal can then be summarized as

$$\theta = \sum_{k=1}^N U_k = \sum_{k \in S} U_k + \sum_{k \notin S} U_k \equiv X + (\theta - X),$$

highlighting in particular that *a posteriori* only $\theta - X$ is unknown.

One can construct a prior as a hierarchical model defined by

$$U_1, \ldots, U_N \overset{\text{iid}}{\sim} M_{c-1}(1, \phi)$$

with an underlying hyperparameter $\phi = (\phi_j, \ j = 1, \ldots, c)$, with $\sum_j \phi_j = 1$. In a second level we assume the hyperprior, $\phi \mid a \sim D_{c-1}(a), a = (a_1, \ldots, a_c) \in \mathbb{R}_+^c$.

Regarding the first level of the hierarchial prior model, we have thus $\theta \mid \phi \sim M_{c-1}(N, \phi)$ and X and $\theta - X$ are by definition *a priori* conditionally independent given ϕ, with distributions of the same type, $X \mid n, \phi \sim M_{c-1}(n, \phi)$ and $\theta - X \mid n, \phi \sim M_{c-1}(N - n, \phi)$. Note also that the hypergeometric sampling model for X can be written as

$$f(x \mid n, \theta) = \frac{\Pi_{j=1}^c C_{x_j}^{N_j}}{C_n^N} = \frac{f(x \mid n, \phi) \, h(\theta - x \mid n, \phi)}{h(\theta \mid \phi)} = \frac{f(x, \theta \mid n, \phi)}{h(\theta \mid \phi)}$$
$$= f(x \mid n, \theta, \phi).$$

Using the second-level information, one can identify the following marginal (or prior predictive) distributions arising from the multinomial-Dirichlet model:

$$\theta \mid a \sim MD_{c-1}(N, a); \ X \mid n, a \sim MD_{c-1}(n, a); \tag{3.1}$$
$$\theta - X \mid n, a \sim MD_{c-1}(N - n, a).$$

We also see that updating of the prior information on ϕ conditional on x is such that $\phi \mid x \sim D_{c-1}(a + x)$. On the other hand, since $\theta - x \mid x, \phi \overset{d}{=} \theta - x \mid \phi \sim M_{c-1}(N - n, \phi)$, we have that $\theta - x \mid x \sim MD_{c-1}(N - n, a + x)$.

In summary, the posterior distribution of $\theta - x$ under hypergeometric sampling is of the same multinomial-Dirichlet type as the prior distribution.

The posterior distribution for the vector θ of group totals is derived from that by translation by x, which of course implies the posterior distribution for the vector of population proportions θ/N (Basu and Pereira, 1982).

Problems

3.1 *Exponential $\wedge$ gamma model.* Let $x_i \sim \text{Exp}(\theta)$, $i = 1, \ldots, n$, i.i.d.

    a. Assuming θ is distributed as $\text{Ga}(\alpha, \beta)$, with α and β fixed, find the posterior distribution $h(\theta \mid x_1, \ldots, x_n)$.

    b. Under the same assumptions, compute the predictive distribution $p(x_{n+1} \mid x_1, \ldots, x_n)$.

    c. Consider now a slightly different situation. Imagine that the exponential random variables represent waiting times for the recurrence of disease in n patients surgically treated at time 0. We are at time a, and all patients are still alive. Some of the n patients may have experienced recurrence. We record their recurrence time x_i (assume patients are not followed up after the recurrence, i.e., we have no further data). Other patients may still be healthy, so we don't know exactly what the recurrence time is. We only know $x_i > a$. Repeat steps (a) and (b) for this case.

3.2 *Binomial (unknown θ, n) $\wedge$ beta/Poisson model.* Consider a binomial sampling model $x \mid \theta, n \sim \text{Bi}(n, \theta)$.

    a. For fixed n and $\theta \sim \text{Be}(a_0, b_0)$, find the marginal distribution $p(x)$. This distribution is known as beta-binomial (cf. Section 3.1).

    b. Assume now that also n is unknown, $h(n) \propto 1/n^2$. Plot the joint posterior distribution $h(n, \theta \mid x)$ for $x = 50$, and $(a_0, b_0) = (1, 4)$.

    Hint: Use a grid on $0.01 \leq \theta \leq 0.99$ and $x \leq n \leq 500$. Use the R function `lgamma(n+1)` to evaluate $\ln(n!)$.

3.3 *Hierarchical Poisson $\wedge$ gamma model.* An animal experiment records tumor counts for mice of two different strains, A and B. Tumor counts are approximately Poisson distributed. The observed tumor counts for $n_A = 10$ mice of strain A and $n_B = 13$ mice of strain B are

$$y_A = (12, 9, 12, 14, 13, 13, 15, 8, 15, 6); \quad n_A = 10$$
$$y_B = (11, 11, 10, 9, 9, 8, 7, 10, 6, 8, 8, 9, 7); \quad n_B = 13.$$

We assume $y_{Ai} \sim \text{Poi}(\theta_A)$, i.i.d., for $i = 1, \ldots, n_A$. And independently $y_{Bi} \sim \text{Poi}(\theta_B)$, i.i.d., for $i = 1, \ldots, n_B$. In parts (a) through (c) we will consider three alternative prior models that reflect our prior information about θ_A and θ_B at different levels.

    a. Find the posterior distributions, means, variances, and 95% credible intervals for θ_A and θ_B, assuming Poisson sampling distributions for each group and the following prior distribution:

$$\theta_A \sim Ga(120, 10), \quad \theta_B \sim Ga(12, 1), \quad h(\theta_A, \theta_B) = h(\theta_A) \cdot h(\theta_B).$$

b. Set up a hierarchical prior for θ_A and θ_B that formalizes the notion that types A and B are similar, that is, a two-level hierarchical model:

$$\theta_A \mid \psi \sim h(\theta_A \mid \psi) \text{ and } \theta_B \mid \psi \sim h(\theta_B \mid \psi)$$
$$\psi \sim h(\psi).$$

Hint: You could, for example, use a hierarchical hyperprior for a common prior mean ψ for θ_A and θ_B.

c. Now modify the prior model from (b) to allow for a positive probability for $\theta_A = \theta_B$. Find $h(\theta_A = \theta_B \mid y)$.

3.4 *Rayleigh $\wedge$ gamma model.* The Rayleigh distribution with p.d.f. $f(x \mid \delta) = \delta x e^{-\delta x^2/2} I_{(0,+\infty)}(x)$ is used for some problems in engineering. Assume $x = (x_i, i = 1, \ldots, n)$ is a realization of a random sample from this model and assume a $Ga(a, b)$ prior distribution for δ.

a. Find the posterior distribution $h(\delta \mid x)$. Argue that the gamma family is the natural conjugate model. Find $E(\delta \mid x)$ and $\text{Var}(\delta \mid x)$.

b. Hypothesis testing for $H_0 : \delta = \delta_0$ can be carried out using incomplete gamma functions. For example, using the Jeffreys prior $h(\delta) \propto \delta^{-1} I_{(0,+\infty)}(\delta)$, the posterior distribution conditional on one observation x from the Rayleigh model is $\delta \mid x \sim Exp(x^2/2)$.

Find the level of relative posterior plausibility of H_0 (recall the definition from Section 1.3.1).

c. Next we compute a Bayes factor. Assume a sample of five measurements from the Rayleigh model gives $\sum_i x_i^2 = 7.54$. Assume that it is desired to test H_0 with $\delta_0 = 2$ on the basis of 50% prior probability for H_0, and adopting a $Ga(0.02, 0.01)$ distribution for the prior under the alternative hypothesis. Note that the prior distribution for $\delta \mid H_1$ is a proper distribution with mean 2 and variance 200, reasonably similar to an improper Jeffreys prior. It is quite flat over most of its support, with the exception of small positive values. Find the Bayes factor $B(x) = \frac{P(H_0|x)}{P(H_1|x)}$.

d. Finally, we consider prediction for Y, with $Y \mid \delta \sim Ray(\delta)$ independently of $(X_1, \ldots, X_n)$. Find the posterior predictive density function $p(y \mid x)$, the point estimate $E(Y \mid x)$ and $P(Y > 1 \mid x)$.

Hint: Use properties of the conditional expectation and integration by parts to prove $E(Y \mid \delta) = \sqrt{\pi/2} \, \delta^{-1/2}$).

3.5 *Uniform $\wedge$ Pareto model.* Let $x = (x_i, i = 1, \ldots, n)$ denote a random sample from a uniform $U(0, \theta)$ model, with density

$$f(x_1, \ldots, x_n \mid \theta) = \theta^{-n} I_{[t,+\infty)}(\theta), \quad t = x_{(n)} \equiv \max_{1 \le i \le n} x_i.$$

a. Recognize $f(x \mid \theta)$ as the kernel of a Pareto distribution for θ. State the parameters of the Pareto kernel.

b. Assuming $\theta \sim Pa(a, b)$ with $a, b > 0$, find $h(\theta \mid x)$.

c. Find the posterior mean, mode, and median for θ.

d. Find a γ-HPD credible interval for θ.

e. Let $y = x_{n+1}$ denote a new observation from the sampling model, assumed independent of the already observed data. Find $p(y \mid x_1, \ldots, x_n)$.

Hint: The solution is best written in two cases, for y below and above some threshold.

3.6 *Normal linear regression (unknown β, Σ).* Consider a normal linear regression model for y_i, $i = 1, \ldots, n$ on x_{ij}, $j = 1, \ldots, k$, with a proper multivariate normal prior on β and three alternative priors on the covariance matrix. Let $y = (y_1, \ldots, y_n)'$ be an $n \times 1$ vector of responses, X an $n \times k$ design matrix (i.e., a matrix with x_{ij} in the ith row and jth column). Let $\beta = (\beta_1, \ldots, \beta_k)$ be a vector of regression coefficients. We assume

$$y \mid \beta, \Sigma \sim N(X\beta, \Sigma)$$
$$\beta \sim N(\mu, T).$$

a. Assume that Σ is known. Let $V_\beta = (X'\Sigma^{-1}X)^{-1}$, and $\hat{\beta} = V_\beta X'\Sigma^{-1}y$. Show that $h(\beta \mid \Sigma, y) = N(m, V)$, with

$$V^{-1} = T^{-1} + V_\beta^{-1} \text{ and } m = V(T^{-1}\mu + V_\beta^{-1}\hat{\beta}),$$

with the last term simplifying to $V_\beta^{-1}\hat{\beta} = X'\Sigma^{-1}y$.

b. We now extend the model by assuming an unknown – but diagonal – covariance matrix:

$$y \mid \beta, \sigma^2 \sim N(X\beta, \sigma^2 I),$$
$$\beta \mid \sigma^2 \sim N(\mu, \sigma^2 R),$$
$$\sigma^2 \sim \text{Inv-}\chi^2(v_0, s_0).$$

Find $h(\tau \mid y)$ for $\tau = 1/\sigma^2$ and $h(\beta \mid \sigma^2, y)$ for fixed R, v_0, s_0.

c. Replace the prior on β by $\beta \sim N(\mu, T)$. Find $h(\tau \mid \beta, y)$.

Note: Together with $h(\beta \mid \sigma^2, y)$ from question (b), this allows us to define an algorithm that alternately simulates from these two complete conditional posterior distributions. The algorithm is known as the Gibbs sampler and will be discussed at length in Chapter 6. See also Problem 6.11.

4

Inference by Monte Carlo Methods

The vast majority of statistical inference problems involve complex models that often leave it unrealistic to consider analytical (or even numerical) solutions for any inference summaries of interest, which in Bayesian inference often take the form of integrals. In this context, classical Monte Carlo methods arise as an attractive alternative. Monte Carlo methods evaluate the relevant inference based on calculations involving simulated random samples from probability distributions, which in turn can be generated from (pseudo-)random variate generators [realizations of a uniform $U(0, 1)$]. Related methods of stochastic simulation have been the subject of extended literature[1] and can now be implemented by several available statistical and mathematical software packages.

This chapter describes the general idea of traditional Monte Carlo methods in its basic version and in importance sampling, as well as some of the specialized versions and variations pertaining to Bayesian inference.

4.1 Simple Monte Carlo

Consider the problem of approximating an integral of the form

$$\int g(\theta)\, h(\theta \mid x)d\theta = E[g(\theta) \mid x], \qquad (4.1)$$

where θ and x can be vectors, assuming the expectation with respect to $h(\theta \mid x)$ exists. Many posterior summaries can be expressed as (4.1) for some integrable function $g(\theta)$. This is the case for posterior moments of the elements of θ, posterior probabilities of subsets of the parameter space, and posterior predictive densities, where $g(\theta)$ is, respectively, θ_i (for the mean of the i-th coordinate of θ), $I_A(\theta)$ for $A \subset \Theta$ and $f(y \mid \theta)$ for fixed y.

---

[1] In particular, the books by Devroye (1986), with a free pdf version of the book and errata available on the author's homepage (www.nrbook.com/devroye); Ripley (1987) and Gentle (2004).

Other quantities of interest can also be expressed using appropriate integrals, including the normalizing constant of a posterior distribution, marginal posterior densities, Bayes factors, and posterior model probabilities.

If one can simulate a random sample $\theta_1, \ldots, \theta_n$ from the posterior distribution $h(\theta \mid x)$, then the simplest Monte Carlo method approximates the integral (4.1) by the sample mean

$$\hat{E}\left[g(\theta) \mid x\right] = \frac{1}{n} \sum_{i=1}^{n} g(\theta_i), \qquad (4.2)$$

which by the strong law of large numbers converges almost surely to $E\left[g(\theta) \mid x\right]$. The precision of the estimator can be evaluated by the (estimated) standard error of the Monte Carlo average, given by

$$\frac{1}{\sqrt{n(n-1)}} \left\{ \sum_{i=1}^{n} \left[g(\theta_i) - \frac{1}{n} \sum_{i=1}^{n} g(\theta_i) \right]^2 \right\}^{1/2}, \qquad (4.3)$$

when $E\{[g(\theta)]^2 \mid x\} < \infty$.

The integral of interest (4.1) can be represented by infinitely many variations involving consistent changes of the triple of parameter space, integrand, and target distribution, (Θ, g, h) (Ripley, 1987). The Monte Carlo estimators related to each of these representations come with different precisions, and corresponding implications for the computational effort (easier or more difficult random variate generation and larger or smaller Monte Carlo sample size) required for getting reliable estimates. This suggests opportunities for more efficient tools to obtain highly precise estimates with a relatively low Monte Carlo sample size.[2]

In summary, if one can generate from the posterior distribution $h(\theta \mid x)$, then the evaluation of integrals of the type (4.1) is straightforward. Note also that a simulated Monte Carlo sample considerably simplifies many otherwise analytically difficult inference summaries. This is the case, for example, for reparametrizations and marginalization, which are simply carried out by the corresponding transformations of the simulated sample and the selection of the components of interest, respectively. The following subsections discuss in more detail the evaluation of posterior probabilities, marginal posterior distributions, credible intervals, and posterior predictive summaries.

Example 4.1 *Phase I clinical trials for chemotherapy agents in cancer*

---

[2] For details on variance reduction techniques for Monte Carlo estimates see, for example, Rubinstein (1981) and Robert and Casella (2004).

Table 4.1 CRM: dose levels, prior probabilities of toxicity π_k^0, and standardized doses δ_k.

	Dose level					
k	1	2	3	4	5	6
Dose (mg/m^2)	10	20	40	60	75	90
Prob(toxicity) π_k^0	0.05	0.10	0.20	0.30	0.50	0.70
Standardized dose δ_k	-1.47	-1.1	-0.69	-0.42	0	0.42

aim to establish the maximum tolerable dose (MTD) that can be administered without excessive probability of a dose-limiting toxicity (DLT). Assuming that higher doses are more effective for the tumor treatment, we wish to find the highest dose possible without excessive toxicity. However, some toxicity has to be tolerated, otherwise the treatment would be ineffective. Investigators might therefore, for example, aim to find the highest dose with probability of DLT less than $\pi^\star = 30\%$. The continual reassessment method (CRM) is one of the first Bayesian model-based designs for such trials (O'Quigley et al, 1990). In its most basic form, this method characterizes the dose–toxicity relationship by simple one-parameter models, such as the hyperbolic tangent model, the logistic model, or the power model. Let δ_k, $k = 1, \ldots, K$ denote the available dose levels in the trial and let π_k be the probability of a DLT at the k-th dose. The hyperbolic tangent model assumes

$$\pi_k(a) = [(\tanh(\delta_k) + 1)/2]^a = \left[\frac{\exp(\delta_k)}{\exp(\delta_k) + \exp(-\delta_k)} \right]^a. \tag{4.4}$$

To highlight the nature of π_k as a function of the unknown parameter a, we write $\pi_k(a)$. Let π_k^0 denote an a priori expert judgement of the expected toxicity at the k-th dose level. Recording doses as standardized dose levels $\delta_k = \tanh^{-1}(2\pi_k^0 - 1)$, we can match the prior mean $E(\pi_k \mid a = 1)$ with the expert prior judgment, i.e., $E(\pi_k \mid a = 1) = \pi_k^0$.

Suppose then that in developing a new agent, $K = 6$ dose levels are to be studied. We assume a hyperbolic tangent dose–toxicity curve with prior distribution $h(a) = Exp(1)$. The targeted toxicity level is set at $\pi^\star = 20\%$. The dose levels and our prior beliefs regarding the probability of toxicity at each dose level are given in Table 4.1. Assume, then, that the first four patients are treated at dose levels $k_i = 3, 4, 4,$ and 5, that is, patient $i = 1$ was treated with dose δ_3, etc. Let $y_i \in \{0, 1\}$ denote an indicator for the i-th patient reporting a DLT. Assume that the observed toxicity outcomes are

$y_i = 0, 0, 0$ *and* 1. *Under* (4.4), *the sampling model is* $f(y_i = 1 \mid k_i = k, a) = \pi_k(a)$.

Let $D_i = (y_1, \ldots, y_i)$ *denote the data up to the ith patient. To carry out the CRM we need to compute* $\bar{\pi}_k \equiv E\{\pi_k(a) \mid D_i\}$ *for* $k = 1, \ldots, K$. *This takes the form of posterior expectations as in* (4.1) *with* $\theta = a$ *and* $g(\cdot) = \pi_k(\cdot)$. *Consider the moment just before the enrollment of the* $(i + 1) = 5$-*th patient and compute* $\bar{\pi}_k$, $k = 1, \ldots, K$. *The posterior distribution* $h(a \mid D_4)$ *is*

$$h(a \mid D_4) \propto e^{-a}(1 - \pi_3(a))(1 - \pi_4(a))^2 \pi_5 =$$
$$e^{-a}(\exp(2\delta_3) + 1)^{-a}(\exp(2\delta_4) + 1)^{-2a}(1 + \exp(-2\delta_t))^{-a}.$$

We use Monte Carlo integration to evaluate $\bar{\pi}_k$. *We generate* $M = 5000$ *samples* $a_m \sim h(a \mid D_4)$, $m = 1, \ldots, M$ *(using, for example, the R macro* sim.x() *in Appendix B) and evaluate* $\widehat{\pi}_k = \frac{1}{M} \sum \pi_k(a_m)$ *using Monte Carlo averages as in* (4.2). *Figure 4.1 shows the posterior estimates and the estimated posterior distributions* $h\{\pi_k(a) \mid D_4\}$. *The CRM method would then call for the next patient to be treated at the highest dose k with* $\widehat{\pi}_k \leq \pi^\star$. *In this case we find* $k^\star = 3$, *which would then be assigned to the next enrolled patient.* ∎

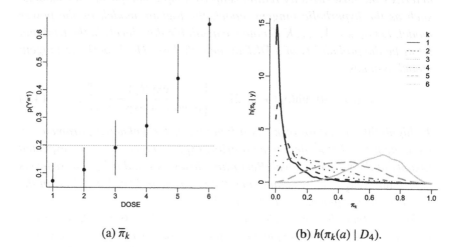

(a) $\bar{\pi}_k$ (b) $h(\pi_k(a) \mid D_4)$.

Figure 4.1 Panel (a) shows the posterior mean toxicities evaluated by Monte Carlo averages $\widehat{\pi}_k$. The vertical line segments show ±0.5 posterior standard deviations. Panel (b) shows the marginal posterior distributions $h(\pi_k \mid D_4)$, evaluated as kernel density estimates of the histograms of $\{\pi_k(a_m); \ m = 1, \ldots, M\}$.

4.1.1 Posterior Probabilities

If $g(\theta) = I_A(\theta)$ is an indicator function for some event A in the parameter space, then the Monte Carlo estimate (4.2) becomes the proportion of simulated samples that fall into A. As a specific example, consider the evaluation of the posterior probability of the shortest HPD set that contains a specific fixed value $\theta_0 \in \mathbb{R}$,

$$P(\theta_0) \equiv P_{h(\theta|x)}(\{\theta : h(\theta \mid x) \geq h(\theta_0 \mid x)\}),$$

which we introduced in Chapter 1 as a way to construct Bayesian hypothesis tests for $H_0 : \theta = \theta_0$ (posterior plausibility). The evaluation of this level of relative posterior plausibility does not require the normalization constant of a univariate $h(\theta \mid x)$. The corresponding Monte Carlo estimate becomes

$$\hat{P}(\theta_0) = \frac{1}{n}\#\{\theta_i, \ 1 \leq i \leq n : L(\theta_i \mid x)\,h(\theta_i) \geq L(\theta_0 \mid x)\,h(\theta_0)\}. \tag{4.5}$$

4.1.2 Credible Intervals

Consider now a Monte Carlo sample $(\theta_i, \ 1 \leq i \leq n)$ from a univariate posterior distribution $h(\theta \mid x)$, with cumulative distribution function $H(\theta \mid x)$, and assume that we wish to summarize the posterior distribution with a credible interval $R(\gamma)$ at level γ. The construction of such an interval requires complete knowledge of the posterior distribution. In the case of an unknown normalization constant, one could exploit the Monte Carlo sample to obtain an approximation of the credible interval from corresponding empirical quantiles.

A Monte Carlo approximation of a central γ-credible interval $R_*(\gamma)$ is obtained by sorting the Monte Carlo sample and using empirical quantiles. Specifically, letting $(\theta_{(i)}, 1 \leq i \leq n)$ denote the ordered sample, the Monte Carlo estimate of $R_c(\gamma)$ is

$$\hat{R}_*(\gamma) = (\theta_{(\ell)}, \theta_{(h)}) \text{ with } \ell = \left[n\left(\frac{1}{2} - \frac{\gamma}{2}\right)\right], \ h = \left[n\left(\frac{1}{2} + \frac{\gamma}{2}\right)\right], \tag{4.6}$$

where $[n\alpha]$ is the integer part of $n\alpha$.

The best interval summary of a unimodal, possibly asymmetric distribution is the HPD interval $R_0(\gamma) = \{\theta : h(\theta \mid x) \geq k_\gamma\}$, where k_γ is the largest threshold such that the posterior probability of $R_0(\gamma)$ is at least γ. The definition makes this interval more difficult to evaluate than intervals with fixed, predetermined tail areas, even if a closed-form expression for the posterior density of θ is available. Chen and Shao (1999) propose a Monte

Carlo approach to approximate $R_0(\gamma)$ which is extremely simple to implement. Based on an ordered Monte Carlo sample $(\theta_{(i)}, 1 \le i \le n)$, credible intervals at level γ can be determined by

$$\hat{R}_i(\gamma) = \left(\theta_{(i)}, \theta_{(i+[n\gamma])}\right), \ i = 1, \ldots, n - [n\gamma],$$

where $[n\gamma]$ denotes the integer part of $n\gamma$. Taking into account the minimum length property of HPD intervals, the Monte Carlo approximation of $R_0(\gamma)$ proposed by Chen and Shao is defined as $\hat{R}_0(\gamma) = R_{i_0}(\gamma)$, with i_0 determined by $i_0 = \arg \min_i \left[\theta_{(i+[n\gamma])} - \theta_{(i)}\right], 1 \le i \le n - [n\gamma].$[3]

Note that the method is straightforward to modify for HPD intervals for parametric functions $\psi(\theta)$. It suffices to apply it to the transformed Monte Carlo sample $(\psi(\theta_i), 1 \le i \le n)$. However, recall that the HPD nature is not invariant under non-linear transformations.

4.1.3 Marginal Posterior Distributions

Assume $\theta = (\theta_1, \ldots, \theta_k) \in \mathbb{R}^k$, $k > 1$, and that the goal is to evaluate marginal posterior densities based on a Monte Carlo sample $\theta_{(i)} = (\theta_{(i)1}, \ldots, \theta_{(i)k})$, $1 \le i \le n$, from $h(\theta \mid x)$ (using subscripts (i) to index samples and $(i)m$ to index components of $\theta_{(i)} \in R^k$). There are several methods one could use.

When the goal is the evaluation of a marginal density, say $h(\theta_j \mid x)$, the simplest method is to select the jth component of each multivariate Monte Carlo sample, create the histogram based on the resulting univariate sample $(\theta_{(1)j}, \ldots, \theta_{(n)j})$, and fit a curve to the histogram using some simple smoothing method. A more sophisticated non parametric smoothing method for the evaluation of the marginal density $h(\theta^{(m)} \mid x)$, where $\theta^{(m)} = (\theta_1, \ldots, \theta_m) \in \mathbb{R}^m$ for some fixed $m = 1, \ldots, k - 1$, is the so-called kernel method. A description can be found in any book on non parametric methods (e.g., Silverman, 1986).

To introduce another method based on conditioning, assume for a moment $k = 2$ and let Θ denote the support of the posterior density $h(\theta_1, \theta_2 \mid x)$ for $\theta = (\theta_1, \theta_2)$. Let $\Theta_{-1}(\theta_1) = \{\theta_2 : (\theta_1, \theta_2) \in \Theta\}$ denote the subset of Θ which constitutes the support of $h(\theta_1, \theta_2 \mid x)$ for fixed θ_1, and let $\Theta_1(\theta_2) = \{\theta_1 : (\theta_1, \theta_2) \in \Theta\}$ denote the support of the conditional density $h(\theta_1 \mid \theta_2, x)$.

---

[3] See Chen et al.(2000, ch. 7) about the asymptotic validity of the approximation $\hat{R}_0(\gamma)$.

For a fixed value θ_{1*} of θ_1, let (assuming Fubini's theorem applies)

$$
\begin{aligned}
h(\theta_{1*} \mid x) &= \int_{\Theta_{-1}(\theta_{1*})} h(\theta_{1*} \mid \theta_2, x) h(\theta_2 \mid x) \, d\theta_2 \\
&= \int_{\Theta_{-1}(\theta_{1*})} h(\theta_{1*} \mid \theta_2, x) \left\{ \int_{\Theta_1(\theta_2)} h(\theta_1, \theta_2 \mid x) \, d\theta_1 \right\} d\theta_2 \qquad (4.7) \\
&= \int_{\Theta} h(\theta_{1*} \mid \theta_2, x) h(\theta \mid x) \, d\theta,
\end{aligned}
$$

which shows that the ordinates of the marginal posterior density for θ_1 can be interpreted as posterior expected values (with respect to θ, including in particular θ_2) of the corresponding ordinates of the conditional posterior density for θ_1.

Generalizing this argument for $\theta = \left(\theta^{(m)}, \theta^{(-m)} \right)$, with $\theta^{(-m)} = (\theta_{m+1}, \ldots, \theta_k)$, we get

$$
h(\theta_*^{(m)} \mid x) = \int_{\Theta} h(\theta_*^{(m)} \mid \theta^{(-m)}, x) h(\theta \mid x) \, d\theta. \qquad (4.8)
$$

The expression implies that the marginal posterior density for $\theta^{(m)} = (\theta_1, \ldots, \theta_m)$ can be approximated with a Monte Carlo estimate based on a random sample of $h(\theta \mid x)$, $\theta_{(i)} = (\theta_{(i)}^{(m)}, \theta_{(i)}^{(-m)})$ with $\theta_{(i)}^{(m)} = (\theta_{(i)1}, \ldots, \theta_{(i)m})$ and $\theta_{(i)}^{(-m)} = (\theta_{(i)m+1}, \ldots, \theta_{(i)k})$, $i = 1, \ldots, n$, as

$$
\hat{h}\left(\theta_*^{(m)} \right) = \frac{1}{n} \sum_{i=1}^{n} h\left(\theta_*^{(m)} \mid \theta_{(i)}^{(-m)}, x \right). \qquad (4.9)
$$

This estimate was proposed by Gelfand and Smith (1990; see also Gelfand et al., 1992). It does not make use of the part $\theta_{(i)}^{(m)}$, $i = 1, \ldots, n$, of the simulated values on which the kernel density estimate is based, but instead requires complete knowledge of the conditional posterior density of $\theta^{(m)}$ given $\theta^{(-m)}$.

Assuming this condition is met, the estimate (4.9) turns out to be more efficient than the estimate obtained by the kernel method, as was shown by Gelfand and Smith (1990). This is because it exploits the knowledge of the model structure as it is embodied in the required conditional distribution. Something similar happens with the following estimate of the posterior mean of $\theta^{(m)}$ that, accounting for (4.9), is given by

$$
\hat{\theta}^{(m)} = \frac{1}{n} \sum_{i=1}^{n} E\left(\theta^{(m)} \mid \theta_{(i)}^{(-m)}, x \right). \qquad (4.10)
$$

This estimator, using the availability of the indicated conditional expectation, is more precise than the classical Monte Carlo estimator obtained from a sample of the marginal distribution of $\theta^{(m)}$, due to properties of conditional expectations.[4]

4.1.4 Predictive Summaries

Noting that the ordinates of the posterior predictive density of Y are the expectations $p(y \mid x) = E_{\theta|x}[f(y \mid \theta, x)]$, one can easily derive the Monte Carlo approximation

$$\hat{p}(y \mid x) = \frac{1}{n} \sum_{i=1}^{n} f(y \mid \theta_i, x) \qquad (4.11)$$

based on a posterior Monte Carlo sample of draws from $h(\theta \mid x)$.

For Monte Carlo estimation of summaries associated with the predictive model $p(y \mid x)$, one needs a random sample from this distribution. This is possible by what is known as the method of composition (Tanner, 1996; section 3.3) if one can simulate from the sampling model for y. The method generates a sample $(y_1, \dots, y_n)$ from $p(y \mid x)$ as follows.

1. Generate an i.i.d. sample of size n from $h(\theta \mid x)$, $(\theta_1, \dots, \theta_n)$.
2. For each i, generate y_i from $f(y \mid \theta_i, x)$, $i = 1, \dots, n$.

Based on this Monte Carlo sample, one can then easily evaluate approximations for various predictive summaries. For example, an estimate of the predictive mean and predictive HPD intervals for future observations $y \in \mathbb{R}$ is obtained in the same way as we did for the posterior mean and HPD credible intervals for θ on the basis of a posterior Monte Carlo sample of θ, as we discussed before.

4.2 Monte Carlo with Importance Sampling

Although there are random variate generators for many specific distributions (see, e.g., Ripley, 1987), it is in many cases not possible to generate an i.i.d. sample from the posterior $h(\theta \mid x)$, making it necessary to consider alternative strategies. One of the possible strategies is based on simulating from a distribution which is "similar" to the desired posterior distribution.

---

[4] The argument is analogous to the Rao–Blackwell theorem, which establishes that the expected value of an estimator conditional on a sufficient statistic is an estimator with equal bias but more efficient than the original one. Even if the context here is not the same, the same term, *Rao–Blackwellization*, which is used for the conditioning is also used for the conditioning in (4.10) and (4.9).

An example of this type of methods is known as importance sampling, which we describe in the following. Until around 1990, importance sampling used to be the method of choice for posterior simulation, but is now much less widely used. We still include it here, for historical context, and also because the underlying ideas remain useful in many applications.

Let $p(\theta)$ be a density whose support, say Θ_p, contains the support of $h(\theta \mid x) = cf(x \mid \theta)h(\theta)$ and which is proposed as a tool for the desired sampling. Assume the quantity of interest is the expectation of $g(\theta)$ with respect to the posterior distribution on θ. It can be written using the distribution $p(\theta)$ as

$$\bar{g} \equiv \int g(\theta) \, h(\theta \mid x) d\theta = \int g(\theta) \, \frac{h(\theta \mid x)}{p(\theta)} \, p(\theta) d\theta,$$

that is, as expected value of the original function g with respect to p, but adjusted by a multiplicative factor $h(\theta \mid x)/p(\theta)$. The latter expectation always exists by the assumption about the support of the distribution $p(\theta)$. In the light of what was discussed in the previous section, the idea of simulating from $p(\theta)$ instead of from $h(\theta \mid x)$ naturally leads to estimating the quantity of interest by $(\Theta_p, (gh)/p, p)$, that is, estimating it as an integral of $(gh)/p$ with respect to p over Θ_p.

Also, this new representation of the quantity of interest requires only that the posterior be known up to a proportionality constant c, and the same is true for $p(\theta)$. In fact,

$$\int g(\theta)h(\theta \mid x)d\theta = \frac{\int g(\theta)f(x \mid \theta)h(\theta)d\theta}{\int f(x \mid \theta)h(\theta)d\theta} \qquad (4.12)$$

$$= \frac{\int g(\theta)\frac{f(x\mid\theta)h(\theta)}{p(\theta)}p(\theta)d\theta}{\int \frac{f(x\mid\theta)h(\theta)}{p(\theta)}p(\theta)d\theta} = \frac{\int g(\theta)w(\theta)p(\theta)d\theta}{\int w(\theta)p(\theta)d\theta},$$

with $w(\theta) = f(x \mid \theta)\,h(\theta)/p(\theta)$. The density $p(\cdot)$ is known as the importance function, possibly because it allows one to better explore the region of the parameter space that is most important for the evaluation of the integral of interest. Accordingly, the process of simulation from this distribution is known as importance sampling.

Assume, then, that $(\theta_1, \dots, \theta_n)$ is an importance sample from $p(\theta)$. Using $w_i = w(\theta_i)$, one can now apply Monte Carlo methods to approximate $E[g(\theta) \mid x]$ as

$$\hat{E}[g(\theta) \mid x] = \frac{1}{\sum_{i=1}^{n} w_i} \sum_{i=1}^{n} w_i g(\theta_i). \qquad (4.13)$$

The form of this estimator shows that importance sampling could be seen as weighted sampling, with the weights w_i for $g(\theta_i)$ known as importance sampling weights. Under appropriate assumptions, that is, in particular that the support of $p(\theta)$ includes the support of $h(\theta \mid x)$ and the integral $\int g(\theta)h(\theta \mid x)d\theta$ exists and is finite, Geweke (1989) shows that with an i.i.d. importance sample θ_i from $p(\theta)$,

$$\frac{1}{\sum_{i=1}^{n} w_i} \sum_{i=1}^{n} w_i g(\theta_i) \quad \rightarrow \quad \int g(\theta)h(\theta \mid x)d\theta \qquad \text{a.s.,}$$

with a Monte Carlo standard error that can be estimated by

$$\widehat{\sigma}_n = \frac{1}{\sum_{j=1}^{n} w_j} \left[\sum_{i=1}^{n} \left\{ g(\theta_i) - \frac{1}{\sum_{j=1}^{n} w_j} \sum_{i=1}^{n} w_i g(\theta_i) \right\}^2 w_i^2 \right]^{1/2}. \tag{4.14}$$

The result assumes a finite variance of the Monte Carlo estimator, that is, of the posterior expected value of the product of $[g(\theta)]^2$ and the importance weight $h(\theta \mid x)/p(\theta)$ (this is identical to the expected value with respect to p of the square of $g(\theta)h(\theta \mid x)/p(\theta)$).

The rate of convergence for the importance sampling estimator depends on the ratio between the importance distribution and the target distribution $h(\theta \mid x)$. Note that the estimator gives more weight to θ values with $p(\theta) < h(\theta \mid x)$ and less when the opposite inequality holds. If the importance ratio is unbounded, as happens if the tails of p are lighter than the tails of $h(\cdot \mid x)$, then the weights can vary substantially and give great importance to few simulated values in a range (tails) with low probability under the target distribution. Depending on the function g, the variance of the estimator could even be infinite, implying far worse performance than an estimator based directly on the target distribution, if that were possible.

In summary, whether Monte Carlo with importance sampling is a promising technique for variance reduction depends on the selected importance sampling density (for more details, see Robert and Casella, 2004). Desirable properties for a good importance sampling density are: (1) easy random variate generation; (2) heavier tails than the target distribution $h(\cdot \mid x)$; and (3) good approximation of $h(\cdot \mid x)$. Shaw (1988) developed a class of univariate distributions that are designed to be suitable as importance functions (see also Smith, 1991). In the case of multivariate parameters, often multivariate normals or Student t distributions are used.[5]

---

[5] The program BAYESPACK provides an R interface for Fortran subroutines that implement numerical integration by importance sampling, based on methods described

Example 4.2 *Recall the setup from Example 4.1. The single-parameter model* (4.4) *was deliberately chosen to allow meaningful inference also with small sample sizes in a phase I trial. Still keeping a parsimonious model, but allowing for some more flexibility Neuenschwander et al (2008) propose a design based on a two-parameter probit regression,*

$$f(y_i = 1 \mid d_i = \delta_k) = \pi_k \text{ with } \pi_k = 1 - \Phi\left[-a - b\ln(\delta_k/\delta^o)\right]. \quad (4.15)$$

Here, a and b are probit regression coefficients and δ^o is a reference dose. The model allows easy interpretation of the parameters, with a determined by the prior odds at the reference dose δ^o, and b determines the shift in log odds for doses away from δ^o. The model is completed with a bivariate normal prior $(a, b) \sim N(\mu, \Sigma)$. We set the prior mean to $\mu = (1.65, 1.327)$ to match a prior expectation $E(\pi_1) = 0.01$ and $E(\pi_K) = 0.95$, respectively, and $\Sigma = I$ to have wide prior support over a range of plausible dose–response curves.

Noting that it is impossible to define a single precise target toxicity $\pi^\star$, Neuenschwander et al (2008) extend the notion of a single target toxicity level $\pi^\star$ to an ordinal scale over four sub-intervals of toxicity probabilities. Neuenschwander et al (2008) partition the range of toxicity probabilities π_k into four intervals: under-dosing, $I_u = (0, 0.20]$; targeted toxicity, $I_t = (0.20, 0.35]$; excessive toxicity, $I_e = (0.35, 0.60]$; and unacceptable toxicity, $I_a = (0.60, 1.00]$. Based on the posterior probabilities of π_k, $k = 1, \ldots, K$, being in these four intervals they propose a pragmatic design that prescribes de-escalation, escalation, and continued enrollment at the current dose, depending on these four probabilities.

Consider a study with a dose grid $\delta = (12.5, 25, 50, 100, 150, 200, 250)$ with reference dose $\delta^0 = 250$. Assume that the first $n = 7$ patients were assigned doses $k_i = 1, 1, 2, 2, 3, 2, 3$, with recorded outcomes $y_i = 0, 0, 0, 0, 1, 0, 1$. We use importance sampling to find $P(\pi_k \in I_t \mid D_n)$ and similar for I_e and I_a, for $k = 1, \ldots, K$. Let $\theta = (a, b)$. We use a bivariate normal importance function $p(\theta) = N(m, V)$, with m being the posterior mode (MAP) and V being the negative inverse of the Hessian of the log posterior at the mode,[6] i.e., $S = -H^{-1}$. Figure 4.2 summarizes posterior inference. The trial design would then determine the dose with maximum $p(\pi_k \in I_t \mid D_n)$, restricting the search to all doses with $p(\pi_k \in I_e \cup I_a \mid D_n) < 0.25$. ∎

by Genz and Kass (1997). The package can be downloaded from
http://cran.r-project.org/src/contrib/Archive/bayespack.
[6] See Section 8.1.1 for more discussion of normal approximations of the posterior distribution.

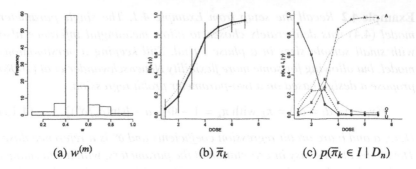

(a) $w^{(m)}$ (b) $\bar{\pi}_k$ (c) $p(\bar{\pi}_k \in I \mid D_n)$

Figure 4.2 Ordinal toxicity intervals: Panel (a) shows the importance sampling weights $w^{(m)}$. Panel (b) shows the posterior estimated probabilities of DLT, $\bar{\pi}_k = E(\pi_k \mid D_n)$ after $n = 7$ patients. The short vertical line segments show ± 1 posterior standard deviation for π_k. Panel (c) plots the posterior probabilities $p(\pi_k \in I \mid D_n)$ for the four intervals $I = I_u, I_t, I_o,$ and I_a (marked with "U," "T," "O," and "A," respectively).

In a similar fashion as in the previous section, we now proceed to describe applications of this method (and variations) for inference related to credible intervals, Bayes factors and marginal posterior densities.[7]

4.2.1 Credible Intervals

For more generality we now assume that the parameter vector in the sampling model is partitioned as $\theta = (\gamma, \phi)$, where γ is a univariate parameter of interest and ϕ is a vector of nuisance parameters (in the discussion corresponding to Section 4.1., there is no ϕ and thus $\theta = \gamma$).

Let (γ_i, ϕ_i), $1 \le i \le n$, denote a random sample from an importance sampling density $p(\gamma, \phi)$, designed for use with a posterior distribution $h(\gamma, \phi \mid x) \propto L(\gamma, \phi \mid x)h(\gamma, \phi)$. The c.d.f. of the marginal posterior distribution of γ in γ_* is then

$$H(\gamma_* \mid x) = E\left[I_{(-\infty,\gamma_*)}(\gamma) \mid x\right]$$

$$= \frac{\int I_{(-\infty,\gamma_*)}(\gamma)\frac{L(\gamma,\phi|x)h(\gamma,\phi)}{p(\gamma,\phi)}p(\gamma,\phi)d\gamma d\phi}{\int \frac{L(\gamma,\phi|x)h(\gamma,\phi)}{p(\gamma,\phi)}p(\gamma,\phi)d\gamma d\phi}.$$

---

[7] Additional discussion can be found in the books by Paulino et al (2018) and Chen et al (2000).

It can be approximated by the weighted Monte Carlo average:

$$\hat{H}(\gamma_* \mid x) = \frac{1}{n} \sum_{i=1}^{n} w_i I_{(-\infty, \gamma_*)}(\gamma_i), \tag{4.16}$$

with weights

$$w_i = \frac{L(\gamma_i, \phi_i \mid x) h(\gamma_i, \phi_i) / p(\gamma_i, \phi_i)}{\frac{1}{n} \sum_{j=1}^{n} L(\gamma_j, \phi_j \mid x) h(\gamma_j, \phi_j) / p(\gamma_j, \phi_j)}.$$

(Note that in variation from (4.13), we now include the normalization of the weights in w_i already.) Denote the sample ordered by the value of γ_i as $(\gamma_{(i)}, \phi_{(i)})$, $1 \le i \le n$, where $\phi_{(i)}$ is the value that was simulated together with $\gamma_{(i)}$ (that is, not the ith order statistic of ϕ, if ϕ were univariate), and let $w_{(i)}$ denote the respective weight for the pair $(\gamma_{(i)}, \phi_{(i)})$. We then define a weighted empirical distribution function of γ as

$$\hat{H}(\gamma_* \mid x) = \begin{cases} 0, & \gamma_* < \gamma_{(1)} \\ \sum_{j=1}^{i} w_{(j)}/n, & \gamma_{(i)} \le \gamma_* < \gamma_{(i+1)}, \\ 1, & \gamma_* \ge \gamma_{(n)} \end{cases}$$

which naturally matches the empirical distribution function if $p(\gamma, \phi) = h(\gamma, \phi \mid x)$ (and thus $w_{(i)} = c$, $\forall i$).

Let $\gamma_\alpha = \inf \{\gamma : H(\gamma \mid x) \ge \alpha\}$ denote the α-quantile of the marginal posterior of γ. Its Monte Carlo estimate is

$$\hat{\gamma}_\alpha = \begin{cases} \gamma_{(1)}, & \alpha = 0 \\ \gamma_{(i)}, & \frac{1}{n} \sum_{j=1}^{i-1} w_{(j)} < \alpha \le \frac{1}{n} \sum_{j=1}^{i} w_{(j)}. \end{cases}$$

The central $1 - \alpha$ credible interval, $R_*(1 - \alpha)$, is (consistently) estimated by

$$\hat{R}_*(1 - \alpha) = \left(\hat{\gamma}_{\frac{\alpha}{2}}, \hat{\gamma}_{1 - \frac{\alpha}{2}} \right). \tag{4.17}$$

Similarly, letting

$$\hat{R}_i(1 - \alpha) = \left(\hat{\gamma}_{\frac{i}{n}}, \hat{\gamma}_{\frac{i + [n(1 - \alpha)]}{n}} \right), \quad i = 1, \ldots, n - [n(1 - \alpha)]$$

denote a sequence of $(1 - \alpha)$ credible intervals for γ, the HPD interval $R_0(1 - \alpha)$ can be estimated by $\hat{R}_0(1 - \alpha) = \hat{R}_{i_0}(1 - \alpha)$, where $\hat{R}_{i_0}(1 - \alpha)$ is the minimum length interval in this sequence.

For credible intervals regarding any real-valued function $\psi(\gamma, \phi)$, it suffices to order the values $\psi_i = \psi(\gamma_i, \phi_i)$ and estimate the quantiles by the same scheme, which requires only the rearrangement of the same weights $w_{(i)}$.

4.2.2 Bayes Factors

Credible intervals are often used as a means to construct Bayesian significance tests, as was mentioned in Chapter 1. However, the idea of comparing statements by their posterior probabilities implies that hypothesis tests
(as well as the usual model comparison procedures) should make use of
Bayes factors, which in general could be complicated ratios of marginal
likelihoods.

Specifically, the Bayes factor in favor of H_0 versus the model H_1 is the
ratio of marginal likelihoods $B(x) = p(x \mid H_0)/p(x \mid H_1)$, where

$$p(x \mid H_k) = \int_{\Theta_k} f(x \mid \theta_k, H_k) h(\theta_k \mid H_k) \, d\theta_k, \; k = 0, 1.$$

This is the ratio of the normalizing constants for $f(x \mid \theta_k, H_k) h(\theta_k \mid H_k)$,
$k = 0, 1$. Therefore the methods that we shall describe for evaluating $B(x)$
are equally applicable for the evaluation of any ratio of normalization constants.

We start by considering the case when the densities with respect to which
we integrate in numerator and denominator are of the same dimension. In
that case notation need not distinguish parameters under H_0 and H_1, and
we write $\theta \equiv \theta_0 = \theta_1$. For simpler notation we also use

$$h(\theta \mid x, H_k) = \bar{h}_k(\theta)/c_k,$$

with support Θ_k. Here, $\bar{h}_k$ is the un-normalized product of prior times likelihood, and $c_k = p(x \mid H_k)$, $k = 0, 1$ is the normalization constant. Assume,
then, that one wishes to evaluate the ratio

$$B(x) = \frac{c_0}{c_1} = \frac{\int_{\Theta_0} \bar{h}_0(\theta) d\theta}{\int_{\Theta_1} \bar{h}_1(\theta) d\theta}$$

for analytically intractable (or difficult to evaluate) c_k.

Let $p_k(\theta)$ denote an importance sampling density for $\bar{h}_k$, assumed completely known, and let $\{\theta_1^{(k)}, \ldots, \theta_{n_k}^{(k)}\}$, $k = 0, 1$, denote corresponding importance samples. Direct application of Monte Carlo with importance sam-
pling for each c_k gives the following approximation:

$$\hat{B}_1(x) = \frac{\hat{c}_0}{\hat{c}_1}, \; \hat{c}_k = \frac{1}{n_k} \sum_{i=1}^{n_k} \frac{\bar{h}_k\left(\theta_i^{(k)}\right)}{p_k\left(\theta_i^{(k)}\right)}, \; k = 0, 1. \qquad (4.18)$$

By the law of large numbers this is a consistent estimator for $B(x)$.

Note that alternatively one could evaluate c_k with independent simple
Monte Carlo methods using sampling from the prior distribution, to give

$\frac{1}{n_k} \sum_{i=1}^{n_k} f\left(x \mid \theta_i^{(k)}, H_k\right)$, with the simulated values now being a random sample of size n_k from the prior $h(\theta \mid H_k)$ on θ under H_k. However, the prior could be substantially different from the likelihood function, in particular over subsets which are *a priori* little plausible, implying that this could be a rather poor estimate of c_k. See Chapter 5 for alternative methods to evaluate c_k.

In the special case of $\Theta_0 \subset \Theta_1$ it is possible to use a Monte Carlo approach for the evaluation of $B(x)$, using only a sample generated from $h_1(\theta)$ (which could be obtained without knowing c_1, as we shall see in Chapter 6). In fact,

$$B(x) = \frac{c_0}{c_1} = \int_{\Theta_1} \frac{\bar{h}_0(\theta)}{c_1} d\theta = E_{h_1}\left[\frac{\bar{h}_0(\theta)}{\bar{h}_1(\theta)}\right].$$

Assume now that $\left(\theta_i^{(1)}, i = 1, \ldots, n_1\right)$ is a random sample from h_1. Then

$$\hat{B}_2(x) = \frac{1}{n_1} \sum_{i=1}^{n_1} \frac{\bar{h}_0\left(\theta_i^{(1)}\right)}{\bar{h}_1\left(\theta_i^{(1)}\right)} \tag{4.19}$$

is a (unbiased and consistent) Monte Carlo estimate of $B(x)$. Note that this approximation is most efficient when the tails of $h_1(\theta)$ are heavier than the tails of $h_0(\theta)$ and less efficient when there is little overlap of $h_0(\theta)$ and $h_1(\theta)$ (that is, small $E_{h_1}[h_0(\theta)]$).

In many problems, the Bayes factor involves densities of different dimension and therefore requires different strategies. We will discuss some in Chapter 7. For a more general discussion of this problem, see the books by Chen et al (2000) and Paulino et al (2018).

4.2.3 Marginal Posterior Densities

As we explained in Section 4.1.3, the evaluation of marginal posterior densities by the conditional approach of Gelfand and Smith (1990) requires full knowledge of the corresponding conditional posterior densities (not just the kernels), which unfortunately is not commonly available, and availability of a Monte Carlo sample from the marginal posterior distribution for $\theta^{(-m)}$. If the latter is not available but it is possible to instead simulate from a substitute $p(\cdot)$ of $h(\theta^{(-m)} \mid x)$, then one can define an importance sampling estimate of the marginal density for $\theta^{(m)}$

$$\hat{h}\left(\theta_*^{(m)} \mid x\right) = \frac{\sum_{i=1}^{n} w_i h\left(\theta_*^{(m)} \mid \theta_{(i)}^{(-m)}, x\right)}{\sum_{i=1}^{n} w_i}, \tag{4.20}$$

where

$$w_i = h\left(\theta_{(i)}^{(-m)} \mid x\right) / p\left(\theta_{(i)}^{(-m)}\right),$$

$i = 1, \ldots, n$. Alternatively, with an argument as in (4.8), one could use $w_i = h\left(\theta_{(i)} \mid x\right) / p\left(\theta_{(i)}\right)$, $i = 1, \ldots, n$, with an importance sampling density $p(\cdot)$ for $h(\theta \mid x)$.

As yet another alternative, one could generate $\theta_{(i)}^{(m)}$, $i = 1, \ldots, n$, by the composition method using $p(\theta^{(-m)})$ and $h(\theta^{(m)} \mid \theta^{(-m)}, x)$. However, since we used $p(\cdot)$ instead of the marginal posterior for $\theta^{(-m)}$, the samples $\theta_{(i)}^{(m)}$ are not a random sample from $h(\theta^{(m)} \mid x)$. Instead, the $\theta_{(i)}^{(m)}$ are a weighted sample of an approximation of $h(\theta^{(m)} \mid x)$, with weights $p_i = w_i / \sum_{i=1}^{n} w_i$, $i = 1, \ldots, n$. To get from this a random sample of size L, say, one could simulate in the spirit of a bootstrap method L values $\theta_{(j)*}^{(m)}$, $j = 1, \ldots, L$, from the discrete distribution $(\theta_{(i)}^{(m)}, p_i)$, $i = 1, \ldots, n$. Smith and Gelfand (1992) therefore used the name weighted bootstrap.

This method to evaluate marginal posterior densities, similar to Gelfand and Smith (1990), does not apply when the normalization constant for the conditional posterior density $h(\theta^{(m)} \mid \theta^{(-m)}, x)$ is unknown. In this case, Chen (1994) proposes a weighted estimator for $h\left(\theta_*^{(m)} \mid x\right)$, based on the following identity

$$
\begin{aligned}
h\left(\theta_*^{(m)} \mid x\right) &= \int_{\Theta_{-m}(\theta_*^{(m)})} h\left(\theta_*^{(m)}, \theta^{(-m)} \mid x\right) d\theta^{(-m)} \\
&= \int_{\Theta} w\left(\theta^{(m)} \mid \theta^{(-m)}\right) \frac{h(\theta_*^{(m)}, \theta^{(-m)} \mid x)}{h(\theta^{(m)}, \theta^{(-m)} \mid x)} h(\theta \mid x) d\theta,
\end{aligned}
\tag{4.21}
$$

where $\Theta_{-m}(\theta^{(m)}) = \{\theta^{(-m)} : (\theta^{(m)}, \theta^{(-m)}) \in \Theta\}$ is the subspace of Θ with fixed $\theta^{(m)}$ and $w(\theta^{(m)} \mid \theta^{(-m)})$ is a completely known conditional density with the same as or greater support than $h(\theta^{(m)} \mid \theta^{(-m)}, x)$, given by $\Theta_m(\theta^{(-m)}) = \{\theta^{(m)} : (\theta^{(m)}, \theta^{(-m)}) \in \Theta\}$. The criteria for selecting the function w are the same as for selecting an importance sampling density.

The form of (4.21) highlights that the normalization constant of the joint posterior distribution (and, *a fortiori*, conditional) cancel out and that the marginal density in question can be unbiasedly estimated based on a sample $\theta_{(i)} = (\theta_{(i)}^{(m)}, \theta_{(i)}^{(-m)})$, $1 \le i \le n$, of $h(\theta \mid x)$, by

$$
\hat{h}\left(\theta_*^{(m)} \mid x\right) = \frac{1}{n} \sum_{i=1}^{n} w\left(\theta_{(i)}^{(m)} \mid \theta_{(i)}^{(-m)}\right) \frac{h\left(\theta_*^{(m)}, \theta_{(i)}^{(-m)} \mid x\right)}{h\left(\theta_{(i)}^{(m)}, \theta_{(i)}^{(-m)} \mid x\right)}.
\tag{4.22}
$$

4.3 Sequential Monte Carlo

Time series data and related models give rise to challenging posterior intergration problems. Some of these problems can be approached by Monte Carlo simulation methods known as sequential Monte Carlo (SMC), which is the subject of this section. We start with a brief review of dynamic state space models, including popular normal dynamic linear models which allow analytic solutions and motivate some of the SMC schemes.

4.3.1 Dynamic State Space Models

With time series data y_t collected over time, it is natural to index parameters correspondingly as θ_t, $t = 1, \ldots, T$. This allows, in particular, introduction of dependence of y_t across time as independent sampling conditional on θ_t, with an evolution of θ_t over time inducing the desired marginal dependence. Assuming normal linear models for both, the sampling model for y_t (observation equation, OE) and the evolution of θ_t over time (evolution equation, EE) this defines the normal dynamic linear model (NDLM)

$$
\begin{aligned}
\text{OE}: \quad y_t &= F_t'\theta_t + v_t, \quad v_t \sim N(0, V_t), \\
\text{EE}: \quad \theta_t &= G_t\theta_t + w_t, \quad w_t \sim N(0, W_t),
\end{aligned}
\tag{4.23}
$$

with $\theta_0 \sim N(m_0, C_0)$. Here, $y_t \in \mathbb{R}^p$ is the observed data, $\theta_t \in \mathbb{R}^q$ is a latent state vector, and F_t and G_t are known design matrices that could possibly include a regression on covariates.

Posterior updating in the NDLM is straightforward by the following finite recursion. Let $D_t = (y_1, \ldots, y_t)$ denote the data up to time t. Conditioning on D_t defines a sequence of posterior distributions, including $h(\theta_t \mid D_{t-1})$ and $h(\theta_t \mid D_t)$, for $t = 1, \ldots, T$. Starting with $h(\theta_0 \mid D_0) = N(m_0, C_0)$, we easily find for $t = 1, \ldots, T$:

$$
\begin{aligned}
\theta_t \mid D_{t-1} &\sim N(a_t, R_t), & a_t &= G_t m_{t-1}, & R_t &= G_t C_{t-1} G_t' + W_t \\
y_t \mid D_{t-1} &\sim N(f_t, Q_t), & f_t &= F_t' a_t, & Q_t &= F_t' R_t F_t + V_t \\
\theta_t \mid D_t &\sim N(m_t, C_t), & m_t &= a_t + A_t e_t & C_t &= R_t - A_t Q_t A_t' \\
& & e_t &= y_t - f_t \text{ and } A_t = R_t F_t Q_t'
\end{aligned}
\tag{4.24}
$$

A similar set of recursive equations obtains the posterior distributions

$$
h(\theta_{t-k} \mid D_t) = N(a_t(-k), R_t(-k)),
$$

for $k = 1, \ldots, t - 1$. Starting with $a_t(0) = m_t$ and $R_t(0) = C_t$ for $k = 0$, and defining $B_t = C_t G'_{g+1} R^{-1}_{t+1}$, we have

$$a_t(-k) = m_{t-k} + B_{t-k}[a_t(-k+1) - a_{t-k+1}],$$
$$R_t(-k) = C_{t-k} + B_{t-k}[R_t(-k+1) - R_{t-k+1}]B'_{t-k}. \tag{4.25}$$

Without the initial prior at $t = 0$, or equivalently, $C_0^{-1} = 0$, the recursive equations determine the maximum likelihood estimate, and are known as the Kalman filter. As posterior updating the same equations are known as forward filtering (FF) for (4.24) and backward smoothing (BS) for (4.25). See, for example, Prado and West (2010: ch. 4) for a detailed discussion of the NDLM and many useful variations, including in particular the case of unknown variances in the observation and evolution equations.

The NDLM (4.23) is a special case of more general dynamic state space models. The characteristic feature is the hidden Markov nature of the model. The data y_t are independent conditional on latent states θ_t, and the prior for the latent $\{\theta_t, t = 1, 2, \ldots\}$ includes a Markov assumption with conditional independence of θ_t and θ_{t-k}, $k > 1$, given θ_{t-1}. The general dynamic state space model is defined by a sampling model for y_t given θ_t and a transition probability for the Markov prior on the states:

$$f(y_t \mid \theta_t) \text{ and } p(\theta_t \mid \theta_{t-1}), \tag{4.26}$$

for $t = 1, 2, \ldots$. The model is completed with the initial prior $h(\theta_0)$. Like the NDLM, the general dynamic state space model gives rise to a sequence of posterior distributions $h_t = h(\theta_t \mid D_t)$, predictive distributions, and more. Many applications include additional (static) parameters ϕ in $f(y_t \mid \theta_t, \phi)$ and/or $p(\theta_t \mid \theta_{t-1}, \phi)$. See Section 4.3.4.

4.3.2 Particle Filter

Short of the special normal and linear features of the NDLM, posterior inference in general dynamic state space models (4.26) is not analytically tractable and posterior simulation is needed. Monte Carlo posterior simulation methods for the sequence of posterior distributions $h_t = h(\theta_t \mid D_t)$ are naturally set up in a sequential fashion, including a step to update a posterior Monte Carlo sample $B_t = \{\theta_{t,i}, i = 1, \ldots, M\}$ from h_t to a Monte Carlo sample B_{t+1} from h_{t+1}. Such methods are known as SMC methods. A good review appears, for example, in Doucet et al (2001) and, more recently, in Doucet and Lee (2018).

For reference, we state the relevant posterior and posterior predictive distributions and define notation,

$$
\begin{aligned}
h_t &\equiv h(\theta_t \mid D_t) & &\text{posterior at time } t, \\
h'_t &\equiv h(\theta_t \mid D_{t-1}) & &\text{prior distribution at time } t, \\
f_t &\equiv p(y_t \mid D_{t-1}) & &\text{forecast distribution.}
\end{aligned}
\tag{4.27}
$$

One of the earliest proposals for SMC is the auxiliary particle filter described by Pitt and Shephard (1999). The algorithm starts with a Monte Carlo sample $B_0 = \{\theta_{0,i}, \; i = 1, \ldots, M\}$ from $h(\theta_0)$, and then iteratively updates B_{t-1} into a Monte Carlo sample $B'_t = \{\theta'_{t,i}\}$ from the prior distribution $h'_t = h(\theta_t \mid D_{t-1})$ and then a Monte Carlo sample $B_t = \{\theta_{t,i}\}$ from the posterior h_t at time t. In other words, the elements of B_0 ("particles") are pushed through a sequence of updating steps to generate the desired Monte Carlo samples from f_t and h_t. The key identities are the representation of h'_t as a convolution of h_{t-1} and the transition model as

$$
h'_t(\theta_t) = h(\theta_t \mid D_{t-1}) = \int p(\theta_t \mid \theta_{t-1}) \, dh_{t-1}(\theta_{t-1})
\tag{4.28}
$$

and posterior updating

$$
h_t(\theta_t) = h(\theta_t \mid D_t) \propto h'_t(\theta_t) f(y_t \mid \theta_t).
\tag{4.29}
$$

Rather than generating Monte Carlo samples from the target distributions, the algorithm generates Monte Carlo samples from importance sampling densities together with corresponding weights $W_t = \{w_{ti}, \; i = 1, \ldots, M\}$ for B_t and $W'_t = \{w'_{ti}, \; i = 1, \ldots, M\}$ for B'_t. Let $\widehat{h_t} \approx h_t$ and $\widehat{h'_t} \approx h'_t$ denote the importance sampling densities. Then $w_{ti} = h_t(\theta_{t,i})/\widehat{h_t}(\theta_{t,i})$ and $w'_{ti} = h'_t(\theta_{t,i})/\widehat{h'_t}(\theta_{t,i})$, and posterior integrals with respect to the target distributions can be approximated as

$$
\int g(\theta_t) h(\theta_t \mid D_t) d\theta_t \approx \frac{1}{\sum w_{ti}} \sum_{i=1}^{M} w_{ti} g(\theta_{t,i}),
$$

with the Monte Carlo average going over all particles $\theta_{t,i} \in B_t$. In particular, this allows us to approximate h'_t by using the representation from (4.28) as

$$
h'_t(\theta_t) \approx \widehat{h'_t}(\theta_t) = \frac{1}{\sum w_{ti}} \sum w_{t-1,i} \, p(\theta_t \mid \theta_{t-1,i}).
\tag{4.30}
$$

A basic particle filter could then proceed as follows. Assume B_{t-1} and W_{t-1} are available. First, generate B'_t by sampling from $\widehat{h'_t}(\theta_t)$. This is done by: (1) sampling $\theta_{t-1,i}$ from B_{t-1} with probabilities proportional to $w_{t-1,i}$; and (2) generate $\theta'_{t,i} \sim p(\theta'_t \mid \theta_{t-1,i})$ and record weights $w'_{ti} = 1/M$. Finally, in step (3), define B_t by setting $\theta_{t,i} \equiv \theta'_{t,i}$ and $w_{ti} \propto f(y_t \mid \theta_{t,i})$ proportional to the likelihood factor for y_t. This is essentially the idea of the auxiliary variable particle filter, except that by combining steps (1) and (3), the algorithm makes the sampling more efficient.

Similar to (4.30), we define

$$h_t \approx \widehat{h}_t \propto \sum_i w_{t-1,i} f(y_t \mid \theta_t) p(\theta_t \mid \theta_{t-1,i}) \qquad (4.31)$$

as a Monte Carlo approximation of h_t, based on B_{t-1} and W_{t-1}. In words, the trick is to (1) augment $\widehat{h}_t(\theta_t)$ to a joint model $\widehat{h}(\theta_t, i)$; (2) approximate $\widehat{h}(\theta_t, i) \approx g(\theta_t, i)$ by replacing θ_t in $f(y_t \mid \theta_t)$ by $\mu_{t,i} = E(\theta'_{t,i} \mid \theta_{t-1,i})$; and (3) generate $(\theta_t, i) \sim g$, and use weights $w_{t,i} = f(y_t \mid \theta_{t,i})/f(y_t \mid \mu_{t,i})$. The main advantage of the algorithm is that we select the term i in h'_t in a way that already anticipates the later multiplication with the likelihood factor. We formally state steps 1 through 3:

1. Augment $\widehat{h}_t(\theta_t)$ in (4.31) to

$$\widehat{h}(\theta_t, i) \propto w_{t-1,i} f(y_t \mid \theta_t) p(\theta_t \mid \theta_{t-1,i}).$$

   Substitute an approximation $f(y_t \mid \theta_t) \approx f(y_t \mid \mu_{t,i})$, for example, using $\mu_{ti} = E(\theta_t \mid \theta_{t-1,i})$, to obtain

$$g(\theta_t, i) \propto w_{t-1,i} f(y_t \mid \mu_{t,i}) p(\theta_t \mid \theta_{t-1,i}). \qquad (4.32)$$

2. Let $g(i) \propto w_{t-1,i} f(y_t \mid \mu_{t,i})$ denote the implied marginal on i under $g(\theta_t, i)$. Generate $i \sim g(i)$ and $\theta_{t,i} \mid i \sim p(\theta_t \mid \theta_{t-1,i})$.

3. Record weights $w_{ti} = \frac{\widehat{h}(\theta_{t,i}, i)}{g(\theta_{t,i}, i)} = \frac{f(y_t \mid \theta_{t,i})}{f(y_t \mid \mu_{t,i})}$.

4.3.3 Adapted Particle Filter

Pitt and Shephard (1999) refer to the algorithm with $f(y_t \mid \mu_{ti}) \approx f(y_t \mid \theta_{ti})$ as the basic adapted particle filter. Exploiting the specific structure of the state space model, we can sometimes construct better adapted schemes. The aim is to achieve weights w_{ti} with minimum variance.

Perfect adaptation, i.e., constant weights, is possible for a state space model with normal sampling model and evolution (indexing the normal model with mean and variance):

$$f(y_t \mid \theta_t) = N(\theta_t, 1) \text{ and } p(\theta_t \mid \theta_{t-1}) = N[\mu(\theta_{t-1}), \sigma^2(\theta_{t-1})], \qquad (4.33)$$

assuming for simplicity unit variance in the sampling model. In this case $g(\theta_t, i)$ in step (i) from before can be replaced by $\widehat{h}$ itself:

$$\widehat{h}(\theta_t, i) \propto w_{t-1,i} N(y_t \mid \theta_t, 1) N(\theta_t \mid \mu(\theta_{t-1,i}), \sigma^2(\theta_{t-1,i})), \qquad (4.34)$$

without the likelihood approximation in $g(\theta_t, i)$. Instead, the normal assumption allows us to use Bayes' theorem and replace the last two factors to obtain

$$\widehat{h}(\theta_t, i) \propto w_{t-1,i} N(\theta_t \mid m_i, v_i) \underbrace{N(y_t \mid \mu(\theta_{t-1,i}), \sigma^2(\theta_{t-1,i}) + 1)}_{\lambda_i}, \quad (4.35)$$

where (m_i, v_i) are the posterior moments in a normal–normal model with sampling model and prior given by those last two factors. In other words, we replace sampling model times prior, $f(y_t \mid \theta_t, \ldots) \times p(\theta_t \mid \theta_{t-1}, \ldots)$, in (4.34) by posterior times marginal, $h(\theta_t \mid y_t, \ldots) \times p(y_t \mid \ldots)$, in (4.35) (cf. Example 2.8). This simplifies the auxiliary particle filter to

1'. $\widehat{h}(\theta_t, i) \propto w_{t-1,i} \lambda_i N(\theta_t \mid m_i, v_i)$
2'. Generate $i \sim \widehat{h}(i) \propto w_{t-1,i} \lambda_i$ and $\theta_t \mid i \sim N(\theta_t \mid m_i, v_i)$.
3'. Record $w_{ti} = 1/M$.

A similar simplification with perfect adaptation is possible for any conjugate sampling model and evolution.

Example 4.3 *Consider an ARCH model with additional independent normal residuals:*

$$f(y_t \mid \theta_i) = N(\theta_t, \sigma^2), \quad f(\theta_{t+1} \mid \theta_t) = N(0, \beta_0 + \beta_1 \theta_t^2). \quad (4.36)$$

With fixed static parameters $(\beta_0, \beta_1, \sigma^2)$, the model is a special case of (4.33) and allows a perfectly adapted particle filter. Let $N(x \mid m, s^2)$ denote a normal p.d.f. with moments (m, s^2), evaluated for x. In this case $\lambda_i = N(y_t \mid 0, \beta_0 + \beta_1 \theta_{t,i}^2 + \sigma^2)$ and (m_i, v_i) are just the posterior moments for θ_{t+1} under the likelihood and prior in (4.36) ∎

In a general dynamic state space model, with arbitrary sampling model $f(y_t \mid \theta_t)$, one can still implement steps (1') and (2') using a second-order Taylor series approximation of $\ln f(y_t \mid \theta_t)$. The expansion is in θ_t (Pitt and Shephard, 1999). See Problem 4.9.

4.3.4 Parameter Learning

Recall the general dynamic state space model from (4.26). Often the model might include unknown static parameters ϕ, in addition to the dynamic parameters θ_t, defining a model:

$$p(y_t \mid \theta_t, \phi) \text{ and } p(\theta_t \mid \theta_{t-1}, \phi), \quad (4.37)$$

completed with a prior on the static parameters and the initial state $(\phi, \theta_0) \sim h(\phi, \theta_0)$. For example, in the ARCH model, $\phi = (\beta_0, \beta_1, \sigma^2)$.

There are several approaches to generalizing particle filter methods to include parameter learning. Liu and West (2001) reduce static parameter learning to the earlier problem by allowing a negligibly small but positive evolution noise for ϕ, thus including it as ϕ_t in the state vector. Polson et al (2008) use a (approximate) sufficient statistic to define the "practical filter." For a review and more detailed discussion see, for example, Prado and West (2010).

Problems

4.1 *Simple Monte Carlo integration.* Implement inference for Example 4.1.

    a. Verify the posterior means $\bar{\pi}_k$ shown in Figure 4.1, and add central 50% credible intervals for π_k, $k = 1, \ldots, K$.

    b. Assume the next patient is treated at dose $k_5 = 3$, and we record no toxicity, $y_5 = 0$. Find the updated posterior means $\bar{\pi}_k = E(\pi_k \mid D_5)$ and determine the treatment allocation $k^\star$ for the next patient.

4.2 *Importance sampling: probit regression.* Refer to Example 4.2.

    a. Based on Figure 4.2 and the design rule as it is summarized in the example, which dose $k^\star$ is assigned to the next, $(n + 1)$-st patient?

    b. Let $\theta = (a, b)$. Evaluate the marginal posterior distributions $h(\pi_k \mid D_n)$ using importance sampling, using a bivariate normal importance function $p(\theta) = N(m, V)$, as in the example. Plot $h(\pi_k \mid D_n)$, $k = 1, \ldots, K$. In the plot indicate the four intervals for under-dosing, target dose, excessive dose, and unacceptable toxicity by vertical dotted lines on the interval boundaries.

    c. Let $\{\theta^{(m)}; m = 1, \ldots, M\}$ denote the importance sample from $p(\theta)$. Figure 4.2(a) shows the importance weights $w^{(m)} \equiv h(\theta^{(m)} \mid y)/p(\theta^{(m)})$ for an importance Monte Carlo sample $\{\theta^{(m)}; m = 1, \ldots, M\}$ of size $M = 100$. Redo the importance sampling estimate, now with $M = 1000$, and plot the histogram of weights. What do you observe?

    d. Now consider an alternative bivariate Student t importance function, $p_2(\theta) = t_2(m, V; \nu)$ with $\nu = 4$. Plot a histogram of the importance sampling weights $w_2^{(m)} = h(\theta^{(m)} \mid y)/p_2(\theta^{(m)})$ and compare.

4.3 *Importance sampling: nonlinear regression.* Let x denote the number of plants per unit area and y denote the yield per plant. To model the relationship between yield and planting density, we use the sampling model

$$f(y_i \mid \theta) = N(\mu_i, \sigma^2) \text{ with } \mu_i = 1/(\alpha + \beta x_i + \gamma x_i^2).$$

Let $\tau = \ln(\sigma^2)$ and $\theta = (\alpha, \beta, \gamma, \tau)$. In this model, $1/\alpha = \lim_{x \to 0} y$ is interpreted as "genetic potential" and $1/\beta$ can be interpreted as "environmental potential."

The model is completed with a non-informative prior $h(\theta) \propto 1$. Use the data set onion in the R package *SemiPar*. The data set includes the variables dens, yield, and location. We use data from location 0 (Purnong Landing) only. Scale $y = $ yield/100 by 100, and standardize x as $x = (d - \bar{d})/s_d$, where d =density, and $\bar{d}$, s_d^2 are the sample mean and variance.

a. Set up a multivariate normal importance sampling density $p(\theta)$. Use a $N(m, V)$ with m being the posterior mode (MAP) and $V = -H^{-1}$ being the negative inverse Hessian of the log posterior at the mode.[8] Carry out importance sampling to estimate the posterior means and standard deviations of θ. Report numerical uncertainties and show a histogram of importance sampling weights.

b. Repeat the same importance sampling estimation with a multivariate Student t distribution with $\nu = 4$ d.f. (see Appendix A). See also the hint for Problem 4.4(b).

c. Why would one recommend the Student t importance function? Explain.

4.4 *Importance sampling: hierarchical model.* Carlin and Gelfand (1991) consider a hierarchical event rate model for the number of pump failures (y_i) over given exposure times (t_i), $i = 1, \ldots, n = 10$. The data are shown in the following table.

y_i	5	1	5	14	5
t_i	94.32	15.72	62.88	125.76	5.24
y_i	19	1	1	4	22
t_i	31.44	1.048	1.048	2.096	10.48

We assume a Poisson regression,

$$y_i \sim \mathrm{Poi}(\lambda_i t_i),$$

with a hierarchical prior for $L_i = \ln(\lambda_i)$:

$$L_i \sim N(\eta, \sigma^2), \text{ and } \eta \sim N(\mu, \tau^2), \gamma \equiv 1/\sigma^2 \sim \mathrm{Ga}(a, b).$$

We fix the hyperparameters at $(\mu, \tau^2, a, b) = (-1, 1, 1, 1)$.
Let $g = \ln(\gamma)$ and let $\theta = (\eta, g, L_1, \ldots, L_n)$ denote the complete parameter vector (now with $g = \ln(\gamma)$). Let $\hat{\theta}$ and S denote mean and covariance matrix of a multivariate normal approximation of the joint posterior distribution $h(\theta \mid y)$ (for example, posterior mode and negative inverse Hessian of the log posterior at the mode, as in Problem 4.3). Under the multivariate $N(\hat{\theta}, S)$

---

[8] We will discuss the use of such multivariate normal approximations in Chapter 8.

distribution for θ let $m = (\hat{\theta}_1, \hat{\theta}_2)$ and V denote the corresponding marginal moments for $\psi = (\eta, g)$.

Let $p_1(\psi) = t_2(m, V; \nu)$ (use $\nu = 2$), and $p_2(L_i \mid \eta, \gamma) \propto N(L_i \mid \eta, \sigma^2) \mathrm{Poi}(y_i \mid t_i e^{L_i})$. Here, $\mathrm{Poi}(y \mid \mu)$ denotes the Poisson probability mass function with rate μ evaluated for y and similar for $N(x \mid \mu, \sigma^2)$. Use an importance sampling density

$$p(\theta) = p_1(\eta, g) \, \Pi_{i=1}^n p_2(L_i \mid \eta, g). \tag{4.38}$$

We can generate from $p(\cdot)$ by first generating $\psi = (\eta, g)$ from the bivariate t distribution $p_1(\psi)$, and then L_i from p_2 using, for example, a grid-based method using evaluation of p_2 on a grid (using the R function `sample()`; see Appendix B).

a. Using the importance sampling function (4.38), find the expression for the importance sampling weights w_i.

Hint: Do not forget the normalization constant in $p_2(L_i \mid \eta, g)$.

b. Let $y = (y_1, \ldots, y_n)$ denote the data. Implement importance sampling to evaluate posterior moments, $\bar{\lambda}_i = E(\lambda_i \mid y)$ and $s_i^2 = \mathrm{Var}(\lambda_i \mid y)$, $i = 1, \ldots, n$. Show a histogram of the importance sampling weights, a table of estimated posterior moments $\bar{\lambda}_i(s_i)$, and corresponding numerical uncertainties.

Hint: To generate from the bivariate t distribution $t_\nu(m, V)$ with $V = LL'$, you could use: $z \sim N_2(0, I)$, $y = Lz$, $u \sim \chi^2(\nu)$, and $\psi = m + \sqrt{\nu/u}\, y$. Then,

$$p(\psi) \propto \left[1 + \frac{1}{\nu}(\psi - m)' V^{-1}(\psi - m) \right]^{-\frac{\nu+2}{2}} = [1 + z'z/u]^{-\frac{\nu+2}{2}}$$

c. Use suitable Monte Carlo methods to evaluate and plot the marginal posterior distributions $h(\lambda_i \mid y)$, $i = 1, \ldots, n$.

d. The problem greatly simplifies with $\lambda_i \sim \mathrm{Ga}(c, \frac{c}{\eta})$. Why?

4.5 The skewed normal distribution defines a skewed continuous random variable. Let $\varphi_{m,s}$ denote a normal p.d.f. with moments (m, s) and let $\Phi(z)$ denote a standard normal c.d.f. The skewed normal can be defined by its p.d.f.,

$$f(x \mid \mu, \sigma, \alpha) \propto \varphi_{\mu,\sigma}(x) \, \Phi\left(\alpha \frac{x - \mu}{\sigma} \right).$$

For $\alpha > 0$ ($\alpha < 0$), the distribution is right (left) skewed. We write $X \sim \mathrm{SN}(\mu, \sigma, \alpha)$ for a skewed normal random variable X. For the following questions use the data set `stockreturns.txt`[9] of (simulated) stock returns. We assume the sampling model

$$x_i \sim \mathrm{SN}(\mu, \sigma, \alpha),$$

[9]   Available on the book's homepage at
sites.google.com/view/computationalbayes/home

$i = 1, \ldots, n$, i.i.d., and complete the model with a conditionally conjugate prior on μ, σ and a gamma prior on α:

$$1/\sigma^2 \sim \mathrm{Ga}(a/2, a\sigma_0^2/2), \quad h(\mu \mid \sigma) = N(\mu_0, \kappa\sigma^2) \text{ and } h(\alpha) = \mathrm{Ga}(c, d),$$

with fixed hyperparameters κ, c, d, μ_0, a, and σ_0^2.

a. Let $\gamma = 1/\sigma^2$. For fixed α suggest an importance sampling strategy to estimate posterior means (conditional on α). Let $p(\mu, \gamma)$ denote the importance sampling density, and let w denote the importance sampling weights. Propose a choice for $p(\cdot)$, and find a bound M such that $w \leq M$.

b. Claim

$$h(\alpha \mid x) = 2E\{\Phi(W)\}$$

where the expectation is with respect to a t-distributed random variable W. Show the claim, and then use the result to find the marginal posterior mode of α over a grid $\alpha \in \{1, 1.1, 1.2, 1.3, 1.4, 1.5\}$.

4.6 In a study, $N = 97$ alcoholics were classified as X_1 – professional situation (with or without employment), X_2 – daily alcohol consumption (yes or no), and X_3 – expression of some phobia (yes or no), as listed in Table 4.2 (from Paulino and Singer, 2006). The aim of the study was inference on possible associations between the three binary variables X_1, X_2, and X_3. We assume a multinomial sampling model for the observed counts, $(n_{ijk}, i, j, k = 0, 1) \sim M_7(N, \theta_{ijk}, i, j, k = 0, 1)$, and complete the model with an improper prior $h(\theta) \propto \Pi_{i,j,k}\theta_{ijk}^{-1}$. The model implies a Dirichlet posterior distribution $h(\theta \mid n) = D_7(A)$ with $A = (10, 24, 6, 12, 13, 17, 4, 7)$.
We are interested in the hypothesis of conditional independence of X_2 and X_3 given X_1, that is

$$H_{IC} : \theta_{ijk} = \theta_{ij\cdot}\theta_{i\cdot k}/\theta_{i\cdot\cdot}, \forall i, j, k \Leftrightarrow \psi_i \equiv \ln \frac{\theta_{i11}\theta_{i22}}{\theta_{i12}\theta_{i21}} = 0, \forall i.$$

In short, $\psi_i = a_i' \ln \theta$ with $a_1 = (1, -1, -1, 1, 0, 0, 0, 0)'$ and $a_2' = (0, 0, 0, 0, 1, -1, -1, 1)'$. The parameters of interest $\psi = (\psi_1, \psi_2)$ have a distribution that is not easily available in closed form.

Table 4.2 observed frequencies n_{ijk}

Professional situation (X_1)	Daily use (X_2)	phobia (X_3) Yes	No
Unemployed	Yes	10	24
	No	6	12
Employed	Yes	13	17
	No	4	7

    a. Use Monte Carlo simulation to estimate $h(\psi_1, \psi_2 \mid n)$. First, generate $M = 10,000$ draws from the Dirichlet posterior distribution $\theta^{(m)} \sim h(\theta \mid n)$, $m = 1, \ldots, M$. Next, compute $\psi^{(m)}$ for each draw. Use the resulting posterior Monte Carlo sample $\psi^{(m)}$, $m = 1, \ldots, M$ to plot a bivariate histogram or contour plot.

    b. Use an approximation of $h(\psi_1, \psi_2 \mid n)$ on a bivariate grid to find a 95% HPD credible region of $\psi = (\psi_1, \psi_2)$.

    c. What evidence does the credible region provide about the hypothesis H_{IC}?

4.7 *Importance sampling.* Let $\widehat{g}_n$ denote the importance sampling estimate (4.13) of the posterior expectation $\bar{g} = \int g(\theta) h(\theta \mid x) d\theta$. Using the central limit theorem, Geweke (1989) shows $n^{1/2}(\widehat{g}_n - \bar{g}) \to N(0, \sigma^2)$, with $\sigma^2 = E\left\{ [g(\theta) - \bar{g}]^2 w(\theta) \right\}$. Convergence is in distribution. Recall the definition of $\widehat{\sigma}_n^2$ in (4.14). Show $n\widehat{\sigma}_n^2 \to \sigma^2$. State the mode of convergence.

    Hint: See the discussion in Geweke (1989).

4.8 *Consensus Monte Carlo.* Consider a large data set y that is too big or just impractical to process at one time. The idea of consensus Monte Carlo (Scott et al, 2016) is to break the prohibitively big data y into small "shards," y_s, $s = 1, \ldots, S$, carry out posterior computation for each shard separately, and then appropriately combine the subset posteriors to recover, or at least approximate, what posterior inference under the complete data could have been.

    Assume $y_s \mid \theta \sim N(\theta, \Sigma_s)$, $s = 1, \ldots, S$, for known Σ_s (for example, $\Sigma_s = \sigma^2 I$), with conjugate prior $h(\theta) = N(m, T)$.

    a. Define a *subset posterior* as $h_s(\theta \mid y) \propto f(y_s \mid \theta) h(\theta)^{1/S}$, i.e., as posterior conditional on the subset y_s under the modified prior $h_s(\theta) \propto h(\theta)^{1/S}$. Show that $h_s(\theta \mid y_s) = N(m_s, V_s)$, and that $h(\theta \mid y) = \Pi_s h_s(\theta \mid y_s) = N(m, V)$. Find m_s, V_s, m, and V.

    b. Let $\theta_s \sim h_s(\theta \mid y)$ denote draws from the subset posteriors, $s = 1, \ldots, S$. Let $\theta = V\left(\sum_s V_s^{-1} \theta_s\right)$. Show that $\theta \sim N(m, V)$, i.e., θ is a draw from the joint posterior.

For multivariate normal posteriors, the described algorithm provides an exact draw from the joint posterior. In general, one can argue that it provides a reasonable approximate draw from the joint posterior that can be obtained by carrying out computation for small shards only.

4.9 *Adapted auxiliary particle filter.* Recall steps (1′), (2′), and (3′) of the perfectly adapted auxiliary particle filter for model (4.33) in Section 4.3.3. Now replace the normal sampling model in (4.33) by a general sampling model $f(y_t \mid \theta_t)$.

    a. Let $\ell(\theta_t) = \ln f(y_t \mid \theta_t)$ denote the log-likelihood factor for θ_t. Find (μ_t, σ_t)

for the quadratic approximation $\ell(\theta_t) \approx -1/(2\sigma_t^2)(\theta_t - \mu_t)^2$, using a Taylor series expansion of $\ell(\theta_t)$.

b. Use this quadratic approximation to derive a variation of (4.35).

c. Using that variation of (4.35), work out appropriate variations (1″), (2″), and (3″) of the adapted particle filter (the weights in step (3″) are no longer constant).

4.10 Consider a stochastic volatility model,

$$y_t = \epsilon_t \beta \exp(\theta_t/2) \text{ and } \theta_{t+1} = \phi\theta_t + \eta_t,$$

with $\epsilon_t \sim N(0, 1)$ and $\eta_t \sim N(0, \sigma_\eta^2)$. For this problem we fix $\phi = 0.9702, \sigma_\eta = 0.178$, and $\beta = 0.5992$ (Pitt and Shephard, 1999: section 4.2).

a. Simulate a data set $y_1, \ldots, y_T$, using $\theta_0 = 0$ and $T = 200$. State the random variate seed that you use. For example, if you use R, use set.seed(1963). Plot y_t versus t as a time series.

b. Let $\ell(\theta_t) = \ln f(y_t \mid \theta_t)$ denote the log-likelihood factor for θ_t. Find (μ_t, σ_t) for the quadratic approximation $\ell(\theta_t) \approx -1/(2\sigma_t^2)(\theta_t - \mu_t)^2$ (see the previous problem).

c. Implement the adapted auxiliary particle filter from the previous problem. As in Section 4.3, let $D_t = (y_1, \ldots, y_t)$ denote the data up to time t. Plot the posterior means $\bar{\theta}_t = E(\theta_t \mid D_t)$ against time, and add posterior medians and 25% and 75% quantiles.

5

Model Assessment

This chapter deals with approaches for model assessment aiming to implement a selection and comparison leading to the choice of the best model(s). We start in Section 5.1 with a description of model diagnostics such as Bayesian p-values associated with various discrepancy measures, residuals, conditional predictive ordinates, and corresponding pseudo-Bayes factors. In Section 5.2 we then consider several measures of predictive performance, known by their acronyms as AIC, SIC (or BIC), DIC, and WAIC, and ways of using Bayes factors for selection and comparison tasks. Finally, in Section 5.3, using Monte Carlo samples to represent posterior distributions in complex models, we review ways of estimating relevant quantities for model assessment in this context.

5.1 Model Criticism and Adequacy

Verifying or critically examining a model is a stage of statistical analysis that aims to evaluate the adequacy of model fitting to data and known features of the problem at hand. In this exercise, we aim to quantify discrepancies with the data, evaluate whether these are or are not due to chance, and ascertain the degree of sensitivity of inference with respect to various elements of the model, and propose ways to revise the model.

Bayesian P-values

Box (1980, 1983) proposed to base a critical analysis of a model on the comparison of the data x and the marginal (or prior predictive) $p(x) = E_h [f(x \mid \theta)]$ by way of marginal p-values $P [p(X) \geq p(x)]$. This approach does not work with improper priors. In particular, it prevents the use of hypothetical replicate data based on simulation from $h(\theta)$. Even when $h(\theta)$ is proper, Monte Carlo methods tend to be in general unstable (Gelfand, 1996), and therefore not reliable, for the evaluation of $p(x)$.

One of the most widely used strategies for a critical model examination is based on the posterior predictive distribution under the model,

$$p(y \mid x) = \int_{\Theta} f(y \mid \theta) h(\theta \mid x) d\theta. \tag{5.1}$$

Here, y are hypothetical future data (see the following for details) and x are the observed data. The data y should expectedly (or not) reflect the observed data in the case of a good (bad) fit of the model. Any systematic discrepancies between the two data sets, y and x, are evidence for some flaw in the model.

The discrepancy between the observed data and data that are observable under the model can be evaluated by summary variables $V(x, \theta)$, which should be chosen to relate to the specific model aspects that the investigator wishes to evaluate. Examples of such variables include standardized mean squared deviations defined as

$$V(x, \theta) = \sum_i \frac{[x_i - E(X_i \mid \theta)]^2}{\text{Var}(X_i \mid \theta)} \tag{5.2}$$

and the actual log-likelihood, $\ln f(x \mid \theta)$, as well as the special cases of statistics $V(x)$ and functions $g(\theta)$ of the parameters only.

The posterior predictive distribution is typically determined by simulation from the joint distribution of (y, θ), conditional on x. Consider, then, $\{(y_k, \theta_k), k = 1, \ldots, m)\}$, a set of values generated from this joint distribution. The comparison of the real data x and predictive data via the summary variable V can be shown graphically by a scatter plot of the values $\{(V(y_k, \theta_k), V(x, \theta_k), k = 1, \ldots, m)\}$, or by a histogram of $\{V(y_k, \theta_k) - V(x, \theta_k), k = 1, \ldots, m\}$. For a model that fits the data well, the points in the scatter plot should be symmetric with respect to the 45-degree line and the histogram should include 0.

One of the summary measures of discrepancy between $V(x, \theta)$ and the distribution of $V(Y, \theta)$ is the posterior predictive p-value, sometimes referred to as the **Bayesian p-value**, defined as

$$P_B = P[V(Y, \theta) \geq V(x, \theta) \mid x]$$
$$= E_{(Y,\theta)}\{I\{V(Y, \theta) > V(x, \theta)\} \mid x\}. \tag{5.3}$$

Note that a very small or very large value of P_B (for example, below 1% or above 99%) implies that $V(x, \theta)$ falls into one or the other extreme tail of the posterior distribution of $V(Y, \theta)$, given x (in both cases, being in general implausible under the model). In this way, both cases are evidence for a bad fit of the model to the data with respect to the characteristics that are reflected in the chosen summary variable. For this reason, the Bayesian p-value can, alternatively, be defined as $P_B = P[V(Y, \theta) \leq V(x, \theta) \mid x]$, which can be regarded as resulting from (5.3) by taking the negative of the chosen variable. Typically, the Bayesian p-value, P_B, is calculated as a proportion of simulated values from the posterior predictive distribution of (Y, θ) given x which satisfy $V(y_k, \theta_k) \geq V(x, \theta_k)$. Such simulated values can be obtained by first generating from $h(\theta \mid x)$ and then future data y from the sampling model.

When the discrepancy measure is a statistic $V(X)$, the posterior predictive evaluation can alternatively be applied separately for each observation, making use of the marginal predictive distributions $p(y_i \mid x)$. The corresponding marginal p-values with respect to $V(X_i)$ are defined as $P_{B_i} = P[V(Y_i) \geq V(x_i) \mid x]$, $i = 1, \ldots, n$, which reduces to $P_{B_i} = P(Y_i \geq x_i \mid x)$ if V is the identity. This is useful to detect outliers and to check whether there is a global correspondence between the model and observed data. p-values centered at extremes or too concentrated in the middle of the range of values are evidence for overdispersion and underdispersion, respectively, relative to the predictive data.

Extreme values of a measure of statistical significance, such as P_B, need not necessarily prompt one to completely abandon the model if the characteristic that is expressed by the corresponding variable V is not of great practical relevance. Even if it were, the features that are subject to criticism resulting from this model inspection should suggest possible directions for model revision to find models that are more adequate for the context of the actual data.

Residuals and Other Measures of Model Adequacy and Diagnostic

Other measures can be constructed by comparing characteristics of the predictive distribution under the model conditional on observed data with other also observed data. This is possible in the context of cross-validation, where one uses a training sample $x = (x_1, \ldots, x_n)$ to generate a posterior distribution $h(\theta \mid x)$, and another sample $y = (y_1, \ldots, y_\ell)$, independent of x, to evaluate the validity of the model by inspection of the corresponding posterior predictive $p(y \mid x)$ or some of its characteristics. For example, the predictive mean and variance for each component Y_j of the vector Y, of which y is a realization, are useful to define normalized *Bayesian predictive residuals*,

$$d_j = \frac{y_j - E(Y_j \mid x)}{\sqrt{\text{Var}(Y_j \mid x)}}, \quad j = 1, \ldots, \ell, \tag{5.4}$$

which can be used, similar to what is done in classical inference, as instruments for informal model validation.

This approach assumes the existence of independent samples, which does, however, not usually happen in practice. Of course, if the original sample is large, there is always the possibility to split it into two parts and use one as a *training sample* to construct a posterior distribution and the other as a *test sample* to obtain a predictive distribution conditional on the earlier sample.

If it is not viable to split the entire sample x to implement such cross-validation, then one can use a *jackknife* (*leave-one-out*) approach which consists of repeating the cross-validation n times, always leaving one observation out of the training subsample. That observation plays then the validation role of the test sample. This is known as **leaving-one-out cross-validation**.

Denote with $x_{(-i)} = (x_1, \ldots, x_{i-1}, x_{i+1}, \ldots, x_n)$, the vector of all observations except x_i. We can obtain the *conditional predictive distributions* $p(y_i \mid x_{(-i)})$,

$$p(y_i \mid x_{(-i)}) = \int f(y_i \mid \theta, x_{(-i)}) \, h(\theta \mid x_{(-i)}) \, d\theta, \qquad (5.5)$$

and the resulting normalized *leaving-one-out Bayesian residuals*,

$$d_i' = \frac{x_i - E(Y_i \mid x_{(-i)})}{\sqrt{\text{Var}(Y_i \mid x_{(-i)})}}, \qquad i = 1, \ldots, n, \qquad (5.6)$$

where the means and variances of the corresponding conditional predictive distributions are calculated analytically or by simulation.

On the basis of these residuals, one can then again proceed with informal validation. The value of $p(y_i \mid x_{(-i)})$ that is calculated for x_i is commonly known as **conditional predictive ordinate** (CPO) and can be used in an informal diagnostic. In fact, the values are evidence of the likelihood of each observation given all other observations, and, therefore, low CPO values correspond to badly fitted observations. In this sense, the higher the sum of the logarithmic CPO values, also known as log pseudo-marginal likelihood (LPML)

$$\text{LPML} = \sum_{i=1}^{n} \ln \text{CPO}_i = \ln \Pi_{i=1}^{n} p(x_i \mid x_{(-i)}), \qquad (5.7)$$

the more adequate is a model. For other diagnostic instruments see, in particular, Gelfand (1996) and Gelman and Meng (1996).

Example 5.1 *Henderson and Velleman (1981) describe a study of the per-formance of car models in terms of fuel consumption. We use a subset of the data from this study. The data report efficiency, E_f, measured as miles per gallon, weight in pounds (X_1), power in horse power (X_4^*), and number of gears in the transmission, at levels 3, 4, or 5, jointly represented by indi-cator variables for 4 (X_2) and 5 (X_3), respectively. After some preliminary analysis they consider normal linear regression models for the transformed response variable $Y = 100/E_f$, gallons per 100 miles (Y here is unrelated to the earlier notation y for the predictive data).*

One of the models involves the explanatory variables X_1, (X_2, X_3), and $X_4 = X_4^*/X_1$ (power per unit weight) in a multiple regression model:

$$M_1 : \mu \equiv E(Y) = \beta_0 + \sum_{j=1}^{4} \beta_j X_j + \beta_5 X_2 X_4 + \beta_6 X_3 X_4,$$

which corresponds to three different regression functions of X_1 and X_4, one for each number of gears, which differ by intercept and slope with respect to X_4.

The regression model $Y_i \overset{iid}{\sim} N(\mu, \sigma^2)$, $i = 1, \ldots, n = 29$, is completed with the usual non-informative prior distribution, $\beta_j \sim N(0, 10^4)$ and $1/\sigma^2 \sim Ga(10^{-3}, 10^{-3})$. Bayesian analysis for this linear regression model under the natural conjugate prior or the usual non-informative prior for (μ, σ^2) can be implemented analytically (see, e.g., Paulino et al., 2018: sec. 4.3).

In the context of this Bayesian regression model we illustrate some of the quantities that were described in this chapter and variations thereof, with μ parametrized in terms of the regression coefficients, by using Monte Carlo simulation. We define reduced models that compete with the de-scribed model by simplifying μ by way of removing the interaction terms (M_2) and also by removing the main effects for the indicators for the num-ber of gears (M_3). Denote by θ the parameter vector, composed of the re-gression coefficients and the residual variance, in each model.

Figure 5.1 shows scatter plots under models M_1 and M_2 of the measures of discrepancy based on the standardized mean squared deviations $V(\cdot, \theta_k)$ from (5.2), calculated with the simulated values θ_k, generated from the pos-terior distribution of θ (given the observed values for Y and $\{X_j\}$) for the actual data versus the predicted data.

The point cloud of the diagrams is in both cases more concentrated in the region above the 45-degree line, indicating that the predictive residuals under the two models tend to be larger than the corresponding residuals under the observed data. The asymmetric nature of the scatter plot with

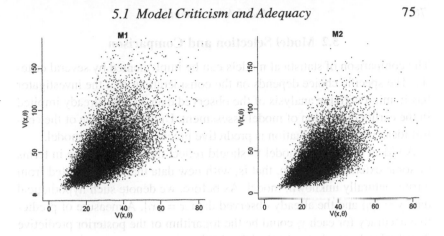

Figure 5.1 Scatterplots for models M_1 and M_2

respect to the 45-degree line seems a little less pronounced for M_2 than for M_1. The Bayesian p-values associated with the standardized mean squared deviations $V(\cdot, \theta_k)$ are evaluated with the observed data and the posterior distribution of $V(Y^*, \theta)$ for the predicted data Y^*. The corresponding Bayesian p-values are tabulated for the three models in Table 5.1, and suggest that the reduced models perform better than the encompassing model, in terms of fitting the data. The sum of the logarithmic CPOs suggest the same, with a slight advantage for model M_2. Following a proposal by Gelfand (1996), these quantities were estimated by the harmonic mean of the assessed sampling density with respect to a simulated sample from the posterior of θ (see Section 5.3.1). ∎

Table 5.1 Diagnostic measures for the competing models

Model	P_B	$\sum \ln \mathrm{CPO}$
M_1	0.844	−27.577
M_2	0.778	−23.665
M_3	0.687	−23.817

It is convenient to distinguish the diagnostic summaries that were discussed in this section from the information criteria in the following section. While the use of these summaries is very similar, the information criteria have a common underlying form and are only meaningful for the comparison of models, whereas many diagnostic summaries in the earlier discussion can also be meaningfully evaluated for individual observations.

5.2 Model Selection and Comparison

The comparison of statistical models can be implemented by several criteria. The specific choice depends on the considerations that the investigator has in mind with the analysis of the observed data, as was already implied in the earlier discussion of model assessment. Undoubtedly one of the central ideas in model evaluation is predictive precision under the model.

An ideal measure of model fit should reflect the predictive use in terms of some external validation, that is, with new data that are generated from a true, naturally unknown, model. As before, we denote such hypothetical data $y = \{y_i\}$ and the already observed data $x = \{x_i\}$. A measure of predictive accuracy for each y_i could be the logarithm of the posterior predictive distribution $\ln p(y_i \mid x) = \ln E_{\theta \mid x}[f(y_i \mid \theta)]$.

Given that the data-generating model is unknown and given the fictitious nature of $\{y_i\}$, we can get an approximation of such a measure by using instead the real data, leading to a posterior predictive intra-sample accuracy measure:

$$
\begin{aligned}
\tilde{A}(x) &= \sum_{i=1}^{n} \ln p(x_i \mid x) = \ln \Pi_{i=1}^{n} p(x_i \mid x) \\
&\simeq \sum_{i=1}^{n} \ln \left[\frac{1}{m} \sum_{k=1}^{m} f(x_i \mid \theta_k) \right],
\end{aligned}
\tag{5.8}
$$

where θ_k, $k = 1, \ldots, m$ are simulated from the posterior distribution $h(\theta \mid x)$.

This type of within-sample approximation of an out-of-sample measure of predictive accuracy is easy to obtain but tends to in general overestimate the measure, because it involves the observed data twice. This issue suggests the use of corrections to $\tilde{A}(x)$, which combined with the application of transformations give rise to distinct measures of predictive performance that are traditionally named information criteria.

5.2.1 Measures of Predictive Performance

We now describe some of these measures that are most widely recommended, practically and theoretically. By the specific form of how all the information criteria are defined, especially by flipping the sign of the corresponding measure of accuracy, the lower the value of these criteria, the better the model.

Akaike Information Criterion (AIC)

The measure of predictive accuracy that is used in the criterion due to Akaike (1973) is based on the approximation of $\tilde{A}(x)$ by the maximum log-likelihood, $\ln f(x \mid \hat{\theta})$, following a plug-in strategy, as is quite typical in frequentist statistics, and penalizing by the number p of parameters in θ, that is,

$$\tilde{A}_{AIC} = \ln f(x \mid \hat{\theta}) - p, \tag{5.9}$$

where $\hat{\theta}$ is the maximum likelihood estimate of θ. The AIC measure of information is obtained from $\tilde{A}_{AIC}$ by a linear transformation as in the likelihood ratio statistic of Wilks, that is

$$AIC = -2 \ln f(x \mid \hat{\theta}) + 2p. \tag{5.10}$$

In summary, the measure is composed of two components, one associated with the goodness of fit of the model, and the other with the complexity of the model, quantified as twice the dimension of the parameter vector. By definition, the criterion does not depend on the sample size but its derivation assumes in fact a large sample context. On the other hand, any weak or strong prior information about the parameters in the sampling model is simply ignored in the AIC, in contrast to Bayesian criteria that are described in the following. For a more detailed discussion about this originally not Bayesian criterion, and particularly about its variants, see Burnham and Anderson (2002: ch. 2 and 6).

Bayesian Information Criterion (SIC/BIC)

Schwarz (1978) proposed a criterion (SIC) to select models by a large sample approximation of the respective marginal distribution of the data $p(x) = E_{h(\theta)} [f(x \mid \theta)]$. The criterion is more commonly known as BIC (Bayes information criterion), possibly because it is based on a weighting of the sampling distribution with the prior density, reflecting an origin that is quite distinct from that of measures of posterior predictive accuracy. For large sample sizes n, $\ln p(x) \simeq \ln f(x \mid \hat{\theta}) - (p/2) \ln n$, where $\hat{\theta}$ is the maximum likelihood estimate of θ. The BIC criterion is defined as

$$BIC = -2 \ln f(x \mid \hat{\theta}) + p \ln n. \tag{5.11}$$

The criterion considers models with large values of the mentioned approximation of $p(x)$ to be preferable, or equivalently, models with small values of BIC. For moderate and large samples, the term in the BIC related to the model dimension is larger than the corresponding term in the AIC, thus heavily penalizing more complicated models.

To avoid simulation-based maximization, Carlin and Louis (2009) suggested a modification of this criterion using the posterior mean of the log-likelihood instead of the maximum. This modified version of the BIC is thus defined as

$$\text{BIC}^{CL} = -2E_{\theta|x}\left[\ln f(x \mid \theta)\right] + p \ln n. \tag{5.12}$$

Deviance Information Criterion (DIC)

Keeping in mind that the prior distribution and the type of model structure tend to affect the degree of over-fitting, the DIC criterion proposed by Spiegelhalter et al (2002) modified the measure of predictive accuracy $\tilde{A}_{AIC}$ in two aspects related to its two components. The maximum likelihood estimate $\hat{\theta}$ is substituted by a Bayesian estimate $\bar{\theta}$ (usually the posterior mean of θ) and the number of parameters is replaced by an effective dimension of the model, p_D, defined by the following argument.

For a definition of model complexity, Spiegelhalter et al (2002) start with a relative information measure for the sampling model, defined as $-2\ln\left[f(x \mid \theta)/g(x)\right]$, where $g(x)$ denotes some function of only the data, used for standardization. For example, $g(x) = f(x \mid \tilde{\theta})$ where $\tilde{\theta}$ is an estimate of θ in a saturated model, implying that the information measure could be seen as a parametric function associated with the likelihood ratio statistic. Seen as a function of θ given the data x, this measure is often called Bayesian **deviance** and denoted $D(\theta)$.

Accordingly the value of this relative information measure for the same distribution when θ is estimated by $\bar{\theta}$ is denoted $D(\bar{\theta})$, and thus the amount of information about the sampling distribution that the estimation of θ by $\bar{\theta}$ does not account for is described by the difference:

$$D(\theta) - D(\bar{\theta}) = -2\ln\frac{f(x \mid \theta)}{f(x \mid \bar{\theta})}, \tag{5.13}$$

which is now independent of the normalizing factor $g(x)$. Since θ is unknown and a random variable under a Bayesian perspective, Spiegelhalter et al (2002) substitute $D(\theta)$ by its posterior expectation $\overline{D(\theta)} = E_{\theta|x}\left[D(\theta)\right]$, and define the **effective number of parameters** by

$$p_D = \overline{D(\theta)} - D(\bar{\theta}). \tag{5.14}$$

This definition is justified in the following. In words, p_D is the difference between posterior mean deviance and deviance under the posterior mean when $\bar{\theta} = E(\theta \mid x)$. This quantity naturally depends on the data, the parameter focus, and the prior information.

Alternatively other Bayesian estimates of θ and $D(\theta)$ could be used, with naturally different results than under the posterior means. One advantage of the earlier definition is easy computation. As long as the model includes a closed-form likelihood function, one can always use the approximation

$$p_D \simeq \frac{1}{m} \sum_{k=1}^{m} D(\theta_k) - D\left(\frac{1}{m} \sum_{k=1}^{m} \theta_k\right), \tag{5.15}$$

where θ_k are a Monte Carlo sample from $h(\theta \mid x)$. Another advantage is the fact that $p_D \geq 0$ for any model with log-concave likelihood (by Jensen's inequality).

In some standard models (without hierarchical structure) with a likelihood dominating the prior, it can be shown that p_D is approximately equal to the actual number of parameters. The interpretation of p_D as a measure of dimensionality of the model attempts to extend the same notion to more complex models for which it is not easy to determine the number of parameters, such as models that include latent variables. However, in some models such as finite mixture models or some hierarchical models the implied p_D can be negative. See, for example, Celeux et al (2006).

Using p_D as a measure of model complexity (and for the moment ignoring the standardization function g), the corresponding measure of predictive accuracy becomes

$$\tilde{A}_{\text{DIC}} = \ln f(x \mid \bar{\theta}) - p_D. \tag{5.16}$$

This leads to the DIC criterion (deviance information criterion) proposed by Spiegelhalter et al (2002) as

$$\text{DIC} = D(\bar{\theta}) + 2p_D = \overline{D(\theta)} + p_D = 2\overline{D(\theta)} - D(\bar{\theta}). \tag{5.17}$$

In practice, the normalizing factor in the deviance is usually omitted (that is, $g(x) = 1$) when the Bayesian models under consideration are all based on the same sampling model and differ only in the parametric structure. Otherwise, one must be careful because the DIC measure depends on the chosen function $g(\cdot)$. Regarding this, it is by no means straightforward to determine the maximum likelihood for the saturated structure in most multiparameter models.

Widely Applicable Information Criterion (WAIC)

The measure of intra-sample predictive accuracy associated with the WAIC (widely applicable information criterion) criterion, due to Watanabe (2010), does not involve plug-in approximations as the previously discussed criteria, and as such is more Bayesian than that used by the DIC. It is evaluated with an overfitting correction as

$$\tilde{A}_{\text{WAIC}} = \tilde{A}(x) - p_W = \sum_{i=1}^{n} \ln E_{\theta|x}\left[f(x_i \mid \theta)\right] - p_W. \tag{5.18}$$

Just like $\tilde{A}(x)$ previously, also the complexity penalty term involves an expression in terms of the individual data. One of the proposals for p_W is similar to the one used in the DIC, expressed as

$$p_{W_1} = -2\sum_{i=1}^{n}\{E_{\theta|x}\left[\ln f(x_i \mid \theta)\right] - \ln E_{\theta|x}\left[f(x_i \mid \theta)\right]\}$$

$$\simeq -2\sum_{i=1}^{n}\left\{\frac{1}{m}\sum_{k=1}^{m} \ln f(x_i \mid \theta_k) - \ln\left[\frac{1}{m}\sum_{k=1}^{m} f(x_i \mid \theta_k)\right]\right\}, \tag{5.19}$$

with $p_{W_1} \geq 0$ by construction.

Another proposal for p_W is based on the posterior variance of $\ln f(x_i \mid \theta)$ for all data points, and defined as

$$p_{W_2} = \sum_{i=1}^{n} \text{Var}_{\theta|x}\left[\ln f(x_i \mid \theta)\right]$$

$$\simeq \sum_{i=1}^{n}\left\{\frac{1}{m-1}\sum_{k=1}^{m}\left[l_k(x_i) - \bar{l}(x_i)\right]^2\right\}, \tag{5.20}$$

where $l_k(x_i) = \ln f(x_i \mid \theta_k)$ and $\bar{l}(x_i) = \frac{1}{m}\sum_{k=1}^{m} l_k(x_i)$.

Using any of these proposals for the complexity penalty term, interpreted as "effective model dimensionality," depending on either data or prior information, Gelman et al. (2014a, 2014b) propose a transformation of Watanabe's information criterion to the same scale as other proposals, being expressed by

$$\text{WAIC} = -2\sum_{i=1}^{n} \ln E_{\theta|x}\left[f(x_i \mid \theta)\right] + 2p_W. \tag{5.21}$$

5.2.2 Selection by Posterior Predictive Performance

Bayesian analysis is usually based on a given model and, consequently, related inference is of a conditional nature. However, unavoidable uncertainty about any of the components of a Bayesian model are a sufficiently strong reason to consider a range of possible joint models for data and parameters, which is then subject to some preliminary screening.

After the inspection and assessment of the models, one should then proceed with a comparison aiming to select the best models with respect to the adopted criteria. This stage of statistical analysis need not necessarily culminate in the selection of a single model as this might lead to misleading conclusions. To the contrary, one should certainly discard some models with unacceptable performance with respect to the chosen criteria, but keep the remaining ones for further consideration.[1]

The traditional practice of carrying out model selection by way of hypotheses tests has slowly been changing over the last 40 years, perhaps due to an increasing understanding of the limitations of such a process as compared to the optimization of other measures of model performance.

Application of the earlier described information criteria respects the parsimony paradigm that requires that the selected models should combine an adequate representation of the data (with a good fit) to as simple a structure as possible (low dimensionality). The paradigm was expressed way back (in the fourteenth century) as **Occam's razor**: "shave away all that is unnecessary."

Keeping in mind the need to control the number of models under consideration, a strategy in the spirit of this principle should be guided by the following desiderata: Drop any model that predicts the data worse than nested simpler models or much worse than the model that produces the currently best prediction. The strategy is compatible with several ways of evaluating the quality of predictions, be it by diagnostic summaries, by information criteria, or others.

Use of Diagnostic Summaries

In the face of several competing models, diagnostic tools or measures of model adequacy such as the Bayesian p-value or standardized Bayesian residuals (obtained by cross-validation or by jackknife) are useful to comparatively evaluate competing models in terms of their performance. For

---

[1] This could even include the implementation of the desired inference by appropriate combination of the selected models, known as Bayesian model averaging.

example, using the sum of squares (or of absolute values) of these residuals, one should favor models that report smaller values.

Another means of evaluating comparative adequacy among several models is the sum of the log conditional predictive ordinates, with the idea of
selecting the models with the highest values. When comparing two models,
H_1 versus H_2, by means of CPO one can use

$$\text{PBF} = \Pi_{i=1}^{n} \frac{p(x_i \mid x_{(-i)}, H_1)}{p(x_i \mid x_{(-i)}, H_2)} \equiv \Pi_{i=1}^{n} Q_i. \qquad (5.22)$$

This is known as the pseudo-Bayes factor (PBF). Keeping in mind that the
product of CPOs for each model is used as a substitute for the respective
marginal likelihood (recall the definition of the Bayes factor), then values
of the pseudo-Bayes factor greater (less) than 1 are evidence for model
H_1 (H_2). Besides this, since observations with Q_i greater (less) than 1 are
evidence for H_1 (H_2), a plot of $\ln(Q_i)$ versus i is useful to visualize which
observations are better fit by which of the two competing models.

Use of Information Criteria

In the context of model comparison the relevant quantities are not the actual values of the predictive performance measures in absolute terms, but
the relative values within the set of the, say, J models under consideration.
Thus for each of these measures the differences across pairs of models are
most useful. Let IC generically denote one of the measures that were introduced in the previous subsection. Since all measures were defined such
that smaller values correspond to better models, it is useful to determine
for each model the differences $r_j(IC) = IC_j - IC_{\min}$, $j \in J$.

The evaluation of these differences allows an easier comparison and
ranking of the models under consideration. The smaller r_j the higher the
degree of empirical evidence for model j, with the best model corresponding to $r_j = 0$. We will use $j = o$ (as in "optimal") to denote the index of the
best model. For example, the differences r_j for DIC are:

$$r_j(\text{DIC}) = \text{DIC}_j - \text{DIC}_o,$$
$$\text{DIC}_j = E_{\theta_j|x}[D_j(\theta_j)] + p_{D_j} = 2E_{\theta_j|x}[D_j(\theta_j)] - D_j(E_{\theta_j|x}[\theta_j]).$$

Considering the respective differences under the BIC criterion, using

$\{p_j^*\}$ for the dimension of the parameter vectors under each model, we get:

$$r_j(\text{BIC}) = \text{BIC}_j - \text{BIC}_o = -2 \ln \frac{f_j(x \mid \hat{\theta}_j) n^{-p_j^*/2}}{f_o(x \mid \hat{\theta}_0) n^{-p_o^*/2}}$$

$$\simeq -2 \ln \frac{p_j(x)}{p_o(x)} = -2 \ln B_{jo}(x). \tag{5.23}$$

That is, the differences $r_j(\text{BIC})$ are related with the Bayes factor between the two models under comparison, say H_j and H_o, in the sense that for large sample sizes they can be approximated by $-2 \ln B_{jo}(x)$, using an argument of Schwarz (1978).

Example 5.2 *Continuing with the earlier example, consider now comparative evaluation of the three multiple regression models with respect to their predictive performance. The PBF for the pairwise comparisons are* PBF(M_1/M_2) = 0.809; PBF(M_1/M_3) = 0.941, *and* PBF(M_2/M_3) = 1.164. *These values support the earlier result that M_2 was the best and M_1 the worst of the three models, in terms of this criterion based on conditional predictive ordinates.*

A comparison with respect to the information criteria shown in Table 5.2, reports model M_2 as the best in terms of the Bayesian summaries DIC and WAIC, which, however, is dominated by M_3 under the BIC. The latter is no surprise, knowing that BIC favors the more parsimonious models.

Table 5.2 DIC, BIC and WAIC criteria for models M_1, M_2 and M_3

Model	DIC (p_D)	BIC (p)	WAIC (p_{W_2})
M_1	48.69 (8.27)	67.36 (8)	46.77 (5.38)
M_2	47.32 (6.19)	61.33 (6)	46.70 (4.78)
M_3	47.58 (4.12)	56.93 (4)	47.40 (3.48)

Pooling the results here and in the previous example, the applied criteria show that the overall best of the three models is the one with intermediate complexity as measured by the number of parameters. ∎

5.2.3 *Model Selection Using Bayes Factors*

The methods for model selection that were discussed in the previous subsection are useful for screening, with the aim of retaining for further consideration those models that are found to perform well with respect to the available information. But there is no concern that any model stands for the reality under study.

In contrast, some methods correspond to a perspective (possibly controversial) that the set of considered models must include a so-called true model, in the sense of being the one that generated the observed data (or, at least, which constitutes a sufficiently good approximation of the true model). The method of using Bayes factors to select one of a finite number of models fits into this perspective. This and other aspects that could be criticized should not prevent one from using this method in some contexts, with due caution.

Any set of Bayesian models $\mathcal{M} = \{M_j, \; j \in J\}$ (with different sampling models and prior distributions) implies a set of corresponding prior predictive models

$$p(x \mid M_j) \equiv p_j(x) = \int f_j(x \mid \theta_j) h_j(\theta_j) \, d\theta_j, \quad j \in J. \tag{5.24}$$

If J is a discrete set of indicators for the members of a set of models that is assumed to contain the unknown true model, the global predictive distribution is

$$p(x) = \sum_{j \in J} P(M_j) p(x \mid M_j), \tag{5.25}$$

where $P(M_j)$ is the prior probability of M_j being the true model and is updated in the face of data x to

$$P(M_j \mid x) = P(M_j) p(x \mid M_j) / p(x), \quad j \in J. \tag{5.26}$$

The Bayes factor in favor of M_k versus M_j is thus the ratio

$$B_{kj}(x) = \frac{P(M_k \mid x) / P(M_j \mid x)}{P(M_k) / P(M_j)} = \frac{p(x \mid M_k)}{p(x \mid M_j)}, \tag{5.27}$$

and the posterior odds for M_k are

$$\frac{P(M_k \mid x)}{1 - P(M_k \mid x)} = \frac{P(M_k)}{\sum_{j \neq k} P(M_j) B_{jk}(x)}, \tag{5.28}$$

where $B_{jk}(x) = 1/B_{kj}(x)$ is the Bayes factor in favour of M_j versus M_k. The formula for these odds becomes $(\sum_{j \neq k} B_{jk}(x))^{-1}$ when one uses a uniform prior over the space of models. Simple examples of the application of this method can be found in Paulino et al (2018).

In general, the evaluation of prior predictive distributions, and thus of Bayes factors, requires simulation – see the preceding chapter and the next section. Model comparison based on Bayes factors requires the use of practical rules for the choice of thresholds on the strength of evidence in favor of a model. One such rule is proposed by Kass and Raftery (1995).

5.3 Further Notes on Simulation in Model Assessment

Following Chapter 4, Sections 5.1 and 5.2 already included some recommendations on the use of stochastic simulation to evaluate diagnostic summaries and measures of fit and predictive performance by means of Monte Carlo methods. In this section we complete these recommendations with the discussion of some additional questions related to simulation-based implementations of such Bayesian inference.

To define the context of the discussion, assume that one has a Monte Carlo sample $\{\theta_{(j)}^\star; \ j = 1, \ldots, m\}$ from some posterior distribution $h(\theta \mid x)$, which was previously generated by some simulation method. The following subsections describe some aspects of simulation specifically related to model assessment.

5.3.1 Evaluating Posterior Predictive Distributions

Let y denote a new data set, independent of the already observed data. The predictive density $p(y \mid x)$ can be estimated, as suggested in Section 4.1.4, by

$$\hat{p}(y \mid x) = \frac{1}{m} \sum_{j=1}^{m} f(y \mid \theta_{(j)}^\star).$$

Using a similar argument, for the estimation of a conditional predictive density

$$p(x_i \mid x_{(-i)}) = \int f(x_i \mid \theta, x_{(-i)}) \, h(\theta \mid x_{(-i)}) \, d\theta,$$

one can, in principle, simulate $\{\theta_{(j)}^\star; \ j = 1, \ldots, m\}$ for each posterior distribution $h(\theta \mid x_{(-i)})$. However, this is impractical for high-dimensional x. An ideal, more practicable method should obtain the desired density estimate using only a single sample $\{\theta_{(j)}^\star; \ j = 1, \ldots, m\}$ from $h(\theta \mid x)$.

Gelfand (1996) suggests to use the harmonic mean of the set $\{f(x_i \mid x_{(-i)}, \theta_{(j)}^\star), \ j = 1, \ldots, m\}$ to estimate $p(x_i \mid x_{(-i)})$. Indeed, noting

$$p(x)h(\theta \mid x) = h(\theta)f(x \mid \theta) = h(\theta)f(x_i \mid x_{(-i)}, \theta)f(x_{(-i)} \mid \theta),$$

we get

$$p(x_i \mid x_{(-i)}) = \frac{p(x)}{p(x_{(-i)})} = \left[\int \frac{1}{f(x_i \mid x_{(-i)}, \theta)} \, h(\theta \mid x) \, d\theta \right]^{-1},$$

and thus, if $\{\theta_{(j)}^\star; j = 1, \dots, m\}$ is a sample from $h(\theta \mid x)$, we have

$$\hat{p}(x_i \mid x_{(-i)}) = \left[\frac{1}{m} \sum_{j=1}^{m} \frac{1}{f(x_i \mid x_{(-i)}, \theta_{(j)}^\star)} \right]^{-1}. \tag{5.29}$$

The expression simplifies in the case of $(X_1, \dots, X_n)$ being conditionally independent, in which case $f(x_i \mid x_{(-i)}, \theta) = f(x_i \mid \theta)$.

Note that a similar argument allows us to estimate moments of the posterior predictive distribution (and, in particular, standardized Bayesian residuals), based on sample moments for each simulated value from $h(\theta \mid x)$, as well as other diagnostic summaries.

5.3.2 Prior Predictive Density Estimation

The evaluation of Bayes factors requires the prior predictive (or marginal) distribution $p(x)$. We review some approaches that have been proposed in the literature to obtain it, assuming it exists.

If $\{\theta_{(j)}^\star; j = 1, \dots, m\}$ is a prior sample from $h(\theta)$, then by the definition of $p(x)$ it follows that the same can be approximated as

$$\hat{p}(x) = \frac{1}{m} \sum_{j=1}^{m} f(x \mid \theta_{(j)}^\star).$$

This estimate of $p(x)$ has been shown, however, to be in general very inefficient, as we already mentioned in Section 4.2.2.

Newton and Raftery (1994) suggested the harmonic mean of $\{f(x \mid \theta_{(j)}^\star)\}$, that is

$$\hat{p}(x) = \left[\frac{1}{m} \sum_{j=1}^{m} \frac{1}{f(x \mid \theta_{(j)}^\star)} \right]^{-1}, \tag{5.30}$$

with $\{\theta_{(j)}^\star; j = 1, \dots, m\}$ being a posterior sample from $h(\theta \mid x)$. Assuming that $h(\theta)$ is a proper distribution, the result is easily shown by using Bayes' theorem to write

$$\frac{1}{p(x)} = \int \frac{1}{p(x)} \, h(\theta) \, d\theta = \int \frac{1}{f(x \mid \theta)} \, h(\theta \mid x) \, d\theta,$$

which motivates the estimation of $p(x)$ by the harmonic mean. However, also this estimator is numerically unstable due to possibly small values of $f(x \mid \theta)$.

Gelfand and Dey (1994) suggested a generalization of (5.30) which gives rise to a more stable estimator. The generalization uses a (proper) distribution $g(\theta)$, which should be a good approximation of the posterior $h(\theta \mid x)$ and should be easy to generate from (for example, a multivariate normal posterior approximation with mean and covariance matrix based on a posterior Monte Carlo sample). Then use

$$\frac{1}{p(x)} = \int \frac{1}{p(x)} g(\theta) \, d\theta = \int \frac{g(\theta)}{f(x \mid \theta) \, h(\theta)} \, h(\theta \mid x) \, d\theta.$$

Using a posterior Monte Carlo sample, $\{\theta^\star_{(j)}, j = 1, \ldots, m\}$, a corresponding estimator for $p(x)$ is

$$\hat{p}(x) = \left[\frac{1}{m} \sum_{j=1}^{m} \frac{g(\theta^\star_{(j)})}{f(x \mid \theta^\star_{(j)}) \, h(\theta^\star_{(j)})} \right]^{-1}. \tag{5.31}$$

More discussion of this and other prior predictive density estimates can be found in Kass and Raftery (1995).

5.3.3 *Sampling from Predictive Distributions*

Suppose we want to sample from the posterior predictive distribution $p(y \mid x)$, for $y = (y_1, \ldots, y_{n^\star})$. If for each element $\theta^\star_{(j)}$ of a posterior Monte Carlo sample $\{\theta^\star_{(j)}\}_{j=1}^{m}$ from $h(\theta \mid x)$ we simulate a data set $y^\star_{(j)}$ from $f(y \mid \theta^\star_{(j)})$, then marginally, $y^\star_{(j)}$ is a sample from $p(y \mid x)$. In particular, $y^\star_{r,(j)}$, the r-th element of the sample $y^\star_{(j)}$, is an observation for $p(y_r \mid x)$. This posterior predictive sampling scheme is useful, in general, for the investigation of model adequacy, including in particular the use of standardized Bayesian residuals d_r.

But how can one sample from the conditional posterior predictive distribution $p(y_i \mid x_{(-i)})$? By a similar argument, one could use a sample $\{\theta^{\star\star}_{(j)}\}_{j=1}^{m}$ from $h(\theta \mid x_{(-i)})$ and then, for each $\theta^{\star\star}_{(j)}$, obtain a sample from $f(y_i \mid \theta^{\star\star}_{(j)})$. However, clearly this would be computation-intensive and inefficient for large sample sizes.

The question arises, then, how to sample from $h(\theta \mid x_{(-i)})$ for all i, without having to repeat the entire scheme for each observation. Note that for each $\theta^\star_{(j)}$, we have for $x = (x_i, x_{(-i)})$,

$$h(\theta^\star_{(j)} \mid x_{(-i)}) = \frac{p(x_i \mid x_{(-i)})}{f(x_i \mid x_{(-i)}, \theta^\star_{(j)})} \, h(\theta^\star_{(j)} \mid x) \propto \frac{1}{f(x_i \mid x_{(-i)}, \theta^\star_{(j)})} \, h(\theta^\star_{(j)} \mid x).$$

Thus if one resamples $\{\theta^\star_{(j)}\}^m_{j=1}$, with probabilities proportional to $\omega_j = \{f(x_i \mid x_{(-i)}, \theta^\star_{(j)})\}^{-1}$ and with replacement, the resulting sample is approximately a sample from $h(\theta \mid x_{(-i)})$. Often $h(\theta \mid x_{(-i)}) \approx h(\theta \mid x)$ and thus the resampling might become unnecessary.

Finally, to sample from the marginal predictive $p(x)$, assuming it is proper, one can generate $\tilde{\theta}_j$ from $h(\theta)$ and then $\tilde{x}_j$ from $f(x \mid \tilde{\theta}_j)$.

Problems

5.1 Replicate Example 5.1. The data are available in R as the data frame `mtcars`. Evaluate P_B and the log pseudo-Bayes factor (5.22).

5.2 Let y_i be the number of misprints on page i of the book *Bayesian Theory* by Bernardo and Smith (2000). Consider two alternative models:

$$\text{Model } H_1: y_i \mid \lambda \sim Poi(\lambda \cdot N_i), \quad i = 1, \ldots, n$$
$$\lambda \sim Ga(1, \beta)$$

$$\text{Model } H_2: y_i \mid \theta \sim Bin(N_i, \theta)$$
$$\theta \sim Be(1, \beta - 1)$$

where N_i is the number of characters per page, $\beta > 1$ is a fixed hyperparameter, and the gamma distribution is parametrized such that $E(\lambda) = 1/\beta$. That is, under both models $1/\beta$ is interpreted as the expected number of typos per word.

a. Find the Bayes factor $B = p(y \mid H_2)/p(y \mid H_1)$ for choosing between competing models H_1 and H_2.

b. Consider the following data

N_i	5607	5878	6200	5460	5576
y_i	0	1	0	0	1
(ctd.)	5772	5770	6009	6027	5793
	0	0	1	0	0

Fix $1/\beta = 0.0001$ and evaluate the Bayes factor.

c. Let $V(Y, \theta) = \sum_i I(Y_i = 0)$ denote the number of typo-free pages. Using V evaluate a Bayesian p-value for models H_1 and H_2.

5.3 For the following data we will consider two competing models: H_1: a linear regression, versus H_2 : a quadratic regression.

x_i	−1.9	−0.39	0.79		−0.20	0.42	−0.35
y_i	−1.7	−0.23	0.50		−0.66	1.97	0.10
(ctd.)	0.67	0.63	−0.024	1.2			
	0.60	1.13	0.943	2.6			

Model H_1:

$$y_i = \beta_1 + \beta_2 x_i + \epsilon_i, \quad i = 1, \ldots, n; \quad \epsilon_i \sim N(0, 1)$$
$$\beta_1 \sim N(0, 1), \quad \beta_2 \sim N(1, 1),$$

with β_1 and β_2 *a priori* independent.
Model H_2:

$$y_i = \gamma_1 + \gamma_2 x_i + \gamma_3 x_i^2 + \epsilon_i, \quad i = 1, \ldots, n; \quad \epsilon_i \sim N(0, 1)$$
$$\gamma_1 = N(0, 1), \quad \gamma_2 \sim N(1, 1), \quad \gamma_3 \sim N(0, 1),$$

with $\gamma_1, \gamma_2, \gamma_3$ *a priori* independent.

a. Find the marginal distributions $p(y \mid H_1) = \int f(y \mid \beta, H_1) h(\beta) \, d\beta$. and $p(y \mid H_2) = \int f(y \mid \gamma, H_2) h(\gamma) \, d\gamma$.

b. Write down the Bayes factor $B = p(y \mid H_2)/p(y \mid H_1)$ for comparing model H_1 versus model H_2 and evaluate it for the given data set.

c. We now replace the prior distributions by improper constant priors: $h(\beta) = c_1$ in model H_1; and $h(\gamma) = c_2$ in model H_2. We can still formally evaluate integrals[2] $\int f(y \mid \beta, H_1) h(\beta) \, d\beta$ and $\int f(y \mid \gamma, H_2) h(\gamma) \, d\gamma$ and define a Bayes factor,

$$\tilde{B} = \frac{\int f(y \mid \gamma) h(\gamma) \, d\gamma}{\int f(y \mid \beta) h(\beta) \, d\beta}.$$

Show that the value of the Bayes factor $\tilde{B}$ depends on the – arbitrarily chosen – constants c_1 and c_2.

d. Evaluate the Bayes factor using the harmonic mean estimator (5.31) and compare with the exact evaluation from **b.**

5.4 Refer to Problem 5.3. Evaluate the log pseudo-Bayes factor (5.22), BIC, AIC, WAIC, and DIC to compare the two models.

---

[2] Although the marginal distributions might be improper, i.e., meaningless.

6

Markov Chain Monte Carlo Methods

As discussed in Chapter 4, the implementation of Bayesian inference often involves the use of simulation-based methods, based on a Monte Carlo sample of values that are generated from a typically multivariate posterior distribution, $h(\theta \mid x)$, $\theta \in \Theta$. The use of simulation-based methods is one way of dealing with the analytically often intractable form of Bayesian inference summaries. Depending on the complexity of the posterior distribution $h(\cdot)$, the evaluation of posterior summaries like $E[g(\theta) \mid x]$ can be carried out by classical Monte Carlo (MC) methods, by generating i.i.d. samples from the target distribution itself, or from some appropriate importance sampling distribution, whose construction involves the target distribution.

For more complex problems it has become more common, especially since the 1990s, to use more general MC methods based on the simulation of a (homogeneous) Markov chain that is constructed to have an ergodic distribution $\pi(\theta)$ equal to the target distribution, $\pi(\theta) \equiv h(\theta \mid x)$. Such methods, known as **Markov chain Monte Carlo** (MCMC), thus use dependent samples of θ, implying also more complex asymptotics and the need for larger simulation sample sizes compared to classical MC methods.

The rediscovery of MCMC methods[1] by statisticians in the 1990's (in particular, Gelfand and Smith, 1990) led to considerable progress in simulation-based inference methods and, in particular, Bayesian analysis for models that were too complex for earlier methods.

Given the nature of MCMC methods, it is not possible to fully understand them and the details of their application in Bayesian statistics without a knowledge of basic results for Markov chains which are therefore summarized in the following section, in a very brief form given the nature

---

[1] The earlier literature includes Metropolis et al (1953), Hastings (1970) and Geman and Geman (1984).

of this text.[2] For simplicity, we use in this section (and beyond) a generic notation for the states of a chain. In the following sections we describe the most commonly used methods, including Metropolis–Hastings chains, Gibbs samplers, slice sampling, and Hamiltonian Monte Carlo. The last section is dedicated to implementation questions related to MCMC methods, including the question of one versus multiple parallel chains and convergence diagnostics.

6.1 Definitions and Basic Results for Markov Chains

A **stochastic process** is a set of random variables that are defined over the same probability space $\{U(t), t \in T\}$, where T is some subset of $\mathbb{R}$ which, without loss of generality, may be considered as a set of temporal indexes. When this set T is $T = \{0, 1, 2, \ldots\}$, then the stochastic process is usually written as $\{U_n, n \geq 0\}$. This is the typical setup in stochastic simulation. The set $\mathcal{U}$ of values of the variables U_n is known as **state space**.

Knowing the past and present states of a process generally informs about the plausibility of future states. When conditional on a given present state, the plausibility of future states does not depend on the past, and we say that the process has **Markov dependence**. A process $\{U_n, n \geq 0\}$ with this conditional independence property is known as a **Markov chain**, and can be defined by

$$U_{n+1} \perp (U_0, \ldots, U_{n-1}) \mid U_n \Leftrightarrow$$
$$P(U_{n+1} \in A \mid U_0 = u_0, \ldots, U_n = u) = P(U_{n+1} \in A \mid U_n = u) \equiv P_n(u, A),$$

for all events A and $n \geq 0$. The probability $P_n(u, A)$ is known as (one-step) **transition function** at time n. Equivalently, considering $A = (-\infty, v]$, a Markov chain can be defined by the conditional distribution functions

$$F_{U_{n+1}}(v \mid U_0 = u_0, \ldots, U_n = u) = F_{U_{n+1}}(v \mid U_n = u) \equiv F_n(u, v),$$

for all $v, u \in \mathcal{U}$. When the transition function is invariant with respect to n, we write $P(u, A)$ (or $F(u, v)$) and the Markov chain is called **homogeneous**. In the upcoming discussion we are only interested in homogeneous Markov chains, and will therefore henceforth not explicitly indicate the qualifier homogeneous.

For a discrete state space, the Markov chain is entirely defined by the

---

[2] For more discussion of this issue, see Ross (2014) and Tierney (1996) and references therein.

conditional probabilities $P(u, \{v\})$, i.e.

$$P(U_{n+1} = v \mid U_0 = u_0, \ldots, U_n = u) =$$
$$P(U_{n+1} = v \mid U_n = u) \equiv p(u, v), \forall n \geq 0, u, v \in \mathcal{U}.$$

In the case of a finite state space the transition probabilities $p(\cdot, \cdot)$ can be recorded as a matrix P of probabilities for one step. When $\mathcal{U}$ is uncountably infinite and $F(u, v)$ is absolutely continuous, then the transition function can be defined by a density $p(u, v) = \frac{\partial F(u,v)}{\partial v}$.

For the moment we assume a discrete Markov chain. We have

$$P(U_{n+1} = v) = \sum_u P(U_n = u)p(u, v) = \sum_u P(U_0 = u)p^n(u, v),$$

where $p^n(u, v) = P(U_n = v \mid U_0 = u) = \sum_u p^{n-1}(u, z)p(z, v)$, $n \geq 1$ defines a transition function for n steps (in matrix form the product P^n). The construction of a Markov chain is therefore completely determined by the transition function, as long as an initial distribution is given.

We say that a probability distribution $\pi(u), u \in \mathcal{U}$ is a **stationary distribution** if

$$\pi(v) = \sum_u \pi(u)p(u, v).$$

In particular, an initial distribution $P(U_0 = u) = \pi(u)$ is stationary if and only if the marginal distribution of U_n is invariant across n, i.e. $P(U_n = u) = \pi(u), \forall n \geq 0$.

The existence and uniqueness of stationary distributions depends upon whether the chain has certain characteristics known as irreducibility and recurrence. A chain is **irreducible** if the chain can within a finite number of transitions reach any state, starting from any initial state. A chain is said to be **recurrent** if it returns infinitely many times to any starting state. It is said to be **positive recurrent** if the expected time of the first return to any state u is finite for all states u. Irreducibility implies positive recurrence if $\mathcal{U}$ is finite.

An irreducible and recurrent Markov chain (with discrete $\mathcal{U}$) has a unique stationary distribution. On the other hand, if there is a stationary distribution $\pi(v)$ such that $\lim_{n \to \infty} p^n(u, v) = \pi(v)$, then the stationary distribution is unique and $\lim_{n \to \infty} P(U_n = v) = \pi(v)$. In that case, independently of the initial distribution, for large enough n the marginal distribution of U_n is approximately π.

Convergence to the stationary distribution π is not guaranteed for an irreducible and positive recurrent chain. However, with the additional condition of **aperiodicity**, defined as $\min\{n \geq 1 : p^n(u, u) > 0\} = 1$ (it suffices if there exists u such that $p(u, u) > 0$), such a chain is then called **ergodic** and has a limiting behavior $p^n(u, v) \xrightarrow[n \to \infty]{} \pi(v)$ for all $u, v \in \mathcal{U}$, thus assuring convergence of $P(U_n = u)$ to $\pi(u)$ for all u.

In addition, if $g(U)$ is a function defined on the state space of an ergodic Markov chain with finite expectation under π, then we have

$$\frac{1}{n} \sum_{t=1}^{n} g(U_t) \xrightarrow[n \to \infty]{} E_\pi[g(U)], \text{ a.s.}$$

This result, commonly known as **ergodic theorem**, generalizes the strong law of large numbers to Markov chains with the stated characteristics. Under additional conditions also an extension of the central limit theorem holds, that is, convergence (in distribution) to a normal distribution for the sequence $\sqrt{n}\left[\frac{1}{n}\sum_{t=1}^{n} g(U_t) - E_\pi[g(U)]\right]$.

When the states of a chain are absolutely continuous random variables, the definition of the described properties needs to be modified to refer to events $A \subseteq \mathcal{U}$ instead of individual states, similar to the definition of a transition function, and are subject to some measure theoretic technical details. For example, the description of the dynamics of a chain involves the condition of visits to an event A with positive probability. A probability measure Π is said to be stationary if for any event A,

$$\Pi(A) = \int_{\mathcal{U}} P(u, A)\Pi(du),$$

which in terms of densities corresponds to

$$\pi(v) = \int_{\mathcal{U}} p(u, v)\pi(u)du.$$

Convergence results for chains with uncountably infinite state spaces are analogous to the earlier statements, with the difference that the results require stronger conditions.[3]

Another property of Markov chains that is of practical importance in the analysis of the limiting behaviour concerns the reversibility of the probabilistic dynamics. Specifically, a chain is said to be **reversible** if for any event A and state u in the state space $\mathcal{U}$ (discrete or not),

$$P(U_{n+1} \in A \mid U_n = u) = P(U_{n+1} \in A \mid U_{n+2} = u).$$

---

[3] For example, positive Harris recurrence is required for ergodicity – see e.g. the book Paulino et al (2018) and references therein.

Reversibility of a chain with transition function $p(\cdot, \cdot)$ and stationary distribution $\pi(\cdot)$ is equivalent to

$$\pi(u)p(u, v) = \pi(v)p(v, u), \quad \forall u, v \in \mathcal{U}. \qquad (6.1)$$

This condition is known as **detailed balance condition**. It can be interpreted as a balance implied by the chain in the sense that being in u and passing to v and being in v and passing to u are equally plausible, for every pair (u, v) of states. In particular, a chain that satisfies this condition for a probability density π is not only reversible but also has the same π as stationary distribution.

6.2 Metropolis–Hastings Algorithm

In this and the following sections we continue to use the notation that was introduced in Section 6.1. Considering the usually multivariate nature of the states of the discussed chains, we change the "time" index to a superindex for the random vectors, such as $U^{(t)}$, reserving the subindex for the elements of the vector (generally scalars), $U_j^{(t)}$ when needed. Note that this deviates from the notation in Chapters 4 and 5. In fact, letting U represent the k-dimensional parameter θ ($k \geq 2$), then $U^{(t)}$ and $U_j^{(t)}$ denote what was then denoted by $\theta_{(t)}$ and $\theta_{(t)j}$.[4] We continue to denote the stationary distribution by $\pi(u), u \in \mathcal{U}$.[5]

The fundamental element of the Metropolis–Hastings algorithm is a conditional distribution $q(\tilde{u} \mid u) \equiv q(u, \tilde{u})$ which plays the role of generating the simulated values. The basic requirement for $q(\cdot \mid \cdot)$, sometimes referred to as proposal or instrumental distribution, is easy random variate generation. The values $\tilde{u}$ that are generated from this distribution are subject to stochastic inspection, based on $q(\cdot \mid \cdot)$ and $\pi(\cdot)$, which determines whether $\tilde{u}$ is accepted or rejected, in the sense that a rejected $\tilde{u}$ is replaced by the most recent accepted value. The process is described in the following algorithm.

---

[4]　Note that for $k = 1$, $U^{(t)}$ corresponds to θ_t in these earlier chapters, reserving $\theta_{(t)}$ for the t-th smallest value of a sample $(\theta_1, \ldots, \theta_n)$.

[5]　For convenience, we will use the term "density function" to refer to a distribution independently of the nature of its support. That is, in the case of discrete random variables it represents the probability mass function.

Algorithm 1 Metropolis–Hastings (M-H) Algorithm

---

1. Given $u^{(t)}$, $t = 0, 1, 2, \ldots$ generate a value $\tilde{U} \sim q(\tilde{u} \mid u^{(t)})$.
2. Evaluate the M-H ratio $R(u^{(t)}, \tilde{U})$, with $R(u, \tilde{u}) = \frac{\pi(\tilde{u})q(u|\tilde{u})}{\pi(u)q(\tilde{u}|u)}$,
   and record the probability $\alpha(u, \tilde{u}) = \min\{R(u, \tilde{u}), 1\}$.
3. Accept as the next state of the chain

$$U^{(t+1)} = \begin{cases} \tilde{U}, & \text{with probability } \alpha(u^{(t)}, \tilde{U}) \\ u^{(t)}, & \text{with probability } 1 - \alpha(u^{(t)}, \tilde{U}). \end{cases} \tag{6.2}$$

Several notes about the algorithm are stated in the following.

Note 1: support of π. The acceptance probability for $\tilde{u}$ in iteration $t + 1$ requires $\pi(u^{(t)}) > 0$. This is guaranteed $\forall t \in \mathbb{N}$ if the initial value $u^{(0)}$ of the chain satisfies it, as all simulated values with $\pi(\tilde{u}) = 0$ are rejected due to $\alpha(u^{(t)}, \tilde{u}) = 0$. We set $R(u, \tilde{u}) = 0$ when $\pi(\tilde{u}) = 0 = \pi(u)$. Thus, once within the support of π, the chain does not leave from it almost surely.

Note 2: normalizing constants. The nature of the M-H ratio shows that the algorithm can be implemented when $\pi(\cdot)$ and $q(\cdot \mid u)$ are known up to normalizing constants, that is, factors that do not involve u in the case of $q(\cdot \mid u)$. On the other hand, values of $\tilde{u}$ with $\pi(\tilde{u})/q(\tilde{u} \mid u^{(t)})$ greater than the same ratio for the previous value, $\pi(u^{(t)})/q(u^{(t)} \mid \tilde{u})$, are always accepted, as $\alpha(u^{(t)}, \tilde{u}) = 1$.

Note 3: repetitions. A chain $\{u^{(t)}\}$ generated by this algorithm can include repetitions, and it is a special case of a Markov chain, as the distribution of $U^{(t+1)}$ conditional on all previous values depends only on $U^{(t)}$. Convergence of this chain to a target distribution $\pi(u)$ depends, as can be expected, on the proposal distribution.

Note 4: transition function. As this is the most common case in applications, we consider here only the absolutely continuous case (with respect to Lebesgue measure) with uncountably infinitely many states, in which case $\pi(u)$ is a density of the stationary distribution.

Let $Q(\cdot, \cdot)$ denote the transition function of a Markov chain, with density $q(\cdot \mid \cdot)$, i.e., $Q(u, d\tilde{u}) = q(\tilde{u} \mid u)d\tilde{u}$. In that case, step 3 of the M-H algorithm defines a transition function,

$$P(u, d\tilde{u}) \equiv P\left[U^{(t+1)} \in d\tilde{u} \mid U^{(t)} = u\right] = \alpha(u, \tilde{u})q(\tilde{u} \mid u)d\tilde{u} + r(u)\delta_u(d\tilde{u}), \tag{6.3}$$

where $\delta_u(d\tilde{u})$ denotes a Dirac measure in $d\tilde{u}$ and $r(u) = 1 - \int \alpha(u, \tilde{u})q(\tilde{u} \mid u)\, d\tilde{u}$ is the probability that the chain remains in u. The transition function

(6.3) is characterized by a transition density

$$p(u, \tilde{u}) = \alpha(u, \tilde{u})q(\tilde{u} \mid u) + r(u)\delta_u(\tilde{u}), \qquad (6.4)$$

which, by definition of α and δ_u, satisfies the detailed balance condition with π, $\pi(u)p(u, \tilde{u}) = \pi(\tilde{u})p(\tilde{u}, u)$. Thus, an M-H chain is reversible with a stationary distribution precisely equal to the desired target distribution π.

Note 5: convergence. Convergence of an M-H Markov chain to the stationary distribution π depends on the regularity conditions that were discussed in the previous section.

Let $S = \{u : \pi(u) > 0\}$ denote the support of π. The use of a proposal distribution $q(\cdot \mid \cdot)$ with $q(\tilde{u} \mid u) > 0$, $\forall (u, \tilde{u}) \in S \times S$ guarantees that the chain $\{U^{(t)}\}$ is irreducible with respect to π. Since π is a stationary distribution of the M-H chain, it is therefore positive recurrent (and also Harris recurrent), and the ergodic theorem of Section 6.1 applies. [6]

In summary, for an M-H chain that converges to a target distribution π, the states of the chain beyond a certain time can be considered as approximate simulations from π, even if in the implementation they were generated from the proposal distribution. This implies that summaries of π can be determined empirically from a (computer-generated) sample from the chain.

∎

The perhaps most attractive feature of the M-H algorithm is its versatility, considering the few and weak requirements for π and q to guarantee convergence of the chain to π. Note, however, that the mere fact of convergence does not yet imply that the algorithm is efficient in the sense of achieving practical convergence in a relatively small number of iterations. That is, it does not necessarily describe a fast mixing Markov chain.

A well-chosen instrumental distribution should generate values that cover the support of the target distribution in a reasonable number of iterations, and the proposals should be neither accepted nor rejected too often. These features are related to the dispersion of the proposal distribution that generates the simulated values. Specifically, if q is too dispersed relative to π, the proposed values are rejected frequently and the support of π can only be representatively sampled after many iterations, implying slow convergence. In the opposite case of narrow dispersion, only a small subset of S is visited across many iterations, with a high acceptance rate that might be falsely interpreted as quick convergence, when in fact a large number of additional iterations is needed to explore other parts of S. For these reasons

---

[6] See e.g. Tierney (1994) or Robert and Casella (2004). If additionally the chain is aperiodic – and this is guaranteed if $r(u) > 0$, $\forall u \in S$ – then one can prove convergence (in a suitable sense) of the n-step transition function, $P^n(u, \cdot)$, to Π as $n \to \infty$.

one should always start with a preliminary analysis of π, such that q could be chosen to approximate the target distribution as well as possible.

Given the generic nature of the M-H algorithm, we now describe two of the most commonly used special cases. [7]

Independence M-H Algorithm

As implied by the name of the algorithm, the proposal distribution is independent of the current state, i.e., $q(\tilde{u} \mid u) = q(\tilde{u})$. This implies the acceptance probability

$$\alpha(u^{(t)}, \tilde{u}) = \min\left\{\frac{\pi(\tilde{u})\, q(u^{(t)})}{\pi(u^{(t)})\, q(\tilde{u})}, 1\right\}, \ t \geq 0.$$

Similar to what we noted about the general M-H algorithm, ergodicity of the chain $\{U^{(t)}\}$ requires that the support of the proposal distribution q, now without conditioning, contain the support of π.

For instance consider simulation from a posterior distribution, i.e., $\pi(\theta) = h(\theta \mid x) \propto L(\theta \mid x)h(\theta)$ and the states are $\{U^{(t)} \equiv \theta^{(t)}\}$. An illustration of an independence M-H chain in this context is the special case with $q(\theta) = h(\theta)$. In this case the support of q covers the support of π, even if the two distributions could be very different. Also, in this case, the M-H ratio reduces to a likelihood ratio $R(\theta^{(t)}, \tilde{u}) = \frac{L(\tilde{u}|x)}{L(\theta^{(t)}|x)}$.

Random Walk M-H Algorithm

This algorithm is defined by an instrumental distribution $\tilde{U} = U^{(t)} + \varepsilon_t$, where ε_t is a random error with distribution q^* independent of $U^{(t)}$. This defines a random walk with transition density $q(\tilde{u} \mid u) = q^*(\tilde{u} - u)$. Usual choices for q^* include uniform distributions on a ball centered around the origin, Gaussian, and Student t distributions.

Note that if the proposal distribution is symmetric, i.e., $q(\tilde{u} \mid u) = q(u \mid \tilde{u})$, then the M-H ratio simplifies to $R(u, \tilde{u}) = \frac{\pi(\tilde{u})}{\pi(u)}$, highlighting that the target distribution need only be known up to a normalization constant. Symmetry occurs when $q^*(y)$ depends on y only through $|y|$. When a chain is based on a random walk $\tilde{U} \sim q^*(|\tilde{u} - u^{(t)}|)$ this becomes the Metropolis algorithm introduced in Metropolis et al (1953) in the context of a problem of the physics of particles with a discrete state space.[8]

---

[7] See, e.g., Givens and Hoeting (2005) for other cases.
[8] Nicholas Metropolis and Stanislaw Ulam were jointly the founders of what they named Monte Carlo methods.

6.3 Gibbs Sampler

The generic character of the M-H algorithm was evident in its description in the previous section, in particular in the fact that it was not necessary to even indicate the dimension of u in the target distribution $\pi(u)$. In contrast, the Gibbs sampler algorithm, [9] which is the subject of this section, is specifically designed for k-dimensional distributions ($k \geq 2$).

The algorithm constructs a Markov chain that is set up to converge to a desired target distribution $\pi(u)$, $u = (u_1, u_2, \ldots, u_k) \in \mathcal{U}$. This is implemented by iteratively sampling from the conditional distributions (typically univariate) given all other elements, also referred to as full conditional distributions. The algorithm successively replaces the elements of a state vector u in cycles of k steps, with the j-th step replacing u_j by a value sampled from the conditional distribution $\pi(v_j \mid \{u_i, i \notin j\})$, $j = 1, 2, \ldots, k$. For example, assuming $k = 3$, a cycle of three steps substitutes the current state u by $v = (v_1, v_2, v_3)$ with

$$(u_1, u_2, u_3) \overset{\text{step 1}}{\longrightarrow} (v_1, u_2, u_3) \overset{\text{step 2}}{\longrightarrow} (v_1, v_2, u_3) \overset{\text{step 3}}{\longrightarrow} (v_1, v_2, v_3).$$

In general, given a currently imputed state $u^{(t)} = (u_1^{(t)}, \ldots, u_k^{(t)})$ one transition of the Gibbs generates iteratively the values $u^{(t+1)}$ for the next state vector of the chain using the full conditional distributions

$$
\begin{aligned}
U_1^{(t+1)} &\sim \pi(u_1 \mid u_2^{(t)}, u_3^{(t)}, \ldots, u_k^{(t)}) \\
U_2^{(t+1)} &\sim \pi(u_2 \mid u_1^{(t+1)}, \ldots, u_k^{(t)}) \\
&\downarrow \\
U_{k-1}^{(t+1)} &\sim \pi(u_{k-1} \mid u_1^{(t+1)}, u_2^{(t+1)}, \ldots, u_{k-2}^{(t+1)}, u_k^{(t)}) \\
U_k^{(t+1)} &\sim \pi(u_k \mid u_1^{(t+1)}, u_2^{(t+1)}, \ldots, u_{k-1}^{(t+1)}).
\end{aligned}
\tag{6.5}
$$

The next transition repeats the k-step cycle, now starting from $u^{(t+1)}$. The scheme is summarized in Algorithm 2, below.

Example 6.1 *Let $x = (x_i, i = 1, \ldots, n)$ be a random sample from a Weibull model with unknown scale and shape parameters denoted δ and α, respectively. The likelihood function is*

$$L(\delta, \alpha \mid x) = (\delta \alpha)^n (\Pi_{i=1}^n x_i)^{\alpha-1} e^{-\delta \sum_i x_i^\alpha}, \quad \delta, \alpha > 0.$$

Assume that δ and α are a priori independent with gamma, $Ga(a, b)$, and

---

[9] The name for this method originated from Geman and Geman (1984) in an application to inference for so-called Gibbs random fields, referring to the physicist J. W. Gibbs.

Algorithm 2 Gibbs sampler

1. Given a current state $u^{(t)} = (u_1^{(t)}, \ldots, u_k^{(t)})$, starting with $t = 0$, generate each component, $u_j^{(t+1)}$, of the next state vector for the chain using

$$U_j^{(t+1)} \sim \pi(u_j^{(t+1)} \mid u_1^{(t+1)}, \ldots, u_{j-1}^{(t+1)}, u_{j+1}^{(t)}, \ldots, u_k^{(t)}),$$

for $j = 1, 2, \ldots, k$.
2. At the end of k steps, take $u^{(t+1)} = (u_1^{(t+1)}, \ldots, u_k^{(t+1)})$ and repeat step 1 for $t \equiv t + 1$.

---

log-normal, $LN(c, d)$ distributions, respectively, with fixed hyperparameters, $a, b, d > 0$ and $c \in \mathbb{R}$.

The joint posterior density has the kernel

$$h(\delta, \alpha \mid x) \propto \alpha^{n+c/d-1} \left(\prod_{i=1}^{n} x_i \right)^{\alpha} e^{-(\ln \alpha)^2/2d} \, \delta^{a+n} e^{-\delta\left(b + \sum_i x_i^{\alpha}\right)}.$$

This implies complete conditional distributions proportional to

1. $h(\delta \mid \alpha, x) \propto \delta^{a+n} e^{-\delta\left(b + \sum_i x_i^{\alpha}\right)}$;
2. $h(\alpha \mid \delta, x) \propto \alpha^{n+c/d-1} \left(\prod_{i=1}^{n} x_i \right)^{\alpha} e^{-\left[\frac{(\ln \alpha)^2}{2d} + \delta \sum_i x_i^{\alpha}\right]}$.

Thus, the complete conditional distribution for δ is $Ga(a + n, b + \sum_i x_i^{\alpha})$ and the generation of values for δ for any given α can be carried out by a computation-efficient gamma random variate generator. The complete conditional distribution for α does not appear in a standard form, thus requiring the use of more sophisticated methods of random variate generation. For example, adaptive rejection sampling based on the concave nature of the log-normal density. See also Note 4 in this section, and Appendix B for generic grid-based random variate generation. ∎

Let u generically denote the currently imputed state vector at the beginning of the j-th step. The Gibbs sampler proceeds as if it were generating a vector $\tilde{u} = (u_1, \ldots, u_{j-1}, \tilde{u}_j, u_{j+1}, \ldots, u_k)$ with

$$\tilde{U} \mid u \sim q_j(\tilde{u} \mid u) = \begin{cases} \pi(\tilde{u}_j \mid u_{-j}), & \text{if } \tilde{u}_{-j} = u_{-j} \\ 0, & \text{otherwise.} \end{cases} \tag{6.6}$$

The term Gibbs sampler refers not only to the described version. There are many variations about the sequential updates and about the simulation. Among others, this includes the following:

Gibbs Sampler with Blocking

Although the typical description of the Gibbs sampler uses univariate full conditional distributions, the scheme can include a more flexible number of steps in the cycle, with each step using the conditional distribution for a subvector of any dimension. This variation has the particular advantage of allowing us to group higher correlated variables together, such that generating from the complete conditional distributions for the entire subvector can accelerate convergence of the algorithm. It is usually used whenever the complete conditional posterior distribution for any subvector of the parameter vector is available for efficient random variate generation.

Gibbs Sampler with Hybridization

In general, there might be no known efficient random variate generators for some of the complete conditional distributions. In such cases, one can always resort to other transition probabilities that can then be combined with the Gibbs sampler to define a hybrid Gibbs sampler. An example is the use of M-H transition probabilities as discussed, for example, in Givens and Hoeting (2005, Section 7.2.5).

After this brief introduction to some variations, it is helpful to highlight some of the aspects of the Gibbs sampler algorithms in general.

Note 1: no proposal distribution. As shown, random variate generation in the Gibbs sampler is based on the target distribution itself. This avoids the often difficult problem of finding a "good" proposal distribution, as it is needed in the M-H algorithm. However, generating a single variable in each iteration of the Gibbs sampler is not a good device for fast mixing over the support of the target distribution.

Note 2: Gibbs and M-H algorithms. Despite differences between the Gibbs and the M-H algorithms, there is a close connection that is best seen in (6.6). Consider step j of a cycle of the Gibbs sampler starting with $u^{(t)}$. Simulation involves the conditional distribution $q_j(\tilde{u} \mid u) = \pi(\tilde{u}_j \mid u_{-j})$ with $\tilde{u}$ being a vector that differs from u only in the j-th component, that is $\tilde{u}_{-j} = u_{-j}$. The distribution $q_j(\tilde{u} \mid u)$ plays the role of a proposal distribution. By the definition of a joint distribution, and earlier introduced notation, we can write $\pi(u) = \pi(u_{-j})\pi(u_j \mid u_{-j})$, where the first and second factor refer, respectively, to the marginal distribution for U_{-j} and the conditional distribution for U_j given U_{-j}. The factors are also exactly the distributions of $\tilde{U}_{-j}$ and the conditional distribution of U_j given $\tilde{U}_{-j}$. Thus,

$$\frac{\pi(\tilde{u})}{\pi(u)} = \frac{\pi(\tilde{u}_j \mid u_{-j})}{\pi(u_j \mid \tilde{u}_{-j})} \equiv \frac{q_j(\tilde{u} \mid u)}{q_j(u \mid \tilde{u})},$$

implying for this step the M-H ratio

$$R_j(u, \tilde{u}) = \frac{\pi(\tilde{u}) \, q_j(u \mid \tilde{u})}{\pi(u) \, q_j(\tilde{u} \mid u)} = 1.$$

Each cycle of the Gibbs sampler can therefore be seen as a composition of k M-H transition probabilities, with acceptance probability for each step equal to 1. Note that when alternatively an entire cycle of the Gibbs sampler was interpreted as a single M-H transition function, a corresponding global acceptance probability could be calculated for the transition density between the initial and the final step of the cycle. This acceptance probability would not reduce to a constant 1.[10]

Note 3: bivariate case. The definition of the Gibbs sampler in the bivariate case consists of the steps $U_1^{(t+1)} \sim \pi_1(\cdot \mid u_2^{(t)})$ and $U_2^{(t+1)} \sim \pi_2(\cdot \mid u_1^{(t+1)})$ for $t \geq 0$, and highlights clearly that the sequence $\{(U_1^{(t)}, U_2^{(t)})\}$ defines a Markov chain. Also each of the subsequences is a Markov chain, e.g., $U_2^{(t)}$ is a Markov chain with transition density

$$P(u_2, \tilde{u}_2) = \int \pi_1(w \mid u_2) \pi_2(\tilde{u}_2 \mid w) \, dw,$$

which depends on the past only through the previous value of U_2. In other words, the definition of the marginal densities and the transition density for U_2 implies

$$\pi_2(\tilde{u}_2) = \int \pi_2(\tilde{u}_2 \mid w) \pi_1(w) \, dw =$$

$$\int \left[\int \pi_2(\tilde{u}_2 \mid w) \pi_1(w \mid u_2) \, dw \right] \pi_2(u_2) \, du_2 = \int P(u_2, \tilde{u}_2) \pi_2(u_2) \, du_2,$$

which shows that π_2 is a stationary distribution for the subchain $U_2^{(t)}$.

One of the basic conditions for convergence of a multivariate $\{U^{(t)}\}$ is that the support $\mathcal{U}$ of the joint distribution $\pi(\cdot)$ be the Cartesian product of the supports $\mathcal{U}_j$ of the marginal distributions $\pi_j(\cdot)$. This implies that the chain is irreducible and, in the bivariate case, the same holds for the marginal subchains. If, additionally, the transition function is absolutely continuous with respect to Lebesgue, with the density taking the form of a

---

[10] It suffices to consider the case $k = 2$ and the corresponding transition density $P(u, \tilde{u}) = \pi_1(\tilde{u}_1 \mid u_2) \pi_2(\tilde{u}_2 \mid \tilde{u}_1)$, where π_j refers to the marginal distribution of the element U_j of the pair (here conditional on the other element). In this case the M-H acceptance ratio $\pi(\tilde{u}_1)/\pi(\tilde{u}_1 \mid u_2) \pi(u_1 \mid \tilde{u}_2)/\pi(u_1)$.

product of complete conditional densities,

$$p(u, v) = \pi_1(v_1 \mid u_2, \ldots, u_k) \pi_2(v_2 \mid v_1, u_3, \ldots, u_k) \times \ldots$$
$$\times \pi_k(v_k \mid v_1, v_2, \ldots, v_{k-1}),$$

the chain is (Harris) recurrent, implying that π is the stationary distribution of the chain $\{U^{(t)}\}$ and its marginals are the limiting distributions of the respective subchains, with the resulting applicability of the ergodic theorem.[11]

In summary, the structure and convergence of the Gibbs sampler highlight that the full conditional distributions suffice to characterize and generate from the joint distribution. It is helpful to explore (counter-)examples for the incompatibility of conditional distributions to appreciate the relevance of the conditions that assure convergence to the target distribution in a Gibbs sampler (see also Paulino et al., 2018 and the references therein). In particular, one needs to be careful with the normalization constant in the complete conditional distributions. In particular, an (improper) infinite normalization constant makes the existence of a proper joint distribution impossible, a condition which is not always detected by inspection of the generated Markov chains, but it occurs not uncommonly with Bayes models with improper prior distributions (see also Robert and Casella, 2004: ch. 10, and references therein).

Note 4: The simulation from complete conditional distributions depends naturally on the specific structure of these conditionals. In the simplest case, resorting to the inverse c.d.f. method or efficient *ad hoc* methods for certain known distributions might allow efficient random variate generation for the corresponding steps in the Gibbs sampler. In more complicated cases, the required sampling is still possible with more sophisticated approaches described in the references that were indicated in the introduction to Chapter 4.

In many statistical inference problems, the target distribution can be difficult to evaluate; for example, if it involves analytically intractable integrals. As a consequence, no easy method for random variate generation for the steps in the Gibbs sampler might be available. One often successful method (like in missing data problems) is to augment the target distribution $\pi(u)$ to $f(u, Z)$ by introducing additional latent variables Z such that

---

[11] And also convergence of the n-step transition function to π if the chain is additionally aperiodic.

$\pi(u)$ remains the marginal distribution of the joint $f(u, Z)$. [12] In some cases, the augmented model $f(u, Z)$ allows a much easier implementation of the Gibbs sampler, now involving the distributions $f(u \mid z)$ and $f(z \mid u)$.

Example 6.2 *Consider a diagnostic test for some disease with a binary outcome (positive or negative). Taking a random sample of N patients, let X be the number of positive results, and assume that $X \mid \phi \sim Bi(N, \phi)$. Most diagnostic tests are subject to classification errors implying that the probability of a positive can be written as $\phi = \alpha\sigma + (1 - \alpha)(1 - \varepsilon)$, where $\theta = (\alpha, \sigma, \varepsilon)$ and α is the prevalence of the disease, σ is the sensitivity of the test (probability of a true positive), and ε is the specificity of the test (probability of a true negative).*

The vector θ is typically unknown and is the parameter vector of interest in the inference problem. However, given the obvious overparametrization of the sampling model, it is not possible to report inference on θ (or functions of θ, except ϕ, for example) without additional data (e.g., from a further test regarded as a gold standard) or a priori information related to the type of diagnostic test and the disease under consideration. Suppose that one only has access to such prior information, represented as independent beta distributions for the components of θ, with fixed hyperparameters. The posterior distribution takes the following analytically intractable form:

$$h(\theta \mid x) \propto f(x \mid \theta)\alpha^{a_p-1}(1 - \alpha)^{b_p-1}\sigma^{c_s-1}(1 - \sigma)^{d_s-1}\varepsilon^{c_e-1}(1 - \varepsilon)^{d_e-1},$$

$\theta \in (0, 1)^3$. Intending to implement posterior inference using MCMC, the Gibbs sampler is not a particularly easy approach for this posterior distribution because the conditional posterior distributions are complicated, requiring specialized random variate generation methods. However, the implementation of a Gibbs sampler is greatly facilitated by the following model augmentation with latent data. Let $Y = (X, Z_1, Z_2)$, where Z_1 (resp. Z_2) are unobserved (latent) data that report the number of individuals with true positive (negative) results. A model for Y that remains consistent with the observed data X is defined as

$$f(y \mid \theta) = f(x \mid \theta)f(z_1 \mid x, \theta)f(z_2 \mid x, \theta),$$

where now $Z_1 \mid x, \theta \sim Bi(x, \alpha\sigma/\phi)$ and $Z_2 \mid x, \theta \sim Bi(N-x, (1-\alpha)\varepsilon/(1-\phi))$.

Note that the parameters of the conditional distributions for the latent variables correspond to the so-called positive predicted values $V_+ = \alpha\sigma/\phi$

---

[12] The construction of $f(u, Z)$ could also be referred to as demarginalization or augmentation of $\pi(u)$.

and negative predicted values $V_- = (1 - \alpha)\varepsilon/(1 - \phi)$. The posterior density, now with the augmented data y, is then

$$h(\theta \mid y) \quad \propto \quad f(x \mid \phi)(V_+)^{z_1}(1 - V_+)^{x-z_1}(V_-)^{z_2}(1 - V_-)^{N-x-z_2} \times$$
$$\alpha^{a_p-1}(1 - \alpha)^{b_p-1}\sigma^{c_s-1}(1 - \sigma)^{d_s-1}\varepsilon^{c_e-1}(1 - \varepsilon)^{d_e-1}.$$

The expression is considerably simplified to a product of three beta densities. In fact, if we introduce a transformation of the data from $y = (x, z_1, z_2)$ to $y^* = (m, z_1, z_2)$, where $m = z_1 + N - x - z_2$ is the number of individuals in the sample who have the disease, we find from $f(y \mid \theta)$ that

$$f(y^* \mid \theta) = f(m \mid \theta)f(z_1 \mid m, \theta)f(z_2 \mid m, \theta),$$

such that $M \mid \theta \sim Bi(N, \alpha)$, $Z_1 \mid m, \theta \sim Bi(m, \sigma)$ and $Z_2 \mid m, \theta \sim Bi(N - m, \varepsilon)$.

This factorization of the likelihood, considering factorization of the joint prior and of the binomial and beta factors, implies that the components of θ are also a posteriori independent, with the following distributions:

$$\alpha \mid y \sim Be(A_p, B_p), \quad A_p = a_p + m = a_p + z_1 + N - x - z_2,$$
$$B_p = b_p + N - m = b_p + x - z_1 + z_2$$
$$\sigma \mid y \sim Be(C_s, D_s), \quad C_s = c_s + z_1, \ D_s = d_s + N - x - z_2$$
$$\varepsilon \mid y \sim Be(C_e, D_e), \quad C_e = c_e + z_2, \ D_e = d_e + x - z_1.$$

These are the complete conditional distributions for the parameters conditional on the augmented data y. Since the parts z_1 and z_2 of the augmented data are not observed, one needs to impute these based on the parameters. The latter can be done using the respective sampling distributions conditional on the observed part x of the data. This leads to a Gibbs type algorithm for the joint posterior distribution $h(\theta, z_1, z_2 \mid x)$, defined by the following two steps.

Data Augmentation

1. *Imputation step: given $\theta^{(0)} = (\alpha^{(0)}, \sigma^{(0)}, \varepsilon^{(0)})$, compute $V_+^{(0)} = V_+(\theta^{(0)})$ and $V_-^{(0)} = V_-(\theta^{(0)})$ and generate*

$$z_1^{(1)} \sim Bi(x, V_+^{(0)}), \ z_2^{(1)} \sim Bi(N - x, V_-^{(0)}).$$

2. *Posterior step: based on $(z_1^{(1)}, z_2^{(1)})$, generate from the posterior distribution for θ given the augmented data. That is, generate $\theta^{(1)}$ as*

$$\alpha^{(1)} \sim Be(A_p, B_p), \ \sigma^{(1)} \sim Be(C_s, D_s), \ \varepsilon^{(1)} \sim Be(C_e, D_e).$$

Starting from $\theta^{(1)}$ repeat the cycle of the two steps repeatedly.

This algorithm was introduced, still without any reference to the Gibbs sampler, by Tanner and Wong (1987) under the aforementioned title, where they prove that $h(\theta \mid x, z_1^{(t)}, z_2^{(t)})$ converge as $t \to \infty$ to $h(\theta \mid x)$, under quite general conditions.

∎

6.4 Slice Sampler

As we saw, complex target distributions π can complicate conditional random variate generation even when pointwise evaluation of the density function $\pi(u)$ in any $u \in \mathcal{U}$ remains possible. In this case, yet another strategy to implement MCMC is to introduce an auxiliary variable Z with the aim of facilitating simulation of a chain for $(U, Z) \sim f(u, z) = \pi(u)f(z \mid u)$. Here, Z should be chosen such that the chain for the augmented distribution $f(u, z)$ converges and such that the exploration of the support $\mathcal{U}$ of the corresponding subchain and the evaluation of the desired summaries of π are possible.

Defining Z such that $Z \mid U = u \sim U(0, \pi(u))$, we get $(U, Z) \sim U(\mathcal{S})$ where $\mathcal{S} = \{(u, z) : u \in \mathcal{U}, z \in [0, \pi(u)]\}$ and $U(\mathcal{S})$ refers to a uniform distribution over the set $\mathcal{S}$. Thus one way of obtaining a MC sample from π is to generate a Markov chain with the stationary distribution being precisely the multivariate uniform on $\mathcal{S}$.

The slice sampler is an iterative method to generate a random walk on $\mathcal{S}$, moving alternating in two directions using uniform distributions. In the first step over the real line using $Z \mid U = u \sim U(0, \pi(u))$ and in the second step over $\mathcal{U}$ using $U \mid Z = z \sim U(\mathcal{S}(z))$, with $\mathcal{S}(z) = \{u \in \mathcal{U} : \pi(u) \geq z\}$ – note that the marginal density $f(z)$ is therefore proportional to Lebesgue measure of $\mathcal{S}(z)$.

If the chain converges, this method thus generates an approximate sample from π by considering the corresponding subchain, requiring only the evaluation of π in the locations simulated by the uniform distribution. Actually, the sampling schemes only requires π up to a normalization constant[13].

In summary, the sampling algorithm is defined as follows.

---

[13] In fact, writing $\pi(u) = c\pi^*(u)$ and letting $Z^* = Z/c$, the approach is equivalent to using $(U, Z^*) \sim U(\{(u, z^*) : u \in \mathcal{U}, z^* \in [0, \pi^*(u)]\})$, implying $Z^* \mid U = u \sim U(0, \pi^*(u))$ and $U \mid Z^* = z^* \sim U(\{u : \pi^*(u) \geq z^*\})$.

Algorithm 3 Slice Sampler

Given $(u^{(t)}, z^{(t)})$, starting with $t = 0$, simulate

1. $z^{(t+1)} \sim U(0, \pi(u^{(t)}))$;
2. $u^{(t+1)} \sim U(\{u : \pi(u) \geq z^{(t+1)}\})$;
   and repeat the cycle of these two steps incrementing t each time; note
   that $\pi(u)$ here denotes the density or its kernel, whichever is easier to
   evaluate.

We conclude with a few more comments about this approach whose
name is attributed to Neal (1997) and which goes back to work published
in Neal (2003) and Damien et al (1999).

Note 1: univariate case. For univariate U the slice sampler can be easily
illustrated by a graphical representation of the density $\pi(u)$ with U and Z
marked on the horizontal and vertical axes, respectively (see Figure 6.1).
The point $(u^{(t)}, \pi(u^{(t)})$ defines on the vertical axis a slice over which the

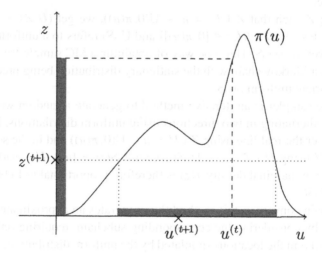

Figure 6.1 Slice sampler for a univariate distribution $\pi(u)$.

value $z^{(t+1)}$ is generated. The intersection of the line $Z = z^{(t+1)}$ with $\pi(u)$
defines the point(s) that delimit the horizontal slice $\mathcal{S}(z^{(t+1)})$ (an interval
or union of intervals) over which $u^{(t+1)}$ is generated. In practice, the main
difficulty with this algorithm is the second step since the support $\mathcal{S}(z)$ of the
distribution on the horizontal slice could be complicated for a multimodal
$\pi(u)$, which might need the use of other simulation methods in this step

(e.g., rejection sampling). In any case, by the nature of the algorithm it works better than many other algorithms (such as, for example, M-H) with multimodal target densities, in the sense of an efficient exploration of the support of such target distribution.

Note 2: slice sampler and Gibbs. The structure of the slice sampler for univariate $\mathcal{U}$ highlights that it can be seen as a special case of a two-step Gibbs sampler for the model augmentation of $\pi(u)$ to $f(u, z) = \pi(u)f(z \mid u)$, a uniform in $\mathcal{S}$. The sequence $\{U^{(t)}\}$ is therefore a Markov chain with transition density $P(u, \tilde{u}) = \int f(z \mid u)f(\tilde{u} \mid z)\,dz$ and stationary distribution $\pi(u)$.

This interpretation remains essentially valid also for multivariate target distributions, except for a naturally larger number of steps. As a consequence, the convergence conditions for a slice sampler can be seen to follow from those for the Gibbs sampler, based on the introduction of a vector of auxiliary variables to deal with more complex target distributions (for a discussion, see, for example, Robert and Casella, 2004).

6.5 Hamiltonian Monte Carlo

6.5.1 Hamiltonian Dynamics

A common problem with some of the earlier discussed MCMC schemes is the often local nature of the transitions. For example, with a Metropolis–Hastings random walk transition function, we often only move a small step in the parameter space. With a Gibbs sampler we only update one parameter at a time. High posterior correlations can lead to very slowly mixing Markov chains. An interesting alternative that can allow us to quickly move around the parameter space is Hamiltonian Monte Carlo (Neal, 2011). The basic idea is very simple. There are three important steps to the construction. Let $\pi(\theta)$ denote the target distribution of interest, e.g., a posterior distribution $h(\theta \mid x)$.

First, we add a (entirely artificial) time index to θ, making it $\theta(t)$. Eventually, after the transition, we will drop the t index again to obtain the new parameter values.

Next, we start the construction with a differential equation system for $d\theta(t)/dt$ that is known to keep a given target function invariant. That is, if we simulate transitions following the solution of this system, then these transitions would keep the target function unchanged. If we use $\ln \pi$ as the target function, then this gives us transitions that move along equal contour lines of $\pi(\theta)$. Such a differential equation system is, for example,

Hamilton's equations of Hamiltonian mechanics. All we need to do is to equate potential energy with the log posterior distribution. Then we simulate Hamiltonian dynamics. We are guaranteed that the simulated states have all equal posterior density. That is, we move on contours of the joint posterior distribution.

There is one more clever twist to the setup. Let $N(x \mid m, S)$ denote a multivariate normal p.d.f. for the random vector x with mean m and covariance matrix S. We first augment the probability model to $\pi(\theta, p) = \pi(\theta) N(p \mid 0, I)$, using a multivariate normal distribution for p (and it could be any other – but this makes the following derivations easiest). The notation p for the additional variable is chosen in anticipation of the upcoming interpretation of the augmented model. Note that this model augmentation is unusual in the sense that θ and the latent variable p are independent. That will turn out to greatly simplify the algorithm. Let

$$H(\theta, p) = -\ln \pi(\theta) + \frac{1}{2}p'p \qquad (6.7)$$

denote the negative log augmented target distribution (ignoring constant factors). We use $H(\theta, p)$ as the target function (potential) for the Hamiltonian equations, interpreting θ as location and p as momentum. That is all! All we have left to do is to state the equations and then implement an approximate numerical solution to the differential equation. Let $\theta = (\theta_1, \ldots, \theta_d)$ and $p = (p_1, \ldots, p_d)$ denote the two d-dimensional location and momentum. Hamilton's equations are

$$\frac{d\theta_i}{dt} = \frac{\partial H}{\partial p_i} \text{ and } \frac{dp_i}{dt} = -\frac{\partial H}{\partial \theta_i}. \qquad (6.8)$$

Changing $(\theta(t), p(t))$ according to these equations leaves the potential unchanged. Since we set the potential to be the log (augmented) target distribution we are guaranteed to move on equal probability contours. That is the trick. The particular choice (6.7) simplifies the equations further, with

$$\frac{d\theta_i}{dt} = \frac{\partial H}{\partial p_i} = p_i \text{ and } \frac{dp_i}{dt} = -\frac{\partial H}{\partial \theta_i} = \frac{\partial \ln \pi}{\partial \theta_i}.$$

There is a beautiful interpretation of the setup. In the application of (6.8) to mechanics, the parameters θ become the location of an object and p is the momentum (that is, velocity × mass). For example, think of the object as a ball on a slope. Then $\ln \pi(\theta)$ is the potential, that is the energy due to location, and $\frac{1}{2}p^2$ is the kinetic energy. It is good to think of the object as a ball, as we entirely ignore friction. Hamiltonian mechanics describes how a ball in location θ and with momentum p at time t will move. Its movement is determined by keeping the sum of potential and kinetic energy constant. Compare this to Figure 6.2, later.

Leapfrog Approximation

To implement Hamiltonian dynamics we use a discretization of the differential equation system (6.8) known as the leapfrog method. Starting from $(\theta(t), p(t))$ we generate $(\theta(t + \epsilon), p(t + \epsilon))$ by using a discrete approximation over two subintervals of length $\epsilon/2$ each:

$$p_i\left(t + \frac{\epsilon}{2}\right) - p_i(t) + \frac{\epsilon}{2}\frac{\partial \ln \pi(\theta(t))}{\partial \theta_i}$$

$$\theta_i(t + \epsilon) = \theta_i(t) + \epsilon\, p_i\left(t + \frac{\epsilon}{2}\right)$$

$$p_i(t + \epsilon) = p_i\left(t + \frac{\epsilon}{2}\right) + \frac{\epsilon}{2}\frac{\partial \ln \pi(\theta(t + \epsilon))}{\partial \theta_i}. \tag{6.9}$$

Let $T_\epsilon(\theta(t), p(t)) = (\theta(t + \epsilon), p(t + \epsilon))$ denote the discrete approximation implemented in (6.9). It is easily verified that the approximation is perfectly reversible, that is, $T_{-\epsilon}(\theta(t + \epsilon), p(t + \epsilon)) = (\theta(t), p(t))$ again, or $T_{-\epsilon}(\theta, p) = T_\epsilon^{-1}(\theta, p)$. Even easier than turning back time, all we have to do to send the ball back to where it came from is to turn it around. That is, $p \equiv -p$, or $T_\epsilon^{-1}(\theta, p) = T_\epsilon(\theta, -p)$. Note that the time index in $\theta(t)$ and $p(t)$ is only used for the implementation of $T_\epsilon(\cdot)$. After the last step in (6.9), we drop the time index again.

Example 6.3 Logistic regression. *In a toxicity study for some new compound, various dose levels of the compound are administered to batches of animals. Let $i = 1, \ldots, k$ index the batches, let x_i index the dose for the i-th batch, let n_i denote the number of animals in the i-th batch, and y_i the number of animals in the i-th batch that show a response. We assume that y_i is a binomial random variable, $y_i \sim Bi(n_i, \pi_i)$, where π_i is the probability of response at dose x_i. We assume $\pi_i = 1/\left(1 + e^{\alpha + \beta x_i}\right)$. This is known as a logistic regression model. The probabilities π_i define the sampling model (likelihood).*

We complete the model with a prior $h(\alpha, \beta) = N(0, cI)$, where I is a (2×2) identity matrix, and $c = 100$, i.e., a very vague prior. We observe *the following data:*

i	Dose x_i	Number animals n_i	Number responses y_i
1	−0.86	6	1
2	−0.30	5	2
3	−0.05	5	3
4	0.73	5	5

*In this example, we use (6.9) to define transitions that leave the augmented
log posterior (6.7) invariant. For the moment these are* deterministic *transitions – we will later add randomness. This will be easy. Let $\theta = (\alpha, \beta)$
denote the parameter vector. Let $\bar{\pi}_i = 1 - \pi_i$ and $\bar{y}_i = n_i - y_i$ denote
the probabilities and number of non-responses. Then $f(y \mid \theta) = \Pi_i \pi_i^{y_i} \bar{\pi}_i^{\bar{y}_i}$,
$h(\theta) = N(0, I)$ and*

$$\ln h(\theta \mid y) = c - \frac{\alpha^2 + \beta^2}{2} - \sum_i y_i \ln\left(1 + e^{\alpha + \beta x_i}\right) - \sum_i \bar{y}_i \ln\left(1 + e^{-\alpha - \beta x_i}\right).$$

with gradient

$$\nabla \ln h(\theta \mid y) = \begin{pmatrix} -\alpha \\ -\beta \end{pmatrix} - \sum_i y_i \bar{\pi}_i \begin{pmatrix} 1 \\ x_i \end{pmatrix} + \sum_i \bar{y}_i \pi_i \begin{pmatrix} 1 \\ x_i \end{pmatrix}.$$

*Using (6.9) with target distribution $\pi(\theta) = h(\theta \mid y)$, we implement $M = 8$
steps of size $\epsilon = 0.1$. The transitions are deterministic, and we expect to
stay on a constant level of the augmented model (6.7). The algorithm requires an initial value of p. Think of θ as the location of a ball on log posterior contours, and p as the momentum that you give the ball by kicking it.
Hamiltonian mechanics and the approximation in (6.9) describes the trajectory of the ball over M small time intervals of length ϵ. In this analogy
you have to think of the posterior distribution as a valley, with the posterior
mode being the lowest point. This is because $\ln h(\theta \mid y)$ appears in (6.7)
with negative sign. Figure 6.2 shows a contour plot of the log posterior
"valley," and three possible trajectories. All start at $\theta = (-2, -4)$, kicking
the ball with $p = (1, 0), (1, -3),$ and $(1, 1.4)$. On the four-dimensional contours of the augmented model $H(\theta, p)$ the trajectories would move along
contour lines. Next we will introduce a random transition function, building on this deterministic transition of the leapfrog approximation, which we
will then use in Problem 6.12 to implement MCMC posterior simulation for
this example.*

■

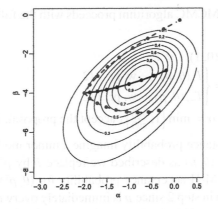

Figure 6.2 Log posterior $\ln h(\theta \mid y)$ with trajectories for $M = 8$ steps of the leapfrog approximation (6.9). All trajectories start at the same point θ, and correspond to three different initial values for p.

6.5.2 Hamiltonian Monte Carlo Transition Probabilities

Recall that (exact) Hamiltonian dynamics leaves the augmented probability model $h(\theta, p)$ invariant. However, the approximation $T_\epsilon(\cdot)$ does not – with the approximation error depending on the step size. But this is not a problem for our application. We use T_ϵ to generate a proposal in a Metropolis–Hastings transition probability. Starting with (θ, p), we generate a proposal $(\tilde{\theta}, \tilde{p})$ with

$$(\tilde{\theta}, \tilde{p}) = \begin{cases} T_\epsilon(\theta, p) & \text{w. pr. } \frac{1}{2} \\ T_{-\epsilon}(\theta, p) & \text{w. pr. } \frac{1}{2}. \end{cases} \tag{6.10}$$

By the earlier comment, the proposal distribution is symmetric, leaving the acceptance probability $\alpha = \min(1, R)$ with $\ln(R) = H(\tilde{\theta}, \tilde{p}) - H(\theta, p)$. In this implementation, a possible approximation error in (6.9) is a feature, not a problem, as it allows us to move across contour lines of $H(\cdot)$.

The final trick of Hamiltonian Monte Carlo is particularly clever. We alternate the M-H step (6.10) with a Gibbs transition probability by generating p from the complete conditional under $\pi(\cdot)$,

$$p \sim \pi(p \mid \theta) = N(0, I).$$

Here, we exploit the fact that location and momentum are independent in (6.7), making the Gibbs step particularly easy.

In summary, the MCMC algorithm proceeds with the following two transition probabilities.

1. Generate $p_i \sim N(0, 1)$, $i = 1, \ldots, d$.

2. Generate $(\tilde{\theta}, \tilde{p}) = \begin{cases} T_\epsilon(\theta, p) & \text{w. pr. } 1/2 \\ T_{-\epsilon}(\theta, p) & \text{w. pr. } 1/2 \end{cases}$.

   With probability $\alpha = \min\left\{1, \frac{\pi(\tilde{\theta})}{\pi(\theta)}\right\}$, accept the proposal, $\theta \equiv \tilde{\theta}$.

To justify the acceptance probability imagine a minor modification of step 2. After generating $(\tilde{\theta}, \tilde{p})$ as described we replace $\tilde{p}$ by $p^\dagger \sim \pi(p \mid \tilde{\theta})$ and recognize α as the M-H acceptance probability for $(\tilde{\theta}, p^\dagger)$. Finally, we do not need to record p in step 2 since p is immediately overwritten in step 1 of the next iteration. Also, if desired, T_ϵ can be changed to implement multiple leapfrog steps. The algorithm remains unchanged (and the approximation error increases with multiple steps).

The algorithm can be further simplified by noting that $p_i(t + \epsilon)$ in the last step in the leapfrog approximation (6.9), that is T_ϵ or $T_{-\epsilon}$ in step 2, is not needed. The value $p_i(t + \epsilon)$ is never used in the MCMC described here. It is immediately replaced by a new value, $p_i \sim N(0, 1)$ in step 1 of the following iteration. The first two lines of (6.9) can be collapsed into

$$\theta_i(t + \epsilon) = \theta_i(t) + \epsilon \left\{ p_i(t) + \frac{\epsilon}{2} \frac{\partial \ln \pi(\theta(t))}{\partial \theta_i} \right\}. \tag{6.11}$$

And, even easier, we can further collapse (6.11) with $p_i \sim N(0, 1)$ in step 1 to get

$$\theta_i(t + \epsilon) \mid \theta_i(t) \sim N\left\{ \theta_i(t) + \frac{\epsilon^2}{2} \frac{\partial \ln \pi(\theta(t))}{\partial \theta_i}, \epsilon^2 \right\}.$$

That is, we replace steps 1 and 2 with a single step.

1'. Generate a proposal,

$$\tilde{\theta}_i \mid \theta \sim N\left\{ \theta_i + \frac{\epsilon^2}{2} \frac{\partial \ln \pi(\theta)}{\partial \theta_i}, \epsilon^2 \right\}.$$

Accept with probability $\alpha = \min\{1, R\}$ with acceptance ratio

$$R = \frac{\pi(\tilde{\theta})}{\pi(\theta)} \Pi_{i=1}^d \frac{N\left\{ \theta_i \mid \tilde{\theta}_i + \frac{\epsilon^2}{2} \frac{\partial \ln \pi(\tilde{\theta})}{\partial \theta_i}, \epsilon^2 \right\}}{N\left\{ \tilde{\theta}_i \mid \theta_i + \frac{\epsilon^2}{2} \frac{\partial \ln \pi(\theta)}{\partial \theta_i}, \epsilon^2 \right\}},$$

the first factor being the ratio of target distributions and the second factor the ratio of proposal distributions for the proposed and the reciprocal moves. This and other simplifications are discussed by Welling and Teh

(2011). In particular, they observe the following clever interpretation of the last version of the HMC algorithm. First, letting $\delta = \epsilon^2$, rewrite the proposal distribution as

$$\tilde{\theta}_i = \theta_i + \frac{\delta}{2} \frac{\partial \ln \pi(\theta)}{\partial \theta_i} + \sqrt{\delta} Z$$

where $Z \sim N(0, 1)$ is a standard normal random variable. Stated in this form, note that for large δ the gradient term dominates, whereas for small δ the standard normal term dominates.

6.6 Implementation Details

As we discussed before, MCMC methods aim to iteratively generate the states of a Markov chain such that it approaches its limiting distribution with increasing number of iterations. And the chain is set up such that this limiting distribution equals a desired target distribution $\pi(u)$. If, in a given iteration t, the chain is already in (or "close to") its limiting distribution, then the generated states at that time and beyond can be used as approximate draws from the target distribution, which in our discussion is usually a posterior distribution $h(\theta \mid x)$.

However, subsequent realizations of the same chain (over time) are not a random sample from the target distribution, because of the serial correlation of the generated vectors $\theta^{(t)}$. This is the main difference to classical MC methods that we discussed in Chapter 4. While the summaries of the MC sample are the same, the quantification of the corresponding numerical uncertainty requires different summaries – for example, the sample standard deviation of the ergodic averages is not the same as the standard error in the i.i.d. case.[14] Also, the asymptotic justification of the ergodic averages introduces additional requirements.

Besides the importance of understanding convergence conditions for the previously described MCMC schemes, it is equally important that these conditions are not immediately useful from an implementation point of view. This is the case, because the practical verification of these conditions is often problematic and also because the methods themselves do not include diagnostics about when simulation can be considered sufficient to evaluate the desired inference summaries.

---

[14] One strategy is to use the mentioned sample standard error after a correction factor that accounts for the serial correlations (see, e.g., Robert and Casella, 2004: chapter 12). Another option, mentioned below, is to sufficiently thin out the chain such that the remaining states can be considered as a random sample.

For these reasons it is in practice necessary to resort to empirical diagnostics to evaluate the simulation output to understand when practical convergence is achieved (with the desired target), keeping in mind that no such methods are exact. Without such diagnostics it is difficult to have any confidence in the reported summaries.

Single Chain Versus Multiple Chains

Many diagnostics aim to monitor convergence of the chain to its stationary distribution or of the ergodic averages to the corresponding expectations. Naturally, approaches differ about the extent to which they make use of the simulation output, and whether they use a single long chain or multiple, parallel independent chains. The latter two choices are described in the following.

Single Chain Approach

Let $\theta^{(0)} = (\theta_1^{(0)}, \ldots, \theta_k^{(0)})$ denote the initial state of the chain.

- Generate one long realization of the chain of size $t = \ell + k^\star m$ iterations, where

  - ℓ is the number of initial iterations used to reach practical convergence (as determined by one of the diagnostics in the following). These initial iterations are also known as initial burn-in, and can be longer or shorter depending on whether the chain is faster or slower mixing for a specific model;
  - m is the desired MC sample size, and k^* is the spacing between states of the chain $\{\theta^{(t)}\}$ that are being saved, aiming to mitigate serial auto-correlation between the saved states such that the resulting MC sample is approximately i.i.d. ($k^\star$ can be determined from a plot of auto-correlations across different lags).

- In summary this results in extracting from the original chain a subset of m realizations $\theta^{(\ell+k^\star)}, \theta^{(\ell+2k^\star)}, \ldots, \theta^{(\ell+mk^\star)}$, which we shall now denote $\theta_{(1)}, \ldots, \theta_{(m)}$, where $\theta_{(j)} \equiv \theta^{(\ell+jk^\star)}$, and which shall be used to evaluate the desired inference summaries as discussed in Chapters 4 and 5.

The question arises of how to choose the sample size m, the number of initial iterations ℓ and the spacing $k^\star$ between iterations. Since the choices are highly dependent on the particular details in each problem, there are no general answers. Note that the value of ℓ in particular is dependent on the initial state of the chain and the level of mixing. The simulation sample size m is dependent on the desired precision for the inference summaries. The spacing $k^\star$ is highly dependent on the correlation structure and is meant to achieve faster convergence of ergodic averages, although at the cost of reduced efficiency (the ergodic average after thinning out has less precision than the total average (after burn-in) – see MacEachern and Berliner, 1994).

Multiple Chains

- Generate m chains with t^* (usually, $t^* \ll t$) iterations each, starting with m initial values, usually generated to be distinct and well separated across the support of the target distribution.
- Use the final iterations $\theta^{(t^*)}$ of each chain to form a MC sample $\theta_{(1)}, \ldots, \theta_{(m)}$ – the choice of t^*, beyond some initial burn-in, and the choice of m are subject to similar considerations as before.

Both approaches have their advantages and limitations, which explains the great variety of choices that are found in the literature. [15] The first scheme allows us to reduce the computational cost and can lead to a chain closer to $h(\theta \mid x)$ than schemes using multiple chains, using the same total number of iterations. The second scheme makes it easier to control convergence to $h(\theta \mid x)$ by reducing dependence on the initial states and allows a more direct exploration of the target support. It is more likely to detect if the apparent convergence of a chain is merely an indication that it is trapped around some local mode, far from the target distribution. If this is the case, one can reparametrize the model (difficult in general) or one can change the initial values. In summary, the scheme with multiple chains seems by and large appropriate for an exploratory evaluation before running one long chain for definite inference.

Convergence diagnostics

A variety of methods have been proposed to diagnose convergence. Some are already included as default in specific or more general software for Bayesian inference. Others can be added by writing problem-specific code for a given inference problem. Keeping with the scope of this text, we limit the discussion to a brief review of some of the most widely used methods.

The most widely used tools to monitor convergence to the stationary distribution are plots of simulated values across iterations, known as trajectory (or trace) plots, and the analysis of such plots across different time windows to inspect any changes in the mixing of the chain over the support of the target posterior distribution. Another tool is the superposition of

---

[15] The issue is discussed at length by Geyer (1992) and in the following discussion, where many pros and cons of each method are presented.

estimated marginal posterior densities based on increasing numbers of iterations to detect when the estimate stabilizes. Yet another type of method is the use of non-parametric tests to verify if the process appears to become stationary. For example, one could use a Kolmogorov–Smirnov test for the univariate marginal distributions across two subsamples corresponding to non-overlapping ranges of iterations in the thinned-out chain.

To monitor convergence of ergodic averages for scalar functions $g(\theta)$, given by $S_m = \sum_{i=1}^{m} g(\theta_{(i)})/m$ (recall Chapter 4), one possible approach is to graph the cumulative sums $D_\ell = \sum_{i=1}^{\ell} [g(\theta_{(i)}) - S_m]$, $\ell = 1, \ldots, m$. For fast-mixing chains this summary tends to look like noise centered around zero, in contrast to slowly mixing chains for which this plot appears more regular with long excursions to values far from zero. One possible variation of this graphical summary is to use ergodic averages of conditional means when g is a function of only a subset of the parameters, say $g(\alpha)$ for $\theta = (\alpha, \beta)$. That is, $S_m^c = \sum_{i=1}^{m} E[g(\alpha) \mid \beta_{(i)}]$, where the conditional means are used, which in the case of a Gibbs sampler are often readily available.

There are other methods to verify convergence based on different ideas which appeared in the literature around the same time (beginning of the 1990's), which are often known by the respective author names. These are the methods of Gelman–Rubin, Raftery–Lewis, Geweke, and Heidelberger–Welch. A comparative description of these methods appears in Cowles and Carlin (1996). All are implemented in the R packages CODA (acronym for COnvergence Diagnostic and output Analysis) developed by Best et al (1995) and Plummer et al (2006) and BOA (Bayesian Output Analysis) by Smith (2007). Chapter 9 of this text discusses Bayesian software and includes examples of the use of these packages with MCMC methods.

Problems

Most of the following problems require programming to implement MCMC simulation. See Appendix B for some suggestions on how to implement such simulation in R. Later, in Chapter 9, we will discuss public domain software to implement MCMC for most problems. However, it is useful to implement MCMC and understand implementation details for at least some more stylized problems. It is therefore recommended not to use MCMC software, such as OpenBUGS, JAGS, or Stan in the following problems.

A large number of good case studies can be found in the manuals for BUGS and R-INLA, including some substantially more complex inference problems than the following exercises. See `www.openbugs.net/ Examples/` and also the problem set in Chapter 9.

6.1 *Metropolis–Hastings.* Verify that the transition function (6.4) does indeed satisfy the detailed balance condition (6.1).

6.2 *Data augmentation.* The table below shows the observed frequencies y_j related to the observed phenotype defined by the blood group of an individual, for a sample of $n = 435$ individuals. Here $j \in \{1, 2, 3, 4\}$ indexes the four blood groups O, A, B, AB.

j	Blood group	Frequency y_j	Probability p_j
1	O	176	r^2
2	A	182	$p^2 + 2pr$
3	B	60	$q^2 + 2qr$
4	AB	17	$2pq$

The probabilities p_j are determined by the laws of genetics, with p, q, and r being the probabilities of the genes of type A, B, and O, respectively, with $p + q + r = 1$.

a. Find the likelihood function $f(y \mid \theta)$ under this model for $\theta = (p, q)$ and using $r = 1 - p - q$.

b. The observed phenotype (blood group) depends on the genotype which cannot be directly observed. Following is the relationship between genotype and phenotype:

k	Phenotype	Genotype	Probability p_j
1	O	OO	r^2
2	A	AA	p^2
3	A	AO	$2pr$
4	B	BB	q^2
5	B	BO	$2qr$
6	AB	AB	$2pq$

Let $z_i \in \{1, \dots, 6\}$ denote the unobserved genotype for individual i, $i = 1, \dots, n$, and let $z = (z_1, \dots, z_n)$. Write a complete data likelihood $f(y \mid z, \theta)$.

c. Using the latent variables z from (b) and completing the model with a suitable prior $h(\theta)$, propose a Gibbs sampling scheme to generate $(\theta, z) \sim h(\theta, z \mid y)$.

6.3 *Binomial (unknown θ, n) ∧ beta/Poisson model.* Refer to Problem 3.2. Find the conditional posterior distributions $h(\theta \mid n, x)$ and $h(n \mid \theta, x)$. As before, use $x = 50$, and $(a_0, b_0) = (1, 4)$.

a. Describe and implement a Gibbs sampling algorithm to generate $(n_m, \theta_m) \sim h(n, \theta \mid x)$. Plot the joint posterior $h(n, \theta \mid x)$, and plot on top of the same figure the simulated posterior draws (n_m, θ_m), $m = 1, \dots, 50$ (connected by line segments showing the moves).

Hint: Use the R function `sample(.)` to generate from $h(n \mid \theta, x)$. When evaluating $h(n \mid \theta, x)$, evaluate the function first on the log scale over a grid on n, subtract the maximum (to scale it), and then only exponentiate (to avoid numerical problems). See Appendix B.

   b. In the same problem implement Metropolis–Hastings posterior simulation. Add the simulated posterior draws on top of the plot from (a).

6.4 *Missing data.* Consider a bivariate normal sampling model:

$$(x_i, y_i) \sim N(\mu, \Sigma), i = 1, \ldots, n.$$

Here, $\mu = (\mu_1, \mu_2)$ is the (bivariate) mean and Σ is the (2×2) covariance matrix. We assume an improper prior,

$$h(\mu, \Sigma) \propto |\Sigma|^{-(d+1)/2},$$

where $d = 2$ is the dimension of μ.

   a. *Posterior distribution:* Let $y = \{x_i, y_i, \ i = 1, \ldots, n\}$ denote the observed data. Find the posterior distribution $h(\mu \mid \Sigma, y)$ and $h(\Sigma \mid y)$.

   b. *Missing data posterior:* Assume we observe the following data

i	1	2	3	4	5	6	7	8	9	10	11	12
x	1	1	−1	−1	2	2	−2	−2	−	−	−	−
y	1	−1	1	−1	−	−	−	−	2	2	−2	−2

with missing observations marked as "−".

Let y denote the observed data. Let $z = \{x_9, \ldots, x_{12}, y_5, \ldots, y_8\}$ denote the missing data. Find $p(z \mid \Sigma, \mu, y)$ and $h(\mu, \Sigma \mid y, z)$.

Hint: Write $h(\mu, \Sigma \mid y, z)$ as $h(\Sigma \mid y, z) \cdot h(\mu \mid \Sigma, y, z)$.

   c. *Data augmentation – algorithm.* Using the conditional posterior distributions found in part (b), describe a data augmentation scheme to implement posterior simulation from $h(\mu, \Sigma \mid y)$.

- Set up a Gibbs sampler for $h(\mu, \Sigma, z \mid y)$. Let $\theta^k = (\mu^k, \Sigma^k, z^k)$ denote the simulated Monte Carlo sample, $k = 1, \ldots, K$.
- Simply drop the z^k. The remaining (μ^k, Σ^k) are an MC sample from $h(\mu, \Sigma \mid y)$.

   d. *Data augmentation – simulation.* Implement the data augmentation described in part (c). Plot trajectories of generated μ_j, $j = 1, 2$, against iteration number and estimated marginal posterior distributions $h(\mu_j \mid y)$.

   e. *Convergence diagnostic.* Propose some (ad hoc) convergence diagnostic to decide when to terminate posterior simulation in the program used for part (d).

(The answer need not be perfect – any reasonable, practical, creative suggestions is fine. See Section 9.6 for more discussion of convergence diagnostics.)

6.5 We consider a hierarchical event rate model with a Poisson sampling model $y_i \sim Poi(\lambda_i t_i)$, and a prior model

$$\lambda_i \sim Ga(\alpha, \beta) \text{ and } \beta \sim Ga(c, d),$$

where (α, c, d) are fixed hyperparameters.[16]

a. Find the conditional posterior distributions:

    1. $h(\lambda_i \mid \beta, \lambda_j, j \ne i, y)$.
    2. $h(\beta \mid \lambda_1, \ldots, \lambda_n, y)$.

b. Using the data from Problem 4.4, implement a Gibbs sampler to simulate from the posterior in the above model.

c. Alternatively, marginalize with respect to λ_i to find the marginal likelihood $f(y_i \mid \beta)$ and $h(\beta \mid y)$.

6.6 Assume that x, y are jointly distributed random variables with support $(0, B)$, with conditional p.d.f.

$$f(x \mid y) \propto e^{-xy}, \quad 0 < x < B, \tag{6.12}$$
$$f(y \mid x) \propto e^{-xy}, \quad 0 < y < B. \tag{6.13}$$

a. Propose a Gibbs sampler to generate an MC sample from $f(x, y)$ (this is easy – there are no tricks).

b. Now consider $B = \infty$, that is, the support for x and y is the entire positive real line. Show that there is no (proper) joint distribution $f(x, y)$ with conditionals (6.12) and (6.13).

c. Justify the statement "Under the setup of (b) we can not apply the Gibbs sampler."

6.7 *Probit regression.* Consider a probit regression model for a binary response y_i on covariates x_i, $i = 1, \ldots, n$. Let $\Phi(\cdot)$ denote the standard normal c.d.f.

$$P(y_i = 1 \mid x_i) = \Phi(x_i'\beta), \tag{6.14}$$

where $\beta = (\beta_0, \beta_1, \beta_2)$ and $x_i = (1, x_{i1}, x_{i2})$. We observe the following data.[17] These are historical data – do you recognize them?

---

[16] Compare with Problem 4.4 for a variation of the same problem.
[17] The (identical) data are available as `oring.dta` on the book homepage
    `sites.google.com/view/computationalbayes/home`

x_{i1}	x_{i2}	y_i	x_{i1}	x_{i2}	y_i	x_{i1}	x_{i2}	y_i	x_{i1}	x_{i2}	y_i
66	50	0	70	100	0	53	200	1	75	200	1
70	50	1	57	200	1	67	200	0	75	200	1
69	50	0	63	200	1	75	200	0	76	200	0
68	50	0	70	200	1	70	200	0	58	200	1
67	50	0	78	200	0	81	200	0	31	200	0
72	50	0	67	200	0	76	200	0			
73	100	0	53	200	1	79	200	0			

Let $y = (y_1, \ldots, y_n)$ denote the observed data. Assuming an improper prior $h(\beta) = 1$, find the marginal posterior distributions $h(\beta_j \mid y)$, $j = 0, 1, 2$ and plot the posterior predictive probability $p(y_{n+1} = 1 \mid y, x_{n+1})$ as a function of x_{n+1}.

Start by introducing latent scores z_i to replace (6.14) by

$$y_i = I(z_i > 0) \text{ and } z_i \sim N(x_i'\beta, 1). \tag{6.15}$$

Here, $I(A)$ is the indicator function of event A. Then,

a. Show that (6.15) is equivalent to (6.14).
b. Find the conditional posterior $h(z_i \mid \beta, y)$ and $h(\beta \mid z, y)$.
c. Propose a Gibbs sampling scheme to simulate from the posterior distribution $h(\beta, z \mid y)$.
d. Plot a histogram of simulated β values as an estimate of $h(\beta_j \mid y)$.
e. Show that $E\{h(\beta_j \mid y, z)\} = h(\beta_j \mid y)$. With respect to which distribution is the expectation?
f. Use (e) to produce estimates of $h(\beta_j \mid y)$.
g. Argue why the estimate in (f) is "better" than (d). How do you formalize "better"?
h. Plot $P(y_{n+1} = 1 \mid x_{n+1}, y)$.
    Fix $x_{n+1,2} = 100$ and plot the posterior predictive probability $P(y_{n+1} = 1 \mid x_{n+1}, y)$ for a grid of values for $x_{n+1,1}$, say $30 < x_{n+1,1} < 80$.

6.8 *Probit regression.* Refer to Example 4.2 in Section 4.2. Use Gibbs sampling with data augmentation to implement inference in this application, using latent variables similar to Problem 6.7. Plot $h(a \mid y)$ and $h(b \mid y)$.

6.9 *Mixture model.* Consider the following mixture of normal models for an unknown density $g(x)$:

$$g(x) = \sum_{j=1}^{J} w_j N(\mu_j, \sigma^2), \tag{6.16}$$

with a Dirichlet prior on the weights

$$(w_1, \ldots, w_J) \sim D(\alpha, \alpha, \ldots, \alpha),$$

i.e., $h(w) \propto \Pi_{j=1}^{J} w_j^{\alpha-1}$ and independent normal priors for the normal locations,

$$\mu_j \sim N(0, \tau),$$

$j = 1, \ldots, J$, independently. Here α and τ are fixed hyperparameters. Use, for example, $\alpha = \tau = 1$. Complete the prior with a gamma prior on the precision, $(1/\sigma^2) \sim Ga(a, b)$.

We use the mixture of normal priors for a density estimation problem, i.e., we assume a sampling model

$$x_i \sim g(x_i), \quad i = 1, \ldots, n, \quad \text{i.i.d.}$$

with prior (6.16) for $g(\cdot)$.

a. *Joint posterior.* Let $\mu = (\mu_1, \ldots, \mu_J)$, $w = (w_1, \ldots, w_J)$, and $x = (x_1, \ldots, x_n)$. Find the joint posterior distribution $h(\mu, w, \sigma \mid x)$ (up to a normalizing constant is fine).

b. *Hierarchical model.* Rewrite (6.16) as a hierarchical model using indicators $s_l \in \{1, \ldots, J\}$:

$$f(x_i \mid s_i = j, \mu, w, \sigma^2) = \ldots \text{ and } P(s_i = j \mid \mu, w, \sigma^2) = \ldots \quad (6.17)$$

What are the appropriate probabilities to substitute in ...?

c. *Gibbs sampling.* Using the hierarchical model (6.17), define a Gibbs sampling scheme to simulate from the posterior distribution $h(w, \mu, s, \sigma \mid x)$. State the list of complete conditional posterior distributions that are sampled in each iteration of the Gibbs sampler.

d. *Metropolis–Hastings.* Now consider posterior simulation *without* using the hierarchical model extension, i.e., using the original posterior distribution $h(\mu, w \mid x)$ without the model augmentation with the latent indicators s_i.

Define an MCMC scheme with the following transition probabilities:

- For each j, $j = 1, \ldots, J$, update μ_j by ...
- Update w by ...
- Update σ^2.

e. *Data.* Use the dataset `galaxy` in R. You can get it as the data `galaxies` in the package `MASS`.

Estimate $g(x)$ using a mixture of $J = 5$ normals using the Gibbs part (c). Show:

1. convergence diagnostic to judge practical convergence. You can use an implementation from the R package `coda` or `boa` (see Section 9.6 for more discussion of convergence diagnostics);
2. estimated $g(x)$ on a grid (use, $0, 0.01, 0.02, \ldots, 0.99, 1.0$);

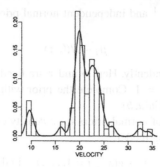

Figure 6.3 Galaxy data. The histogram shows the data points. The curve shows a kernel density estimate.

    3. trajectory plot of $\ln h(w, \mu, s, \sigma \mid x)$ against iteration (up to a constant is okay);

    4. trajectory plot of σ against iteration.

  f. Do the same using the Metropolis–Hastings of (d). Estimate $g(x)$ using a mixture of $J = 5$ normals using the M-H.

6.10 This problem describes a real inference problem that arises in bioinformatics research. The probability model is more complex than other examples, but does not introduce any serious difficulties. [18]

  Likelihood (sampling model). Let x_i, $i = 1, \ldots, n$, denote a set of multinomial random variables, with outcomes $x_i \in \{1, \ldots, N\}$. Let $y = (y_1, \ldots, y_N)$ denote a contingency table summarizing the multinomial experiment, i.e., y_j is the frequency of outcome j. Let $\pi_j = P(x_i = j)$ denote the unknown probability of observing outcome j, $\sum \pi_j = 1.0$. We write

$$y \sim M_{N-1}(n; \pi_1, \ldots, \pi_N).$$

Prior. Due to the nature of the experiment we believe *a priori* that some of the π_j are much larger than others. We refer to this subset of outcomes with much larger probability as the "prevalent" outcomes A_1, and to the set of not so likely outcomes as "rare" outcomes A_0. We will formally define A_0 and A_1 in the following.

Parametrization. To define a prior probability model for $\theta = (\pi_1, \ldots, \pi_N)$ it is convenient to introduce latent indicators z_j, and a change of variables for

---

[18] The problem is a stylized form of the analysis for SAGE data discussed by Morris et al (2003).

the π_j:

$$\pi_j = \begin{cases} \pi^* q_j & \text{if } z_j = 1 \\ (1 - \pi^*) r_j & \text{if } z_j = 0, \end{cases} \tag{6.18}$$

with $\sum q_j = 1$ and $\sum r_j = 1$ (let $q_j = 0$ if $z_j = 0$, and $r_j = 0$ if $z_j = 1$). In words, the latent variable z_j is an indicator for outcome j being a prevalent outcome, i.e., $A_1 = \{j : z_j = 1\}$ and $A_0 = \{j : z_j = 0\}$. The probability of observing some prevalent outcome is π^*, with π^* close to 1.0; q_j is the probability of outcome j given that we observe a prevalent outcome, and r_j is the probability of j given a rare outcome. For later reference we define

$$M_1 = \#A_1 \text{ and } M_0 = N - M_1$$

as the number of prevalent and rare outcomes, respectively.

Prior probability model $h(z, \pi^*, q, r)$. We assume

$$P(z_j = 1) = \rho, \tag{6.19}$$

a beta prior on the total probability of prevalent outcomes:

$$\pi^* \sim Be(a^*, b^*), \tag{6.20}$$

and a Dirichlet prior for the partitioning of π^* into the cell probabilities π_j, $j \in A_1$. Let $\tilde{q}_h$, $h = 1, \ldots, M_1$ denote the non zero weights q_j:

$$(\tilde{q}_1, \ldots, \tilde{q}_{M_1}) \sim D_{M_1-1}(a_1, \ldots, a_1). \tag{6.21}$$

The use of equal Dirichlet parameters a_1 reflects the symmetric nature of prior beliefs about $(q_1, \ldots, q_{M_1})$. Similarly for r_j, $j \in A_0$:

$$(\tilde{r}_1, \ldots, \tilde{r}_{M_0}) \sim D_{M_0-1}(a_0, \ldots, a_0). \tag{6.22}$$

Hyperparameters. The hyperparameters ρ, a^*, b^*, a_1, a_0 are fixed. Use, for example,

$$\rho = 0.1, a^* = 9, b^* = 1, a_1 = 0.1, \text{ and } a_0 = 10.$$

Data. posted on the book homepage[19] as `sage.dta`. The file gives the observed values $x_i \in \{0, N\}$, $i = 1, \ldots, n$, with $n = 700$ and $N = 77$.

a. *Joint probability model.* Write out the joint probability model

$$p(\pi^\star, q_1, r_1, \ldots, q_N, r_N, z_1, \ldots, z_N, y_1, \ldots, y_N).$$

[19] `sites.google.com/view/computationalbayes/home`

b. *Graphical model* (optional).[20] Show a graphical model representation of the probability model. Use circles for each random variable, and connect any two r.v.'s that are *not* conditionally independent given all other variables.

c. *Conditional posterior distributions.* Find the complete conditional posterior distributions $h(z_j \mid \ldots)$, $h(\pi^* \mid \ldots)$, $h(q \mid \ldots)$, and $h(r \mid \ldots)$. Here … denotes "all other parameters and the data y."

d. *Marginalizing with respect to q and r.* Find the posterior distribution $p(z \mid \pi^*, y)$, marginalizing with respect to q and r.

e. *MCMC I.* Consider a Gibbs sampling scheme based on sampling from the complete conditional posterior distributions found in (c), i.e., an MCMC scheme with steps: $z_i \sim p(z_i \mid \ldots)$; $\pi^* \sim h(\pi^* \mid \ldots)$; $q \sim h(q \mid \ldots)$; $r \sim h(r \mid \ldots)$.
Show that MCMC I violates irreducibility (of course, do not implement MCMC I – it would not work).

f. *MCMC II.* Implement a Gibbs sampling scheme based on sampling from the conditional posterior distributions found in part (d): $z_i \sim p(z_i \mid z_{-i}, \pi^*, y)$, $i = 1, \ldots, n$; $q \sim h(q \mid \ldots)$; $r \sim h(r \mid \ldots)$; and $\pi^* \sim h(\pi^* \mid \ldots)$. Show trajectories of simulated values $\pi^{*(t)}$ against iteration t; a boxplot of the (marginal) posterior distributions $h(\pi_j \mid y)$ (use one figure with multiple boxplots, e.g., using the R command `boxplot(.)`); a plot of the posterior means $E(\pi_j \mid y)$ against the maximum likelihood estimates $\hat{\pi}_j = y_j/n$. In the latter include the 45-degree line and discuss the shrinkage pattern that you (should) see.

g. *MCMC III.* Consider the following MCMC scheme. We describe the MCMC by constructive definition of the transition function, i.e., $h(\theta^{t+1} \mid \theta^t)$:

1. Metropolis–Hastings step to change z_i, q, r, $i = 1, \ldots, N$: Generate a proposal (z_i', q', r') using $p(z_i' = 1) = 0.5$, $q' \sim h(q \mid z', \ldots, y)$ and $r' \sim h(r \mid z', \ldots, y)$, where z' is the currently imputed z, with z_i replaced by z_i', i.e., $z' = (z_1, \ldots, z_{i-1}, z_i', z_{i+1}, \ldots, z_N)$.
   Compute an appropriate acceptance probability α, and set $(z_i, q, r) \equiv (z_i', q', r')$ with probability α and keep (z_i, q, r) unchanged otherwise.
2. $\pi^* \sim h(\pi^* \mid \ldots)$

Find the correct expression for the acceptance probability α (in step 1) (no need to implement MCMC III).

6.11 *Normal linear regression* (see also Problem 3.6). Consider a normal linear regression model $y_i = x_i'\beta + \epsilon_i$, $i = 1, \ldots, n$, with $\epsilon_i \sim N(0, \sigma^2)$, independently. Here, $y_i \in \mathbb{R}$ is the response and $x_i = (x_{i1}, \ldots, x_{ip}) \in \mathbb{R}^p$ is a covariate vector. Letting X denote the $(n \times p)$ design matrix with x_i in the ith row and

---

[20] This was not discussed in the text.

$\epsilon = (\epsilon_1, \ldots, \epsilon_n)$, we can alternatively write the model as

$$y = X\beta + \epsilon. \qquad (6.23)$$

We complete the model with a prior. Let $\tau^2 = 1/\sigma^2$ denote the residual precision:

$$h(\tau^2) = \text{Ga}(v_0/2, v_0\sigma_0^2/2) \text{ and } h(\beta) = N(\beta_0, \Sigma_0), \qquad (6.24)$$

independently. That is, we assume an informative prior for β (for example, this could be based on historical data from a related earlier study). Here, $X \sim \text{Ga}(a, b)$ denotes a gamma distribution with mean $E(X) = a/b$.

a. State the joint posterior $h(\beta, \tau^2 \mid y)$ (up to a normalizing constant is okay). No need to simplify.

b. Find the conditional distribution $h(\beta \mid \tau^2, y)$. Use notation $\widehat{\beta}$ for the least squares solution. Recognize the distribution as a well-known parametric family.

c. Find $h(\tau^2 \mid \beta, y)$. You can use notation $\text{RSS}(\beta) = (y - X\beta)'(y - X\beta)$. Recognize the distribution as a well-known parametric family.

d. Propose a Gibbs sampling posterior MCMC scheme based on the conditionals from (b) to generate a Monte Carlo sample,

$$(\beta^{(m)}, \tau^{2(m)}) \sim h(\beta, \tau^2 \mid y), m = 1, \ldots, M.$$

6.12 *Hamiltonian Monte Carlo.* Refer to Example 6.3 in Section 6.5.1.

a. *Posterior.* Plot the posterior distribution $h(\alpha, \beta \mid y)$. Use a contour plot (or heatplot, or any other format that allows you to add the points for the simulations from part (b)).

b. *Hamiltonian Monte Carlo.* Let $\theta = (\alpha, \beta)$. Propose a Hamiltonian Monte Carlo algorithm to simulate a Monte Carlo sample:

$$\theta_m \sim h(\theta \mid y),$$

$m = 1, \ldots, M$ (the θ_m need not be independent, as in any MCMC). Use $M = 100$.

1. Describe the algorithm by stating all transition probabilities.
2. Implement the algorithm.
3. Plot θ_m by adding them to the plot from part (a).

c. *Metropolis–Hastings.* Implement a Metropolis–Hastings MCMC to generate $\theta_m \sim h(\theta \mid y)$, $m = 1, \ldots, M$.

1. Describe the algorithm by stating all transition probabilities.
2. Plot θ_m by adding them to the plot from part (a).

6.13 *Approximate Bayesian computation (ABC).* Consider a posterior $h(\theta \mid y) \propto h(\theta) \cdot f(y \mid \theta)$ in a statistical inference problem with data y and unknown parameters θ. We set up the following MCMC simulation. Let $q(\tilde{\theta} \mid \theta)$ denote a proposal distribution, for example $q(\tilde{\theta} \mid \theta) = N(\theta, cI)$, a multivariate normal centered at θ.

Start with θ_0. For $i = 1, \ldots, M$, simulate the following transition function.

1. $\tilde{\theta} \sim q(\tilde{\theta} \mid \theta_i)$;
2. $\tilde{z} \sim f(\tilde{z} \mid \tilde{\theta})$, using the sampling distribution under $\tilde{\theta}$.
3. Let

$$\theta_{i+1} = \begin{cases} \tilde{\theta} & \text{w. pr. } a = \min\{1, A(\theta_i, \tilde{\theta})\} \\ \theta_i & \text{w. pr. } 1 - a, \end{cases} \tag{6.25}$$

with

$$A(\theta_i, \tilde{\theta}) = \frac{h(\tilde{\theta})}{h(\theta_i)} \frac{I\{d(\tilde{z}, y) < \epsilon\}}{1} \frac{q(\theta_i \mid \tilde{\theta})}{q(\tilde{\theta} \mid \theta_i)},$$

where $d(z, y)$ is some distance measure for two (hypothetical or actually observed) data sets z and y, for example, $d(z, y) = \|z - y\|^2$.
Find the stationary distribution $\pi(\theta)$ for this Markov chain.

Hint: Introduce a variable z_i, initializing with $z_0 \sim f(z_0 \mid \theta_0)$, and then modify (6.25) to a proposal distribution for an augmented state vector (θ_i, z_i), find the stationary distribution $\pi(\theta, z)$ for the Markov chain with this augmented state vector. Finally, argue that the desired $\pi(\theta)$ is the marginal under $\pi(\theta, z)$.[21]

6.14 Thall et al (2003) consider inference for a phase I oncology trial for the combination of two cytotoxic agents. Here, we focus on estimating the dose–response surface $\pi(x; \theta) = P(y = 1 \mid x = (x_1, x_2), \theta)$ for the probability of toxicity ($y = 1$) as a function of the doses of the two agents (x_1 and x_2). We assume standardized doses, $0 \leq x_j \leq 1$, and let $y_i \in \{0, 1\}$ denote an indicator of the i-th patient recording toxicity after being treated with combination therapy with doses x_{i1} and x_{i2} of the two agents. The response surface is indexed by unknown parameters $\theta = (a_1, b_1, a_2, b_2, a_3, b_3)$,

$$\pi(x, \theta) = \frac{a_1 x_1^{b_1} + a_2 x_2^{b_2} + a_3 \left(x_1^{b_1} x_2^{b_2}\right)^{b_3}}{1 + a_1 x_1^{b_1} + a_2 x_2^{b_2} + a_3 \left(x_1^{b_1} x_2^{b_2}\right)^{b_3}}. \tag{6.26}$$

The model is chosen to allow easy incorporation of information about single-agent toxicities. For $x_2 = 0$ the model reduces to the single-agent dose–toxicity curve $\pi((x_1, 0), \theta) \equiv \pi_1(x_1, \theta)$ and similarly for π_2. The parameters (a_3, b_3) characterize the two-agent interactions.

---

[21] This is one of the variations of ABC. See Marin et al (2012) for a review.

We complete the model with independent gamma priors:

$$a_j \sim Ga(\alpha_{1j}, \alpha_{2j}) \text{ and } b_j \sim Ga(\beta_{1j}, \beta_{2j}),$$

$j = 1, 2$ as an informative prior with hyperparameters $(\alpha_{1j}, \alpha_{2j}, \beta_{1j}, \beta_{2j})$, $j = 1, 2$ are chosen to match the known single-agent toxicity curves as closely as possible with prior means $E(a_1, b_1, a_2, b_2) = (0.4286, 7.6494, 0.4286, 7.8019)$ and marginal variances $(0.1054, 5.7145, 0.0791, 3.9933)$. These moments were carefully elicited by Thall et al (2003). For the interaction parameters, we use a log-normal prior $\ln a_3 \sim N(\mu_{a3}, \sigma_{a3}^2)$ and $\ln b_3 \sim N(\mu_{b3}, \sigma62_{b3})$. As default choices we propose to use $\mu_{a3} = \mu_{b3} = 0.25$ and $\sigma_{a_3}^2 = \sigma_{b_3}^2 = 3$.

Let $Y_n = (x_i, y_i; \ i = 1, \ldots, n)$ denote observed indicators for toxicity y_i for n patients treated at dose combinations $x_i = (x_{i1}, x_{i2}), i = 1, \ldots, n$.

a. Find hyperprior parameters to match the described prior information.
b. Propose a Hamiltonian Monte Carlo scheme for posterior simulation. Find $\partial \ln h(\theta \mid Y_n)/\partial\theta_j$ and describe the transition probabilities.
   Hint: In the derivation of the gradient it is useful to use notation like $\pi_i \equiv \pi(x_i, \theta)$, $\bar{\pi}_i = (1 - \pi_i)$., and $\bar{y}_i = 1 - y_i$. Use $x_{i3} = (x_{i1}^{b_1} x_{i2}^{b_2})$ (keeping in mind that the definition of x_{i3} involves b_1 and b_2).
c. Using the data set CTX.dta from the book's homepage[22] implement posterior simulation. Plot the estimated mean toxicity surface $\bar{\pi}(x) = E\{\pi(x; \theta)\}$ over a grid for $(x_1, x_2) \in [0, 1]^2$ (the expectation is with respect to $h(\theta \mid x)$).

6.15 *Getting it all right diagnostic* (Geweke, 2004). Let $f(y \mid \theta)$ and $h(\theta)$ denote sampling model for data y and a prior for parameters θ in a Bayesian inference problem. Let $h(\theta \mid y) \propto h(\theta)f(y \mid \theta)$ denote the posterior distribution and let $p_{\theta,y}(\theta, y)$ denote the joint probability model on (θ, y).
Almost all MCMC posterior simulation schemes can be described as generating a sequence θ_m using some transition kernel $q(\theta_m \mid \theta_{m-1}, y)$. That is, $P(\theta_m \in A \mid \theta_{m-1}) = \int_A q(\theta_m \mid \theta_{m-1}, y)d\theta_m$ (for fixed y – we only indicate y in the kernel in anticipation of the next construction). The transition kernel $q(\cdot)$ is constructed such that it has unique invariant distribution $\pi(\theta) \equiv h(\theta \mid y)$. Consider the following Markov chain in $x = (\theta, y)$. Initialize with $\theta_0 \sim h(\theta)$ and $y_0 \sim f(y \mid \theta_0)$. Set $m = 0$, and iterate over the following steps, $m = 1, \ldots, M$:

1. Generate $\theta_m \sim q(\theta_m \mid \theta_{m-1}, y_{m-1})$.
2. Generate $y_m \sim f(y_m \mid \theta_m)$.

a. Find the invariant distribution for this Markov chain.
b. Let $P^{(n)}(x_0, A) = P(x_n \in A \mid x_0)$ denote the n-step transition probability

---

[22] sites.google.com/view/computationalbayes/home

under this chain. Show that $P^{(n)} \to p_{\theta,y}$ in total variation norm. That is,

$$\lim_{n\to\infty} \|P^{(n)}(x_0, \cdot) - p_{\theta,y}\| = 0$$

in total variation norm, for *all* x_0. You may assume that $q(\theta_m \mid \theta_{m-1}, y_{m-1}) > 0$ for all $\theta_m \in \Theta$ in the parameter space Θ (and all θ_{m-1}, y_{m-1}); and similarly $f(y \mid \theta) > 0$ for all $y \in X$ in the sample space X and $\theta \in \Theta$. Use at most three sentences.

c. Can you suggest an alternative way of generating an MC sample $x_n \sim p_{\theta,y}(\theta, y)$? [23]

Hint: There is a very easy answer.

---

[23] Geweke (2004) uses ergodic Monte Carlo averages under (a) and under (b) to construct an interesting diagnostic.

7

Model Selection and Trans-dimensional MCMC

Earlier (Sections 4.2.2. and 4.2.3) we discussed how the evaluation of the marginal likelihood function (or prior predictive distribution) for model selection can be implemented by means of importance sampling. Since the 1990s, various methods have been proposed in the literature to implement such schemes.[1] This works for problems with moderate dimensional parameter vectors, but breaks down in higher dimensional problems. More complex problems usually require the use of Markov chain Monte Carlo (MCMC) methods to generate posterior Monte Carlo samples (or, to be more precise, approximate posterior samples), as discussed in previous chapters. Using such posterior Monte Carlo samples, one can then approximately evaluate the marginal likelihood function. It is convenient to distinguish two cases. The first case is when the simulated values are generated from the parameter space for each model separately. The other case is when the simulated values are generated from the model space, that is, model indicators (separately or jointly with the parameter space). A popular algorithm to implement the latter is reversible jump MCMC (RJ).

In the following discussion, M_j (or for short, j, when the context clarifies the use) will denote competing models, and θ_j will denote parameters that index the sampling distribution under model M_j, and we will use notation $f(y \mid \theta_j, M_j)$ or for short $f_j(y \mid \theta_j)$ for the sampling model under model M_j, $h(\theta_j \mid M_j)$, or $h_j(\theta_j)$ for the prior under model M_j, $p(x \mid M_j)$, or $p_j(x)$ for the marginal under model M_j, and $h(M_j)$ or just $h(j)$ for the prior model probability.

7.1 MC Simulation over the Parameter Space

Besides the basic Monte Carlo methods that we already discussed in Sections 4.2.2. and 4.2.3, methods that correspond to the first of the above cases include those by Chib (1995) and Chib and Jeliazkov (2001). The

---

[1] See Chen et al (2000) and Andrieu et al (2004) for useful reviews of these methods.

latter methods approximate the posterior distribution of the parameters in each model, $h(\theta_j \mid y, M_j)$, by Gibbs and Metropolis–Hastings samplers, respectively. Importantly, the evaluation includes normalization constants which then allow the evaluation of the marginal distribution $f(y \mid M_j)$ via Bayes' theorem (written as candidate's formula, as explained in the following).

We describe the approach for the evaluation of the marginal likelihood function $f(x)$ for one model, dropping for the moment the explicit conditioning on the model indicator M_j. The method of Chib (1995) uses the factorization of the joint posterior distribution of a parameter vector θ into factors corresponding to $b \geq 2$ subvectors $\theta_{(i)}$, $i = 1, \dots, b$, assuming that the complete conditional posterior distributions for all subvectors are available in closed form. The Gibbs sampler is carried out $b-1$ times to estimate the first $b - 1$ factors of

$$h(\theta_{(1)}, \theta_{(2)}, \dots, \theta_{(b)} \mid y) = h(\theta_{(1)} \mid y)\, h(\theta_{(2)} \mid \theta_{(1)}, y) \times \dots$$
$$\times h(\theta_{(b)} \mid \theta_{(b-1)}, \dots, \theta_{(1)}, y) \equiv \Pi_{i=1}^{b} h(\theta_{(i)} \mid \theta_{(1)}, \dots, \theta_{(i-1)}, y). \quad (7.1)$$

Details of this approach are explained in Chib (1995), including variations for the case when complete conditionals are not available for all blocks. We only briefly summarize the approach. Let $\theta_{-(1)}$ denote the θ vector with the subvector $\theta_{(1)}$ removed. First, note that $h(\theta_{(1)}^* \mid y) = \int h(\theta_{(1)}^* \mid \theta_{-(1)}, y) h(\theta_{-(1)} \mid y) d\theta_{-(1)}$ allows an approximate evaluation of $h(\theta_{(1)}^* \mid y)$ as a Monte Carlo average of $h(\theta_{(1)}^* \mid \theta_{-(1)}, y)$ over a posterior Monte Carlo sample $\{\theta_{(1)}, \theta_{-(1)}\}$ (discarding the $\theta_{(1)}$ values in the Monte Carlo sample without using them). Assume that the posterior Monte Carlo sample is generated by MCMC simulation. Assuming $b > 2$, to evaluate reduced conditional ordinates like $h(\theta_{(2)}^* \mid \theta_{(1)}^*, y)$ continue running the same MCMC, but now keeping $\theta_{(1)}$ fixed at $\theta_{(1)}^*$. In a Gibbs sampler implementation this is easily done by skipping one transition probability, without any additional programming. Using the resulting posterior sample $\{\theta_{(1)}^*, \theta_{(2)}, \theta_{-(1,2)}\}$, we then approximate $h(\theta_{(2)}^* \mid \theta_{(1)}^*, y)$ as the Monte Carlo average over the posterior sample of $h(\theta_{(2)}^* \mid \theta_{(1)}^*, \theta_{-(1,2)}, y)$. A similar scheme allows the evaluation of all reduced conditional ordinates in (7.1).

Once the posterior density for θ is evaluated at a given point, say, θ^*, (e.g., some value with high posterior plausibility), the marginal distribution can be estimated via an inversion of Bayes' theorem (also known as candidate's formula). Using, for computational reasons, log transformed densities, we have

$$\ln \hat{p}(y) = \ln f(y \mid \theta^*) + \ln h(\theta^*) - \ln \hat{h}(\theta^* \mid y),$$

where $\hat{h}(\theta^* \mid y) = \Pi_{i=1}^{b-1} \hat{h}(\theta_{(i)}^* \mid \theta_{(1)}^*, \ldots, \theta_{(i-1)}^*, y) \times h(\theta_{(b)}^* \mid \theta_{(i)}^*, i \neq b, y)$.

The evaluation of $\hat{h}(\theta^* \mid y)$ by this method requires closed-form expressions for all complete conditional distributions. In general this might not be available. Chib and Jeliazkov (2001) propose an alternative approach for such cases, using instead a Metropolis–Hastings proposal distribution $q(\tilde{\theta} \mid \theta)$ with closed form expression.

7.2 MC Simulation over the Model Space

Methods corresponding to the second case mentioned at the beginning of this chapter include, in particular, many popular methods for variable selection. Consider variable selection in a normal linear regression with response variable Y and p explanatory variables x_j. There are 2^p models. To make variable selection feasible we proceed with a preliminary selection of a smaller class of appropriate models in a first step. In a second step we then select the members in this class that best fulfill the criteria of the particular inference problem or we proceed using all models by means of a weighting scheme for the particular inference of interest. Naturally there are various criteria and methods that can be used for such constructions.

The SSVS Method

Consider variable selection in a normal linear regression model with a linear predictor $\eta = \sum_{j=1}^{p} \beta_j x_j$. George and McCulloch (1993) propose a method known as SSVS (stochastic search variable selection), based on a hierarchical prior structure with the first level defining for each regression coefficient a mixture of two zero mean normals. The variances are fixed (on the basis of some preliminary fit) such that one of the two terms in the mixture is tightly concentrated around 0 and the other term is diffuse. More specifically, introducing a binary parameter v_j corresponding to each β_j

$$\beta_j \mid v_j \sim \begin{cases} h_1(\beta_j) \equiv N(0, b_j^2) & \text{if } v_j = 0 \\ h_2(\beta_j) \equiv N(0, a_j^2 b_j^2) & \text{if } v_j = 1, \end{cases} \tag{7.2}$$

where b_j and a_j are fixed values of small and large magnitude, respectively. Assuming conditional independence the implied prior distribution for $\beta = (\beta_j, j = 1, \ldots, p)$ in the first level of the hierarchical model is a multivariate normal $\beta \mid v \sim N_p(0, B_v)$, with $B_v = \text{diag}\left[(1 - v_j)b_j^2 + v_j a_j^2 b_j^2\right]$ being a diagonal matrix.[2]

At the second level of the hierarchy, the SSVS model assumes an inverse

---

[2] George and McCulloch (1993, 1997) consider more general multivariate normal prior distributions, including correlations in B_v and dependence on a sampling variance σ^2.

gamma prior distribution for σ^2 with fixed hyperparameters. More importantly, for the indicators v_j the model assumes $v_j \sim \text{Ber}(w_j)$, implying the mixture prior

$$h(\beta_j \mid w_j) = (1 - w_j)h_1(\beta_j) + w_j h_2(\beta_j),$$

where $w_j = P(v_j = 1)$ is the prior probability for a non-zero estimate for β_j, i.e., for including x_j in the model. This way, each of the 2^p models is identified by a vector of latent indicators $v = (v_1, \ldots, v_p)$. The prior model probabilities are written as the product of p Bernoulli probabilities, $\text{Ber}(w_j)$, with $\{w_j\}$ representing the prior beliefs about including each covariate.

Once the hierarchical model is completely specified, SSVS proceeds by using a Gibbs sampler [3] to generate a sequence $(\beta^{(t)}, \sigma^{(t)}, v^{(t)})$, $t = 1, \ldots, T$, that approximates the joint posterior distribution, with mainly the subsequence $v^{(t)}$, $t = 1, \ldots, T$, being of interest. Inspection of this sequence allows in particular the identification of a subset of covariates with the highest inclusion probabilities, which indicate the most promising models in the light of the data and the assumed prior. Note that any specific value of v might not occur with high frequency in the sample, simply due to the limited size of the sample (T can be much less than 2^p when p is large). In summary, the nature of SSVS is mainly an exploratory tool to restrict the class of models for further consideration. Only when a small number of covariates makes it practicable (say, $p < 7$), can a similar process be used to assess the posterior distribution for v, rather than just restricting the set of models under consideration.

Several approaches that are in some way related have appeared in the literature. For example, Kuo and Mallick (1998) use a linear predictor of the form $\eta = \sum_{j=1}^{p} v_j \beta_j x_j$, making the variable selection explicit, and a prior distribution for β that is independent of v. Dellaportas et al (2002) keep a dependent prior for β and v, but use the latter type of linear predictor.

The earlier-described hierarchical prior in the SSVS is not conjugate for normal linear models (given any subset of included covariates). A conjugate prior is achieved by scaling B_v with σ^2 Hoff(2009: ch. 9). With this change in the prior $p(\beta \mid v, \sigma^2)$, it becomes possible to evaluate the kernel of the marginal posterior distribution for v, $h^*(v \mid y) = c^{-1}h(v \mid y)$ (George and McCulloch, 1997), from which one can then directly generate a Markov chain in v, without involving (β, σ^2). For example, one could

---

[3]   See George and McCulloch (1993, 1997) for recommendations about the choice of the tuning parameters, the complete conditional posterior distributions, and extension to other families such as generalized linear models.

implement a Gibbs sampler using the complete conditional distributions $h(v_j \mid v_{-j}, y)$.

Relying on a predefined subset of models, for example the subset M_G of models that occur in a preliminary sample $v_{(k)}$, $k = 1, \ldots, K$, one can then obtain an estimate of the posterior probability for each model via h^* using

$$\hat{h}(v \mid y) = \hat{c} \, h^*(v \mid y) \equiv \frac{\hat{h}(M_G \mid y)}{h^*(M_G \mid y)} \, h^*(v \mid y), \qquad (7.3)$$

where

$$h^*(M_G \mid y) = \sum_{v \in M_G} h^*(v \mid y), \quad \hat{h}(M_G \mid y) = \frac{1}{K} \sum_{k=1}^{K} I_{M_G}(v_{(k)}).$$

In (7.3) the histogram estimate $\widehat{h}(M_g \mid y)$ is used to estimate c by matching it with the unnormalized $h^*(M_G \mid y)$. By explicitly using information from the particular model specification, such estimates are naturally more precise than an estimate using the relative frequency of models in a Gibbs sampler Monte Carlo sample, obtained from the original form of the SSVS. The difference between these two evaluations can be more noticeable in problems with large p.

MC^3 *Method*

Generating a Markov chain with a stationary distribution given by the kernel $h^*(v \mid y)$ can be done by an M-H algorithm with some proposal distribution[4] $q(\tilde{v} \mid v^{(t)})$ for any $v^{(t)}$. Using the special case of a Metropolis algorithm with symmetric proposal q, the acceptance ratio for a proposal $\tilde{v}$ generated from q simplifies to $R(v^{(t)}, \tilde{v}) = h^*(\tilde{v} \mid y)/h^*(v^{(t)} \mid y)$. A simple example of this class of Metropolis algorithms uses a proposal distribution that is only non-zero for $\tilde{v}$ that differs from $v^{(t)}$ in only one component, $q(\tilde{v} \mid v^{(t)}) = 1/p$, where p is the dimension of the least parsimonious model corresponding to $v = 1_p$ with all 1s. This algorithm was proposed for models with discrete data by Madigan and York (1995) under the name MC^3, (Markov chain Monte Carlo model composition). Raftery et al (1997) used MC^3 Bayesian model averaging in multiple regression with a conjugate (normal-gamma) prior on (β, σ^2).

---

[4] Under suitable conditions, this algorithm can be implemented very computation efficiently, similar to what happens in a Gibbs sampler (George and McCulloch, 1997).

Bayesian Lasso, Horseshoe, and Dirichlet–Laplace Model

The SSVS model (7.2) can be characterized as a scale mixture of normals $h(\beta_j) = \int N(0, b_j^2 \gamma_j) dG(\gamma_j)$ with respect to a discrete mixing measure $G(\gamma_j) = w_j \delta_1 + (1 - w_j) \delta_{a_j^2}$. Here, δ_x denotes a point mass at x. The mixture can be alternatively written as a hierarchical model:

$$h(\beta_j \mid \gamma_j) = N(0, b_j^2 \gamma_j) \text{ and } \gamma_j \sim G(\gamma_j).$$

Several other approaches, including the Bayesian lasso (Park and Casella, 2008), the horseshoe (Carvalho et al, 2010) and the Dirichlet–Laplace model (Bhattacharya et al, 2015) use similar scale mixture of normal constructions. The Bayesian lasso uses

$$h(\beta_j \mid \sigma^2, \gamma_j) = N(0, \sigma^2 \gamma_j) \text{ and } \gamma_j \sim \text{Exp}(\lambda^2/2).$$

Marginalizing with respect to γ_j the implied prior $h(\beta_j \mid \sigma^2) = \frac{\lambda}{2\sigma} e^{-\lambda|\beta_j|/\sigma}$ is the double exponential distribution. The log double exponential prior density introduces the L_1 penalty that is characteristic for the popular lasso method (Tibshirani, 1996). Thus, the Bayesian lasso gives an interpretation of the lasso as the maximum *a posteriori* estimate in a corresponding Bayes model. The horseshoe prior uses

$$h(\beta_j \mid \gamma_j) = N(0, \gamma_j^2) \text{ and } \gamma_j \mid \tau \sim C^+(0, \tau),$$

completed with $\tau \mid \sigma \sim C^+(0, \sigma)$, where $C^+(0, s)$ denotes a Cauchy distribution with scale s and truncated to the positive half-line. The name "horseshoe" derives from the implied prior on the shrinkage coefficient in writing $E(\beta_j \mid y)$ as shrinking the maximum likelihood estimator to zero. In a stylized setup the prior on that shrinkage coefficient is a $\text{Be}(1/2, 1/2)$ distribution which takes the shape of a horseshoe. Finally, the Dirichlet–Laplace prior has

$$h(\beta_j \mid \gamma_j, \psi_j, \tau) = N(0, \psi_j \gamma_j^2 \tau^2), \quad \psi_j \sim \text{Exp}\left(\frac{1}{2}\right), \quad (\gamma_1, \ldots, \gamma_p) \sim \text{D}(a)$$

with $a = (a, \ldots, a)$ and $\tau \sim \text{Ga}(pa, \frac{1}{2})$. Here, $\text{D}(a)$ denotes a symmetric Dirichlet distribution with all parameters equal to a. The *a priori* independent scaling coefficients ψ_j imply marginally double exponential distributions, like in the Bayesian lasso. The main feature of the Dirichlet–Laplace prior are the scaling coefficients γ_j with the dependent Dirichlet prior. The Dirichlet–Laplace prior is most suitable for a massive sparse signal, that is, a context with $p \to \infty$, but only a few non-zero β_j. Using $a = p^{-(1+\beta)}$ the Dirichlet prior introduces a similar mechanism as the horseshoe prior.

This is because the Dirichlet distribution with total mass $pa < 1$ piles up probability mass in the corners of the simplex, leading to effective variable selection.

MC Simulation over the Model Space: Beyond Variable Selection

When the class of models M_υ (or υ, for short) under consideration is such that it is possible to evaluate $p(y \mid \upsilon)$ (typically obtained by eliminating parameters via appropriate integration), then it is possible to work in the context of the model space only, requiring only a prior distribution $h(\upsilon)$. This is the case, for example, under SSVS and MC^3 for variable selection under a conjugate hierarchical prior.

Using MCMC allows, then, to generate a Markov chain $\upsilon^{(t)}, t = 1, 2, \ldots$ which converges to the posterior distribution $h(\upsilon \mid y) \equiv P(M_\upsilon \mid y)$, the posterior probability for model M_υ. One could, for example, adopt an M-H algorithm that generates in iteration $t+1$ a proposal $\tilde\upsilon$ from $q(\cdot \mid \upsilon^{(t)})$, which is accepted with probability

$$\alpha(\upsilon^{(t)}, \tilde\upsilon) = \min\left\{1, \frac{p(y \mid \tilde\upsilon)\, h(\tilde\upsilon)}{p(y \mid \upsilon^{(t)})\, h(\upsilon^{(t)})} \times \frac{q(\upsilon^{(t)} \mid \tilde\upsilon)}{q(\tilde\upsilon \mid \upsilon^{(t)})}\right\}.$$

In the case of rejection, we keep $\upsilon^{(t+1)} = \upsilon^{(t)}$. A simple estimate of the posterior probability of each model is then given by the inclusion probability in the Monte Carlo sample that is generated by this chain. On the basis of these posterior probabilities, one can estimate Bayes factors as a ratio of the posterior odds versus the prior odds between any pair of models.

The efficiency of the algorithm depends not only on the appropriate proposal distribution, but also on a fast evaluation of the marginal likelihood. Note that in the case of analytically available exact marginal likelihood, one can obtain alternative posterior estimates in the subclass $\mathcal{B}_s$ of models that appear in the Monte Carlo sample by way of the standardization

$$\hat h(\upsilon \mid y) = \frac{p(y \mid \upsilon)\, h(\upsilon)}{\sum_{\upsilon \in \mathcal{B}_s} p(y \mid \upsilon)\, h(\upsilon)},$$

with the corresponding advantages of its use in Bayesian model averaging.

7.3 MC Simulation over Model and Parameter Space

Consider now the general model selection problem, beyond the specific example of variable selection. Let $\mathcal{M} = \{M_j, j \in J\}$ denote the set of models under consideration. For each M_j let $\theta_j \in \Theta_j$ denote a parameter vector of dimension p_j. The joint model and parameter space is then defined as $\mathcal{N} = \bigcup_{j \in J} \left[\{M_j\} \times \Theta_j \right]$ and the aim is to develop a simulation method for the target distribution being the posterior distribution of the pairs (model, parameters):

$$h(M_j, \theta_j \mid y) \propto f(y \mid M_j, \theta_j) \, h(\theta_j \mid M_j) \, h(M_j) \equiv h^*(M_j, \theta_j \mid y), \quad (7.4)$$

where $\sum_{k \in J} \int f(y \mid M_k, \theta_k) \, h(\theta_k \mid M_k) \, h(M_k) d\theta_k$ is the reciprocal of the normalization constant, and h^* is an un-normalized version of the posterior distribution. The aim is then to simulate from (7.4) using computer simulation.

The Pseudo-Prior Method of Carlin–Chib

Carlin and Chib (1995) achieve the desired simulation by setting up a Gibbs sampler over a larger space, namely the product space $\mathcal{M} \times \Pi_{k \in J} \Theta_k$. That is, they set up a super parameter vector $\omega = (M, \theta_1, \ldots, \theta_J)$ that includes in addition to the parameters for the chosen model $M = M_j$ also parameters for all other models $k \neq j$. The vectors θ_k, $k \neq j$ remain hypothetical in the sense that they are not used in the evaluation of the likelihood. However, the prior probability model is defined over the entire super parameter vector, including what Carlin and Chib refer to as "pseudo-priors" for the parameters θ_k, $k \neq j$. See the following for details. The output is a Markov chain of states $(M, \theta_1, \ldots, \theta_J)$, from which we keep for each j the subsample $(M = M_j, \theta_j)$.

In this description we assumed that all models in $\mathcal{M}$ use different parameter vectors, which are assumed *a priori* independent, given the model, and are concatenated to a composite parameter vector $\theta = (\theta_1, \ldots, \theta_J)$, such that for each model $f(y \mid M_j, \theta) = f(y \mid M_j, \theta_j)$ and $h(\theta \mid M_j) = h(\theta_j \mid M_j) \times \Pi_{k \neq j} h(\theta_k \mid M_j)$, with proper prior distributions. The factors $h(\theta_k \mid M_j)$ are the pseudo-priors. Their role is to allow the construction of transition probabilities across models M and $\tilde{M}$. See the following.

Upon convergence this Gibbs sampler algorithm generates a sample from the posterior distribution $h(M, \theta \mid y)$ which implies for each model

$$h(M_j, \theta \mid y) \propto f(y \mid M_j, \theta_j) \, h(\theta_j \mid M_j) \, \Pi_{k \neq j} h(\theta_k \mid M_j) \, h(M_j)$$
$$\equiv h^*(M_j, \theta \mid y), \quad (7.5)$$

implying that the prior distributions $h(\theta_k \mid M_j)$ for the parameters corresponding to models $k \neq j$ are not required to specify (M_j, θ_j). Further, one can easily show that the marginal likelihood for each model can be written as

$$f(y \mid M_j) = E_\theta \Big[f(y \mid M_j, \theta) \mid M_j \Big] = E_{\theta_j} \Big[f(y \mid M_j, \theta_j) \mid M_j \Big],$$

from which one can see that for the purpose of model comparison via Bayes factors the choice of the pseudo-priors is irrelevant.

The pseudo-prior method makes use of the complete conditional distributions for the $J + 1$ blocks

$$\forall M \in \mathcal{M} \quad h(M \mid \theta, y) = \frac{h^*(M, \theta \mid y)}{\sum_{k \in J} h^*(M_k, \theta \mid y)} \tag{7.6}$$

$$\forall j \in J \quad h(\theta_j \mid \theta_{-j}, M, y) = \begin{cases} h(\theta_j \mid M_j, y), & M = M_j \\ h(\theta_j \mid M_k), & M = M_k, \; k \neq j. \end{cases} \tag{7.7}$$

The simulation based on these distributions is more efficient if, for each model M_j, one has conjugacy of the likelihood and the respective prior $h(\theta_j \mid M_j)$, and if one chooses pseudo-priors $h(\theta_k \mid M_j)$, $k \neq j$, that are similar to $h(\theta_k \mid M_k, y)$. Note that under conjugacy for model M_j one can exactly evaluate the posterior distribution for the respective parameter and the marginal likelihood $f(y \mid M_j)$ and, on the basis of the latter, evaluate the posterior probability of M_j, which allows a separate and easy evaluation of the posterior quantities.

Once a Monte Carlo sample $\{(M^{(t)}, \theta^{(t)})\}$ from $h(M, \theta \mid y)$ is available, it can be used to evaluate posterior probabilities for each model $h(M_j \mid y)$ (as relative sample frequencies of $M = M_j$) and, therefore, Bayes factors between any pair of models. Inference related to $h(\theta_j \mid M_j, y)$ is obtained from the subsample of $\theta^{(t)}$ consisting of the components $\theta_j^{(t)}$ associated with model M_j.

For details about the implementation, see Carlin and Louis (2009: section 4.5.1). Dellaportas et al (2002) propose a modification of the pseudo-prior method for the special case of variable selection.

A Metropolized Pseudo-Prior MCMC

This approach was proposed by Dellaportas et al (2002) with the aim of reducing the computational effort of the Carlin and Chib method related to the generation from $(\#\mathcal{M} - 1)$ pseudo-priors in each cycle of the Gibbs sampler (here $\#\mathcal{M}$ is the number of models under consideration). This is achieved by hybridizing the Gibbs sampler by substituting $h(M \mid \theta, y)$ in the step of the model updating with a proposal distribution that is independent of the parameters θ. Let $q(M_{j'} \mid M_j)$ denote the proposal distribution when the current model is M_j. The "Metropolization" of the model updating step then creates a sampler that is independent of the current parameters.

In $h(M_\ell, \theta \mid y)/h(M_k, \theta \mid y)$, $k \neq \ell$, all other pseudo-priors cancel out and only the pseudo-priors $h(\theta_k \mid M_\ell)$ and $h(\theta_\ell \mid M_k)$ remain. Also, recall that $h^*(\cdot)$ denotes the un-normalized product of prior times likelihood. Thus, the M-H acceptance ratio for a proposals $M_j \longrightarrow M_{j'}$ is

$$R(M_j, M_{j'}) = \frac{h^*(M_{j'}, \theta_{j'} \mid y) \, h(\theta_j \mid M_j) \, q(M_j \mid M_{j'})}{h^*(M_j, \theta_j \mid y) \, h(\theta_{j'} \mid M_j) \, q(M_{j'} \mid M_j)},$$

highlighting that in each iteration only one pseudo-prior is needed. Thus, each cycle of the hybrid MCMC consists of the following three steps:

1. Given a current model M_j, generate a value $h(\theta_j \mid M_j, y)$.
2. Propose a transition to $M_{j'}$ by generating from $q(M_{j'} \mid M_j)$ and generate a value from $h(\theta_{j'} \mid M_j)$.
3. Accept the proposal with probability

$$\alpha(M_j, M_{j'}) = \min\{1, R(M_j, M_{j'})\}.$$

More details about this method, including in particular the choice of proposal distribution, are found in Dellaportas et al (2002).

7.4 Reversible Jump MCMC

Reversible jump MCMC (RJ) is another method to set up simulation from (7.4). As the perhaps most widely used approach of this type, we discuss it in more detail. RJ is due to Green (1995) and implements an M-H algorithm to generate from the posterior distribution on the pair (model, parameter), defined over the space $\bigcup_{j \in J} \{M_j, \Theta_j\}$. Without loss of generality, assume $\Theta_j = \mathbb{R}^{p_j}$. The RJ defines a process that can jump between models of different dimensions, including a mapping between model-specific parameters. By trans-dimensional simulation the algorithm generates a sample from the joint posterior distribution of an indicator M for a model in a given set and a parameter θ which takes values in the set $\bigcup_{j \in J} \Theta_j$ such that $\theta \in \Theta_j$ (i.e., $\theta = \theta_j$) when $M = M_j$. The set J of model indicators is allowed to be infinite.

The transition from a current state (M_j, θ_j) to $(\tilde{M}, \tilde{\theta}_{\tilde{M}})$ follows an M-H transition probability that is implemented with a proposal distribution which is composed of two factors related to the jump between models (q_m)

followed by a generation of a parameter for the proposed model (q_p), defined as

$$q(\tilde{M}, \tilde{\theta}_{\tilde{M}} \mid M_j, \theta_j) = q_m(\tilde{M} \mid M_j, \theta_j) \, q_p(\tilde{\theta}_{\tilde{M}} \mid M_j, \theta_j, \tilde{M}).$$

Assume $\tilde{M} = M_{j'}$. The proposal distribution q_m is in many cases selected to be independent of the parameters under the current model, θ_j. That is, $q_m(\tilde{M} \mid M_j, \theta_j) = q_{jj'}$ is a function of only j, j'. The distinguishing feature of the RJ method is in the proposal distribution q_p, wich has to accommodate the transition from model M_j to $\tilde{M}$, including a possible change in dimension of the parameter vector. Details are introduced in the following.

In short, the reversible jump builds on an M-H algorithm by adding two important elements. First, we introduce dimension padding by adding auxiliary variables. Second, each transition probability can include a deterministic transformation. The latter is important to create a well-mixing Markov chain. For example, consider an RJ for a normal linear regression that allows the use of a line with (M_2) or without (M_1) intercept, that is $E(y_i \mid x_i)$ is $\alpha + \beta x_i$ under M_2 or βx_i under M_1. It is important to adjust the currently imputed value of the slope β when we propose to add a new intercept $\alpha \neq 0$ in the line. That is essentially all that is to be said about the RJ. The rest are details.

We first introduce the RJ for the simple problem of regression with and without an intercept. Of course, one would not really use RJ in this problem. But it provides an easily understood context with all the same details that are needed in any RJ. Let $f(y \mid \alpha, \beta, M_2)$ and $f(y \mid \beta, M_1)$ denote the likelihood function under the model with and without intercept, respectively, and let $h(\alpha, \beta \mid M_2), h(\beta \mid M_1)$, and $h(M)$ denote the prior distributions. In terms of the earlier general notation for model-specific parameter vectors $\theta_1 = (\beta)$ and $\theta_2 = (\alpha, \beta)$.

Move up: Assume the current state is $\omega = (M_1, \theta_1)$. Propose a new model $\tilde{M}$ with $P(\tilde{M} = 2) = q_{12}$ and $P(\tilde{M} = 1) = q_{11} = 1 - q_{12}$. If $\tilde{M} = M_1$, continue with the usual MCMC step, without change of dimension. Otherwise $\tilde{M} = M_2$ and:

1. Generate $(\tilde{\beta}, \tilde{\alpha})$ by:
   (a) generating an *auxiliary variable $u \sim q(u)$*;
   (b) using a *deterministic mapping* $(\tilde{\beta}, \tilde{\alpha}) = T(\beta, u)$.

2. Accept the proposal $(\tilde{\beta}, \tilde{\alpha})$ with probability $A_{up} = \min\{\rho_{up}, 1\}$ and ratio

$$\rho_{up}(\beta, u, \tilde{\beta}, \tilde{\alpha}) = \frac{h(\tilde{M})}{h(M_1)} \frac{h(\tilde{\beta}, \tilde{\alpha} \mid \tilde{M})}{h(\tilde{\beta} \mid M_1)} \frac{f(y \mid \tilde{\alpha}, \tilde{\beta})}{f(y \mid \beta)} \frac{q_{21}}{q_{12} \, q(u)} \left| \frac{\partial T(\beta, u)}{\partial(\beta, u)} \right|.$$

$$\text{prior ratio} \times \text{likelihood} \times \text{proposal} \times \text{Jacobian}$$

3. With probability A_{up}, set $\omega = (\tilde{M}, \tilde{\beta}, \tilde{\alpha}) = (M_2, \theta_2)$.

Move down: Similarly, assume the current state is (M_2, θ_2). Propose a new model $\tilde{M}$ with $P(\tilde{M} = 2) = q_{22}$ and $P(\tilde{M} = 1) = q_{21} = 1 - q_{22}$. If $\tilde{M} = M_2$, continue with the usual MCMC step, without change of dimension. Otherwise:

4. Compute $(\tilde{\beta}, u) = T^{-1}(\beta, \alpha)$.
5. Acceptance probability $A_{down} = \min\{1, \rho_{down}\}$, with

$$\rho_{down} = 1/\rho_{up}(\tilde{\beta}, u, \beta, \alpha).$$

The inclusion of the auxiliary variable in step 1(a) achieves the desired dimension padding and allows transdimensional MCMC. The use of the deterministic mapping in step 1(b) allows us to design algorithms with better mixing. For example, in the application to a regression with and without intercept, the slope β should be adjusted when proposing to add an intercept and vice versa. In general, both moves, up and down, could involve auxiliary variables, set up such that the dimensions of current state and proposal, possibly both augmented by auxiliary variables, match. A general RJ algorithm can include more than two types of transition probabilities. The only condition is that for the proposal generated by any transition probability there needs to be a matching reciprocal type of transition probability that could generate a proposal to come back. If we were to propose, for example, an up-move of no return, that is, with no possibility to reverse the proposal, then formally in ρ_{up} the proposal probability in the numerator would evaluate as zero, leaving acceptance probability $A_{up} = 0$. That is, the algorithm would never accept such a move of no return. It is therefore usually best to design RJ moves in reciprocal pairs. Examples are the up and down move, birth and death moves that add or remove a term in a mixture model, and many more.

A similar trans-dimensional MCMC algorithm could be implemented for any posterior distribution over variable-dimension parameter spaces. In practice, the use of a good mapping $T(\cdot)$ is critical to achieve a reasonably fast-mixing Markov chain. That is, the construction requires a good estimate for proposed parameters $\tilde{\theta}$ in the proposed model $\tilde{M}$. In many more complex problems, the lack of a good mapping makes the implementation of RJ impractical, since proposed moves would be almost always rejected. One class of problems in which RJ has been found to be viable are mixture models. It is reasonably easy to construct proposals for the parameters of a larger (smaller) size mixture when proposing moves up (down) (Richardson and Green, 1997). See also problem 7.2 at the end of the chapter.

Finally, note the similarities between RJ and the pseudo-prior algorithm. Consider an RJ transition probability that involves a proposal to move from a current state vector $\theta \in \Theta_j$ to a proposal $\tilde{\theta} \in \Theta_{j+1}$. Assume the transition probability involves an auxiliary variable generated from $q(u)$ and a deterministic mapping $T(\theta, u)$. The same elements can be used to construct a suitable pseudo-prior $h(\theta_{j+1} \mid \theta_j, M_j)$. The only formal difference is that the RJ does not require a finite number of competing models M_j, whereas the pseudo-prior method does.

RJ with General "Up" and "Down" Moves.

For reference we include a description of a general RJ that involves "up" and "down" moves similar to the earlier stylized example. For example, in the mixture of normal problem the "up" move could involve splitting a term in the mixture into two new terms, and the "down" move could involve merging two terms.

Consider an RJ for a generic target distribution $\pi(\theta)$ on a variable-dimension parameter space $\Theta = \cup_n \Theta_n$ with $\Theta_n \subseteq \mathbb{R}^n$. We let $\theta \in \Theta$ denote the state vector and write θ_n when we want to highlight $\theta_n \in \Theta_n$. We let $\pi_n(\theta_n) = \pi(\theta \mid \Theta_n)$ denote the target distribution restricted to Θ_n and assume that it has a density $f_n(\theta_n)$. That is, $\pi_n(F_n) = \int_{F_n} f_n(\theta) \, d\theta$ for any event $F_n \subseteq \Theta_n$.

We consider an RJ including transition probabilities $P_u(\theta, A)$ to propose a move from $\theta \in \Theta_n$ to $\theta \in \Theta_{n+1}$ (**"up"**), and $P_d(\theta, A)$ to move from $\theta \in \Theta_{n+1}$ to $\theta \in \Theta_n$ (**"down"**). For easier notation we assume that the jump in dimension is from n to $n + 1$ and $n - 1$, respectively (little changes if it were transitions from Θ_n to Θ_{n+d} and Θ_{n-d}, respectively). For the following construction the reader might find it helpful to keep in mind the specific example of a mixture of normal model with split ("up") and merge ("down") moves. And there might be other transition probabilities that involve moves within Θ_n. For example, in a mixture of normal problem, we might include Gibbs sampling transition probabilities to update locations and weights for a fixed size mixture (like in Problem 6.9). In the following, we only focus on P_u and P_d which move across dimensions. We construct general RJ transition probabilities in this problem.

Algorithm 4 Reversible Jump (RJ).

Assume the current state is $\theta_n \in \Theta_n$. Let $q_{n,n-1} = \frac{1}{2}$ if $n \geq 2$ and $q_{n,n-1} = 0$ for $n = 1$.

Move up: With probability $1 - q_{n,n-1}$, propose an "**up** move," P_u.

1. Select one of N_n^{up} possible moves. For example, in a mixture problem one might select the term to be split. Let $q_{up,m}(\theta_n)$ denote the probability of selecting move m, $m = 1, \ldots, N_n^{up}$. For example, $q_{up,m} = 1/N_n^{up}$.
2. Generate an auxiliary variable $u \sim q_{aux}(\theta_n)$. Often, q_{aux} involves a truncation. Do not forget the normalization constant if it is a function of θ_n.
3. Use a deterministic function to define a proposal $\tilde{\theta}_{n+1} = T(\theta_n, u)$. Record $J = \det(\partial T / \partial \theta_n \partial u)$.
4. Evaluate the acceptance probability $A_{up}(\theta_n, \tilde{\theta}_{n+1}) = \min\{1, \rho(\theta_n, \tilde{\theta}_{n+1})\}$

$$\rho(\theta_n, \tilde{\theta}_{n+1}) = \underbrace{\frac{\pi(\tilde{\theta}_{n+1})}{\pi(\theta_n)}}_{\text{target}} \underbrace{\frac{q_{n+1,n}}{q_{n,n+1}} \frac{q_{down,m'}(\tilde{\theta}_{n+1})}{q_{up,m}(\theta_n)}}_{\text{proposal}} \underbrace{\frac{1}{q_{aux}(u)}}_{\text{auxiliary}} |J|. \qquad (7.8)$$

See the following for the details of the down move.
5. With probability A_{up} set $\theta = \tilde{\theta}_{n+1}$, otherwise $\theta = \theta_n$.

Move down: With probability $q_{n,n-1}$, carry out a "**down** move," P_d.

1. We select one of N_n^{down} possible down moves with probabilities $q_{down,m}(\theta_n)$, $m = 1, \ldots, N_n^{down}$. For example, in a mixture problem, one might select two adjacent terms to be merged. Let m' denote the selected move.
2. Record $(\tilde{\theta}_{n-1}, u) = T^{-1}(\theta_n)$.
3. Compute the acceptance probability

$$A_d(x_n, \tilde{\theta}_{n-1}) = \min\left\{1, \frac{1}{\rho(\tilde{\theta}_{n-1}, \theta_n)}\right\}.$$

4. With probability A_d set $\theta = \tilde{\theta}_{n-1}$, otherwise keep $\theta = \theta_n$.

Note how we had to carefully record all moves in steps 1 through 3 and account for the corresponding proposal probabilities in (7.8).

Nothing much changes if the "down" move also involves an auxiliary $v \in \mathbb{R}^q$. It only complicates notation.

Problems

As in Chapter 6, most of the problems require some programming to implement MCMC simulation. See Appendix B for some suggestions on how to implement such simulation in R.

7.1 *Normal linear regression – variable selection.* Use the setup and notation of Problem 6.11.

   a. Let $\bar{\beta} = E(\beta \mid \tau^2, y)$ and $V = \text{Var}(\beta \mid \tau^2, y)$ denote the posterior mean and covariance matrix for β conditional on τ^2. Let $\text{RSS}(\beta) = \sum_i (y_i - \varpi_i'\beta)^2$ denote the residual sum of squares for β. Prove the following result

$$f(y \mid \tau^2) \propto |V|^{\frac{1}{2}} h(\bar{\beta}) \tau^{\frac{n}{2}} \exp\left(-\frac{\tau^2}{2}\text{RSS}(\bar{\beta})\right), \qquad (7.9)$$

   as a function of τ^2. That is, the proportionality constant is a function of y. *Hint:* You could use Bayes' theorem for $h(\beta \mid y, \tau^2)$ and substitute for $\beta = \bar{\beta}$.

   b. Now consider variable selection. Let $\gamma = (\gamma_1, \ldots, \gamma_p)$ denote a vector of indicators $\gamma_j \in \{0, 1\}$, let $p_\gamma = \sum_j \gamma_j$, and let X_γ denote the $(n \times p_\gamma)$ submatrix of X with the columns selected by $\gamma_j = 1$. Similarly, let β_γ denote the subvector of β selected by γ, and similar for $\beta_{0\gamma}$ and $\Sigma_{0,\gamma}$. We change model (6.23) to include variable selection by using

$$y = X_\gamma \beta_\gamma + \epsilon, \qquad (7.10)$$

   with $\epsilon = (\epsilon_1, \ldots, \epsilon_n)$, and a modified prior $h(\beta_\gamma \mid \gamma) = N(\beta_{0,\gamma}, \Sigma_{0,\gamma})$ and hyperprior $h(\gamma_j = 1) = \pi$, $j = 1, \ldots, p$, independently across j.

   Use (7.9) to find $h(\gamma \mid \tau^2, y)$.

   c. Propose a posterior MCMC scheme to generate a posterior Monte Carlo sample $(\gamma^{(m)}, \tau^{2(m)}) \sim h(\gamma, \tau^2 \mid y)$.
   How would you augment the Monte Carlo sample with $\beta^{(m)} \sim h(\beta \mid \gamma^{(m)}, \tau^{2(m)}, y)$, if desired?

7.2 *Variable selection.* Ročková and George (2014) propose the following implementation of SSVS for a Gaussian linear model:

$$f(y \mid \beta, \sigma) = N(X\beta, \sigma^2 I),$$

where $y = (y_1, \ldots, y_n)$ is a response vector, and X is an $(n \times p)$ matrix of covariates.
We use the following SSVS prior for the regression coefficients β. Let

$$\text{cov}(\beta) = D_{\sigma,\gamma} = \sigma^2 \text{diag}(a_1, \ldots, a_p) \text{ with } a_i = (1 - \gamma_i)v_0 + \gamma_i v_1$$

denote the prior covariance matrix for β. Here, $\gamma_j \in \{0, 1\}$, v_0 is small such that $\beta_j \approx \sqrt{v_0}$ is practically dropping the jth covariate; and v_1 is large.

That is, $\gamma = (\gamma_1, \ldots, \gamma_p)$ has the interpretation of a vector of indicators for variable selection. We assume that

$$h_\beta(\beta \mid \sigma, \gamma) = N(0, D_{\sigma,\gamma}),$$

with $h_\gamma(\gamma_j = 1 \mid \theta) = \theta$. The model is completed with hyperpriors,

$$h_\sigma(\sigma^2 \mid \gamma) = \text{IGa}(\nu/2, \nu\lambda/2), \quad h_\theta(\theta) = \text{Be}(a, b),$$

and ν_0, ν_1 are fixed hyperparameters.

Ročková and George introduce an EM-type (Dempster et al, 1977) iterative algorithm to maximize $h(\beta, \theta, \sigma \mid y)$. Let $(\beta^{(t)}, \theta^{(t)}, \sigma^{(t)})$ denote the parameter vector after t iterations. The algorithm proceeds by iteratively maximizing

$$Q(\beta, \theta, \sigma \mid \beta^{(t)}, \theta^{(t)}, \sigma^{(t)}, y) = E_\gamma \left[\ln h(\beta, \theta, \sigma, \gamma \mid y) \right]. \quad (7.11)$$

The expectation (E_γ) is with respect to $h(\gamma \mid \beta^{(t)}, \theta^{(t)}, \sigma^{(t)}, y)$, using the currently imputed values $(\beta^{(t)}, \theta^{(t)}, \sigma^{(t)})$. That is, remove γ from $\ln h(\beta, \theta, \sigma, \gamma \mid y)$ by marginalizing with respect to $h(\gamma \mid \beta^{(t)}, \theta^{(t)}, \sigma^{(t)}, y)$. As a result, the Q function has no argument γ anymore – it is removed by the expectation, leaving a function of (β, θ, σ) only.

In the context of the general EM algorithm, the evaluation of Q is known as the E-step, and the maximization of Q with respect to β, θ, σ is known as the M-step. The maximization defines $(\beta^{(t+1)}, \theta^{(t+1)}, \sigma^{(t+1)})$.

It can be shown that $(\beta^{(t)}, \theta^{(t)}, \sigma^{(t)})$ converges to the mode of $p(\beta, \theta, \sigma \mid y)$.

a. Find $h(\gamma \mid \beta, \theta, \sigma, y)$.

b. Show that $h(\gamma \mid \beta, \theta, \sigma, y)$ is independent across γ_j, $j = 1, \ldots, p$.

For the next two questions, factor the posterior distribution and the Q function in (7.11) as

$$h(\beta, \theta, \sigma, \gamma \mid y) = C \times f(y \mid \beta, \sigma, \gamma) \times h_\sigma(\sigma^2) \times h_\beta(\beta \mid \sigma^2, \gamma)$$
$$\times h_\gamma(\gamma \mid \theta) \times h_\theta(\theta)$$
$$Q = E_\gamma[\ln h(\cdot \mid y)] = \ln C$$
$$+ Q_y(\beta, \sigma) + Q_\sigma(\sigma^2) + Q_\beta(\beta, \sigma^2) + Q_\gamma(\theta) + Q_\theta(\theta).$$

Here, $Q_y = E_\gamma[\ln f]$ and $Q_x = E_\gamma[\ln h_x]$ $(x = \gamma, \sigma, \beta, \theta)$ and recall again that the expectation is with respect to $h(\gamma \mid \beta^{(t)}, \theta^{(t)}, \sigma^{(t)}, y)$. Note that, for example, the only argument of Q_y is just θ, after taking the expectation with respect to γ.

c. Find Q_y, Q_σ and Q_θ.

d. Find Q_β and Q_γ.

7.3 *Mixture model.* Recall the mixture of normal model (6.16) from Problem 6.9. Let $\theta = (J, w_1, \ldots, w_J, \mu_1, \ldots, \mu_J, \sigma^2)$.

$$g_\theta(x) = \sum_{j=1}^{J} w_j N(\mu_j, \sigma^2). \quad (7.12)$$

We now complete the model with a prior on J. Let $\text{Poi}^+(\lambda)$ denote a Poisson distribution restricted to positive integers. We assume

$$J \sim \text{Poi}^+(\lambda).$$

Use $\lambda = 5$.

a. *Joint posterior.* Let $\mu = (\mu_1, \ldots, \mu_J)$, $w = (w_1, \ldots, w_J)$, and $x = (x_1, \ldots, x_n)$, and let $\theta = (\mu, w, \sigma^2, J)$ denote the complete parameter vector. Find the joint posterior distribution $h(\theta \mid x)$.

b. *Hierarchical model.* Rewrite the mixture as a hierarchical model using indicators $s_i \in \{1, \ldots, J\}$.

$$f(x_i \mid s_i = j) = N(\mu_j, \sigma^2) \text{ and } P(s_i = j \mid w, J) = w_j. \qquad (7.13)$$

Let $s_{-i} = (s_1, \ldots, i-1, s_{i+1}, \ldots, n)$.
Find $h(\mu_j \mid s, w, x)$, $h(s_i \mid s_{-i}, \mu, w, J, x_i)$, and $h(w \mid s, J, x)$.

c. *Reversible jump MCMC.* Propose a RJ MCMC for posterior simulation across variable J.

    1. *Split move.* Propose a transition probability for incrementing J, i.e., $\tilde{J} = J + 1$.

    Describe the construction of a proposal (step by step), and state the acceptance probability for the proposal.

    Hint: You could: (1) select a term j to split; assume without loss of generality $j = J$ (rearrange indexes if needed, to simplify notation); (2) generate a bivariate auxiliary variable (u, v); (3) define $T(\theta, u, v)$ by $\tilde{\mu}_J = \mu_J + u$, $\tilde{\mu}_{J+1} = \mu_J - u$, $\tilde{w}_J = w_J v$ and $\tilde{w}_{J+1} = w_J(1 - v)$.

    2. *Merge move.* Propose a transition probability for decrementing J, i.e., $\tilde{J} = J - 1$ ("merge move"). Describe the construction of a proposal (step by step) and state the acceptance probability for the proposal.

d. *Implementation.* Implement an RJ using the complete conditional distributions from part (b) and the RJ move from (c).

    Use the data set `galaxy` in R. You can get it, for example, in the R package `ElemStatLearn`. The data is shown in Figure 6.3.

    • Plot J against iteration (trajectory of imputed J).
    • Estimate $\bar{g}(x) = E[g_\theta(x) \mid x]$ for x on a grid x.
    • Evaluate convergence diagnostics for σ^2, $g_{10} = g_\theta(10)$, $g_{20} = g_\theta(20)$, and $G_{30} = \int_{30}^{\infty} g_\theta(s)ds$.[5]

7.4 *Pseudo-prior.* The following example is about inference in a clinical trial using a historical control. The trial is a study of a proposed treatment for uterine papillary serous carcinoma, a very rare disease. The study drug is administered in three doses, including 0 (control), 1, and 2. To facilitate a study in a

---

[5] Use the R package *boa* or *coda* (or any other) for convergence diagnostics. See Section 9.6.

realistic time frame we consider pooling with historical data on control. Let y_i denote the outcome (PFS, progression free survival, in months) for the ith patient, numbering all patients, including patients from the historical study as $i = 1, \ldots, n$, with $n = 56$, including $n_0 = 40$ patients in the historical data and $n_1 = 16$ in the new study. Let $I_i \in \{0, 1\}$ denote an indicator for a patient to be in the historical study and $z_i \in \{0, 1, 2\}$ for the dose of the study drug. All patients in the historical data are on control, i.e., $z_i = 0$, $i = 1, \ldots, n_0$. We use a Weibull regression with (or without in part (b)) a study effect. That is, a sampling model

$$y_i \sim \text{Weib}(\lambda, a), \text{ with } \ln \lambda = \beta_0 + \beta_1 z_i + \beta_2 I_i.$$

a. Set up a prior $\beta_j \sim N(m_j, s_j^2)$, $j = 0, 1, 2$, with $m_2 = 0$, $s_0 = 0.1$ and $s_1 = s_2 = 0.5$. Determine suitable values for m_0 and m_1 to match expert opinion that PFS at doses $z = 0, 1, 2$ should be around 7, 11, and 14 months (you might not be able to exactly match these means). The data are in the file `uterine.txt` which is linked on the book's homepage.[6] In addition to z_i, y_i, and I_i, the file reports an indicator s_i for observed event time ($s_i = 1$) versus censoring time ($s_i = 0$). Carry out posterior inference.

b. Now we change the prior on β_2, the study effect. Let δ_x denote a point mass at x. We assume

$$\beta_2 \sim \begin{cases} \delta_0 & \text{if } M = 0 \\ N(m_2, s_2^2) & \text{if } M = 1, \end{cases}$$

with $h(M = 1) = 0.5$. That is, $\beta_2 = 0$ under model $M = 0$, and $\beta_2 \sim N(m_2, s_2^2)$ under model $M = 1$. The modified model allows for pooling of all data ($\beta_2 = 0$), with prior probability 0.5. Implement posterior MCMC with a pseudo-prior mechanism for transdimensional MCMC across $M = 0$ and $M = 1$.

c. Alternatively, evaluate a Bayes factor for model $M = 0$ versus $M = 1$. Use an appropriate Monte Carlo strategy to approximate the Bayes factor (see Section 4.2.2).

7.5 *RJ: multivariate mixture model.* Zhang et al (2004) develop an RJ algorithm for a multivariate mixture of a normal model,

$$y_i \mid K, \mu, \Sigma, w \sim \sum_{k=1}^{K} w_k N(\mu_k, \Sigma_k). \tag{7.14}$$

Here, $y_i = (y_{i1}, \ldots, y_{iD})'$ is a D-dimensional response vector. The covariance matrix Σ_k is represented by its singular value decomposition $\Sigma_k = E_k \Lambda_k E_k'$, where $E_k = (e_1^k, \ldots, e_D^k)$ is an orthogonal matrix with columns equal to the

---

[6] `sites.google.com/view/computationalbayes/home.`

eigenvectors of Σ_k, and $\Lambda_k = \mathrm{diag}(\kappa_{k1}, \ldots, \kappa_{kD})$ is a diagonal matrix with the corresponding eigenvalues. We assume that $E_k = E$ is fixed across components and thus $\Sigma_k = E\Lambda_k E'$. We fix E using the SVD, $S = E\Lambda E'$, of the empirical covariance matrix S, and complete the prior specification for Σ_k by assuming

$$\kappa_{kd}^{-1} \sim \mathrm{Ga}(a/2, b/2).$$

The model is completed with $K \sim \mathrm{Poi}^+(\lambda)$, $\mu_j \sim N(0, B)$ and $w \sim D_{K-1}(a)$, with fixed hyperparameters λ, B, and a.

For fixed K, MCMC transition probabilities to update w, μ and κ are very similar to the univariate mixture model, as in Problem 7.3. However, updating K requires an RJ-type move. Let $\omega = (w, \mu, \kappa)$ denote the parameters except for K.

We make a random choice to propose a *combine* or a *split* move. Let q_{Kd} and $q_{Ku} = 1 - q_{Kd}$ denote the probability of proposing a combine and a split move, respectively, for a currently imputed point configuration of size K. We use $q_{Kd} = 0.5$ for $K \geq 2$, and $q_{Kd} = 0$ for $K = 1$. In the following transition probabilities, let $\mu_{kd}^\star = e_d' \mu_k$ and $y_d^\star = e_d' y$ denote the coordinates of μ_d and y_d in the eigenvector basis.

Split move: We randomly select a component j to split into two new components. The probability of choosing component j is $q_{Ks}(j) = \frac{1}{K}$. Without loss of generality, assume that component $j = 1$ is split into new components $j_1 = 1$ and $j_2 = 2$ (relabeling components $2, \ldots, K$ into $3, \ldots, K + 1$). We define new parameters $\tilde{\omega}$:

$$\tilde{w}_1 = w_1 \alpha, \qquad\qquad \tilde{w}_2 = w_1(1 - \alpha)$$

$$\tilde{\mu}_{1d}^\star = \mu_{1d}^\star - \sqrt{\tfrac{\tilde{w}_2}{\tilde{w}_1}} \kappa_{1d}^{1/2} r_d \quad \tilde{\mu}_{2d}^\star = \mu_{1d}^\star + \sqrt{\tfrac{\tilde{w}_1}{\tilde{w}_2}} \kappa_{1d}^{1/2} r_d$$

$$\tilde{\kappa}_{1d} = \beta_d(1 - r_d^2)\tfrac{w_1}{\tilde{w}_1}\kappa_{1d} \quad \tilde{\kappa}_{2d} = (1 - \beta_d)(1 - r_d^2)\tfrac{w_1}{\tilde{w}_2}\kappa_{1d},$$

where $\alpha \sim \mathrm{Be}(1, 1)$, $\beta_d \sim \mathrm{Be}(1, 1)$ and $r_d \sim \mathrm{Be}(2, 2)$ are auxiliary variables. For later reference, let $q_u(\alpha, \beta, r) = p(\alpha)\Pi_d p(\beta_d)p(r_d)$.

Let $\theta = (w_1, \mu_1, \kappa_{1d})$ and $u = (\alpha, r, \beta)$ denote the current state (ignoring the terms that are not affected by the split) and the auxiliary variables, and let $\tilde{\theta} = (\tilde{w}_1, \tilde{w}_2, \tilde{\mu}_1, \tilde{\mu}_2, \tilde{\kappa}_{1d}, \tilde{\kappa}_{2d})$ denote the proposal. In short, the split proposes

$$\tilde{\theta} = T(\theta, u).$$

It is easy to verify that the marginal moments $E(y_d^\star)$ and $\mathrm{cov}(y_d^\star)$ remain unchanged under the proposed extended mixture.

Combine move: We randomly select a pair (j_1, j_2) of components to merge. The probability of choosing (j_1, j_2) is $q_{Kc}(j_1, j_2) = \frac{2}{K(K-1)}$, $j_1 < j_2$. Without loss of generality, assume $(j_1, j_2) = (1, 2)$ are merged to form the new component $j = 1$. The following deterministic transformation defines parameter values after the merge. To highlight the relationship with the earlier split move (and simplify the answer to the following question), we label the current state vector $\tilde{\omega}$ and the proposal ω:

$$w_1 = \tilde{w}_1 + \tilde{w}_2 \tag{7.15}$$
$$w_1\mu_1 = \tilde{w}_1\tilde{\mu}_1 + \tilde{w}_2\tilde{\mu}_2$$
$$w_1(\kappa_{1d} + \mu_{1d}^{\star 2}) = \tilde{w}_1(\tilde{\kappa}_{1d} + \tilde{\mu}_{1d}^{\star 2}) + \tilde{w}_2(\tilde{\kappa}_{2d} + \tilde{\mu}_{2d}^{\star 2}),$$

and the implied auxiliary variables

$$\alpha = \ldots, \quad \frac{\beta_d}{1 - \beta_d} = \ldots \text{ and } \left\{ \sqrt{\frac{\tilde{w}_1}{\tilde{w}_2}} + \sqrt{\frac{\tilde{w}_2}{\tilde{w}_1}} \right\} r_d = \ldots \tag{7.16}$$

Here, we wrote the equations for μ_1, κ_{1d}, and β_d without the final simplification – just for beauty, and to highlight how to derive them as the inverse of the split. For later reference we denote the mapping of (7.15) and (7.16) as

$$S(\tilde{\theta}) = (\theta, u).$$

a. Fill in the missing expressions ... on the r.h.s. of (7.16) and show that $S = T^{-1}$.
b. Find the acceptance ratio for the *split move*.
c. Find the acceptance ratio for a *merge move*.
d. See Dellaportas and Papageorgiou (2006) for an alternative RJ for a multivariate normal mixture of normals. Discuss the relative advantages and limitations of the two posterior simulation schemes.

7.6 *Detail balance for RJ.* In this problem we verify the detail balance condition for the RJ MCMC with general "up" and "down" transition probabilities (in Section 7.4).

To verify detail balance for this general RJ, we start with the general statement of DB.

$$\int_A \sum_m q_m(\theta) P_m(\theta, B) \pi(d\theta) = \int_u \sum_m q_m(\theta) P_m(\theta, A) \pi(d\theta)$$

for any (measureable) $A, B \subset \Theta$. We only worry about transdimensional moves, $A = F_{n+1} \in \Theta_{n+1}$ and $B = F_n \in \Theta_n$:

$$\int_{F_{n+1}} \sum_m q_m(\theta_{n+1}) P_m(\theta_{n+1}, F_n) \pi(d\theta_{n+1}) =$$
$$\int_{F_n} \sum_m q_m(\theta_n) P_m(\theta_n, F_{n+1}) \pi(d\theta_n) \tag{7.17}$$

Complete the argument to verify (7.17).
Hint: Your argument could proceed along the following steps. (1) A sufficient condition for (7.17) is that the equation holds for pairs (m, m') of matching down and reciprocal up moves, P_d and P_u. (2) Write P_u as an integral over u. (3) Use the densities f_n and f_{n+1}, write $\theta_{n+1} = T(\theta_n, u)$, and

use indicators for F_n and F_{n+1} to replace the range of integration. (4) Use a change of variables to make both sides into integrals over (θ_n, u). (5) Finally, argue that equality of the integrands is a sufficient condition for equality of the integrals, and verify that the RJ acceptance probability satisfies the latter condition.

8

Methods Based on Analytic Approximations

Since the 1980s, investigators have aimed to find efficient, and preferably simple, approaches to overcome the technical problems of calculus that arise in Bayesian inference. A variety of strategies have been proposed, including in particular multivariate normal approximations of posterior distributions, the Laplace approach, numerical quadrature methods, classical Monte Carlo methods, and Markov chain Monte Carlo (MCMC) methods.

Advances in data collection give rise to the need for modeling ever more complex data structures. This includes, spatio-temporal models, dynamic linear models, generalized linear mixed models, generalized additive models, log-Gaussian Cox processes, geo-additive models, and more. All these models are part of a much larger class of models known as latent Gaussian models (LGMs). See, for example, Blangiardo and Cameletti (2015). Theoretically, it is always possible to implement MCMC algorithms for such LGMs. However, such implementations come with many problems in terms of convergence and computation time.

Recently, Rue et al (2009) developed an analytical approach based on integrated and nested Laplace approximations (INLAs), which allows deterministic approximation of marginal posterior distributions in these models. The method provides a particularly efficient implementation of Bayesian inference in LGMs. The INLA approach has two major advantages over MCMC techniques. The first is computation time. Using INLA one can get results within seconds or minutes in models that would take hours or even days for inference using MCMC algorithms. The second advantage is that INLA treats LGMs in a unified way, allowing substantial automation of inference, independent of the specific model.

To better understand the methods proposed by Rue et al (2009), this chapter starts with a review of the main techniques for analytical approximation that were developed to implement Bayesian inference, and then presents the INLA method and its implementation in an associated R package.

8.1 Analytical Methods

8.1.1 Multivariate Normal Posterior Approximation

One possible strategy to overcome computational problems that arise in Bayesian inference is based on asymptotic properties of the posterior distribution. In fact, for large n and under certain regularity conditions, the posterior distribution for a k-dimensional parameter vector θ is approximately multivariate normal (Walker, 1969).

Consider a posterior density $h(\theta \mid x)$, written as

$$h(\theta \mid x) \propto \exp\{\ln h(\theta) + \ln f(x \mid \theta)\}.$$

Using a Taylor series expansion of second order for the logarithm of the two terms in the previous expression, around the respective maxima (assuming those are unique), we get

$$\ln h(\theta) = \ln h(m_0) - \frac{1}{2}(\theta - m_0)^t H_0 (\theta - m_0) + R_0 \qquad (8.1)$$

$$\ln f(x \mid \theta) = \ln f(x \mid \hat{\theta}_n) - \frac{1}{2}(\theta - \hat{\theta}_n)^t H(\hat{\theta}_n)(\theta - \hat{\theta}_n) + R_n,$$

where m_0 is the prior mode and $\hat{\theta}_n$ is the maximum likelihood estimate of θ given the data x,

$$H_0 = -\left.\frac{\partial^2 \ln h(\theta)}{\partial \theta_i \partial \theta_j}\right|_{\theta = m_0}, \qquad H(\hat{\theta}_n) = -\left.\frac{\partial^2 \ln f(x \mid \theta)}{\partial \theta_i \partial \theta_j}\right|_{\theta = \hat{\theta}_n}$$

and R_0, R_n, are the remainders of the respective series expansions. Subject to certain regularity conditions, which guarantee that the remainder terms are small for large n (see, e.g., Bernardo and Smith, 1994), we get

$$h(\theta \mid x) \propto \exp\left\{-\frac{1}{2}(\theta - m_n)^t H_n (\theta - m_n)\right\},$$

$$H_n = H_0 + H(\hat{\theta}_n),$$

$$m_n = H_n^{-1}(H_0 m_0 + H(\hat{\theta}_n)\hat{\theta}_n). \qquad (8.2)$$

This expansion suggests that the posterior distribution can be approximated, for large enough sample size and subject to regularity conditions, by a multivariate normal distribution $N_k(m_n, \hat{\Sigma}_n)$ with mean m_n and covariance matrix $\hat{\Sigma}_n = H_n^{-1}$.

With increasing sample size the prior precision, represented by H_0, is completely dominated by $H(\hat{\theta}_n)$, which arises from the data, that is $H_n \approx H(\hat{\theta}_n)$. Thus, also $m_n \approx \hat{\theta}_n$, and one can use it to approximate the posterior distribution by a multivariate normal, centered at the maximum likelihood estimate and covariance matrix $\hat{\Sigma} = \left[H(\hat{\theta}_n) \right]^{-1}$, that is, the inverse of the observed information matrix. [1]

The two separate expansions (around separate modes) in (8.1) are useful to note the asymptotic match with the observed information matrix. Alternatively, one can consider one expansion of the log posterior $\ln h(\theta \mid x)$ around its mode m_n, that is, around the posterior mode. Assume, then, a sequence of posterior distributions $\{h_n(\theta \mid x), n = 1, 2, \ldots\}$ for θ and that $L_n(\theta \mid x) = \ln h_n(\theta \mid x)$ and m_n are such that

$$L_n'(m_n) = \partial L_n(\theta \mid x)/\partial \theta|_{\theta=m_n} = 0$$

and

$$\Sigma_n = (-L_n''(m_n))^{-1},$$

where $[L_n''(m_n)]_{ij} = (\partial^2 L_n(\theta \mid x)/\partial \theta_i \partial \theta_j)|_{\theta=m_n}$. Bernardo and Smith (1994: ch. 5) prove that, under some conditions on $h_n(\theta \mid x)$ and for sufficiently large n, the posterior distribution can be approximated by a multivariate normal distribution $N(m_n, \Sigma_n)$.

This approach has the advantage that practically all posterior summaries can be calculated based on a Gaussian route. However, a major problem arises in the need to verify, for each application, the adequacy of this multivariate normal posterior approximation.

Example 8.1 *Assume that X follows a binomial distribution with parameters n (known) and θ, and that θ is assumed to follow a beta prior with parameters (a_0, b_0). We know that the posterior for θ is again a beta distribution with parameters (a_n, b_n), where $a_n = a_0 + x$ and $b_n = b_0 + n - x$. Thus*

$$h_n(\theta \mid x) \propto \theta^{a_n-1}(1 - \theta)^{b_n-1}, \quad 0 \le \theta \le 1.$$

Of course, if one wishes to make inference on θ or any function of θ, for example, the logit, that is, $\rho = \ln\left(\frac{\theta}{1-\theta}\right)$, one need not resort to sophisticated computational methods, as exact solutions are readily available. However, the example is useful to illustrate the earlier methods.

We find $\ln h_n(\theta \mid x) \propto (a_n - 1) \ln \theta + (b_n - 1) \ln(1 - \theta)$ and thus

$$L_n'(\theta) = \frac{(a_n - 1)}{\theta} - \frac{(b_n - 1)}{(1 - \theta)}, \quad L_n''(\theta) = -\frac{(a_n - 1)}{\theta^2} - \frac{(b_n - 1)}{(1 - \theta)^2} \qquad (8.3)$$

---

[1] Since the observed information matrix $H(\hat{\theta}_n)$ converges to the Fisher information matrix, one can also define an approximation with the inverse of the Fisher information matrix as covariance matrix.

and

$$m_n = \frac{(a_n - 1)}{a_n + b_n - 2}, \quad -\{L_n''(m_n)\}^{-1} = \frac{(a_n - 1)(b_n - 1)}{(a_n + b_n - 2)^3}. \quad (8.4)$$

It is easy to verify that the regularity conditions are satisfied, and therefore the posterior distribution can be well approximated, for large n, by a normal distribution, $N(m_n, \sigma_n^2)$, with $\sigma_n^2 = -\{L_n''(m_n)\}^{-1}$.

In the case of a uniform prior ($a_0 = b_0 = 1$), we have

$$m_n = \frac{x}{n}, \quad \sigma_n^2 = \frac{x/n(1 - x/n)}{n},$$

that is, the posterior distribution for θ given $X = x$ can be approximated by a normal distribution, $N(x/n, (x/n)(1 - x/n)/n)$. Note the duality of this result with what is obtained – by the central limit theorem – about the asymptotic distribution of X/n given θ. In fact, we know that for $X \sim Bi(n, \theta)$ and large n the distribution of X/n given θ is well approximated by a normal distribution $N(\theta, \theta(1 - \theta)/n)$.

If approximate inference on the log odds ρ is desired, one could proceed with several approaches. Start by verifying that the exact posterior distribution for ρ can be obtained by a simple transformation. In fact, note

$$h_n(\rho \mid x) \propto e^{a_n\rho}(1 + e^\rho)^{-(a_n+b_n)}, \quad \rho \in \mathbb{R}. \quad (8.5)$$

The posterior mean of ρ evaluated from (8.5) is $\psi(a_n) - \psi(b_n)$ where the function $\psi(x)$ is the derivative of the logarithm of $\Gamma(x)^2$. We find

$$\ln h_n(\rho \mid x) \propto a_n\rho - (a_n + b_n)\ln(1 + e^\rho)$$

$$L_n'(\rho) = a_n - (a_n + b_n)\frac{e^\rho}{(1 + e^\rho)}, \quad L_n''(\rho) = -(a_n + b_n)\frac{e^\rho}{(1 + e^\rho)^2}, \quad (8.6)$$

and thus

$$m_n = \ln \frac{a_n}{b_n} \text{ and } -\{L_n''(m_n)\}^{-1} = \frac{1}{a_n} + \frac{1}{b_n}. \quad (8.7)$$

In summary, the posterior distribution for ρ can be approximated by a normal distribution, $N(\ln(a_n/b_n), 1/a_n + 1/b_n)$. In the case of a vague prior ($a_0 = b_0 = 0$), we get:

$$m_n = \ln \frac{\hat{\theta}}{1 - \hat{\theta}}, \quad \sigma_n^2 = \frac{1}{n\hat{\theta}(1 - \hat{\theta})} \text{ with } \hat{\theta} = x/n.$$

That is, the posterior for ρ given $X = x$ can be approximated by a normal

---

2 See Gradshteyn and Ryzhik (2007: 943) for integral representations and series expansions of this function.

distribution $N(m_n, \sigma_n^2)$. Note again the duality of this result with the one obtained, by the central limit theorem, for the asymptotic distribution of $\ln \frac{X/n}{1-X/n}$ given θ. In fact, we know that for $X \sim Bi(n, \theta)$, the distribution of $\ln \frac{X/n}{1-X/n}$ given θ is well approximated, for large n, by an $N\left(\ln\left(\frac{\theta}{1-\theta}\right), \frac{1}{n\theta(1-\theta)}\right)$ distribution.

∎

8.1.2 *The Classical Laplace Method*

Tierney and Kadane (1986) proposed an analytic approach to evaluate expressions of the form

$$E[g(\theta) \mid x] = \int g(\theta)h(\theta \mid x)\,d\theta, \qquad (8.8)$$

using the Laplace method to approximate integrals. This method consists, essentially, of the following: Assume that ψ is a regular function of a k-dimensional parameter θ and that $-\psi$ has a maximum in $\hat{\theta}$. The Laplace method approximates integrals of the form

$$I = \int f(\theta) \exp(-n\psi(\theta))d\theta, \qquad (8.9)$$

by a series expansion of ψ around $\hat{\theta}$. In general, an expansion up to second order suffices. This is what is used in the following argument.

- Consider first the case $k = 1$.

  Expanding $\psi(\theta)$ around $\hat{\theta}$ up to second order and substituting it in $\exp(-n\psi(\theta))$, we get

  $$\exp(-n\psi(\theta)) \approx \exp\left(-n\psi(\hat{\theta}) - \frac{n(\theta - \hat{\theta})^2}{2}\psi''(\hat{\theta})\right),$$

  using $\psi'(\hat{\theta}) = 0$.

  Note that the exponential function is proportional to the density function of a normal distribution with mean $\hat{\theta}$ and variance $(n\psi''(\hat{\theta}))^{-1}$, and therefore

  $$\int_{-\infty}^{+\infty} \exp\left(-\frac{n\psi''(\hat{\theta})}{2}(\theta - \hat{\theta})^2\right) = \left(2\pi(n\psi''(\hat{\theta}))^{-1}\right)^{\frac{1}{2}}.$$

  Thus the integral I in (8.9) can be approximated by

  $$I \approx \hat{I}\{1 + O(n^{-1})\}, \qquad (8.10)$$

where

$$\hat{I} = \sqrt{2\pi} n^{-\frac{1}{2}} \hat{\sigma} f(\hat{\theta}) \exp(-n\psi(\hat{\theta}))$$

and $\hat{\sigma} = [\psi''(\hat{\theta})]^{-1/2}$.

- In the k-dimensional case a similar argument leads to $\hat{I}$ of the form,

$$\hat{I} = (2\pi)^{\frac{k}{2}} n^{-\frac{k}{2}} \det(\hat{\Sigma})^{\frac{1}{2}} f(\hat{\theta}) \exp(-n\psi(\hat{\theta})),$$

where $\hat{\Sigma}^{-1} = \nabla^2 \psi(\hat{\theta})$ is the Hessian matrix of ψ in $\hat{\theta}$.

Of course, higher-order expansions of f and ψ would obtain better approximations, for example:

$$\int f(\theta) e^{-n\psi(\theta)} d\theta = \sqrt{(2\pi)} \sigma e^{-n\hat{\psi}} \left\{ \hat{f} + \frac{1}{2n} \left[\sigma^2 \hat{f}'' - \sigma^4 \hat{f}' \hat{\psi}''' + \right. \right.$$

$$\left. \left. + \frac{5}{12} \hat{f}(\hat{\psi}''')^2 \sigma^6 - \frac{1}{4} \hat{f} \hat{\psi}^{(4)} \sigma^4 \right] \right\} + O(n^{-2}), \quad (8.11)$$

where $\hat{f}, \hat{\psi}$, etc., are the respective functions evaluated in $\hat{\theta}$, which is, as already mentioned, a value where the maximum of $-\psi(\theta)$ is achieved and $\sigma^2 = [\psi''(\hat{\theta})]^{-1}$.

Assume, then, that one wants to evaluate the posterior expected value of some function $g(\theta)$ of the parameters. By (8.8) we see that $E[g(\theta) \mid x]$ can be obtained as a ratio of two integrals, that is,

$$E[g(\theta) \mid x] = \frac{\int g(\theta) f(x \mid \theta) h(\theta) d\theta}{\int f(x \mid \theta) h(\theta) d\theta}. \quad (8.12)$$

The basic idea is to apply separate Laplace approximations to the numerator and denominator integrals and consider the ratio of these approximations. Tierney and Kadane (1986) obtain the following two corresponding approximations for $E[g(\theta) \mid x]$.

- Use the Laplace approximation for $\exp(-n\psi(\theta)) = f(x \mid \theta) h(\theta)$, in numerator and denominator, with $f(\theta) = g(\theta)$ in the numerator and $f(\theta) = 1$ in the denominator of (8.12) to get

$$E[g(\theta) \mid x] = g(\hat{\theta})[1 + O(n^{-1})]. \quad (8.13)$$

Note that this corresponds to approximating $E[g(\theta) \mid x]$ by the mode $g(\hat{\theta})$, where $\hat{\theta}$ is the posterior mode, since $\hat{\theta}$ was defined as the point of maximum of $-\psi(\theta)$.

- Assuming that $g(\theta)$ is positive almost everywhere and, to simplify, that θ is a real-valued parameter, we get

$$E[g(\theta) \mid x] = (\sigma^\star/\hat{\sigma})\exp\{-n[\psi^\star(\theta^\star) - \psi(\hat{\theta})]\}(1 + O(n^{-2})).$$

To arrive at this approximation, consider

$$E[g(\theta) \mid x] = \frac{\int \exp\{-n\psi^\star(\theta)\}d\theta}{\int \exp\{-n\psi(\theta)\}d\theta}, \qquad (8.14)$$

where

$$-n\psi(\theta) = \ln h(\theta) + \ln f(x \mid \theta),$$
$$-n\psi^\star(\theta) = \ln g(\theta) + \ln h(\theta) + \ln f(x \mid \theta). \qquad (8.15)$$

Define $\hat{\theta}$, $\theta^\star$ and $\hat{\sigma}$, $\sigma^\star$ such that

$$-\psi(\hat{\theta}) = \sup_{\theta}\{-\psi(\theta)\}, \quad \hat{\sigma} = [\psi''(\theta)]^{-1/2}|_{\theta=\hat{\theta}},$$
$$-\psi^\star(\theta^\star) = \sup_{\theta}\{-\psi^\star(\theta)\}, \quad \sigma^\star = [\psi^{\star''}(\theta)]^{-1/2}|_{\theta=\theta^\star}. \qquad (8.16)$$

Assuming that $\psi(\cdot)$, $\psi^\star(\cdot)$ are sufficiently regular functions, the Laplace approximations for the numerator and denominator integrals in (8.14) (using in both cases $f(\theta) = 1$) are, respectively,

$$\sqrt{2\pi}\sigma^\star n^{-1/2}\exp\{-n\psi^\star(\theta^\star)\} \text{ and } \sqrt{2\pi}\hat{\sigma}n^{-1/2}\exp\{-n\psi(\hat{\theta})\}.$$

From there we get the following approximation for $E[g(\theta) \mid x]$,

$$E[g(\theta) \mid x] \approx (\sigma^\star/\hat{\sigma})\exp\{-n[\psi^\star(\theta^\star) - \psi(\hat{\theta})]\}. \qquad (8.17)$$

The approximation errors for the two integrals are of order n^{-1}. However, the relevant terms of the two errors are identical and therefore cancel out in the ratio. Therefore the final approximation has a relative error of order n^{-2}.

To arrive at the previous approximation, we imposed a quite restrictive condition, namely that g be positive almost everywhere. One can proceed in various ways for approximations with real-valued function g in more general problems. Tierney et al (1989) suggest to start with an approximation of the moment-generating function of $g(\theta)$ ($E[\exp\{sg(\theta)\}]$), using Laplace approximation for positive functions, and then from there to obtain an approximation of the expected value of $g(\theta)$ as the derivative of the logarithm of the moment generating function in $s = 0$. The error for this approximation is of order $O(n^{-2})$.

Another approach, proposed by Tierney et al (1989), is to rewrite the integrands in (8.12) such that the expectation $E[g(\theta) \mid x]$ can be written as

$$E[g(\theta) \mid x] = \frac{\int f_N(\theta) \exp\{-n\psi_N(\theta)\} d\theta}{\int f_D(\theta) \exp\{-n\psi_D(\theta)\} d\theta}, \qquad (8.18)$$

with appropriate f_N, f_D, ψ_N, and ψ_D,[3] and then use the Laplace approximation (8.11) for both integrals.

Example 8.2 *Getting back to the first example, if one wishes to estimate $g(\theta) = \rho = \ln \frac{\theta}{1-\theta}$, one could use a Laplace approximation. Since $g(\theta)$ can take negative values, we either use the first approximation that corresponds to estimating the mean by the mode, obtaining*

$$E(\rho \mid x) = \ln \frac{a_n - 1}{b_n - 1},$$

or we use one of the alternative approaches proposed by Tierney et al (1989).

Using the approach in (8.18) with $\psi_N = \psi_D = \psi$, that is, $-n\psi = \ln h(\theta) + \ln f(x \mid \theta)$; $f_N(\theta) = g(\theta)$; $f_D(\theta) = 1$, we get

$$E(\rho \mid x) = \ln \frac{a_n - 1}{b_n - 1} + \frac{1}{2n} \frac{(a_n - b_n)}{(a_n - 1)(b_n - 1)}$$
$$- \frac{1}{n^2} \frac{(a_n - 1)(b_n - 1)}{(a_n + b_n - 2)} [(a_n - 1)^2 - (b_n - 1)^2]. \qquad (8.19)$$

Compare this result, for specific values of a_n and b_n, with the exact value.

Tanner (1996) suggests obtaining an approximation of the mean of ρ based on the transformation

$$\lambda = \frac{1}{2} \ln \frac{b_n \theta}{a_n(1 - \theta)}.$$

It is easily seen that the distribution of λ is the distribution of Fisher's z with probability density function

$$h(\lambda) \propto \frac{e^{2a_n\lambda}}{(2b_n + 2a_n e^{2\lambda})^{(a_n+b_n)}},$$

with approximate mean

$$\frac{1}{2} \ln \left[\frac{1 - (2a_n)^{-1}}{1 - (2b_n)^{-1}} \right].$$

---

[3] For example, if one were to use $\psi_N = \psi_D$; $f_N(\theta) = g(\theta)$; $f_D(\theta) = 1$ then (8.18) would reduce to (8.13) only. See Tierney et al (1989) or Robert (1994) for more details.

Thus we obtain as approximate posterior mean for ρ,

$$\ln \frac{a_n - 0.5}{b_n - 0.5},$$

which is more precise than the previous estimates.   ∎

These ideas are easily extended to the multiparameter case, with immediate application to the evaluation of marginal posterior distributions, posterior moments, and predictive densities.

Assume $\theta \in \Theta = R^k$ and that we wish to find the marginal posterior distribution for θ_1. Partition the parameter vector as $\theta = (\theta_1, \theta_{-(1)})$ where $\theta_{-(1)} = (\theta_2, ..., \theta_k) \in \Theta_{-(1)}$. The marginal posterior distribution for θ_1 can be written as the ratio of two integrals:

$$h_1(\theta_1 \mid x) = \int_{\Theta_{-(1)}} h(\theta_1, \theta_{-(1)} \mid x) d\theta_{-(1)} \tag{8.20}$$

$$= \frac{\int_{\Theta_{-(1)}} h(\theta_1, \theta_{-(1)}) f(x \mid \theta_1, \theta_{-(1)}) d\theta_{-(1)}}{\int_{\Theta} h(\theta) f(x \mid \theta) d\theta}. \tag{8.21}$$

Applying Laplace approximation to the numerator and denominator integrals in (8.20), we obtain the approximation

$$h_1(\theta_1 \mid x) \approx \left(\frac{\det(\hat{\Sigma}^*(\theta_1))}{2\pi n \det(\hat{\Sigma})} \right)^{1/2} \frac{h(\theta_1, \hat{\theta}_{-(1)}) f(x \mid \theta_1, \hat{\theta}_{-(1)})}{h(\hat{\theta}) f(x \mid \hat{\theta})}, \tag{8.22}$$

where $\hat{\theta}$ maximizes $h(\theta) f(x \mid \theta)$, and $\hat{\Sigma}$ is the negative inverse of the corresponding Hessian matrix evaluated in $\hat{\theta}$, $\hat{\theta}_{-(1)}$ maximizes $h(\theta_1, \theta_{-(1)}) f(x \mid \theta_1, \theta_{-(1)})$ for fixed θ_1, and $\hat{\Sigma}^*(\theta_1)$ is the negative inverse of the corresponding Hessian matrix evaluated in $\hat{\theta}_{-(1)}$.

In Section 8.3 we will see how this result becomes useful in the INLA approach proposed by Rue and collaborators.

Using similar arguments, one can further show that (8.17) remains valid when $\theta \in R^k$ with

$$\hat{\sigma} = |\nabla^2 \psi(\hat{\theta})|^{-1/2} \quad \text{and} \quad \sigma^\star = |\nabla^2 \psi^\star(\theta^\star)|^{-1/2},$$

where

$$[\nabla^2 \psi(\theta)]_{ij} = \frac{\partial^2 \psi(\theta)}{\partial \theta_i \partial \theta_j} \quad \text{and} \quad [\nabla^2 \psi^\star(\theta)]_{ij} = \frac{\partial^2 \psi^\star(\theta)}{\partial \theta_i \partial \theta_j}.$$

For more discussion of this method, see the references cited in the book by Paulino et al (2018). Despite being a powerful technique, the approach has some limitations. In the multivariate case the application can become difficult and impractical, in particular when the integrands are multimodal and/or the derivatives are difficult to obtain. In many problems, even with moderate dimension parameter vectors, it is convenient to consider reparametrizations for better approximations.

8.2 Latent Gaussian Models (LGM)

The class of models known as LGMs can be represented by a hierarchical three-level structure. The first level is the top-level sampling model,

$$x \mid \theta, \psi \sim f(x \mid \theta, \psi) - \Pi_{i=1}^{n} f(x_i \mid \theta, \psi), \tag{8.23}$$

The second level assumes that the parameter vector θ follows a Gaussian Markov random field (GMRF), with respect to an undirected graph $\mathcal{G} = (\mathcal{V} = \{1, ..., n\}, \mathcal{E})$ (Rue and Held, 2005), that is

$$\theta \mid \psi \sim N(0, \Sigma(\psi))$$
$$\theta_l \perp \theta_m \mid \theta_{-(lm)}, \qquad \forall \{l, m\} \notin \mathcal{E} \tag{8.24}$$

where $\theta_{-(lm)}$ is the vector θ without the components θ_l and θ_m, implying that θ_l and θ_m are conditionally independent if they do not share an edge. The third level specifies a prior distribution $h(\psi)$ for unknown hyperparameters ψ, including hyperparameters in the covariance matrix of θ and in the sampling model (8.23).

Many problems allow partitioning the hyperparameter vector ψ into $\psi = (\psi_1, \psi_2)$ such that the LGM can be stated as

$$\begin{aligned} x \mid \theta, \psi &\sim f(x \mid \theta, \psi) = \Pi_{i=1}^{n} f(x_i \mid \theta_i, \psi_2) & \text{(sampling model for } x\text{)} \\ \theta \mid \psi &\sim N(0, \Sigma(\psi_1)) & \text{(GMRF prior for } \theta\text{)} \\ \psi &\sim h(\psi) & \text{(hyperprior,)} \end{aligned}$$

The notation θ_i in the sampling model indicates that x_i only depends on one or a few components of the latent field, e.g., θ_i. Most components of θ will not be observed. Also ψ_1 is a vector of hyperparameters for the covariance matrix and ψ_2 are, for example, dispersion parameters. In such models, the vector θ could be very high dimensional, in contrast to ψ which usually is low dimensional $(1 - 5)$.

Example 8.3 *In a longitudinal study, n patients with the same disease were assigned to two different treatments. Clinical evaluations were recorded at three different times after treatment. The aim of the study was to evaluate whether the disease developed differently between the two groups, whether*

*this depends on age, duration of the disease before treatment, or on an-
other time-dependent covariate that was recorded at the same three times
as the clinical evaluations of the disease.*

A Bayesian analysis of this regression problem with repeat measurements is easily implemented as an LGM. Let X_{jk} denote the result of the
clinical evaluation of patient j (with $j = 1, ..., n$) at time k (with $k = 1, 2, 3$).
Let $z_j = (z_{1,j}, z_{2,j}, z_{3,j})$ denote the covariate vector of treatment, age, and
duration of the disease, respectively, for patient j, and let z_{jk} denote the
time-dependent covariate.

We assume the following model for X_{jk}:

- $X_{jk} \sim N(\mu_{jk}, \sigma^2)$, independent conditional on the parameters
- $\mu_{jk} = \beta_0 + \beta_1 z_{1,j} + \beta_2 z_{2,j} + \beta_3 z_{3,j} + \beta_4 z_{jk} + a_j + b_{jk}$
- $a_j \stackrel{iid}{\sim} N(0, \sigma_a^2)$, $b_{jk} \stackrel{iid}{\sim} N(0, \sigma_b^2)$, where $a = (a_j, j = 1, ..., n)$ and $b = (b_{jk}, j = 1, ..., n, k = 1, 2, 3)$ are random effects at the level of patients and at the level of repeat measurements within a patient (see Section 9.2.1 on including b_{jk}). The random effects are introduced to induce de-pendence that arises from the longitudinal nature of the data;
- $\beta = (\beta_1, \beta_2, \beta_3, \beta_4)$, $\beta_0, \beta_i, i = 1, ..., 4 \stackrel{iid}{\sim} N(0, \sigma_\beta^2)$;
- Let $\tau = 1/\sigma^2$, $\tau_a = 1/\sigma_a^2$, $\tau_b = 1/\sigma_b^2$, and $\tau_\beta = 1/\sigma_\beta^2$ denote the preci-sions. We assume $\tau \sim Ga(c, d)$ and $\tau_x \sim Ga(c_x, d_x)$ for $x = a, b, \beta$.

The model can be written as a three-level hierarchical model. Let $N(x \mid m, s^2)$ indicate an $N(m, s^2)$ density for the random variable X.

1. $X \mid z, \theta, \psi \sim f(x \mid z, \theta, \psi) = \Pi_{j,k} N(x_{jk} \mid \mu_{jk}, 1/\psi_2)$;
2. $\theta = (\beta_0, \beta, a, b)$ with $\theta \sim N(0, \Sigma(\psi_1))$, *i.e.* $\theta \mid \psi \sim GMRF(\psi_1)$;
3. $\psi = (\psi_1, \psi_2)$ with $\psi_1 = (\tau_\beta, \tau_a, \tau_b)$, *assuming that the parameters are a priori independent and* $\psi_2 = \tau$.

■

Note that the assumed prior independence of the fixed effects parameters
is not needed. One of the attractive properties of the GMRF (see Rue and
Held, 2005) is that the precision matrix $Q = \Sigma^{-1}$ is sparse. In fact, one can
show

$$\theta_l \perp \theta_m \mid \theta_{-(lm)} \Leftrightarrow Q_{lm} = 0,$$

where Q_{lm} is the lm element of the precision matrix Q. This has computational advantages when using numerical methods that are specifically designed for sparse matrices.

An alternative way to state the LGM, and which is central to the INLA approach, is based on recognizing the model as a special case of a regression model with additive structure (Fahrmeir and Tutz, 2001). In these models, the dependent variable (X_i) is assumed to have an exponential family distribution with mean μ_i that is linked to a predictor η_i with additive structure (see the following) via a link function $g(\mu_i) = \eta_i$, and the sampling model can still additionally be controlled by hyperparameters ψ_2. The general form of the predictor is

$$\eta_i = \beta_0 + \sum_{j=1}^{n_\beta} \beta_j z_{ji} + \sum_{k=1}^{n_f} w_{ki} f^{(k)}(u_{ki}) + \epsilon_i, \qquad (8.25)$$

where β_0 is an intercept, $\beta = (\beta_1, ..., \beta_{n_\beta})$ is a vector of linear coefficients for the covariates z, and the functions $(f^{(1)}, ..., f^{(n_f)})$ of covariates u can represent non linear effects of continuous covariates, seasonal effects, and random effects of various natures. These functions can have associated weights $(\{w_{ki}\})$, fixed and known for each observation. Random effects without specific structure are included as ϵ_i.

A latent Gaussian model is then obtained by assuming for $\theta = \{\beta_0, \{\beta_j\}, \{f^{(k)}(u_{ki})\}, \{\eta_i\}\}$ a multivariate normal prior with precision matrix $Q(\psi_1)$, that is, a GMRF. This parametrization of θ, including η_i, is useful since it allows one to link each observation with one component of the random field.

The definition of the latent Gaussian model is completed with the specification of a final hyperprior for the model hyperparameters (ψ_1, ψ_2).

8.3 Integrated Nested Laplace Approximation

In LGMs, the posterior distribution of interest is

$$h(\theta, \psi \mid x) \propto h(\theta \mid \psi) h(\psi) \Pi_i f(x_i \mid \theta_i, \psi)$$

$$\propto h(\psi) |Q(\psi)|^{n/2} \exp\left(-\frac{1}{2} \theta^T Q(\psi) \theta + \sum_i \ln(f(x_i \mid \theta_i, \psi))\right).$$

The principal aim of INLA is to obtain an analytic expression for the marginal posterior distributions of the latent parameters and the hyperparameters in the Gaussian model.

The marginal distributions can be written as:

$$h(\theta_i \mid x) = \int h(\theta, \psi \mid x) d\psi = \int h(\psi \mid x) h(\theta_i \mid \psi, x) d\psi$$

$$h(\psi_k \mid x) = \int h(\psi \mid x) d\psi_{-(k)},$$

where $\psi_{-(k)}$ denotes the vector ψ without the component ψ_k. The evaluation of these distributions requires first estimates of $h(\psi \mid x)$ and $h(\theta_i \mid \psi, x)$ to then obtain

$$\tilde{h}(\theta_i \mid x) = \int \tilde{h}(\psi \mid x)\tilde{h}(\theta_i \mid \psi, x)d\psi \qquad (8.26)$$

$$\tilde{h}(\psi_k \mid x) = \int \tilde{h}(\psi \mid x)d\psi_{-(k)}, \qquad (8.27)$$

where $\tilde{h}(. \mid .)$ is an approximation of the respective density. The approximation of marginal posterior distributions (8.26) and (8.27) is then implemented in three steps: an approximation for $h(\theta_i \mid \psi, x)$; an approximation for $h(\psi \mid x)$; and finally numerical integration. The name INLA comes from exactly these steps. Note that

$$h(\psi \mid x) = \frac{h(\theta, \psi \mid x)}{h(\theta \mid \psi, x)} \propto \frac{h(\psi)h(\theta \mid \psi)f(x \mid \theta, \psi)}{h(\theta \mid \psi, x)}.$$

If $\tilde{h}(\theta \mid \psi, x)$ were a Gaussian approximation for $h(\theta \mid \psi, x)$ with mode $\widehat{\theta}(\psi)$, then an approximation for $h(\psi \mid x)$ can be obtained by

$$\tilde{h}(\psi \mid x) \propto \frac{h(\psi)h(\theta \mid \psi)f(x \mid \theta, \psi)}{\tilde{h}(\theta \mid \psi, x)}\bigg|_{\theta=\widehat{\theta}(\psi)},$$

which is the Laplace method as proposed by Tierney and Kadane (1986) for the approximation of the marginal posterior (proceeding similar to the argument in (8.22)). Regarding the approximation $\tilde{h}(\theta \mid \psi, x)$, using

$$h(\theta \mid \psi, x) \propto \exp\left\{-\frac{1}{2}\theta^T Q\theta - \sum_i \ln(f(x_i \mid \theta_i, \psi))\right\},$$

one can obtain a normal approximation for $h(\theta \mid \psi, x)$ by an iterative process, considering a second-order Taylor series expansion of $\ln(f(x_i \mid \theta_i, \psi)) = g_i(\theta_i \mid \psi)$ around the ith component $\mu_i^{(0)}(\psi)$ of an initial value for the mean vector $\mu^{(0)}(\psi)$. See Rue et al (2009) for details.

Regarding the approximation of $h(\theta_i \mid \psi, x)$ in (8.26), there are several possible approaches:

1. Directly use a normal approximation for $h(\theta \mid \psi, x)$ and a Cholesky decomposition for the precision matrix $Q(\psi_1)$, that is, $Q(\psi_1) = L(\psi_1)L^T(\psi_1)$, where $L(\psi_1)$ is a lower triangular matrix, to obtain marginal variances. In this way, the only additional work is to calculate the marginal variances. However, this normal approximation for $h(\theta_i \mid \psi, x)$ is generally not very good.

2. Let θ_{-i} denote θ without θ_i; then

$$h(\theta_i \mid \psi, x) = \frac{h(\theta_i, \theta_{-i} \mid \psi, x)}{h(\theta_{-i} \mid \theta_i, \psi, x)} \propto \frac{h(\psi)h(\theta \mid \psi)f(x \mid \theta, \psi)}{h(\theta_{-i} \mid \theta_i, \psi, x)}.$$

Using a normal approximation for $h(\theta_{-i} \mid \theta_i, \psi, x)$, an estimate for $h(\theta_i \mid \psi, x)$ is then

$$\tilde{h}(\theta_i \mid \psi, x) \propto \left. \frac{h(\psi)h(\theta \mid \psi)f(x \mid \theta, \psi)}{\tilde{h}(\theta_{-i} \mid \theta_i, \psi, x)} \right|_{\theta_{-i} = \widehat{\theta_{-i}}(\theta_i, \psi)}, \tag{8.28}$$

where $\widehat{\theta_{-i}}(\theta_i, \psi)$ is the mode of $\tilde{h}(\theta_{-i} \mid \theta_i, \psi, x)$. This approach gives a better approximation than the earlier one, but the complication is that it needs re-calculation for each θ and ψ, since the precision matrix depends on θ_i and ψ.

3. To overcome this problem, Rue et al (2009) suggested several modifications that lead to alternative Laplace approaches which they call complete Laplace approximation and simplified Laplace approximation.

   Under the complete approach, one avoids the optimization, using instead of the mode the conditional mean $E(\theta_{-i} \mid \theta_i)$ based on a normal approximation $\tilde{h}(\theta \mid \psi, x)$. Besides this, only the θ_j which are "close" are used, using the intuition that only those should impact the marginal posterior distribution for θ_i. Such a region of interest around θ_i is constructed by considering θ_j to be close to θ_i if $|a_{ij}(\psi)| > 0.001$, with a_{ij} defined by

$$\frac{E(\theta_j \mid \theta_i) - \mu_j(\psi)}{\sigma_j(\psi)} = a_{ij}(\psi)\frac{\theta_i - \mu_i(\psi)}{\sigma_i(\psi)},$$

where $\mu_i, \sigma_i, \mu_j, \sigma_j$, are based on the Gaussian approximation $\tilde{h}(\theta \mid \psi, x)$.

   Finally, the simplified approach is based on a third-order Taylor series expansion of the log numerator and denominator in (8.28), substituting again for θ_{-i} the conditional expectation (instead of the mode). In the numerator, the third-order terms allow correcting the approximation with respect to asymmetry. Details of this approach are explained by Rue et al (2009).

Naturally, the computational details in the implementation of these methods are non-trivial. An extensive description of some of these details are given by Rue et al (2009) and Blangiardo et al (2013). An efficient implementation of this approach is available in the public domain package R-INLA (see www.r-inla.org).

8.4 Variational Bayesian Inference

8.4.1 Posterior Approximation

Variational Bayesian inference (VB) (Jordan et al, 1999) implements approximate posterior inference by approximating the joint posterior distribution $h(\theta \mid x)$ within a predefined class of distributions $\mathcal{D}$ (variational family).

The most widely used variational family $\mathcal{D}$ is the class of independent distributions, $\mathcal{D} = \{q : q(\theta) = \Pi_j q_j(\theta_j)\}$, known as the mean-field variational family. Here, independence is across the elements or subvectors of $\theta = (\theta_1, \ldots, \theta_p)$. We briefly review the setup of VB, in particular mean-field VB. For a more extensive recent review see, e.g., Blei et al (2017).

The criterion to select the best approximation within a variational family $\mathcal{D}$ is Kullback–Leibler (KL) divergence. That is,

$$q^* = \arg\min_{q \in \mathcal{D}} KL\{q(\theta)\|h(\theta \mid x)\}. \qquad (8.29)$$

Recall that KL is defined as $KL(q(\theta)\|h(\theta \mid y)) = E_q \ln\{q(\theta)/h(\theta \mid y)\}$, with the expectation being with respect to $q(\theta)$. Using Bayes theorem to substitute $h(\theta \mid x)$ and noting that $E_q p(x) = p(x)$, we find

$$KL\{q(\theta)\|h(\theta \mid x)\} = E_q\{\ln(q(\theta)\} - E_q\{\ln[f(x \mid \theta)h(\theta)]\} + \ln p(x) \qquad (8.30)$$
$$= E_q\{\ln[q(\theta)/h(\theta)]\} - E_q\{\ln[f(x \mid \theta)]\} + \ln p(x).$$

All expectations are with respect to $q(\theta)$. Therefore, (8.29) is equivalent to maximizing

$$q^* = \arg\max_q \underbrace{\left\{ E_q[\ln f(x \mid \theta)] - KL(q(\theta)\|h(\theta)) \right\}}_{ELBO}. \qquad (8.31)$$

The criterion is known as evidence lower bound (ELBO). This is because (8.30) can be stated as

$$KL\{q(\theta)\|h(\theta \mid x)\} = KL\{(q(\theta)\|h(\theta)\} - E_q[\ln f(x \mid \theta)] + E_q[\ln p(x)]$$
$$= \ln p(x) - \text{ELBO} \geq 0,$$

and therefore $\ln p(x) \geq \text{ELBO}$ (and "evidence" is another name for the marginal distribution $p(x)$). Equation (8.31) also reveals the nature of VB as another form of balancing maximization of the (log-) likelihood and shrinkage toward the prior.

8.4.2 Coordinate Ascent Algorithm

An easy algorithm to find q^* is an iterative conditional maximization known as coordinate ascent variational inference (CAVI). By assumption, $q \in \mathcal{D}$ factors as $q(\theta) = \Pi_{j=1}^{p} q_j(\theta_j)$. CAVI is defined as iterative optimization of q_j, keeping all other q_k, $k \neq j$, at their currently imputed choice. The algorithm repeatedly cycles over $j = 1, \ldots, p$, until q^* remains unchanged for an entire cycle. As a greedy optimization, the algorithm delivers a local optimum only. Most importantly, the optimization of q_j in each step is easy. Let $h(\theta_j \mid \theta_{-j}, x)$ denote the complete conditional posterior distribution of θ_j given the remaining parameters, and let $E_{-j}(\cdot)$ denote an expectation over θ_{-j} with respect to $q_{-j}(\theta_{-j}) = \Pi_{k \neq j} q_k(\theta_k)$, that is, an expectation with respect to the current solution for q_k, $k \neq j$. Then the optimal choice for q_j at each step of the CAVI is given by

$$q_j^*(\theta_j) \propto \exp\{E_{-j} \ln h(\theta_j \mid \theta_{-j}, x)\}. \qquad (8.32)$$

Blei et al (2017) give an elegant and easy argument for this result. The optimization is with respect to $KL\{q(\theta) \| h(\theta \mid y)\}$ in (8.29). Using $h(\theta \mid x) = h(\theta_j \mid \theta_{-j}, x) \, h(\theta_{-j} \mid x)$ and the assumed factorization of $q(\theta)$ we have

$$E\{\ln h(\theta \mid x)\} = E_j\{E_{-j} \ln h(\theta_j \mid \theta_{-j}, x)\} + E_{-j} \ln h(\theta_{-j} \mid x).$$

Dropping terms that do not depend on q_j, we are left with optimizing q_j with respect to

$$\text{ELBO}(q_j) \equiv E_j\{E_{-j} \ln h(\theta_j \mid \theta_{-j}, x)\} - E_j \ln q_j(\theta_j).$$

Here, E_{-j} is defined as before, and E_j is an expectation with respect to q_j. Note that $\text{ELBO}(q_j) = -KL\{q_j(\theta_j) \| q_j^*(\theta_j)\}$ for the q_j^* from (8.32). As such, it is maximized for $q_j = q_j^*$. That is all. In summary, the algorithm is as shown in Algorithm 5.

Algorithm 5 Coordinate Ascent Algorithm (CAVI)

Input: posterior $h(\theta \mid x)$; variational family $\mathcal{D} = \{q : q(\theta) = \Pi_j q_j(\theta_j)\}$; initial solution $q^* \in \mathcal{D}$
Output: variational approximation $q^*(\theta) = \Pi \, q_j^*(\theta_j)$

1: **repeat**
2:     **for** $j = 1$ to p **do**
3:         $q_j^* \propto \exp\{E_{-j} \ln h(\theta_j \mid \theta_{-j}, x)\}$.
4:     **end for**
5: **until** no change

The optimization becomes particularly easy when $h(\theta_j \mid \theta_{-j}, x)\}$ is an exponential family model. In that case,

$$h(\theta_j \mid \theta_{-j}, x) \propto a(\theta_j) \exp(\eta_j' t(\theta_j)), \tag{8.33}$$

with $\eta_j = \eta_j(\theta_{-j}, x)$ being some function of (θ_{-j}, x). If we use a variational family $\mathcal{D}$ with q_j in the same exponential family as (8.33), then line 3 in the algorithm greatly simplifies. First, taking the expectation E_{-j} requires only $E_{-j}[\eta_j(\theta_{-j}, x)]$. Second, and most important, recording q_j^* we only need to record the updated hyperparameters η_j. Since the (unconstrained) solution q^* is in $\mathcal{D}$, the use of the assumed family $\mathcal{D}$ constitutes no restriction.

This situation arises quite commonly in conditionally conjugate models, including in particular hierarchical models with conditionally conjugate model choices. The simplification is best appreciated in an example. We outline the steps for an example from Gelfand et al (1990), which also appears as the `rats` example in the OpenBUGS manual, `www.openbugs.net/w/Examples`.

Example 8.4 *Gelfand et al (1990) discuss this example of a hierarchical normal/normal model. The data are weights for n = 30 young rats, measured weekly for J = 5 weeks. The data are given in table 3 of Gelfand et al (1990). Let y_{ij} denote the recorded weight for rat i in week j. Let x_j denote the measurement times in days. We assume a normal sampling model,*

$$y_{ij} \mid \alpha_i, \beta_i, \sigma_y \sim N(\mu_{ij}, \tau_y) \text{ with } \mu_{ij} = \mu + \alpha_i + \beta_i x_j,$$

with a normal prior for animal-specific growth curve parameters

$$\alpha_i \sim N(\mu_\alpha, \tau_\alpha) \text{ and } \beta_i \sim N(\mu_\beta, \tau_\beta),$$

where the second parameter of the normal distribution is the precision (using the parametrization from WinBUGS). The model is completed with a hyperprior

$$\tau_y \sim Ga(\gamma_y, \delta_y), \tau_\alpha \sim Ga(\gamma_\alpha, \delta_\alpha), \tau_\beta \sim Ga(\gamma_\beta, \delta_\beta) \text{ and } p(\mu_\alpha) = p(\mu_\beta) = c,$$

with fixed hyperparameters $(\gamma_y, \delta_y, \gamma_\alpha, \delta_\alpha, \gamma_\beta, \delta_\beta)$, and assuming independence across parameters in the hyperprior.

Let $\omega = (\mu_\alpha, \mu_\beta, \tau_y, \tau_\alpha, \tau_\beta, \alpha_i, \beta_i, i = 1, \dots, n)$ denote the complete parameter vector, and let $\theta_i = (\alpha_i, \beta_i)$ denote the animal-specific random effects. In a slight abuse of notation, let $N(x \mid m, P)$ indicate a multivariate normal distribution for the random variable x with mean m and precision matrix P and similarly for $Ga(x \mid c, d)$ (note the use of the precision matrix instead of the covariance matrix as the second parameter in the normal *distribution). We use a variational family $\mathcal{D}$ with variational distributions of the form*

$$q(\omega) = \Pi_i\, N(\theta_i \mid m_i, P_i)\, \Pi_{x=y,\alpha,\beta}\, Ga(\tau_x \mid c_x, d_x)\, \Pi_{x=\alpha,\beta}\, N(\mu_x \mid m_x, P_x).$$

The rationale for this choice will be evident in a moment, when we work out the updates (8.32). As before, let E_{-x} denote an expectation under q with respect to all parameters except for x (where the symbol x here is a placeholder for any of the parameters). Let $h(\omega \mid y)$ denote the joint posterior distribution, and let $h(x \mid \omega_{-x}, y)$ denote the complete conditional posterior for parameter x. For reference, we note the joint posterior. Let $y_i = (y_{ij}, j = 1, \ldots, J)$ denote the repeat measurements for animal i. Let X denote the $(J \times 2)$ design matrix for the linear regression for one animal, let $H = XX'$, and let $\hat{\theta}_i$ denote the least squares fit for the θ_i. Also, let $T = \mathrm{diag}(\tau_\alpha, \tau_\beta)$ and $\mu = (\mu_\alpha, \mu_\beta)$, and let $N = nJ$ denote the total sample size. We have

$$h(\omega \mid y) \propto \Pi_{x=y,\alpha,\beta}\, Ga(\tau_x \mid \gamma_x, \delta_x)\, \Pi_i\, N(y_i \mid X\theta_i, \tau_y I)\, N(\theta_i \mid \mu, T) =$$

$$\Pi_{x=y,\alpha,\beta}\, Ga(\tau_x \mid \gamma_x, \delta_x)\, \tau_y^{\frac{N}{2}-n}\, \Pi_i\, N(\hat{\theta}_i \mid \theta_i, \tau_y H)\, N(\theta_i \mid \mu, T),$$

with $h(\mu_\alpha) = h(\mu_\beta) = c$ being subsumed in the proportionality constant. Following (8.32) we find then the following updating equations by first deriving the complete conditional posterior $h(x \mid \omega_{-x}, y)$ for each parameter and then $E_{-x} \ln h(x \mid \omega_{-x}, y)$, where, again, x is a placeholder for any of the parameters and E_{-x} is an expectation with respect to ω_{-x} under the variational distribution q. Taking the latter expectation, keep in mind the independence under q, which greatly simplifies the evaluation. We start with the update for $q(\theta_i)$. Below we write ω_{-i} as short for $\omega_{-\theta_i}$ and similar for E_{-i}. Note that $h(\theta_i \mid \omega_{-i}, y) = N(\bar{\theta}_i, \bar{V})$, with

$$\bar{V} = T + \tau_y H \text{ and } \bar{\theta}_i = \bar{V}^{-1}(T\mu + \tau_y H\hat{\theta}_i).$$

Therefore, $\ln h(\theta_i \mid \omega_{-i}, y) = c - \frac{1}{2}\theta_i'\bar{V}\theta_i + \theta_i'\bar{V}\bar{\theta}_i$. Let $\bar{\tau}_x = c_x/d_x$ $(x = \alpha, \beta, y)$, $\bar{T} = \mathrm{diag}(\bar{\tau}_\alpha, \bar{\tau}_\beta)$ and $\bar{\mu} = (m_\alpha, m_\beta)$ denote expectations under q_{-i}. Also, let $P_i = E_{-i}\bar{V} = \bar{T} + H\bar{\tau}_i$. Then,

$$E_{-i} \ln h(\theta_i \mid \omega_{-i}, y) = c - \frac{1}{2}\theta_i' P_i \theta_i + \theta_i'\,_{-i}\left\{T\mu + \tau_y H\hat{\theta}_i\right\}$$

$$= c - \frac{1}{2}\theta_i' P_i \theta_i + \theta_i'\,_i P_i^{-1}(\bar{T}\bar{\mu} + \bar{\tau}_y H\hat{\theta}_i) \quad (8.34)$$

and therefore by (8.32), $q^*(\theta_i) = N(m_i, P_i)$ with $m_i = P_i^{-1}(\bar{T}\bar{\mu} + \bar{\tau}_y H\hat{\theta}_i)$ and P_i as above.

Similar simplifications apply for updating $q(\tau_y)$ $q(\tau_\alpha)$, $q(\tau_\beta)$, $q(\mu_\alpha)$, *and* $q(\mu_\beta)$. *In all cases it turns out that the expectation under* q_{-x} *in the equivalent of* (8.34) *is easy. This is no coincidence. Because the complete conditional distributions are exponential families,* $\ln h(x \mid \omega_{-x}, y)$ *always reduces to an expression of the type* $t(x)\eta_x(\omega_{-x})$, *and the expectation of* $\eta_x(\cdot)$ *is usually easy since* q_{-x} *includes independence across all other parameters.* ∎

In Problem 8.6 we consider a finite mixture. VB for mixture models has been generalized to infinite mixture of normal models by several recent papers, including those by Blei and Jordan (2006) and Lin (2013), who also introduce a sequential scheme to accommodate big data.

8.4.3 Automatic Differentiation Variational Inference

Implementing Algorithm 5 requires careful consideration of the target distribution and problem-specific choice of a suitable variational family $\mathcal{D}$. Alternatively, Kucukelbir et al (2017) develop an implementation of variational inference that lends itself to automation. The two key elements of the algorithm are the use of a transformation to map all original parameters to the real line, and the use of mean-field independent normal variational family $\mathcal{D}$, now indexed only by the normal location and scale parameters for the p independent univariate normal distributions, $\eta = (\mu_1, \ldots, \mu_p, \sigma_1, \ldots, \sigma_p)$. One more mapping transforms to a multivariate standard normal distribution, making it possible to evaluate the expectations that appear in the ELBO and using gradient ascent with automatic differentiation to carry out the optimization.

The algorithm is implemented in Stan, a public domain program that implements posterior MCMC using Hamiltonian Monte Carlo. See Section 9.4 for a brief introduction to Stan and Problem 9.6 in the same chapter for an example of using variational inference in STAN.

Problems

8.1 *Normal approximation.* Under a particular genetic model, animals of a given species should be one of four specific phenotypes with probabilities $p_1 = (2 + \theta)/4$, $p_2 = (1 - \theta)/4$, $p_3 = (1 - \theta)/4$ and $p_4 = \theta/4$, respectively. Let $y_1, \ldots, y_4$ denote the number of animals of each phenotype, and $N = y_1 + \ldots + y_4$. Assuming multinomial sampling and a Be(a, b) prior on θ the posterior density $h(\theta \mid y)$ takes the form

$$h(\theta \mid y) \propto (2 + \theta)^{y_1} (1 - \theta)^{y_2 + y_3 + b - 1} \theta^{y_4 + a - 1}, \quad 0 \le \theta \le 1,$$

that is,

$$L(\theta \mid y) \equiv \ln h(\theta \mid y) = C + y_1 \ln(2 + \theta) + (y_2 + y_3 + b - 1) \ln(1 - \theta) +$$
$$+ (y_4 + a - 1) \ln(\theta)$$
$$L'(\theta) = \frac{y_1}{2 + \theta} - \frac{y_2 + y_3 + b - 1}{1 - \theta} + \frac{y_4 + a - 1}{\theta}$$
$$-L''(\theta) - \frac{y_1}{(2 + \theta)^2} + \frac{y_2 + y_3 + b - 1}{(1 - \theta)^2} + \frac{y_4 + a - 1}{\theta^2},$$

where C is the log normalization constant. Answer (a) through (d) below using the following two data sets: $N = 197, y = (125, 18, 20, 34)$ and $N = 20$, $y = (14, 0, 1, 5)$.

a. Find a (truncated) normal approximation, $N(m, V), 0 \le \theta \le 1$, by solving $H' = 0$ to determine m and using $V^{-1} = -H''(m)$. Let $p_1(\theta)$ denote the p.d.f. Let m_1 and V_1 denote posterior mean and variance under the truncated normal approximation (use simulation to find the moments of the truncated normal – note that $m_1 \ne m$, due to the truncation).

b. As an alternative approximation, find a beta distribution, $\mathrm{Be}(a, b)$, by matching mean and variance (obtained as in part (a)). Let $p_2(\theta)$ denote the beta p.d.f. Let $m_2 \,(= m$, by construction) and $V_2 = V$ denote the posterior moments under the beta approximation.

c. Now use p_1 and p_2 as importance sampling densities to carry out importance sampling to evaluate the posterior mean and variance. Let (m_3, V_3) and (m_4, V_4) denote the approximate posterior moments, using importance sampling densities p_1 and p_2, respectively.

d. With p_2 as the importance sampling density, carry out importance sampling to find the normalization constant for $h(\theta \mid y)$. Then use numerical integration on a grid over $0 \le \theta \le 1$ (for example, as a Rieman sum, or using the trapezoidal rule) to evaluate posterior mean and variance. Let (m_0, V_0) denote the estimates.

Make a table to compare (m_j, V_j), $j = 0, 1, \ldots, 4$.

8.2 *LGM.* Refer to Example 8.3. Identify the three levels of the LGM. That is, state the probability models $f(x_i \mid \theta_i, \psi_2)$, $p(\theta \mid \psi)$, and $h(\psi)$.

8.3 *LGM (Rue et al, 2009).* Consider a stochastic volatility model for daily pound–dollar exchange rates, with sampling model

$$y_t \mid \eta_t \sim N(0, \exp(\eta_t)),$$

$t = 1, \ldots, n_d$, log variances $\eta_t = \mu + f_t$, prior

$$f_t \mid f_1, \ldots, f_{t-1}, \phi \sim N(\phi f_{t-1}, 1/\tau),$$

and hyperpriors

$$\tau \sim \text{Ga}(1, 0.1), \quad \mu \sim N(0, 1), \quad \text{and } \phi = 2\frac{e^{\phi'}}{1 + e^{\phi'}} - 1, \quad \text{with } \phi' \sim N(3, 1).$$

Show how the model can be stated as an LGM. Identify the three levels of the LGM. That is, state the probability models $f(x_i \mid \theta_i, \psi_2)$, $p(\theta \mid \psi)$, and $h(\psi)$.

8.4 (Rue et al. 2009). Let $y_i \in \{0, 1\}$ denote indicators for pre-malignant ($y_i = 1$) versus malignant ($y_i = 0$) incidences of cervical cancer, $i = 1, \ldots, n_d$. Let $d_i \in \{1, \ldots, 216\}$ and $a_i \in \{1, \ldots, 15\}$ index geographical region and age group of the ith case. Rue and Held (2005) use a logistic binary regression for $p_i \equiv P(y_i = 1)$,

$$\text{logit}(p_i) = \eta_i = \mu + f^a_{a_i} + f^s_{d_i} + f^u_{d_i}$$

where $f^a = (f^a_1, \ldots, f^a_A)$, $A = 15$, is a smooth effect of age groups, $f^s = (f^s_1, \ldots, f^s_S)$, $S = 216$, is a smooth spatial field of geographic region effects, and $f^u = (f^u_1, \ldots, f^u_S)$ are district-specific random effects. For f^a we assume a second-order random walk model with precision κ_a,

$$f^a \mid \kappa_a \propto (\kappa_a)^{(15-2)/2} e^{-\frac{\kappa_a}{2} \sum_{j=3}^{15} (f^a_j - 2f^a_{j-1} + f^a_{j-2})^2}.$$

For f^s we assume a conditional autoregressive model $f^s \sim \text{CAR}(0, \kappa_s, G)$, where G is a $(S \times S)$ binary adjacency matrix with $G_{st} = 1$ if district s is neighboring district t. Subject to some constraints, the CAR model implies a multivariate normal prior for $f^s \mid \kappa_s \sim N(0, \Sigma(\kappa_s, G))$. This is all that is needed in this problem. The random effects f^u_d are independent $N(0, 1/\kappa_u)$. The model is completed with independent $\text{Ga}(1, 0.01)$ priors for κ_a, κ_s, and κ_u, and $\mu \sim N(0, 0.01)$, with the second parameter of the normal distribution being a precision here (matching the parametrization used in INLA).

Show how the model can be stated as an LGM. Identify θ, ψ, and the three levels of the LGM. That is, state the probability models $f(x_i \mid \theta_i, \psi_2)$, $p(\theta \mid \psi)$, and $h(\psi)$.

8.5 *Variational Bayes.* For Example 8.4 in Section 8.4.2, find the updating equations for $q(\tau_y)$ $q(\tau_\alpha)$, $q(\tau_\beta)$, $q(\mu_\alpha)$, and $q(\mu_\beta)$.

8.6 *Variational Bayes: mixture model.* Consider a mixture of normal model $f(x \mid \theta) = \sum_{k=1}^K \pi_k N(x \mid \mu_k, \sigma^2)$, with $\theta = (\pi, \mu, \sigma^2)$, where $\mu = (\mu_1, \ldots, \mu_K)$ and $\pi = (\pi_1, \ldots, \pi_K)$. Let $\gamma = 1/\sigma^2$. We complete the model with conditionally conjugate priors $h(\mu_k) = N(0, \tau)$, $h(\gamma) = \text{Ga}(a, b)$ and $\pi \sim D_{K-1}(\alpha, \ldots, \alpha)$, with fixed hyperparameters (τ, a, b, α) and prior independence.

a. Find the complete conditional posterior $h(\theta_j \mid \theta_{-j}, x)$ for μ_k, π_k and γ.

b. For the moment, fix $\sigma^2 = 1$ and $\pi = (1/K, \ldots, 1/K)$. Consider the mean-field variation family $\mathcal{D}$ with $q(\mu_k) = N(m_k, s_k)$, $q(c_i = k) = \phi_{ik}$, and derive one iteration of CAVI, that is, find the updating equations for (m_k, s_k)

and ϕ_{kj}.

Hint: See the discussion in Blei et al (2017).

c. Now include γ and π in the parameter vector. Extend $\mathcal{D}$ by defining $q(\gamma) =$ Ga(c, d) and $q(\pi) = $ D$(e_1, \dots, e_K)$. Find the updating equations for c, d, and e.

8.7 In R, load the package MASS which provides the data set galaxies. Scale the data as x = c(scale(galaxies)). Assume a mixture of $K = 5$ normal models, $f(x_i \mid \theta) = \sum_{k=1}^{K} \pi_k N(\mu_k, \sigma^2)$ with $\theta = (\mu, \pi, \sigma^2)$. Complete the model with priors as in the previous problem, using $\tau = a = b = c = d = e = 1$. Use variational inference to generate an approximate Monte Carlo posterior sample, $\Theta = \{\theta^m, \ m = 1, \dots, M\}$ with $\theta^m \sim h(\theta \mid x)$, approximately.

a. At each iteration, evaluate the ELBO. Plot it against the iteration.

b. Use Θ to approximate the posterior predictive distribution

$$\widehat{f}(x) = \frac{1}{M} \sum_m \sum_k \pi_k^m N(\mu_k, (\sigma^m)^2).$$

Plot the data, together with $\widehat{f}$. Add pointwise central 50% credible bounds for $\widehat{f}(x)$.

9

Software

Using computational methods, like those discussed in previous chapters, Bayesian data analysis can be implemented for problems arising from a wide variety of scientific areas. This development has been importantly supported by the generosity of many investigators who have made software implementations of such methods freely available to the scientific community. The software R includes a variety of packages, or sometimes just functions, that can be used for Bayesian inference. Interested readers should consult the page http://cran.r-project.org/web/views/Bayesian.html. One can find there, for example, the package *bayesSurv*, built specifically for Bayesian inference in survival models, for example. Besides these R packages and the four software packages discussed below, there are several other public domain programs for Bayesian inference, including NIMBLE (de Valpine et al, 2017; Rickert, 2018), bayesm (Rossi et al, 2005), and the Bayesian regression software by George Karabatsos (Karabatsos, 2015). Rickert (2018) includes an implementation of inference for Problem 4.4 and 6.5 in NIMBLE.

For this chapter we selected four general-purpose public domain software packages that implement methods based on stochastic simulation. Although they are independent of R, all four can be used through an interface in R. These are OpenBUGS (Thomas et al, 2006), JAGS (Plummer, 2003), Stan (Carpenter et al, 2017), and BayesX (Brezger et al, 2005; Belitz et al, 2013). The chapter includes a brief summary of the principal characteristics of each software and illustrates each in the same example. We also show how to monitor and diagnose convergence of chains using the software packages CODA and BOA. Both are R packages. Finally, we show how the same example can be analyzed using R-INLA (www.r-inla.org).

There are several books that show the use of these software packages, including those by Ntzoufras (2009), Kruschke (2011, 2014), Korner-Nievergelt et al (2015) and Blangiardo and Cameletti (2015). Each of these packages comes with extensive documentation.

9.1 Application Example

Here, we introduce the common example that will be analyzed with the different methods.

Example 9.1 *In a longitudinal study, n patients with the same disease were assigned to two different treatments. A clinical evaluation after the treatment is made at three different time points. The aim of the study is to investigate whether disease progression differs between the two groups and whether it depends on the age of the patient, the duration of the disease prior to treatment, and another longitudinal covariate that is also measured at the same three time points as the clinical evaluation of the disease progression.*

Bayesian inference for regression with repeat measurements can be considered in the context of LGM. In fact, let X_{jk} denote the random variable that represents the clinical evaluation of patient j (with j = 1, ..., n) at time k (with k = 1, 2, 3). Let $z_j = (z_{1,j}, z_{2,j}, z_{3,j})$ denote the vector of covariates including treatment, age, and prior disease duration for patient j, and let z_{jk} denote the time-dependent covariate.

The following model is assumed for X_{jk}:

1. *$X_{jk} \sim N(\mu_{jk}, \sigma^2)$, conditionally independent given the parameters;*
2. *$\mu_{jk} = \beta_0 + \beta_1 z_{1,j} + \beta_2 z_{2,j} + \beta_3 z_{3,j} + \beta_4 z_{jk} + a_j + b_{jk}$;*
3. *$a_j \overset{iid}{\sim} N(0, \sigma_a^2)$, $b_{jk} \overset{iid}{\sim} N(0, \sigma_b^2)$, with $a = (a_j, j = 1, ..., n)$ and $b = (b_{jk}, j = 1, ..., n, k = 1, 2, 3)$ representing random effects at the level of patients and the repeat observations nested within patients, respectively (see Section 9.2.1 on including b_{jk}). The random effects are introduced to represent the dependence structure that arises from the longitudinal nature of the data;*
4. *$\beta = (\beta_1, \beta_2, \beta_3, \beta_4)$, $\beta_0, \beta_i, i = 1, ..., 4 \overset{iid}{\sim} N(0, \sigma_\beta^2)$;*
5. *$\tau = (\sigma^2)^{-1} \sim Ga(c, d), \tau_a = (\sigma_a^2)^{-1} \sim Ga(c_a, d_a)$,*
   $\tau_b = (\sigma_b^2)^{-1} \sim Ga(c_b, d_b), \tau_\beta = (\sigma_\beta^2)^{-1} \sim Ga(c_\beta, d_\beta)$. ∎

9.2 The BUGS Project: WinBUGS and OpenBUGS

The project BUGS (Bayesian inference using Gibbs sampling) was initiated in 1989 as a contract of Andrew Thomas with the Medical Research Council Biostatistics Unit in Cambridge. The project arose out of work that was developed by Spiegelhalter (1986) and Lauritzen and Spiegelhalter (1988) about graphical models and their applications in artificial intelligence, and the recognition of the importance of these structures in the formulation of Bayesian models. It is interesting to note that at the same time, but independently, the seminal work of Gelfand and Smith (1990) was developed in Nottingham, even if this was done with a rather different perspective.

A prototype of BUGS was first publicly presented in the *IV. Valencia Meeting* in 1991. According to Lunn et al (2009), the real push for the development came in 1993 after the *INSERM Workshop on MCMC Methods*, which was followed by a workshop in Cambridge on the use of BUGS, which prompted the book *MCMC in Practice* by Gilks, Richardson and Spiegelhalter in 1996. In the first versions of the software, only Gibbs samplers were used and only for models with log-concave complete conditional posterior distributions. The big step forward was at the beginning of 1996 when the project moved to Imperial College London. The WinBUGS version was developed, which permitted interactive diagnostics and inference. The introduction of Metropolis–Hastings methods allowed dropping the restriction to log-concavity.

The analysis of more complex models was then achieved with the introduction of the slice sampler and the Jump interface for WinBUGS, which allowed the implementation of MCMC with reversible jumps. GeoBUGS was developed for spatial data, PKBugs for pharmacokinetic models, and WBDiff to deal with systems of ordinary differential equations. In 2004, Andrew Thomas started to work on an open-source version of BUGS at the University of Helsinki, giving rise to the project OpenBUGS. OpenBUGS is expected to be the future of the BUGS project after version 1.4.3. was launched as the last version of WinBUGS in 2007. A history of the project, including the technical development, can be read in Lunn et al (2009). The availability of BUGS is without doubt partially responsible for the rapid dissemination of Bayesian ideas at the end of the last century, as was predicted by Lindley. The software BUGS was for many years without any competitors, despite some known limitations of the program, in particular computation times.

The syntax of BUGS is simple and attractive, by using a text definition of a Bayesian inference model. Distributions are indicated by the symbol $\sim$ and logical and/or deterministic relationships by the symbol $< -$. It includes deterministic structures that are typically used in programs, such as `for` loops. Being a declarative language, the sequence of instructions is irrelevant. This implies the inconvenience of not allowing, for example, instructions like *if–then–else*, which is a great limitation of the language. The *step()* function can be used to overcome this limitation, but is unclear programming style.

With WinBUGS not being further developed, it is now advisable to use OpenBUGS. The R2OpenBUGS package, an adaptation of the R2WinBUGS package (Sturtz et al, 2005) by Neal Thomas, serves as the interface between OpenBUGS and R. To analyze Bayesian models in R with R2OpenBUGS, one needs to first write the code to program the statistical model in BUGS. It is useful to do this in OpenBUGS, which includes the possibility to verify the syntax and correct possible errors.

There are various manuals for BUGS, which can be downloaded from the site www.openbugs.net/w/Manuals. The basic manual is OpenBUGS User Manual, which should be consulted to understand how models are defined and to understand the functionality of BUGS. A list of accepted sampling distributions and prior distributions, and how to specify them, is found in appendix I of this manual. In the case of a sampling distribution that is not included in this list, there is the possibility that the user constructs his or her own likelihood. The section Advanced Use of the BUGS Language in the manual explains how to do this. The same approach can be used to specify a prior distribution for a parameter that is not listed in the appendix.

Next we illustrate the use of BUGS with the example that was introduced earlier in this chapter.

9.2.1 Application Example: Using R2OpenBUGS

After opening an R session, install the package using the command

```
install.packages("R2OpenBUGS", dependencies=TRUE,
   repos="http://cran.us.r-project.org")
```

To simplify the commands we will always assume that all files that are needed for the program are saved in the working directory of the R session (use setwd() if needed). The steps to analyze the model in R2OpenBUGS are then the following:

1. Write the code for the model and save it in a file with extension .txt. In this case, we saved it in the file Cexemplo1BUGS.txt.

```
model{
for(i in 1:147){
  X[i]~dnorm(mu[i],tau)
  mu[i]<-beta0+beta[1]*z1[i]+beta[2]*z2[i]
    +beta[3]*z3[i]+beta[4]*z[i]+a[ID[i]]+b[i]
```

```
   b[i]~dnorm(0,tau_b)
}
for(j in 1:49){
   a[j]~dnorm(0,tau_a)
}
for(k in 1:4){
   beta[k]~dnorm(0,0.0001)
}
beta0~dnorm(0,0.0001)
tau~dgamma(0.05,0.05)
tau_a~dgamma(0.05,0.05)
tau_b~dgamma(0.05,0.05)
sigma<-1/sqrt(tau)
sigma_a<-1/sqrt(tau_a)
sigma_b<-1/sqrt(tau_b)
}
```

The first `for` loop corresponds to the statement of the probability model given in item 1 of Section 9.1. In BUGS the second parameter (`tau`) of the normal distribution is the precision (inverse variance). The loop also includes the definition of the linear predictor `mu` and the statement of the model for the random effects `b` that appear in items 2. and 3. of the same section. The number of patients is $n = 49$, but since all were observed at three distinct time points, the total number of observations is 147.

The second `for` loop is the model for the random effects a. Those effects are specific to each patient, who are identified by the variable `ID` in the first loop.

The third `for` loop defines the prior distribution for the fixed effect parameters. After this, the prior distribution for the remaining model parameters are given. All prior distributions reflect vague prior information. Finally, to allow monitoring of standard deviations, those are defined as a function of the respective precisions. Note that the sequence of these commands is completely arbitrary.

To verify the file that defines the model to be used by OpenBUGS, one can use the command

```
file.show("Cexemplo1BUGS.txt")
```

2. Reading in the data. For better convergence of the chains, it is advisable that the covariates that appear in the definition of the linear predictor be centered. If the data file does not yet include centering, this can be done in R.

```
> Cexemplo1<-read.table("Cexemplo1.txt",header=T)
> dim(Cexemplo1)
[1] 147   9
```

```
> head(round(Cexemplo1,4))

    X  gender z1      z2    year     z3  ID        z   all
1  14       1  0 -0.89796    1   2.5979   1  19.1329     1
2  10       2  0 -0.89796    1  -0.4020   2 -13.0671     2
3   8       2  0  0.10204    1  -0.9020   3  -7.3671     3
4  10       2  0 -3.89796    1  -1.2020   4  51.2329     4
5  10       2  0 -7.89796    1  -1.7020   5  18.2329     5
6  20       2  0 -3.89796    1   0.5979   6  -0.8671     6
```

The covariate z is recorded at three time points. The variable ID is a patient identifier with values between 1 and 49. The variable all indexes observations with values between 1 and 147 and is included for convenience, as will be seen later. The variable year is the time of evaluation, with values between 1 and 3, also included for convenience only. The continuous covariates in the file, $z2$, $z3$, and z are already centered. The variable $z1$ is an indicator for the assigned treatment and takes values 0 or 1.

3. Define the vectors of the data matrix to be used by the model. The data must be supplied as a vector, matrix, or list.

```
#Create separate objects for each variable
X<-Cexemplo1$X
ID<-Cexemplo1$ID
z3<-Cexemplo1$z3
z1<-Cexemplo1$z1
z2<-Cexemplo1$z2
z<-Cexemplo1$z
#Create a list of data which will be passed on to OpenBUGS
Cexemplo1.data<-list("X","ID","z1","z2","z3","z")
```

4. Define the parameters that will be monitored.

```
Cexemplo1.params <- c("beta0","beta",
   "tau","tau_a","tau_b","sigma_a","sigma_b","sigma")
```

If one wishes to monitor mu, or any other parameter that was defined in the model specification, for example a, or b, those must appear in the above list.

5. Define the initial values of parameters and hyperparameters in the model. In this case we need to define initial values for beta0, beta, tau, tau_a, tau_b, a, b. Those are defined in a list that needs to include initial values for each chain.

```
Inits<-list(tau=1,tau_a=1,tau_b=1,beta=c(0,0,0,0), b=c(0,0,0,0,
  0,0,0,0,0,0,0,0,0,0,0,0,0,0,0,0,0,0,0,0,0,0,0,0,0,0,0,0,0,0,0,
  0,0,0,0,0,0,0,0,0,0,0,0,0,0,0,0,0,0,0,0,0,0,0,0,0,0,0,0,0,0,0,0,
  0,0,0,0,0,0,0,0,0,0,0,0,0,0,0,0,0,0,0,0,0,0,0,0,0,0,0,0,0,0,0,0,
  0,0,0,0,0,0,0,0,0,0,0,0,0,0,0,0,0,0,0,0,0,0,0,0,0,0,0,0,0,0,0,0,
```

```
0,0,0,0,0,0,0,0,0,0,0,0,0,0,0,0,0,0,0,0),a=c(0,0,0,0,0,0,0,0,0,
0,0,0,0,0,0,0,0,0,0,0,0,0,0,0,0,0,0,0,0,0,0,0,0,0,0,0,0,0,0,0,0,
0,0,0,0,0,0,0,0,0),beta0=0)
```

Using more than one chain, one needs to create a list of the same type for each chain, with different initial values, arranged as objects with names, for examples, "Inits1" and "Inits2", and then define a list of lists using

```
Inits<-list(Inits1,Inits2,...)
```

6. The program OpenBUGS can then be run through R using the function `bugs()`, after having verified that the R2OpenBUGS package is loaded in the current R session.

```
library(R2OpenBUGS)
Cexemplo1_openBUGS.fit<- bugs(data=Cexemplo1.data, inits=list(Inits),
    parameters.to.save=Cexemplo1.params,
    "Cexemplo1BUGS.txt", n.chains=1, n.iter=40000,
    n.burnin=20000, debug=FALSE,save.history=FALSE,DIC=TRUE)
```

It is recommended to verify the arguments for `bugs()` with the command `?bugs()`.

7. To obtain summaries of marginal posterior distributions for the parameters that were declared earlier in the vector `Cexemplo1.params`, write

```
Cexemplo1_OpenBUGS.fit$summary
```

which generates in this case the output (the final column for the 97.5% quantile is cut to fit the page)

	mean	sd	2.5%	25%	50%	75%
beta0	17.4290	1.9208	13.9200	16.1000	17.2800	18.6600
beta[1]	4.2329	2.8568	-2.6160	2.5750	4.4480	6.0600
beta[2]	0.1422	0.1391	-0.1303	0.0474	0.1448	0.2352
beta[3]	4.3456	0.9455	2.3960	3.7600	4.3430	4.9100
beta[4]	-0.1029	0.0366	-0.1726	-0.1281	-0.1046	-0.0798
tau	1.5607	3.6155	0.0636	0.0847	0.1521	1.1012
tau_a	0.0162	0.0038	0.0097	0.0135	0.0159	0.0185
tau_b	2.2989	5.4749	0.0638	0.0870	0.1604	1.4452
sigma_a	8.0226	0.9547	6.4140	7.3560	7.9320	8.5990
sigma_b	2.1790	1.2991	0.2279	0.8318	2.4965	3.3910
sigma	2.2725	1.2624	0.2750	0.9528	2.5640	3.4360
deviance	583.7390	241.1451	37.2990	403.3750	695.3000	782.2000

The output provides summaries of the marginal posterior distributions of the model parameters, including mean, standard deviation, and the 0.025, 0.25, 0.5, 0.75, and 0.975 quantiles. Inspecting these elements one can, for example, report an estimate for β_3 (coefficient of the covariate $z3$) as

4.3456 and a 95% credible interval as (2.396,6.373). To obtain HPD intervals one can use CODA or BOA (as will be demonstrated in the subsections explaining these packages).

8. Some more information is available in `Cexemplo1_OpenBUGS.fit`. Using the command

```
names(Cexemplo1_OpenBUGS.fit)
```

we see the members of this list:

```
 [1]  "n.chains"         "n.iter"
 [3]  "n.burnin"         "n.thin"
 [5]  "n.keep"           "n.sims"
 [7]  "sims.array"       "sims.list"
 [9]  "sims.matrix"      "summary"
[11]  "mean"             "sd"
[13]  "median"           "root.short"
[15]  "long.short"       "dimension.short"
[17]  "indexes.short"    "last.values"
[19]  "isDIC"            "DICbyR"
[21]  "pD"               "DIC"
[23]  "model.file"
```

For example, get information about the DIC with

```
Cexemplo1_OpenBUGS.fit$DIC
[1] 429.7
Cexemplo1_OpenBUGS.fit$pD
[1] -154.1
```

The negative value of p_D could indicate an excessive number of parameters in the model. In this case, this could be due to the inclusion of the random effects b in the model.

9. Finally, it is critical to assess convergence by using some of the methods discussed in Chapter 6. Either the CODA package, or the BOA package in R can be used (see Section 9.6).

10. A complete analysis of the model should include model selection and validation. All this can be done in R. It suffices to have the simulated values of the model parameters. Those values are available in the form of a list, array, or matrix. The latter, for example, is obtained with the command

```
A<-Cexemplo1_OpenBUGS.fit$sims.matrix
dim(A)
[1] 20000      12
head(A)# shows the first 6 rows of A
       beta0 beta[1] beta[2] beta[3] beta[4]    tau
[1,] 15.45   8.683   0.066   4.086  -0.118 0.422
[2,] 16.44   5.370   0.123   4.398  -0.117 0.071
```

```
[3,]  19.35    2.387    0.214    4.675  -0.037 2.613
[4,]  19.12   -0.014    0.152    4.254  -0.084 0.361
[5,]  17.49    3.548    0.068    5.744  -0.104 2.452
[6,]  19.98    3.522    0.384    3.826  -0.106 0.092
      tau_a tau_b sigma_a sigma_b sigma deviance
[1,] 0.017 0.078   7.640   3.589 1.539   536.6
[2,] 0.016 2.567   7.895   0.624 3.749   790.8
[3,] 0.019 0.074   7.169   3.665 0.619   249.5
[4,] 0.016 0.107   7.853   3.061 1.665   570.3
[5,] 0.015 0.079   8.067   3.558 0.639   286.1
[6,] 0.020 3.179   7.058   0.561 3.298   791.9
```

Note that only parameters that were declared in the object Cexemplo1.params appear. To carry out residual analysis, for example, it is important to monitor mu.

If the random effects b are removed (note that the file Cexemplo1BUGS.txt with the model definition and the initial values need to be changed accordingly) we get

```
> exemplo1_OpenBUGS1.fit<- bugs(data=Cexemplo1.data,
    inits=list(Inits1), parameters.to.save=Cexemplo1.params1,
    "Cexemplo1BUGS_semb.txt", n.chains=1,
    n.iter=40000,n.burnin=20000, debug=FALSE,save.history=FALSE,
    DIC=TRUE)
```

```
> exemplo1_OpenBUGS1.fit$summary
             mean      sd     2.5%      25%      50%      75%     97.5%
beta0      17.210   1.763   13.760   16.040   17.190   18.360   20.790
beta[1]     4.781   2.393    0.063    3.186    4.731    6.417    9.495
beta[2]     0.152   0.145   -0.117    0.052    0.149    0.249    0.450
beta[3]     4.146   0.923    2.384    3.527    4.121    4.751    6.053
beta[4]    -0.107   0.036   -0.177   -0.131   -0.107   -0.083   -0.036
tau         0.077   0.011    0.057    0.070    0.077    0.085    0.101
tau_a       0.016   0.004    0.010    0.014    0.016    0.019    0.025
sigma_a     7.974   0.936    6.363    7.319    7.897    8.544   10.020
sigma       3.625   0.265    3.150    3.439    3.608    3.794    4.190
deviance 795.126  12.624  772.600  786.200  794.300  803.200  822.000
```

```
> exemplo1_OpenBUGS1.fit$DIC
[1] 843.2
> exemplo1_OpenBUGS1.fit$pD
[1] 48.03
> A1<-exemplo1_OpenBUGS1.fit$sims.matrix
> dim(A1)
[1] 20000      10
> head(A1)
       beta0 beta[1] beta[2] beta[3] beta[4]      tau
[1,]  20.62 -0.8067  0.1487   4.631 -0.1005  0.0838
[2,]  18.39  2.8580  0.0692   5.767 -0.0569  0.0826
[3,]  19.56  2.5330  0.3619   3.045 -0.1277  0.0784
```

```
[4,]  16.61   6.1660  -0.1078    4.284  -0.1168  0.0827
[5,]  18.11   2.8790   0.1680    4.372  -0.2055  0.0636
[6,]  15.06   5.1330   0.0461    3.707  -0.1142  0.0639
        tau_a  sigma_a  sigma  deviance
[1,]  0.0188    7.291  3.455     773.9
[2,]  0.0141    8.431  3.479     781.4
[3,]  0.0247    6.368  3.572     796.0
[4,]  0.0162    7.844  3.478     783.5
[5,]  0.0251    6.310  3.964     819.5
[6,]  0.0168    7.704  3.955     818.8
```

```
> Cexemplo1_OpenBUGS1$DIC
[1] 843.1
> Cexemplo1_OpenBUGS1$pD
[1] 48.12
```

Note that p_D is now positive, with $p_D = 48.12$.

9.3 JAGS

In 2003 Martyn Plummer, of the International Agency for Research on Cancer, created JAGS (Just Another Gibbs Sampler) as a clone of BUGS written in C++, which fixed certain limitations of BUGS. Models written in BUGS syntax can be used in JAGS, practically without any change. This has the advantage that the same code can be run on both platforms. There are two parts to a model definition in JAGS: the model description (model{}), as in BUGS, and the definition of the data (data{}). The latter can be used, for example, to define transformations of the data, define summary statistics, simulate data sets, etc. The latest version of JAGS was launched in July 2017 (JAGS 4.3.0). To understand how JAGS works, it is important to read the manual (Plummer, 2012). The R package R2jags (https://cran.r-project.org/web/packages/R2jags/R2jags.pdf) serves as an interface between R and JAGS. One of the main advantages of JAGS compared to OpenBUGS is the faster run time.

9.3.1 Application Example: Using R2jags

The following example illustrates how to use R2jags to study the model in the example given in Section 9.1 without the random effects b. The program is installed and loaded with the commands

```
install.packages("R2jags", dependencies=TRUE,
    repos="http://cran.us.r-project.org")

library(R2jags)
```

1. The same model as in OpenBUGS can be loaded as a file, or can be defined in an R *script*, as a function, as follows:

```
exemplo1.model<-function(){
  for(i in 1:147){
    X[i]~dnorm(mu[i],tau)
    mu[i]<-beta0+beta[1]*z1[i]+beta[2]*z2[i]+beta[3]*z3[i]
          +beta[4]*z[i]+a[ID[i]]
  }
  for(j in 1:49){
    a[j]~dnorm(0,tau_a)
  }
  for(k in 1:4){
    beta[k]~dnorm(0,0.0001)
  }
  beta0~dnorm(0,0.0001)
  tau~dgamma(0.05,0.05)
  tau_a~dgamma(0.05,0.05)
  sigma<-1/sqrt(tau)
  sigma_a<-1/sqrt(tau_a)
}
```

2. Reading in the data, the definition of the model variables, the declaration of parameters that are to be monitored, and the definition of initial values is done exactly as before.

```
Cexemplo1.data <- list("X","ID","z3","z1","z2","z")
Cexemplo1.params1 <- c("beta0","beta","tau","tau_a",
 "sigma_a","sigma")

Inits1<-list("tau"=1,"tau_a"=1,"beta"=c(0,0,0,0),
    "a"=c(0, 0, 0, 0, 0, 0, 0, 0, 0, 0, 0, 0, 0, 0, 0,
          0, 0, 0, 0, 0, 0, 0, 0, 0, 0, 0, 0, 0, 0, 0, 0,
          0, 0, 0, 0, 0, 0, 0, 0, 0, 0, 0, 0, 0, 0, 0, 0),
    "beta0"=0)
```

3. Before using R2jags for the first time, we need to set a random variate seed, for example, by the R command

```
set.seed(123)
```

4. To estimate the model in JAGS, use the function `jags()`.

```
exemplo1_JAGS.fit <- jags(data = Cexemplo1.data,
    inits = list(Inits1),  parameters.to.save = Cexemplo1.params1,
    n.chains = 1, n.iter = 40000,
    n.burnin = 20000, model.file = exemplo1.model)
```

5. Summary statistics of the marginal posterior distributions of the parameters are obtained by the command

```
> print(exemplo1_JAGS.fit)
Inference for Bugs model at "C:/Users...model1f5469ec52a3.txt",
fit using jags,
 1 chains, each with 40000 iterations (first 20000 discarded),
  n.thin = 20, n.sims = 1000 iterations saved
           mu.vect sd.vect    2.5%     25%     50%     75%   97.5%
beta[1]      4.751   2.537  -0.248   3.038   4.783   6.507   9.450
beta[2]      0.160   0.143  -0.121   0.069   0.159   0.249   0.447
beta[3]      4.163   0.915   2.467   3.552   4.132   4.777   6.081
beta[4]     -0.107   0.036  -0.177  -0.132  -0.108  -0.081  -0.031
beta0       17.212   1.810  13.561  16.050  17.151  18.387  20.717
sigma        3.676   0.808   3.133   3.441   3.604   3.789   4.267
sigma_a      7.920   1.159   6.289   7.335   7.921   8.529   9.778
tau          0.077   0.013   0.055   0.070   0.077   0.084   0.102
tau_a        0.699  13.406   0.010   0.014   0.016   0.019   0.025
deviance   797.267  28.396 773.207 786.080 794.391 802.998 823.233

DIC info (using the rule, pD = var(deviance)/2)
pD = 403.2 and DIC = 1200.4
DIC is an estimate of expected predictive error
 (lower deviance is better).
```

Note the thinning out of saved simulations (n.thin=20). In fact, one of the arguments of the function jags() is n.thin. Its default value is max(1, floor((n.iter - n.burnin)/1000)); note also the elevated value of *pD*.

6. Another feature of R2jags is the possibility to leave the choice of initial values up to the program, by specifying NULL, as illustrated:

```
exemplo1_JAGS.fit2 <- jags(data = Cexemplo1.data, inits = NULL,
    parameters.to.save = Cexemplo1.params1,
    n.chains = 2, n.iter = 40000,
    n.burnin = 20000, model.file = exemplo1.model)

> print(exemplo1_JAGS.fit2)
Inference for Bugs model at
"C:/Users.../model1f5477c03ee1.txt",
 fit using jags,
 2 chains, each with 40000 iterations (first 20000 discarded),
 n.thin = 20
 n.sims = 2000 iterations saved
           mu.vect sd.vect    2.5%     25%     50%     75%   97.5%
beta[1]      4.859   2.596  -0.346   3.166   4.939   6.604   9.950
beta[2]      0.157   0.139  -0.113   0.068   0.151   0.242   0.453
beta[3]      4.191   0.918   2.422   3.595   4.173   4.805   6.059
beta[4]     -0.105   0.036  -0.175  -0.130  -0.106  -0.081  -0.035
beta0       17.218   1.816  13.857  15.996  17.207  18.435  20.716
sigma        3.659   0.715   3.164   3.436   3.608   3.798   4.235
sigma_a      7.943   1.049   6.363   7.317   7.886   8.587   9.873
tau          0.077   0.012   0.056   0.069   0.077   0.085   0.100
```

```
tau_a        0.507  14.898    0.010   0.014   0.016   0.019   0.025
deviance  796.175  22.494  773.690 786.454 794.169 802.528 822.873
            Rhat  n.eff
beta[1]    1.001   2000
beta[2]    1.003    590
beta[3]    1.001   2000
beta[4]    1.001   2000
beta0      1.001   2000
sigma      1.006   2000
sigma_a    1.040   2000
tau        1.006   2000
tau_a      1.040   2000
deviance   1.022   2000
```

```
For each parameter, n.eff is a crude measure of effective
sample size, and Rhat is the potential scale reduction
factor (at convergence, Rhat=1).

DIC info (using the rule, pD = var(deviance)/2)
pD = 253.1 and DIC = 1049.3
DIC is an estimate of expected predictive error
   (lower deviance is better)
```

Note that there are now two extra columns, "Rhat" and "n.eff," whose meanings are explained in the output.

A plot of simulated parameter values can be obtained by

```
traceplot(exemplo1_JAGS.fit2)
```

7. The plots show obvious convergence problems. If needed, such as in this example, one can continue simulation until convergence using the following command (which can only be used with at least two chains — notice n.chains=2 in the call to jags).

```
exemplo1_JAGS.fit2.upd <- autojags(exemplo1_JAGS.fit2)
```

```
print(exemplo1_JAGS.fit2.upd)
Inference for Bugs model at
"C:/Users.../model1f5477c03ee1.txt",
 fit using jags,
 2 chains, each with 1000 iterations (first 0 discarded)
 n.sims = 2000 iterations saved
          mu.vect sd.vect    2.5%     25%     50%     75%    97.5%
beta[1]     4.681   2.562  -0.227   2.972   4.702   6.345    9.832
beta[2]     0.156   0.143  -0.117   0.059   0.151   0.253    0.440
beta[3]     4.179   0.924   2.410   3.575   4.181   4.771    5.951
beta[4]    -0.106   0.037  -0.178  -0.132  -0.106  -0.081   -0.036
beta0      17.288   1.777  13.735  16.117  17.333  18.443   20.676
sigma       3.631   0.265   3.139   3.444   3.611   3.801    4.210
sigma_a     8.007   0.955   6.314   7.363   7.936   8.582   10.080
tau         0.077   0.011   0.056   0.069   0.077   0.084    0.102
```

```
tau_a     0.016   0.004   0.010   0.014   0.016   0.018   0.025
deviance 795.438  12.641 773.639 786.407 794.608 802.980 823.357
          Rhat n.eff
beta[1]  1.001  2000
beta[2]  1.001  2000
beta[3]  1.001  2000
beta[4]  1.001  2000
beta0    1.001  2000
sigma    1.002  2000
sigma_a  1.001  2000
tau      1.002  2000
tau_a    1.001  2000
deviance 1.002  2000

For each parameter, n.eff is a crude measure of effective
sample size, and Rhat is the potential scale reduction
factor (at convergence, Rhat=1).

DIC info (using the rule, pD = var(deviance)/2)
pD = 79.9 and DIC = 875.4
DIC is an estimate of expected predictive error
  (lower deviance is better).
```

Note the decrease of the values for p_D and DIC. Another function that can be used for the same purpose, and which requires only one chain, is the function update().

In Section 9.6 we will discuss how to evaluate convergence diagnostics for this example, including also for posterior simulation using other packages.

9.4 Stan

In 2010, Andrew Gelman, Columbia University, New York, and collaborators were working on a Bayesian analysis of multi-level generalized linear models, as described by Gelman and Hill (2006). The implementation of these models in WinBUGS or JAGS turned out to be extremely challenging due to the complex model structure. For example, Matt Schofield noted that simulation for a multi-level time series model that was used for a climate model using measurements of growth rings on trees, did not converge even after hundreds of thousands of iterations (Schofield et al, 2016). To resolve the problem, Gelman and collaborators developed a new Bayesian software, which they called Stan, in honor of Stanislaw Ulam, one of the creators of the Monte Carlo methods. The first version was made available for users in August 2012. Stan does not use Gibbs samplers, but instead uses Hamiltonian Monte Carlo (Neal, 2011). With the *no-U-turn sampler* algorithm that they developed (Hoffman and Gelman, 2014), all parameters are simulated in one block. Using this strategy, convergence problems were substantially mitigated. In contrast to BUGS, Stan is written as an imperative language.

Stan allows the use of all basic operators from C++, in addition to a large number of other special functions, including in particular Bessel functions, gamma and digamma functions, and a variety of functions related to inverse functions that are used in generalized linear models. A complete list of the basic operators and special functions that are implemented in Stan is given by Carpenter et al (2017). The list of implemented probability distributions, which also appears in the same reference, is extensive. This allows great flexibility in model construction.

A bit of history of the development of Stan, as well as implementation details, can be found in *Stan Modeling Language: User's Guide and Reference Manual*, which corresponds to version 2.6.2. An interface between R and Stan is implemented in RStan (Stan Development Team, 2014).

9.4.1 Application Example: Using RStan

To install RStan, follow the instructions at https://github.com/stan-dev/rstan/wiki/RStan-Getting-Started.

1. As in the other packages, one has to first define the model in Stan. The model definition is saved in a text file, typically with the suffix .stan. The model definition is a little more elaborate than in the previous packages. Being an imperative language, the sequence of commands is important. For our example, the model definition in Stan, saved in the file exemplo1.stan.txt, is

```
data {
  int<lower=1> J; // length of data
  int<lower=1> N; // number of patients
  real X[J]; // response variable
  real z2[J]; // covariate
  real z3[J]; // covariate
  real z[J]; // covariate
  int<lower=0,upper=1> z1[J]; // z1 takes values 0 and 1
  int<lower=1> ID[J]; // identification
}
parameters {
  real<lower=0> tau;
  real<lower=0> tau_a;
  real beta0;
  real beta[4];
  real a[N];
```

```
}
transformed parameters {
  real<lower=0> sigma_a;
  real<lower=0> sigma;
  sigma_a = sqrt(1/tau_a);
  sigma = sqrt(1/tau);
}
model {
  vector[J] mu;
  for(i in 1:J){
    mu[i] = beta0+beta[1]*z1[i]+beta[2]*z2[i]
      +beta[3]*z3[i]+a[ID[i]]+beta[4]*z[i]};
    beta0 ~ normal(0,100);
    beta ~ normal(0,100);
    tau ~ gamma(0.05,0.05);
    tau_a ~ gamma(0.05,0.05);
    a ~ normal(0, sigma_a);
    X ~ normal(mu, sigma);
  }
generated quantities {
  vector[J] log_lik;
  vector[J] m;
  for(i in 1:J) {
    m[i] = beta0+beta[1]*z1[i]+beta[2]*z2[i]
      +beta[3]*z3[i]+a[ID[i]]+beta[4]*z[i]};
    log_lik[i] = normal_log(X[i] | m[i], sigma);
  }
}
```

We explain the program block by block:

- In the `data` block the data to be used when running Stan have to be declared. For example, J and N are integers with minimum value 1; `z1` is a binary covariate with integer value between 0 and 1. The response variable and the covariates are real vectors. Stan also allows data in the form of a matrix, ordered vectors, arrays, and more.

- The `parameters` block declares all unknown quantities that Stan will estimate. In this case we decided to include the precision parameters `tau` and `tau_a` to be consistent with the earlier model definition. Additionally, we declare variable types for all quantities that are to be estimated. For example, `tau` and `tau_a` are postive reals; `beta` and `a` are real vectors of dimensions 4 and N, respectively.

- In the `transformed parameters` block, all quantities that are functions of the data and/or the parameters have to be declared if they are to be used later. In this case we define `sigma` and `sigma_a` as the square root of the inverse precision parameters.

- The `model` block defines the actual model. The vector `mu` is defined as a function of the covariates and the random effects a. We define the model for the response variable (note that the second parameter of the normal distribution is the standard deviation here). We also define prior distributions for the parameters and hyperparameters in the model. In Stan the definition of prior distributions is not obligatory. In the absence of such definitions, Stan proceeds with uniform prior distributions.

- The `generated quantities` block is not required. Here we define the log-likelihood in a way that individual terms can be saved by Stan. These terms are collected in an object with the name `log-lik`; the simulated values of this object can then be used to calculate the widely applicable information criterion (WAIC) or the LOO (Vehtari et al, 2017), as we shall see.

2. The data are introduced as a list, as before, or if the data are read from a file it suffices to create an object with the variable names, as follows:

```
Cexemplo1<-read.table("Cexemplo1.txt",header=T)
attach(Cexemplo1)
J<-nrow(Cexemplo1)       #J=147
N<-length(unique(ID)) #N=49
# object to be used by Stan
Cexemplo1_data<-c("N","J","X","ID","z3","z2","z1","z")
```

3. Next we can call the function `stan()` from the package `rstan` to simulate from the posterior distribution:

```
library(rstan)
exemplo1.fit_stan <- stan(file="exemplo1.stan.txt",
  data=Cexemplo1_data, iter=40000, chains=2)
```

Call `?stan` to see the arguments of the function `stan`. Particularly useful are the arguments `sample_file` and `diagnostic_file` that allow indicating the names of files where simulated samples of all model parameters and convergence diagnostics can be saved. If these names are not given, these elements are not saved. They can, however, be extracted later.

`rstan` provides information about the execution time for each chain in the following form (here only for one chain):

```
COMPILING THE C++ CODE FOR MODEL 'example1' NOW.

SAMPLING FOR MODEL 'exempl1' NOW (CHAIN 1).

Chain 1, Iteration:     1 / 40000 [  0%]  (Warmup)
Chain 1, Iteration:  4000 / 40000 [ 10%]  (Warmup)
Chain 1, Iteration:  8000 / 40000 [ 20%]  (Warmup)
Chain 1, Iteration: 12000 / 40000 [ 30%]  (Warmup)
Chain 1, Iteration: 16000 / 40000 [ 40%]  (Warmup)
```

```
Chain 1, Iteration: 20000 / 40000 [ 50%]  (Warmup)
Chain 1, Iteration: 20001 / 40000 [ 50%]  (Sampling)
Chain 1, Iteration: 24000 / 40000 [ 60%]  (Sampling)
Chain 1, Iteration: 28000 / 40000 [ 70%]  (Sampling)
Chain 1, Iteration: 32000 / 40000 [ 80%]  (Sampling)
Chain 1, Iteration: 36000 / 40000 [ 90%]  (Sampling)
Chain 1, Iteration: 40000 / 40000 [100%]  (Sampling)
#  Elapsed Time: 46.431 seconds (Warm-up)
#               75.594 seconds (Sampling)
#              122.025 seconds (Total)
```

The execution time for 40,000 iterations is much longer than the execution time in OpenBUGS or JAGS, which for this particular problem is practically instantaneous. However, the number of iterations needed to achieve convergence is lower using Stan. Above we used the same number of iterations, but this was not necessary. In fact, if the number of iterations is not specified in `iter=`, we find convergence after only 2000 iterations in this example.

4. To get summary statistics for the marginal posterior distributions for the parameters of interest, use the command

```
print(exemplo1.fit_stan,
    pars=c("beta0","beta","sigma","sigma_a","tau","tau_a","lp__"))
```

to get (a final column for the 97.5% quantile is cut to fit the page) the following:

```
Inference for Stan model: example1.
2 chains, each with iter=40000; warmup=20000; thin=1;
post-warmup draws per chain=20000, total post-warmup draws=40000.

          mean se_mean   sd    2.5%     25%     50%     75%
beta0    17.22    0.02 1.79   13.67   16.04   17.23   18.41
beta[1]   4.80    0.03 2.52   -0.17    3.12    4.80    6.48
beta[2]   0.16    0.00 0.14   -0.12    0.06    0.16    0.25
beta[3]   4.19    0.01 0.93    2.38    3.55    4.18    4.82
beta[4]  -0.10    0.00 0.04   -0.18   -0.13   -0.11   -0.08
sigma     3.62    0.00 0.26    3.16    3.44    3.61    3.79
sigma_a   8.00    0.01 0.94    6.39    7.34    7.92    8.57
tau       0.08    0.00 0.01    0.06    0.07    0.08    0.08
tau_a     0.02    0.00 0.00    0.01    0.01    0.02    0.02
lp__   -388.89    0.06 6.36 -402.47 -392.90 -388.50 -384.42
         n_eff Rhat
beta0     5771    1
beta[1]   5754    1
beta[2]   7261    1
beta[3]   7555    1
beta[4]  10087    1
sigma    21771    1
```

```
sigma_a 23821     1
tau      21546     1
tau_a    25151     1
lp__     11599     1
```

For each parameter, n_eff is a crude measure of effective sample size, and Rhat is the potential scale reduction factor on split chains (at convergence, Rhat=1).

Here, se_mean is the Monte Carlo standard error of the mean. If no parameters are specified then the summary statistics are given for the marginal posterior distributions of all unknown quantities, including in particular also a, log_lik, m.

The quantity lp_ which appears as the last element in pars= and whose summary statistics are found in the last row of the output, is the log posterior density (un-normalized), which is calculated by Stan for the implementation of Hamiltonian Monte Carlo. It can also be used for model assessment (see, for example, Vethari and Ojanen, 2012).

The print() function provides summary statistics based on all chains that are generated, whereas summary() provides summary statistics for each chain separately.

5. To obtain the simulated parameter values, use the function extract(). With the argument permuted=TRUE, a list of all simulated values for all parameters is created (if only simulated values for some parameters are desired, those need to be given in the argument pars=); using permuted=FALSE, an array is created with the first dimension corresponding to iterations, the second dimension corresponding to chains, and the third dimension corresponding to the parameters. See, for example, the following:

```
#####using permuted=TRUE##############
samples_stan<-extract(exemplo1.fit_stan,
pars=c("beta0", "beta", "sigma", "sigma_a"),
permuted = TRUE, inc_warmup = FALSE, include = TRUE)
> class(samples_stan)
[1] "list"
> names(samples_stan)
[1] "beta0"   "beta"     "sigma"    "sigma_a"
> length(samples_stan$beta0)
[1] 40000 #20000 each chain
> head(samples_stan$beta0)
[1] 16.18767 18.64417 20.43510 16.69809 14.35278 15.39996
> dim(samples_stan$beta)
> head(round(samples_stan$beta,3))

iterations    [,1]  [,2]  [,3]   [,4]
       [1,]  8.994 0.468 2.437 -0.126
```

```
        [2,]    4.310 0.309 4.425 -0.093
        [3,]    2.127 0.079 3.700 -0.156
        [4,]    3.394 0.245 1.680 -0.131
        [5,]   10.541 0.359 3.814 -0.086
        [6,]    8.314 0.357 4.001 -0.068
##########using permuted=FALSE#########
> samples_stan_array<-extract(exemplo1.fit_stan,
+ pars=c("beta0", "beta", "sigma", "sigma_a"),
+ permuted = FALSE, inc_warmup = FALSE, include = TRUE)
> class(samples_stan_array)
[1] "array"
> dim(samples_stan_array)
[1] 20000     2     7 # 20000 each chain
                      # 2 chains, 7 parameters
> samples_stan_array[1:4,1:2,1:3]
, , parameters = beta0

            chains
iterations  chain:1   chain:2
       [1,] 16.29099 17.81893
       [2,] 16.68243 17.31063
       [3,] 16.49383 17.31063
       [4,] 16.20388 16.70740

, , parameters = beta[1]

            chains
iterations  chain:1   chain:2
       [1,] 6.530125 5.718621
       [2,] 4.949012 6.479835
       [3,] 6.000288 6.479835
       [4,] 6.204705 7.421142

, , parameters = beta[2]

            chains
iterations   chain:1    chain:2
       [1,] 0.1718956 0.07575568
       [2,] 0.1657402 0.18286167
       [3,] 0.1793824 0.18286167
       [4,] 0.1347633 0.15160846
```

6. The `traceplot()` function plots the simulated parameter values for each chain. Figure 9.1 is obtained by the following command:

```
traceplot(exemplo1.fit_stan,
   pars=c("beta"), nrow = 5, ncol = 2, inc_warmup = FALSE)
```

7. To obtain the WAIC (Vehtari et al, 2017), proceed as follows, after installing the package `loo` from CRAN:

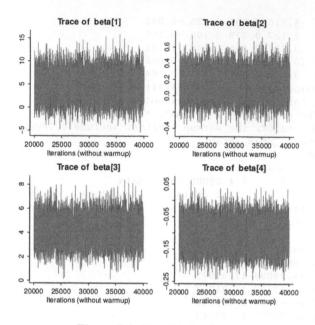

Figure 9.1 Simulated values.

```
> library(loo)
> log_lik1 <- extract_log_lik(exemplo1.fit_stan)
> waic(log_lik1)
Computed from 40000 by 147 log-likelihood matrix

           Estimate    SE
elpd_waic    -422.4   9.9
p_waic         40.5   4.7
waic          844.8  19.8
```

For details on how to use Rstan, see https://cran.r-project.org/web/packages/rstan/vignettes/rstan_vignette.pdf.

9.5 BayesX

BayesX is a program that was developed in the Department of Statistics at Ludwig Maximilian Universität München by Andreas Brezger, Thomas Kneib, and Stefan Lang, with the first versions appearing in 2002. The software is written specifically for structured additive regression models (Brezger et al, 2005). This family of models (STAR), which was introduced in Chapter 8, includes various well-known and widely used regression models, such as generalized additive models (GAM), generalized additive mixed models (GAMM), generalized geoadditive mixed models (GGAMM), dynamic models, spatio temporal models, and more, under one unified framework (Umlauf et al, 2015). BayesX, written in C++, also allows the analysis of regression models when the response variable does not necessarily belong to the exponential family. It also allows the analysis of quantile regression, survival regression by modeling the hazard function (extensions of the Cox model), and analysis of multi-state models and multilevel models. The methodology manual for BayesX (`www.statistik.lmu.de/~bayesx/manual/methodology_manual.pdf`) contains a brief description of the regression models that are allowed in BayesX.

The particular arguments of the BayesX function to implement a statistical model include the specification of a distributional family for the response variable, the estimation method, and other control parameters defined by the function `bayesx.control()`, as will be seen. Similar to the `glm()` function in R, the distributional family that is (implicitly) specified by omission is a Gaussian family. A list of allowed probability distributions in BayesX, besides the usual exponential family distributions, can be found in Umlauf et al (2015). A particular feature of BayesX is that, besides MCMC, BayesX allows us to carry out inference for mixed models using restricted maximum likelihood estimation (REML) and a penalized likelihood method (STEP).

In principle, inference for the STAR models that are implemented in BayesX could also be implemented using WinBUGS/OpenBUGS, or JAGS. However, the BayesX authors report substantial reduction in execution times compared to WinBUGS/OpenBUGS, besides a faster convergence of the Markov chains (Brezger et al, 2005), which have better mixing properties. To simplify the use and subsequent analysis of results from BayesX, Kneib et al (2014) created an R package, also called BayesX, which allows reading and processing results from BayesX. However, with this package, the users still have to read data, adapt the models, and obtain output files using BayesX. To simplify this task, Umlauf et al (2015) introduce a new R package, R2BayesX, which now provides a complete interface between R and BayesX.

The R2BayesX manual can be found at `https://cran.r-project.org/web/packages/R2BayesX/R2BayesX.pdf`. To install R2BayesX it suffices, as usual, to use the commands

```
install.packages("R2BayesX", dependencies=TRUE,
    repos="http://cran.us.r-project.org")
```

9.5.1 Application Example: Using R2BayesX

The syntax used in R2BayesX to implement inference for a Bayesian model is in all aspects very similar to the syntax used in R to implement statistical models.

1. To implement the desired model it suffices, after reading in the data, to write the formula of the model and call the `bayesx()` function.

```
Cexemplo1       <- read.table("Cexemplo1.txt",header=T)
library(R2BayesX)
modelo2_BayesX  <- X~z2+z3+z1+z+sx(ID,bs="re")
exemplo1_BayesX <- bayesx(formula = modelo2_BayesX,
    data = Cexemplo1, family = "gaussian", method = "MCMC",chains=2,
    seed = c(123,456),
    control = bayesx.control(model.name = "bayes2x.estim",
        outfile='C:/...', iterations = 40000L,
        burnin = 20000L,dir.rm=T))
```

Explaining the code:

- The formula that is saved as `modelo2_BayesX` is the formula of the linear predictor for the expected response value. Following the initial model specification, the fixed effects `z2`, `z3`, `z1`, `z` enter linearly in the linear predictor. BayesX is, however, particularly useful to model non linear covariate effects by using the function `sx()`. For example, if we had reason to believe that the covariate `z2` has a non linear effect, and we would like to use a *P-spline* to model this non linear effect, then `z2` should enter in the model with a model statement using `sx(z2,bs="ps")`, where the argument `bs` selects the type of basis for this term. We used it above to specify the random effects. See how the random effect a is introduced using the `sx()` function. Recall that these random effects are patient-specific, with patients indexed by ID. Therefore, the first argument for the function `sx()` is ID. To specify that the random effects are i.i.d. normal with mean zero and standard deviation σ_a, we write `bs="re"`. To specify a model with the random effects b, which we used initially, one would write `sx(all,bs="re")` (recall that `all` indexes all observations with a running index from 1 to 147). A list of all arguments for BayesX can be found in table 4 of Umlauf et al (2015).
- The function `bayesx()` fits the specified model. The function has several arguments, many of which are optional arguments with default choices. The only required arguments are the first two: `formula` and `data`. By

default the distributional family is Gaussian, the method is MCMC,[1] the number of iterations is 12,000, with a `burn-in` of 2000, and thinning out by saving every tenth iteration, and the number of chains is 1. These values, as well as others, can be changed by the argument `control` in the `bayesx.control` function; as usual, to find out the arguments of this function and their use, use the help function in R by typing `?bayesx.control`. The first argument of this function is the `model.name`, which takes the name of the model and is also used to form the name of the files that are used to save the results of the model estimation using BayesX; these files will be saved in the directory specified in `outfile`.

2. Using this code, we get the following output of summary statistics for the marginal distributions of the parameters:

```
> summary(exemplo1_BayesX)
### Chain_1
Call:
bayesx(formula = formula, data = data, weights = weights,
subset = subset, offset = offset, na.action = na.action,
contrasts = contrasts, control = control, model = model,
chains = NULL, cores = NULL)


Fixed effects estimation results:

Parametric coefficients:
              Mean      Sd    2.5%      50%    97.5%
(Intercept) 17.2313  1.8036 13.6702 17.2744 20.7688
z2           0.1557  0.1371 -0.1174  0.1566  0.4250
z3           4.2146  0.9665  2.3040  4.2043  6.2029
z1           4.7691  2.4910 -0.1460  4.7646  9.6957
z           -0.1043  0.0366 -0.1756 -0.1055 -0.0319

Random effects variances:
            Mean     Sd    2.5%     50%   97.5%    Min    Max
sx(ID):re 64.925 15.702 41.081 62.706 99.701 26.824 169.6

Scale estimate:
          Mean     Sd    2.5%     50%   97.5%
Sigma2 13.2389  1.9332  9.9936 13.0804 17.373

N = 147  burnin = 20000  DIC = 194.7823  pd = 48.29928
method = MCMC  family = gaussian  iterations = 40000
step = 10
### Chain_2
Call:
```

---

[1] BayesX also implements REML and STEP; for details, see Umlauf et al (2015)

```
bayesx(formula=formula, data=data, weights=weights,
    subset=subset, offset = offset, na.action = na.action,
    contrasts = contrasts, control = control,
    model = model, chains = NULL, cores = NULL)

Fixed effects estimation results:

Parametric coefficients:
                  Mean      Sd    2.5%      50%   97.5%
(Intercept)   17.1458  1.7125 13.9773 17.0971 20.3820
z2             0.1591  0.1438 -0.1282  0.1612  0.4407
z3             4.1544  0.9413  2.3008  4.1405  6.0312
z1             4.9990  2.5100 -0.2337  5.0116  9.6973
z             -0.1025  0.0351 -0.1751 -0.1016 -0.0367

Random effects variances:
                 Mean      Sd    2.5%     50%   97.5%      Min     Max
sx(ID):re      64.569  15.502  40.542  62.367 101.027   30.008 136.28

Scale estimate:
               Mean      Sd    2.5%     50%   97.5%
Sigma2      13.2323  1.9739  9.9179 13.0191 17.518

N = 147  burnin = 20000   DIC = 195.1921   pd = 48.54314
method = MCMC   family = gaussian   iterations = 40000   step = 10
###
Object consists of 2 models
```

When the argument control gives a file name for the output, folders are automatically created in the indicated directory, one for each chain, containing various files with the simulated parameter values (with file extension .raw) and text files with the summary statistics. In the current example, two folders are created with the names Chain_1_bayes2x.estim and Chain_2_bayes2x.estim. All these data files can later be used for graphical summaries, to evaluate diagnostics, etc.

    3. The command

```
getscript(exemplo1_BayesX)
```

returns an R script to create plots using these files.

    4. Alternatively, the simulated posterior samples of the parameters can be obtained with the samples() function as follows:

```
AA<-samples(exemplo1_BayesX)
> class(AA)
[1] "mcmc.list"
> names(AA)
[1] "Chain_1" "Chain_2"
> length(AA[[1]])
```

```
[1] 10000
> length(AA[[2]])
[1] 10000

plot(AA)
```

The object `AA` is a list that contains in `AA[[1]]` a sample from the posterior distribution of the fixed effect parameters from chain 1, and similarly in `AA[[2]]` for chain 2. Since we save 20,000 iterations and thin out to every tenth, there are 2000 simulated values for each of the five parameters. The order in which the simulated values appear is the same as that in which they were introduced in the formula. Thus `AA[[1]][1:2000]` contains posterior simulated values, starting first with `beta0`; `AA[[1]][2001:4000]` which contains posterior simulated values for `beta1`, the coefficient for the covariate `z2`, etc.

5. The command `plot(AA)` plots the superimposed series of simulated values for each parameter and corresponding marginal posterior density estimates.

6. To get the posterior simulated values of the variances (in this case, the variance of a normal distribution), and the corresponding graphical summaries, write

```
> Va<-samples(exemplo1_BayesX,term = "var-samples")
> length(Va[[1]])
[1] 2000
> plot(Va)
```

Figure 9.2 shows the plot of `plot(Va)`.

7. To get simulated values for the random effects a and for σ_a^2 use the `term="sx(ID)"` argument in the `samples` function. This way one can obtain posterior samples for specific parameters; for example, use `term="z3"` for the parameter corresponding to `z3`.

8. A useful feature is that the folder that is created for the results from each chain also includes a `latex` document with a model summary, including information about the assumed prior distributions and a summary of the results. For example, consulting this document when no specific priors were specified, one finds that diffuse priors were used for the fixed effects, i.i.d. normal random effects, and inverse gamma priors for the variance components with hyperparameters $a = 0.001$ and $b = 0.001$. If desired, the specification of hyperparameters can be adjusted in the `control` argument.

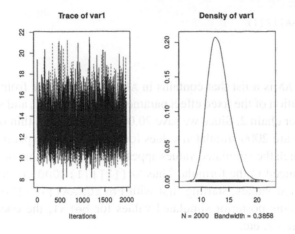

Figure 9.2 Trace plot of simulated values and marginal posterior density for σ^2.

The information from this `latex` document can also be obtained with the command

```
bayesx_logfile(exempl1_BayesX)
```

9.6 Convergence Diagnostics: the Programs CODA and BOA

As already mentioned in Section 6.6, MCMC methods generate realizations from a homogeneous Markov chain with an equilibrium distribution that matches the desired posterior distribution $h(\theta \mid x)$. The aim is then to obtain one (or more) sequence(s) of parameter values which can be considered a representative sample from the joint posterior distribution. To obtain one such sample, it is necessary to assess, based on a given number of iterations t, if the chain is already in (or "close to") the equilibrium state. If that is the case, then the currently imputed states and the following iterations can be considered to be approximate Monte Carlo samples from the posterior distribution $h(\theta \mid x)$, of course correlated due to the Markovian nature of the chain. There are several methods, graphical and based on statistical tests, that allow us to diagnose convergence of the chain or chains to the stationary distribution. Some were already mentioned in Section 6.6. The packages CODA (Plummer et al, 2006) and BOA (Smith, 2007) implement these methods, allowing one to carry out a quick and efficient assessment of convergence.

9.6.1 Convergence Diagnostics

The CODA program as well as BOA allow the evaluation of convergence diagnostics, in particular the methods by Gelman and Rubin (1992), Geweke (1992), Raftery and Lewis (1992), and Heidelberger and Welch (1983), which will be briefly described in the following. A more detailed description can be found in the articles cited in Cowles and Carlin (1996) or Paulino et al (2018).

Gelman and Rubin Diagnostic

Gelman and Rubin suggest using the variance components of multiple parallel chains, initialized from different starting points. The method involves the following steps:

1. Simulate $m \geq 2$ chains, each one with $2n$ iterations, starting from initial points that are generated from a distribution that is overdispersed relative to the target (stationary) distribution.
2. Discard the first n iterations of each chain.
3. Let g denote the scalar quantity of interest that is desired to be estimated (g is typically a function of the parameter θ).
4. On the basis of the simulated values of g, calculate the variance components W and B, that is, the variance within each chain and the variance across chains, respectively.
5. Estimate the mean of g under the target distribution as a sample average of all mn simulated values of g.
6. Estimate V, the variance of $g(\theta)$ under the target distribution, as a weighted average of W and B.
7. Evaluate the *scale reduction factor* $\hat{R} = \sqrt{V/W}$.
8. The ratio converges to 1 as $n \rightarrow \infty$. Values $\hat{R} \approx 1$ are evidence that each of the m sequences of n simulated states is approximating the target distribution.

Geweke's Diagnostic

Let $\theta^t, t = 1, \ldots, N$, be a sequence of states generated by an MCMC simulation and let $g(\theta)$ be a function of θ that is to be estimated. The trajectory $g^1, g^2, \ldots$ formed by $g^t = g(\theta^t)$ defines a time series.

The method of Geweke (1992) is based on the application of usual time series methods to test for the convergence of the simulated sequence. Assuming sufficiently large N, we calculate the sample average $g_a = \frac{1}{n_a} \sum g(\theta^t)$ using the first n_a iterations, as well as the average $g_b = \frac{1}{n_b} \sum g(\theta^t)$ using the last n_b iterations. If the chain is stationary, then the mean of the first part of the chain should be similar to the mean of the latter part of the chain. Letting $N \to \infty$ with fixed n_a/N and n_b/N, one can show that

$$\frac{(g_a - g_b)}{\sqrt{(s_a^2/n_a) + (s_b^2/n_b)}} \to N(0, 1),$$

where s_a^2 and s_b^2 are independent estimates of the asymptotic variances of g_a and g_b, adjusted for the autocorrelation of the time series. Using this statistic, we can now assess whether or not there is evidence for convergence.

Raftery and Lewis Diagnostic

Assume that it is desired to estimate the posterior q-quantile of some function of the parameters, with numerical uncertainty r and probability s to be within the bounds defined by r. The method of Raftery and Lewis calculates the necessary number of iterations N and initial burn-in M needed to achieve the specified criteria. The calculation is based on assuming that a derived binary sequence of indicators of the function being above (1) or below (0), the desired quantile is approximately Markov. Besides N and M the diagnostic reports $N_{\min}$, the minimum size of a pilot sample and refers to $I = (M + N)/N_{\min}$ as the factor of dependence, interpreted as the proportional increase in the number of iterations that can be attributed to the serial dependence. High values of this factor (> 5) are evidence for influential starting values, high correlation between the coefficients of the parameter vector, or a poorly mixing Markov chain over the posterior support. The method should be used with one or more pilot sequences.

Heidelberg and Welch Method

Heidelberg and Welch proposed a test statistic, based on the Cramer-von Mises test, to test the null hypothesis that the simulated Markov chain does come from a stationary distribution.

The convergence diagnostic is applied for each variable that is being monitored, and is evaluated as follows:

1. Generate a chain of size N and define a level α.
2. For each monitored variable, evaluate the test statistic using the N iterations. According to the result of this test, take a decision about rejecting the null hypothesis or not.
3. If the null hypothesis is rejected, evaluate the test statistic again after

discarding the first 10% of iterations. Repeat the process while the null hypothesis is rejected.

4. If we continue to reject the null hypothesis as the remaining number of iterations reaches 50% of the initial N iterations, then the Markov chain simulation has to continue, as the chain has not yet reached equilibrium. In that case CODA reports the test statistic and indicates that the chain has failed the test of stationarity.

5. Otherwise, the part of the chain that passed the stationarity test is used to estimate the mean (m) and asymptotic standard error (s) of the average and a half-width test is applied to that part of the chain as follows. If $1.96s < m\epsilon$, for small ϵ (CODA uses a default of $\alpha = 0.05$ and $\epsilon = 0.1$), then the chain passes the overall test. Otherwise, the condition $1.96s \geq m\epsilon$ means that the Markov chain simulation needs to be continued.

9.6.2 *The CODA and BOA Packages*

The CODA package was originally written for S-PLUS, as part of a biostatistics PhD thesis by Cowles (1994). Later it was taken over by the BUGS team (Best et al, 1995), who created an interface by saving the simulated values from BUGS in a CODA format, which could then later be analyzed by CODA.

The CODA package for R arose from an effort to move the functions that were written for S-PLUS to an R environment. Difficulties in this translation lead to substantial rewriting of the functions, and the creation of the BOA package. The development of the latter started in 2000, exactly when all CODA functions were already rewritten to be used in R. As a consequence, CODA is now available for use in R (Plummer et al, 2006).

Both packages can be directly installed from CRAN with the commands:

```
install.packages("coda",repos="http://cran.us.r-project.org")
install.packages("boa",repos="http://cran.us.r-project.org")
```

Both packages, CODA and BOA from CRAN, have a function `codamenu()` and `boa.menu()`, respectively, which allows using the programs with a menu interface, for casual users with limited knowledge of R. For example, in CODA:

```
> library(coda)
> codamenu()
CODA startup menu

1: Read BUGS output files
2: Use an mcmc object
```

```
3: Quit

Selection: 2

Enter name of saved object (or type "exit" to quit)
1:A1_2_mcmc #ver posteriormente como foi definido.
Checking effective sample size ...OK
CODA Main Menu

1: Output Analysis
2: Diagnostics
3: List/Change Options
4: Quit
```

After reading in the data, the user is presented with a list of analysis options, summary statistics, graphical representations, and convergence diagnostics.

The BOA menu is quite similar. See details of the boa.menu() in Smith (2007).

Alternatively to the menu mode, it is possible to carry out an analysis using R commands. To have an interface between CODA and R such that functions can be used from the R command line, a new R class mcmc was created. BOA accepts the simulated values as a vector or matrix as input parameter, and can save them as an mcmc object.

The latest version of the manuals for CODA and BOA are available from

https://cran.r-project.org/web/packages/coda/coda.pdf
https://cran.r-project.org/web/packages/boa/boa.pdf.

The manuals describe the functions to summarize the MCMC simulation results, including graphical summaries, as well as diagnostic tests for convergence to the limiting distribution of the chains.

The CODA functions require an object of the class mcmc which contains all simulated values for all parameters that are being monitored. Such an object can easily be created using the function as.mcmc() with a matrix of simulation output.

To use the BOA functions, the MCMC simulation output needs to be given in a matrix, with the parameters in the columns and one row for each iteration. A list with row and column names is the argument dimnames() of the class matrix object.

9.6.3 Application Example: CODA and BOA

We illustrate the use of CODA and BOA to study convergence of the chains that were previously simulated using the packages R2OpenBUGS, R2jags, RStan and R2BayesX.

A. Use with R2OpenBUGS

Recall from Section 9.2.1 how the matrix of simulated values for parameters that were previously declared for monitoring can be obtained. It is obtained as the component $sims.matrix of the object A1=Cexemplo1_OpenBUGS.fit. The latter contains all output from the call to bugs(), as is illustrated in the following example:

```
Cexemplo1_OpenBUGS.fit<- bugs(data=Cexemplo1.data,
inits=list(Inits1,Inits2), parameters.to.save=Cexemplo1.params1,
   "Cexemplo1BUGS_semb.txt", n.chains=2, n.iter=40000,
   n.burnin=20000, debug=FALSE,save.history=FALSE,DIC=TRUE)

> A1<-Cexemplo1_OpenBUGS.fit$sims.matrix
> dim(A1)
[1] 40000      10
> head(round(A1,4))
      beta0 beta[1] beta[2] beta[3] beta[4]      tau   tau_a
[1,] 15.73   6.349  0.0098   3.843 -0.1046 0.0819 0.0192
[2,] 18.55   2.689  0.0214   4.742 -0.1315 0.0953 0.0195
[3,] 16.41   6.330  0.2284   4.585 -0.0643 0.0664 0.0218
[4,] 14.18   5.653 -0.1744   4.911 -0.1551 0.0793 0.0127
[5,] 19.86   2.291  0.0826   4.259 -0.1209 0.0875 0.0180
[6,] 19.00   1.449 -0.0214   5.277 -0.0964 0.0778 0.0190
      sigma_a sigma deviance
[1,]   7.207 3.495    797.3
[2,]   7.168 3.240    792.8
[3,]   6.779 3.882    800.5
[4,]   8.883 3.552    781.2
[5,]   7.452 3.381    793.0
[6,]   7.247 3.585    783.9
> class(A1)
[1] "matrix"
```

We see that $A1$ has 40,000 rows (20,000 iterations for each of two chains) and ten columns with the names of the monitored parameters. Note that the states for the first chain are in lines 1 through 20,000, and for the second chain in rows 20,001 through 40,000.

Thus, to use CODA with two chains, we need to define two objects of type mcmc, one for each chain, and then combine them into a single object using the function as.mcmc.list, as is shown in the following example.

```
> library(coda)
```

```
> A1_1chain<-as.mcmc(A1[1:20000,])
> A1_2chain<-as.mcmc(A1[20001:40000,])
> A1_2_mcmc<-as.mcmc.list(list(A1_1chain,A1_2chain))
```

We can plot superimposed trajectories for the two chains, posterior densities (illustrated in Figure 9.3 for the parameters β_1 and β_2), autocorrelations, trajectories of quantiles, and the correlation matrix between the components. The plots are obtained using the following commands:

```
plot(A1_mcmc)
plot(A1_2_mcmc[,2:3])    #only for cols that appear in the figure
autocorr.plot(A1_2_mcmc) #autocorrelation
cumuplot(A1_2_mcmc)      #evaluate quantiles (0.025,0.5,0.975)
crosscorr.plot(A1_2_mcmc)#plot correlation matrix
```

The convergence diagnostics from Section 9.6.1 are easily evaluated with the respective CODA functions.

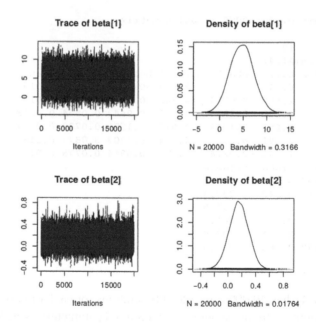

Figure 9.3 Trajectory plots and posterior densities for β_1 and β_2.

1. Gelman and Rubin's Diagnostic

```
> gelman.diag(list(A1_1chain,A1_2chain),
    confidence = 0.95, transform=FALSE, autoburnin=TRUE,
    multivariate=TRUE)
```

```
Potential scale reduction factors:

          Point est. Upper C.I.
beta0             1          1
beta[1]           1          1
beta[2]           1          1
beta[3]           1          1
beta[4]           1          1
tau               1          1
tau_a             1          1
sigma_a           1          1
sigma             1          1
deviance          1          1


Multivariate psrf
1
```

The command included the option autoburnin=TRUE. Therefore, only the second half of the series is used for the evaluation of the scale reduction factor. The factors evaluate to 1, indicating no evidence against convergence of the series. A plot of the evolution of Gelman and Rubin's scale reduction factor versus iteration is obtained by gelman.plot(). Figure 9.4 illustrates this plot for β_1 and β_2.

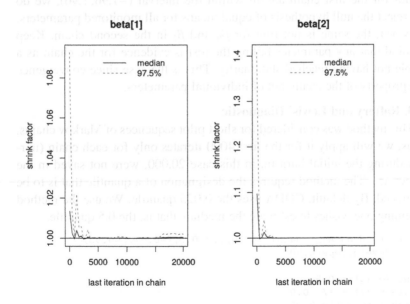

Figure 9.4 Gelman and Rubin's scale reduction factor.

2. Geweke's Diagnostic

```
> geweke.diag(A1_2_mcmc)
[[1]]

Fraction in 1st window = 0.1
Fraction in 2nd window = 0.5

     beta0    beta[1]    beta[2]    beta[3]    beta[4]        tau
  0.003827 -1.383019 -0.608487 -0.695510 -0.948153   0.047654
     tau_a   sigma_a     sigma  deviance
 -0.231638 -0.349071  0.069021 -0.278292


[[2]]

Fraction in 1st window = 0.1
Fraction in 2nd window = 0.5

    beta0 beta[1] beta[2] beta[3] beta[4]      tau
  -2.2450  2.7206  0.6372 -0.5620 -0.5291   0.3862
    tau_a sigma_a   sigma deviance
   0.1276 -0.4537 -0.3752   1.4152
```

The output of this function is the Z-scores for the tests of equal means between the earlier and later part of the series for each variable. Since the values for the first chain are all within the interval $(-1.96, 1.96)$, we do not reject the null hypothesis of equal means for all monitored parameters. However, the same is not true for β_0 and β_1 in the second chain. Keep in mind that any parameter failing the test is evidence for the chain as a whole not having reached stationarity. This is the case since convergence is a property of the chain, not of individual parameters.

3. Raftery and Lewis' Diagnostic

This method was considered for short pilot sequences of Markov chains. Thus, we will apply it for the first 4000 iterates only for each chain (iterates during the initial burn-in, in this case 20,000, were not saved in the object A1). The method requires the designation of a quantile that is to be estimated. By default, CODA uses the 0.025 quantile. We use the method assuming one wishes to estimate the median, that is, the 0.5 quantile.

```
> raftery.diag(A1_1chain[1:4000,],q=0.5,r=0.01,s=0.95,
      converge.eps=0.001)

Quantile (q) = 0.5
Accuracy (r) = +/- 0.01
Probability (s) = 0.95
```

```
You need a sample size of at least 9604 with
these values of q, r and s

#using 10000 iterates
> raftery.diag(A1_1chain[1:10000,],q=0.5,r=0.01,s=0.95)

Quantile (q) = 0.5
Accuracy (r) = +/- 0.01
Probability (s) = 0.95
```

	Burn-in (M)	Total (N)	Lower bound (Nmin)	Dependence factor (I)
beta0	2	9324	9604	0.971
beta[1]	2	9268	9604	0.965
beta[2]	2	9354	9604	0.974
beta[3]	1	9619	9604	1.000
beta[4]	2	9099	9604	0.947
tau	2	9354	9604	0.974
tau_a	2	9520	9604	0.991
sigma_a	2	9558	9604	0.995
sigma	2	9384	9604	0.977
deviance	2	9272	9604	0.965

```
> raftery.diag(A1_2chain[1:10000,],q=0.5,r=0.01,s=0.95)

Quantile (q) = 0.5
Accuracy (r) = +/- 0.01
Probability (s) = 0.95
```

	Burn-in (M)	Total (N)	Lower bound (Nmin)	Dependence factor (I)
beta0	2	9794	9604	1.020
beta[1]	2	9771	9604	1.020
beta[2]	2	9459	9604	0.985
beta[3]	1	9588	9604	0.998
beta[4]	2	9302	9604	0.969
tau	2	9736	9604	1.010
tau_a	2	9406	9604	0.979
sigma_a	2	9399	9604	0.979
sigma	2	9751	9604	1.020
deviance	2	9276	9604	0.966

The dependence factor for both chains is approximately 1, indicating no problems. According to these results, 10,000 iterations would suffice to estimate the median with a tolerance of $r = 0.01$ and a probability of $s = 0.95$ of being within these tolerance limits.

4. Heidelberg and Welch Method

To apply this method we need to fix values for ϵ and α. As mentioned before, CODA uses by default $\epsilon = 0.1$ and $\alpha = 0.05$. The default values

Software

can be changed by using the arguments of the function `heidel.diag()`. Just for illustration, we use $\epsilon = 0.01$.

```
> heidel.diag(A1_2_mcmc, eps=0.01, pvalue=0.05)
[[1]]
```

	Stationarity test	start iteration	p-value
beta0	passed	1	0.503
beta[1]	passed	1	0.052
beta[2]	passed	1	0.592
beta[3]	passed	1	0.822
beta[4]	passed	1	0.504
tau	passed	1	0.402
tau_a	passed	1	0.999
sigma_a	passed	1	0.936
sigma	passed	1	0.435
deviance	passed	1	0.503

	Halfwidth test	Mean	Halfwidth
beta0	passed	17.2739	2.47e−02
beta[1]	passed	4.7013	3.46e−02
beta[2]	failed	0.1565	1.93e−03
beta[3]	passed	4.2236	1.29e−02
beta[4]	passed	−0.1047	4.93e−04
tau	passed	0.0774	1.52e−04
tau_a	passed	0.0163	5.29e−05
sigma_a	passed	7.9973	1.30e−02
sigma	passed	3.6216	3.60e−03
deviance	passed	794.9228	1.72e−01

```
[[2]]
```

	Stationarity test	start iteration	p-value
beta0	passed	2001	0.2585
beta[1]	passed	1	0.0766
beta[2]	passed	1	0.8299
beta[3]	passed	1	0.1795
beta[4]	passed	1	0.8124
tau	passed	1	0.9457
tau_a	passed	1	0.8847
sigma_a	passed	1	0.9781
sigma	passed	1	0.9562
deviance	passed	1	0.5130

	Halfwidth test	Mean	Halfwidth
beta0	passed	17.2694	0.025928
beta[1]	passed	4.6858	0.034335

```
beta[2]   failed       0.1561 0.001879
beta[3]   passed       4.2275 0.012846
beta[4]   passed      -0.1046 0.000507
tau       passed       0.0773 0.000154
tau_a     passed       0.0162 0.000052
sigma_a   passed       8.0069 0.013041
sigma     passed       3.6251 0.003658
deviance  passed     795.0646 0.175413
```

With $\epsilon = 0.01$ the parameter β_2 passed the test of stationarity (for both chains), but failed the half-width test, indicating the need to continue simulation to achieve the desired precision. If we augment ϵ to 0.05, all parameters pass both stationarity and half-width tests.

5. HPD Intervals

Finally, recall that in CODA one can obtain HPD intervals for all monitored parameters, using the function HPDinterval(). This is illustrated here with 95% HPD intervals for each of the chains.

```
> HPDinterval(A1_2_mcmc, prob = 0.95)
[[1]]
                 lower       upper
beta0        13.860000   20.80000
beta[1]       0.036880    9.84600
beta[2]      -0.128400    0.42490
beta[3]       2.487000    6.08700
beta[4]      -0.178200   -0.03300
tau           0.056580    0.10000
tau_a         0.009279    0.02371
sigma_a       6.246000    9.88700
sigma         3.122000    4.14500
deviance    771.400000  820.30000
attr(,"Probability")
[1] 0.95


[[2]]
                 lower       upper
beta0        13.960000   20.87000
beta[1]       0.002304    9.64300
beta[2]      -0.114500    0.42770
beta[3]       2.402000    6.02500
beta[4]      -0.178100   -0.03235
tau           0.055750    0.09912
tau_a         0.009449    0.02374
sigma_a       6.223000    9.83100
sigma         3.122000    4.15300
deviance    771.100000  819.80000
attr(,"Probability")
[1] 0.95
```

We now briefly illustrate how to evaluate the same diagnostics in BOA.

```
A1<-Cexemplo1_OpenBUGS.fit$sims.matrix
                                #results in matrix form
nomes<-list(c(1:20000,1:20000),c("beta0","beta[1]","beta[2]",
            "beta[3]","beta[4]","tau","tau_a",
            "sigma_a","sigma","deviance"))
dimnames(A1)<-nomes
A1_1<-A1[1:20000,]              #define first chain
A1_2<-A1[20001:40000,]         #define a second chain
#-------------------------------------------------#
        #autocorrelation
#-------------------------------------------------#
boa.acf(A1_1,lags=1)
boa.acf(A1_2,lags=1)
#-------------------------------------------------#
        #Geweke's method #
#-------------------------------------------------#
boa.geweke(A1_1, p.first=0.1, p.last=0.5)
boa.geweke(A1_2, p.first=0.1, p.last=0.5)
#-------------------------------------------------#
        #Heidelberg and Welch method #
#-------------------------------------------------#
boa.handw(A1_1, error=0.05, alpha=0.05)
boa.handw(A1_2, error=0.05, alpha=0.05)
#-------------------------------------------------#
                #HPD intervals #
#-------------------------------------------------#
#the function boa.hpd() computes HPD intervals
#for one parameter.
#to find intervals for all (monitored) parameters
#one can use, e.g.
hpd_boa<-function(x)  boa.hpd(x,0.05)
apply(A1_1,2,hpd_boa)
apply(A1_2,2,hpd_boa)
```

B. Using R2jags

1. The output from `jags()` can be converted into an `mcmc` object with the command:

```
exemplo1_JAGS.fit2.mcmc <- as.mcmc(exemplo1_JAGS.fit2 )
```

2. As before, with the `mcmc` object one can then use a variety of commands for convergence diagnostics in CODA:

```
library(coda)
plot(exemplo1_JAGS.fit2.mcmc)
autocorr.plot(exemplo1_JAGS.fit2.mcmc)
gelman.plot(exemplo1_JAGS.fit2.mcmc)
gelman.diag(exemplo1_JAGS.fit2.mcmc)
geweke.diag(exemplo1_JAGS.fit2.mcmc)
```

```
raftery.diag(exemplo1_JAGS.fit2.mcmc)
heidel.diag(exemplo1_JAGS.fit2.mcmc)
```

Note that the object `exemplo1_JAGS.fit2` already includes both chains, and the same is true for the `mcmc` object `exemplo1_JAGS.fit2.mcmc`. Thus it is not necessary to work with separate objects for both chains, as we had to in R2OpenBUGS.

3. The function `jags()` returns the simulated values for the monitored parameters also in matrix form:

```
exemplo1_JAGS.fit2$BUGSoutput$sims.matrix
```

Thus, for using BOA, we proceed exactly as we did in the case of two chains with output from ROpenBUGS.

C. Using RStan

As mentioned before (item 5, section 9.4.1), the simulated parameter values for a chain that is set up using the command `stan()` can be obtained by applying the function `extract()` to the output of `stan()`.

```
> samples_stan_array<-extract(exemplo1.fit_stan,
      pars=c("beta0", "beta", "sigma", "sigma_a", "tau", "tau_a"),
      permuted = FALSE, inc_warmup = FALSE, include = TRUE)
> class(samples_stan_array)
[1] "array"
> dim(samples_stan_array)
[1] 20000    2    9 #20000 cada cadeia, 2 cadeias, 9 parameters
```

To use CODA or BOA, we start by defining matrices for each of the chains.

```
samples_coda_1<-as.matrix(samples_stan_array[1:20000,1,1:9]))
samples_coda_2<-as.matrix(samples_stan_array[1:20000,2,1:9]))
```

For CODA, the matrices are transformed to objects of class `mcmc`:

```
samples_coda_1<-mcmc(samples_coda_1)
samples_coda_2<-mcmc(samples_coda_2)
gelman.diag(list(samples_coda_1,samples_coda_2))
geweke.diag(samples_coda_1)
geweke.diag(samples_coda_2)
raftery.diag(samples_coda_1)
raftery.diag(samples_coda_2)
heidel.diag(samples_coda_1)
heidel.diag(samples_coda_2)
```

For BOA, we need to first define `dimnames` for the row and column names:

```
samples_coda_1<-as.matrix(samples_stan_array[1:20000,1,1:9])
samples_coda_2<-as.matrix(samples_stan_array[1:20000,2,1:9])
dimnames(samples_coda_1)<- list(1:20000,
    c("beta0", "beta[1]","beta[2]", "beta[3]", "beta[4]",
      "sigma", "sigma_a", "tau", "tau_a"))
dimnames(samples_coda_2)<- list(1:20000,
    c("beta0", "beta[1]","beta[2]", "beta[3]", "beta[4]",
      "sigma", "sigma_a", "tau", "tau_a"))
```

We illustrate this with Geweke's diagnostic

```
> boa.geweke(samples_coda_1,p.first=.1,p.last=0.5)
            Z-Score     p-value
beta0    -0.1895212 0.84968432
beta[1]  -1.1536020 0.24866338
beta[2]  -0.3998341 0.68927871
beta[3]  -0.3581599 0.72022368
beta[4]  -1.3735690 0.16957554
sigma    -0.7696775 0.44149123
sigma_a  -1.7314080 0.08337903
tau       0.6671540 0.50467380
tau_a     1.7048218 0.08822767
> boa.geweke(samples_coda_2,p.first=.1,p.last=0.5)
            Z-Score     p-value
beta0    -0.51871293 0.6039609
beta[1]   0.15164978 0.8794632
beta[2]   1.35185008 0.1764233
beta[3]  -0.57649303 0.5642820
beta[4]   0.61505637 0.5385175
sigma    -0.93391998 0.3503452
sigma_a  -0.03298591 0.9736858
tau       1.23723600 0.2159995
tau_a     0.02936042 0.9765771
```

D. Using R2BayesX

Recall (item 4, Subsection 9.5.1) that the function `samples()` applied to the output of `bayesx()` returns the simulated values from the posterior distribution, including the parameters that are indicated in the argument `term`. The argument CODA controls the type and class of the output object.

Thus with the following commands we get a list of type `mcmc`, which can be used for convergence diagnostics in CODA:

```
> AA_coda<-samples(exemplo1_BayesX,
    term=c("linear-samples","var-samples","sd(ID)"),coda=TRUE)
> class(AA_coda)
[1] "mcmc.list"
> names(AA_coda)
[1] "Chain_1" "Chain_2"

#illustrating
```

```
> gelman.diag(AA_coda)
Potential scale reduction factors:

                Point est. Upper C.I.
Intercept           1          1
z2                  1          1
z3                  1          1
z1                  1          1
z                   1          1
                    1          1

Multivariate psrf
1
```

On the other hand, to use BOA for convergence diagnostics, proceed as follows:

```
> AA_boa<-as.matrix(AA_data)
> AA_boa_1<-AA_boa[,1:6]
> AA_boa_2<-AA_boa[,7:12]

#illustrating
> library(boa)
> boa.geweke(AA_boa_1,p.first=0.1,p.last=0.5)
                        Z-Score    p-value
Chain_1.Param.Intercept -0.2281478 0.8195313
Chain_1.Param.z2         1.2278951 0.2194863
Chain_1.Param.z3        -0.2358216 0.8135711
Chain_1.Param.z1         1.1215734 0.2620438
Chain_1.Param.z          0.8195813 0.4124548
Chain_1.Var              0.6110576 0.5411614
> boa.geweke(AA_boa_1,p.first=0.1,p.last=0.5)
                        Z-Score    p-value
Chain_1.Param.Intercept -0.2281478 0.8195313
Chain_1.Param.z2         1.2278951 0.2194863
Chain_1.Param.z3        -0.2358216 0.8135711
Chain_1.Param.z1         1.1215734 0.2620438
Chain_1.Param.z          0.8195813 0.4124548
Chain_1.Var              0.6110576 0.5411614
```

9.7 R-INLA and the Application Example

In Section 8.3. we described the INLA approach to analyzing Bayesian hierarchical models without the use of simulation. Being an approximation method, with this method we need not worry about convergence problems as are inherent in MCMC simulation methods, and discussed in the previous section. However, this does not imply that the obtained posterior approximations are always good. We have to study the quality of the approximation. Rue et al (2009) proposed two strategies to evaluate the approximation error of posterior distributions: one is based on the calculation of the effective number of parameters and the other is based on the Kullback–Leibler divergence criterion. Details of these strategies are discussed in sections 4.1. and 4.2. of the cited article. These strategies are implemented in R-INLA. We will see how to evaluate them. .

As discussed in Chapter 8, the INLA method is designed for Bayesian inference in latent Gaussian models, a large class of models that includes many models from additive GLMMs to log-Gaussian Cox models and spatio-temporal models. Together with the use of stochastic partial differential equations (SPDEs) (Lindgren et al, 2011), one can model all kinds of spatial data, including area referenced data, geo-referenced data, and point process data (Lindgren and Rue, 2015).

The R-INLA software is an R package developed to implement approximate Bayesian inference using INLA. The package is a further development of a stand-alone program INLA. It is written in C using the library GMRFLib (`www.math.ntnu.no/~hrue/GMRFLib/doc/html`) to implement fast and exact simulation for Gaussian random fields.

R-INLA is available for the operating systems Linux, Mac and Windows. On the site `www.r-inla.org`, besides installation instructions for R-INLA, one can find code, examples, articles, and reviews where the theory and application of INLA are discussed, and there are also many other materials of interest, in particular a discussion forum and answers to frequently asked questions.

To install R-INLA directly from R use the command:

```
install.packages("INLA",
 repos="http://www.math.ntnu.no/inla/R/stable")
```

As with any other R package, to load R-INLA in each work session, write

```
library(INLA)
```

As there are frequent updates of R-INLA, one should use

```
inla.upgrade(testing=FALSE)
```

to get the most recent and most stable version of the package.

Using R-INLA there is a large number of probability distributions that can be used for the response variable. The list can be seen with the command

```
> names(inla.models()$likelihood)
```

A complete description of these distributions, with examples, can be found at www.r-inla.org/models/likelihoods. Similarly, to get information about prior distributions for model parameters and structured or not structured random effects, see www.r-inla.org/models/priors and www.r-inla.org/models/latent-models. The lists with the corresponding distributions can also be obtained with the commands

```
> names(inla.models()$prior)
> names(inla.models()$latent)
```

To better understand how R-INLA works, we continue with the application example.

9.7.1 Application Example

1. As in BayesX, using the Bayesian model from Section 9.1, the model is translated into R as the object created by the formula

```
> INLA_formula <- X ~ z1 + z2 + z3 + z +
    f(ID, model="iid",
       hyper=list(prec=list(prior="loggamma",param=c(1,0.005))))
> class(INLA_formula)
[1] "formula"
```

As before, fixed effects that appear linearly in the model have been centered. Using the function f(), which appears in the definition of the formula, we define the structural effects (the various types are defined at www.r-inla.org/models/latent-models). In the case at hand we have only the patient-specific (variable ID) random effects which are introduced in the model as a. The model iid specifies a normal distribution with zero mean and precision τ_a. The prior distribution that is specified in the argument hyper is for $\ln(\tau_a)$. Being a log-gamma it corresponds to a gamma distribution for the precision τ_a.

2. Next we call the inla() function to run the INLA algorithm and obtain the desired results to eventually proceed with Bayesian inference, as follows:

```
> ?inla
> resultado_INLA <- inla(INLA_formula,family="normal",
    control.predictor=list(compute=TRUE),
    control.compute =list(waic=TRUE,dic=TRUE,cpo=TRUE),
    data = Cexemplo1,
    control.family=
      list(hyper=list(prec=list(prior="loggamma",param=c(1,0.005)))))
```

The first line in the above code lists all arguments of the `inla()` function, of which the only required ones are the object that states the formula, in this case `INLA_formula`, and the object that contains the data, in this case `data = Cexemplo1`. By not specifying the other arguments they are assumed by R-INLA to be specified by omission.

The directive `control.predictor=list(compute=TRUE)` specifies to compute the marginal distributions of the linear predictor. There are other arguments for this function, which can be listed by the command

```
?control.predictor
```

`control.family()` declares the prior distributions for the parameters in the family of sampling models. In this case, we declared a prior distribution for the precision parameter τ. See `?control.family` for details on how to do this for parameters of specific distributions.

To compute the WAIC and deviance information criterion (DIC) criteria and also conditional predictive ordinate (CPO), we need to declare

```
control.compute =list(waic=TRUE,dic=TRUE,cpo=TRUE)
```

3. The function `inla()` returns an object of class `inla`, here saved as `resultado_INLA`. This object is a list with many elements that can be explored by the command `names(resultado_INLA)`. Summary results of the INLA approach can be obtained by the command

```
> summary(resultado_INLA)
...
Time used:
   Pre-processing    Running inla Post-processing         Total
          0.1719          0.4375          0.0975        0.7069

Fixed effects:
             mean    sd 0.025quant 0.5quant 0.975quant   mode  kld
(Intercept) 17.250 1.737     13.820   17.251     20.669 17.253    0
z1           4.772 2.448     -0.050    4.770      9.599  4.766    0
z2           0.154 0.138     -0.118    0.154      0.427  0.153    0
z3           4.169 0.908      2.394    4.164      5.972  4.154    0
z           -0.106 0.036     -0.176   -0.106     -0.035 -0.107    0

Random effects:
Name       Model
  ID   IID model

Model hyperparameters:
                                        mean    sd 0.025quant 0.5quant
Precision for the Gaussian observations 0.0789 0.0113    0.0587   0.0782
Precision for ID                        0.0170 0.0039    0.0106   0.0167
                                        0.975quant    mode
```

```
Precision for the Gaussian observations      0.1027 0.0771
Precision for ID                             0.0256 0.0160

Expected number of effective parameters(std dev): 46.38(0.8267)
Number of equivalent replicates : 3.17

Deviance Information Criterion (DIC) ...: 841.57
Effective number of parameters .........: 47.65

Watanabe-Akaike information criterion (WAIC) ...: 844.77
Effective number of parameters ...............: 41.31

Marginal log-Likelihood:  -497.49
Posterior marginals for linear predictor and fitted values computed
```

Compare these results with the corresponding results from simulation methods. In particular, compare the WAIC values with those obtained from RStan.

4. Note that the results also include, for each configuration of hyperparameters, an estimate of the effective number of parameters. This estimate essentially corresponds to the expected number of independent parameters in the model. In our case, we have $7 + 49 = 56$ parameters, but since the random effects are correlated, the effective number of parameters is lower, ≈ 47, as can be seen. As mentioned, this is one of the strategies, proposed in Rue et al (2009), to evaluate the accuracy of the approximation. In particular, if the effective number of parameters is low compared to the sample size, then one expects the approximation to be good. In this case the ratio of sample size (147) and effective number of parameters (46.38) is approximately 3.17, suggesting a reasonably good approximation. In fact, the ratio can be interpreted as the number of "equivalent replicates" corresponding to the number of observations for each expected number of effective parameters.

Another reported quantity is the mean Kullback–Leibler divergence (in the column kld). This value describes the difference between the normal approximation and the simplified Laplace approximation (recall the discussion in Chapter 8 about the various approximation strategies used in INLA) for the marginal posterior distributions. Small values indicate that the posterior distribution is well-approximated by a normal.

5. The default approximation strategy in inla() is the simplified Laplace approach. Other approximation and integration methods can be defined using the argument control.inla in the function inla(). For example, if one wanted the complete Laplace approach used, which is recommended for higher accuracy in the estimation of tails in the marginal distributions, one would use `inla()` with the argument

```
control.inla=list(strategy="laplace",npoints=21)
```

6. Besides the results shown earlier, R-INLA can also report two types of goodness-of-fit measures, namely CPO $p(y_i \mid y_{-i})$ and the probability integral transforms $P(Y_i^{nova} \leq y_i \mid y_{-i})$ (PIT). To add these in the output, just add `cpo=TRUE` in the list of the argument `control.compute` for the function `inla`. The values are then returned as part of the output from `inla`. A list of all possible values can be obtained by the command `names(resultados_INLA)`. Of the 51 possible ones, we list only a few:

```
> names(resultado_INLA)
 [1] "names.fixed"
 [2] "summary.fixed"
 [3] "marginals.fixed"
 [4] "summary.lincomb"
 [5] "marginals.lincomb"
 [6] "size.lincomb"
 [7] "summary.lincomb.derived"
 [8] "marginals.lincomb.derived"
 [9] "size.lincomb.derived"
[10] "mlik"
[11] "cpo"
[12] "po"
[13] "waic"
...
[18] "summary.linear.predictor"
[19] "marginals.linear.predictor"
[20] "summary.fitted.values"
[21] "marginals.fitted.values"
...
[27] "offset.linear.predictor"
...
[51] "model.matrix"
```

One can then save the values of these two measures of fit in an object, for example `CPO_PIT` below, and use, for further analysis, for graphs, etc.

```
> CPO_PIT<-resultado_INLA$cpo
> names(CPO_PIT)
[1] "cpo"      "pit"      "failure"
> class(CPO_PIT)
[1] "list"
> summary(CPO_PIT$cpo)
    Min.   1st Qu.   Median     Mean   3rd Qu.      Max.
0.0003652 0.0486900 0.0741300 0.0673100 0.0905200 0.0924000
> summary(CPO_PIT$pit)
    Min.   1st Qu.   Median     Mean   3rd Qu.      Max.
```

```
0.0004578 0.2769000 0.5046000 0.5013000 0.7493000 0.9961000
> summary(CPO_PIT$failure)
   Min. 1st Qu.  Median    Mean 3rd Qu.    Max.
      0       0       0       0       0       0
```

Extreme CPO values indicate unusual "surprise" observations, and extreme PIT values indicate outliers. A histogram of the PIT probabilities that appears far from uniform is evidence for a model misfit. Corresponding to the information in CPO_PIT$failure above, no observation is considered surprising or discordant.

7. To obtain a graphical representation, one can use the plot() command. The function has various boolean arguments. By default, the arguments are "TRUE." Thus, the command

```
  plot(resultado_INLA)
# or in separate windows
  plot(resultado_INLA,single = TRUE)
```

generates plots of the posterior densities of fixed and random effects, of posterior densities for the precision parameters, of a sequence of means and 0.025 and 0.975 posterior quantiles of the random effects and linear predictors, of the CPO and PIT values, and corresponding histograms. If desired, selected plots can be produced by choosing "FALSE" for the boolean argument corresponding to the graphs that are not wanted. For example, to get only the posterior densities for the precision parameters, use:

```
plot(resultado_INLA,
   plot.fixed.effects = FALSE,
   plot.lincomb = FALSE,
   plot.random.effects = FALSE,
   plot.hyperparameters = TRUE,
   plot.predictor = FALSE,
   plot.q = FALSE,
   plot.cpo = FALSE)
```

to get Figure 9.5.

8. R-INLA works with precision parameters (inverse variance). However, in general, inference for standard deviations is of more interest. It is possible to use a set of functions in INLA to calculate quantiles, expected values of original parameters, and also to obtain samples from marginal posterior distributions. To get posterior means of the standard deviations $\sigma = 1/\sqrt{\tau}$ and $\sigma_a = 1/\sqrt{\tau_a}$, use the following commands:

```
> names(resultado_INLA$marginals.hyperpar)
[1] "Precision for the Gaussian observations"
[2] "Precision for ID"
```

PostDens [Precision for the Gaussian observations]

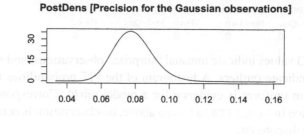

PostDens [Precision for ID]

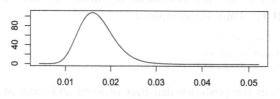

Figure 9.5 Posterior densities for τ and τ_a

```
> tau<-resultado_INLA$marginals.hyperpar$
+"Precision for the Gaussian observations"
> sigma<-inla.emarginal(function(x) 1/sqrt(x), tau)
> sigma
[1] 3.588387
> tau_a<-resultado_INLA$marginals.hyperpar$"Precision for ID"
> sigma_a<-inla.emarginal(function(x) 1/sqrt(x), tau_a)
> sigma_a
[1] 7.813781
```

Alternatively, to get the posterior distribution of random effect standard deviations, one can use the commands:

```
> sigmas<-inla.contrib.sd(resultado_INLA,nsamples=1000)
> names(sigmas)
[1] "samples" "hyper"
> sigmas$hyper
                                  mean      sd    2.5%    97.5%
sd for the Gaussian observations 3.59079 0.25221 3.1267 4.1120
sd for ID                        7.79427 0.88068 6.2625 9.6867
> head(sigmas$samples)
     sd for the Gaussian observations sd for ID
[1,]                        3.407485  8.287859
[2,]                        3.775560  6.945835
```

```
[3,]                               3.912179  9.931287
[4,]                               3.282005 10.068471
[5,]                               3.736729  7.386682
[6,]                               3.808289  9.027061
```

The object `sigmas` above includes in `samples` a vector of posterior simulated standard deviations.

9. To get random samples from marginal posteriors, use the function `inla.rmarginal()` in the following way (illustrated for β_3):

```
> names(resultado_INLA$marginals.fixed) [
1] "(Intercept)" "z1"        "z2"          "z3"          "z"
> dens_z3<-resultado_INLA$marginals.fixed$z3
> amostra_z3<-inla.rmarginal(1000,dens_z3)
> summary(amostra_z3)
   Min. 1st Qu.  Median    Mean 3rd Qu.     Max.
 0.5421  3.5580  4.1580  4.1630  4.7880   7.1570
```

More information about the functions that are used to operate on marginal distributions is obtained via the help command `?inla.marginal`.

10. One of these functions, `inla.hpdmarginal()`, allows getting HPD credible intervals for the model parameters. To obtain these intervals for the parameters corresponding to the fixed effects in the linear predictor, one can either get them individually, or get all in one command, as illustrated here for a 95% interval,

```
> HPD<-NULL
> for(i in 1:5){
    HPD[[i]]<-inla.hpdmarginal
    (0.95, resultado_INLA$marginals.fixed[[i]])}
> HPD
[[1]]
                 low      high
level:0.95 13.82332 20.66469

[[2]]
                 low      high
level:0.95 -0.05260815 9.58653

[[3]]
                 low      high
level:0.95 -0.1184688 0.4263571

[[4]]
                 low      high
level:0.95 2.384431 5.958083

[[5]]
```

```
                    low             high
level:0.95 -0.1759522 -0.03584334
```

and for the model hyperparameters,

```
> names(resultado_INLA$marginals.hyper)
[1] "Precision for the Gaussian observations"
[2] "Precision for ID"
> HPDhyper<-NULL
> for(i in 1:2){
+ HPDhyper[[i]]<-inla.hpdmarginal
+ (0.95, resultado_INLA$marginals.hyper[[i]])}
> HPDhyper
[[1]]
                    low           high
level:0.95 0.0574843 0.1011766

[[2]]
                    low           high
level:0.95 0.009948865 0.02469588
```

As expected, the HPD intervals for the fixed effect parameters practically coincide with the equal tail intervals in the summary results. The same is not true for the precision parameters.

Problems

9.1 *FEV Data.* Rosner (1999) reports on a study of lung capacity and smoking on $n = 654$ youths aged 3 – 19 years. Lung capacity y_i is measured as forced expiratory volume (FEV). Covariates include age (x_{i1}) and an indicator of smoking (x_{i2}). The same data are also analyzed by Chistensen et al. (2011: ch. 7).

Set up a regression of y_i on age (x_{i1}), adjusting intercept and slope for smoking (x_{i2}), that is, a normal linear regression for $y_i = b_0 + b_1 x_{i1} + b_2 x_{i2} + b_3 x_{i1} x_{i2} + \epsilon_{ij}$. The data are available as the data set `fev` in the R package *tmle*. Set up inference using OpenBUGS, JAGS, Stan, or INLA. Does FEV differ by smoking? Does smoking affect the increase of lung capacity with age? Is the interaction term needed?

9.2 Consider any of the examples in the OpenBUGS manual, `www.openbugs.net/w/Examples`. Implement inference in JAGS or Stan or OpenBUGS.

9.3 Consider the *Epilepsy* study reported in the OpenBUGS manual, `www.openbugs.net/Examples/Epil.html`. Implement inference using R-INLA. Show the marginal posterior distributions for the logistic regression coefficients a_j. Compare versus a simplified model without extra-Poisson variation (that is, without the b_{jk} random effect).

9.4 Consider the *Salmonella* dose–response study in the OpenBUGS manual, www.openbugs.net/Examples/Salm.html. Implement inference using R-INLA. Plot the estimated dose-response curve of mean outcome versus dose. Include pointwise 95% credible bands.

9.5 Consider the *surgical institution rating* example in the OpenBUGS manual, www.openbugs.net/Examples/Surgical.html. Implement inference using R-INLA. Show a boxplot of marginal posterior distribution for failure rates r_i, marking posterior mean, median, and quartiles under the dependent model that borrows strength across hospitals.

9.6 *Variational Bayes.* Consider the *rats* example in the OpenBUGS manual, www.openbugs.net/Examples/Rats.html. Code the example in Stan and use the following code fragment to implement posterior inference.

```
# assume the STAN model is coded in the file "rats.stan"
rats_model <- stan_model(file = "rats.stan")
# MCMC posterior simulation
rats_fit <- sampling(rats_model, data=data,
    iter=2000, warmup=1000, chains=4, seed=123)
# use vb() to implement variational inference
rats_fit_vb <- vb(rats_model, data=data,
    output_samples=2000, seed=123)
```

Hint: Use a centered parametrization with an overall mean α_0 and animal-specific offsets $\alpha_i \sim N(0, \sigma_\alpha^2)$. See also the implementation in https://gist.github.com/bakfoo/2447eb7d551ff256706a

Appendix A

Probability Distributions

For reference we include a brief summary of distributions that are used throughout the text. Where multiple parametrizations are in use, the following summary lists the specific parametrizations that are used in the text. We use $f(\cdot)$ generically for probability mass functions for discrete random variables and density functions for continuous random variables. We use $C_k^n = k!(n-k)!/n!$ to denote binomial coefficients, $B(a, b) = \Gamma(a)\Gamma(b)/\Gamma(a+b)$ for the beta function, and in general $B(a) = \Pi_j \Gamma(a_j)/\Gamma(\sum_j a_j)$ for $a = (a_1, \ldots, a_k)$. We write μ, σ^2 for mean and variance, μ_i and σ_i^2 for marginal mean and variance of the i-th component, σ_{ij} for covariance, and Σ for the covariance matrix of a random vector. Notation like $a_\bullet$ indicates summation over all coordinates of a, i.e., $\sum_{i=1}^{c+1} a_i$ when $a = (a_1, \ldots, a_{c+1})$, assuming that the dimension of a is understood from the context. Finally, S_c denotes the c-dimensional simplex and $\mathbb{N}_0$ are the non-negative integers.

Discrete Distributions

Binomial: $x \sim \text{Bi}(n, p)$, $x \in \{0, \ldots, n\}$;
$\quad f(x) = C_x^n p^x(1-p)^{n-x}$, $n \in \mathbb{N}$, $0 < p < 1$
$\quad \mu = np$, $\sigma^2 = np(1-p)$.
Bernoulli: $\text{Ber}(p) = \text{Bi}(n = 1, p)$.

Beta-binomial: $x \sim \text{BeBin}(n, a, b)$, $x \in \{0, \ldots, n\}$
$\quad f(x) = C_x^n B(a + x, b + n - x)/B(a, b)$, $a > 0, b > 0, n \in \mathbb{N}$
$\quad \mu = na/(a + b)$, $\sigma^2 = nab(a + b + n)/[(a + b)^2(a + b + 1)]$.

Note: A $\text{BeBin}(n, a, b)$ distribution is a mixture of a $\text{Bi}(n, \theta)$ with respect to $\theta \sim \text{Be}(a, b)$.

Negative binomial: $x \sim \text{NBin}(r, \theta)$, $x \in \mathbb{N}_0$;
$\quad f(x) = C_x^{x+r-1}(1 - \theta)^r \theta^x$, $0 < \theta < 1$, $r \in \mathbb{N}$;
$\quad \mu = r\theta/(1 - \theta)$ and $\sigma^2 = r\theta/(1 - \theta)^2$.
Geometric: $\text{Geo}(\theta) = \text{NBin}(1, \theta)$.

Beta-negative binomial: $x \sim \text{BeNBin}(r, \alpha, \beta)$, $x \in \mathbb{N}_0$,

$$f(x) = C^{r+x}_{r-1} \frac{B(\alpha + r, \beta + x)}{B(\alpha, \beta)}, \; r \in \mathbb{N}, \; \alpha > 0, \; \beta > 0$$

$\mu = r\frac{\beta}{\alpha-1}$ $(\alpha > 1)$ and $\sigma^2 = \frac{r\beta}{\alpha-1} \left[\frac{\alpha+\beta+r-1}{\alpha-2} + \frac{r\beta}{(\alpha-1)(\alpha-2)} \right]$ $(\alpha > 2)$.

Note: A BeNBin(r, α, β) distribution is the mixture of an NBin(r, θ) distribution with respect to $\theta \sim Be(\alpha, \beta)$.

Poisson: $x \sim \text{Poi}(\lambda)$, $x \in \mathbb{N}_0$;
$f(x) = e^{-\lambda} \lambda^x / x!$, $\lambda > 0$
$\mu = \sigma^2 = \lambda$.

Poisson-gamma: $x \sim \text{PoiGa}(n, \alpha, \beta)$, $x \in \mathbb{N}_0$;

$$f(x) = \frac{\Gamma(\alpha + x)}{x! \Gamma(\alpha)} \left(\frac{\beta}{\beta + n} \right)^\alpha \left(\frac{n}{\beta + n} \right)^x, \; \alpha > 0, \; \beta > 0, \; n \in \mathbb{N}$$

$\mu = n\alpha/\beta$ and $\sigma^2 = n\alpha(\beta + n)/\beta^2$.

Note: A PoiGa(n, α, β) distribution is the mixture of a *Poi*$(n\lambda)$ distribution with respect to $\lambda \sim Ga(\alpha, \beta)$.

Hypergeometric: $x \sim \text{HpG}(N, M, n)$, $x \in \{\underline{n}, \dots, \overline{n}\}$ with $\overline{n} = \min\{n, M\}$, $\underline{n} = \max\{0, n - (N - M)\}$;

$$f(x) = \frac{C^M_x C^{N-M}_{n-x}}{C^N_n}, \; N \in \mathbb{N}, M \in \{0, \dots, N\}, n \in \{1, \dots, N\};$$

$\mu = n\frac{M}{N}$ and $\sigma^2 = n\frac{N-n}{N-1}\frac{M}{N}\left(1 - \frac{M}{N}\right)$.

Continuous Distributions

Uniform: $x \sim \text{U}(\alpha, \beta)$, $\alpha \leq x \leq \beta$;
$f(x) = 1/(\beta - \alpha)$, $\alpha < \beta$, $\alpha, \beta \in \mathbb{R}$;
$\mu = (\beta + \alpha)/2$ and $\sigma^2 = (\beta - \alpha)^2/12$.
Note: We also write U(S) for a uniform distribution over a set S.

Beta: $x \sim \text{Be}(\alpha, \beta)$, $0 \leq x \leq 1$;

$$f(x) = \frac{\Gamma(\alpha + \beta)}{\Gamma(\alpha)\Gamma(\beta)} x^{\alpha-1} (1 - x)^{\beta-1}, \; \alpha > 0, \; \beta > 0;$$

$\mu = \alpha/(\alpha + \beta)$ and $\sigma^2 = \alpha\beta/[(\alpha + \beta)^2(\alpha + \beta + 1)]$.

Normal: $x \sim N(\mu, \sigma^2)$, $x \in \mathbb{R}$;

$f(x) = \frac{1}{\sqrt{2\pi}\sigma} e^{-(x-\mu)^2/2\sigma^2}$, $\mu \in \mathbb{R}$, $\sigma^2 > 0$;

$E(x) = \mu$ and $\text{Var}(x) = \sigma^2$.

Note: Alternative parametrizations use the precision, $1/\sigma^2$, or the standard deviation, σ, as the second parameter. WinBUGS, JAGS, and INLA use precision, STAN and R use standard deviation.

Gamma: $x \sim \text{Ga}(\alpha, \beta)$, $x \geq 0$;

$f(x) = \frac{\beta^\alpha}{\Gamma(\alpha)}, e^{-\beta x} x^{\alpha-1}$, $\alpha > 0$, $\beta > 0$;

$\mu = \alpha/\beta$ and $\sigma^2 = \alpha/\beta^2$.

Exponential: $\text{Exp}(\lambda) = \text{Ga}(1, \lambda)$.

Chi-square: $\chi^2(n) = \text{Ga}(n/2, 1/2)$.

Erlang: $\text{Erl}(k, \lambda) = \text{Ga}(k, \lambda)$, $k \in \mathbb{N}$.

Inverse gamma: $x \sim \text{IGa}(\alpha, \beta)$, $x \geq 0$;

$f(x) = \frac{\beta^\alpha}{\Gamma(\alpha)} e^{-\beta/x} x^{-\alpha-1}$, $\alpha > 0$, $\beta > 0$;

$\mu = \beta/(\alpha - 1)$, $\alpha > 1$ and $\sigma^2 = \beta^2/[(\alpha - 1)^2(\alpha - 2)]$, $\alpha > 2$.

Weibull: $x \sim \text{Weib}(\lambda, k)$, $x \geq 0$;

$f(x) = \frac{k}{\lambda} \left(\frac{x}{\lambda}\right)^{k-1} e^{-(x/\lambda)^k}$, $\lambda > 0$, $k > 0$;

$\mu = \lambda\Gamma(1 + \frac{1}{k})$ and $\sigma^2 = \lambda^2\Gamma(1 + \frac{2}{k}) - \mu^2$.

Note: An alternative parametrization uses $\delta = k/\lambda$ instead of λ.

Rayleigh: $\text{Ral}(\sigma) = \text{Weib}(\lambda = \sigma\sqrt{2}, k = 2)$.

Note: With $\delta = 1/\sigma^2$, we get $f(x) = \delta e^{-\delta x^2/2}$.

Student t: $x \sim t(\lambda, \delta; n)$, $x \in \mathbb{R}$;

$$f(x) = c\left[1 + \frac{(x - \lambda)^2}{\nu\delta}\right]^{-\frac{\nu+1}{2}}, \quad c = [B(\nu/2, 1/2)]^{-1}(\nu\delta)^{-1/2}$$

$\mu = \lambda$, $\nu > 1$ and $\sigma^2 = \frac{\nu}{\nu-2}\delta$, $\nu > 2$.

Gamma-Gamma: $x \sim \text{GaGa}(n, \alpha, \beta)$ $x > 0$;

$$f(x|n, \alpha, \beta) = \frac{\beta^\alpha}{B(n, \alpha)} \frac{x^{n-1}}{(\beta + x)^{\alpha+n}}, \alpha > 0, \beta > 0, n \in \mathbb{N}$$

$\mu = n\beta/(\alpha - 1)$, $\alpha > 1$ and $\sigma^2 = n\beta^2(n + \alpha - 1)/[(\alpha - 1)^2(\alpha - 2)]$, $\alpha > 2$.

Note: A $GaGa(n, \alpha, \beta)$ distribution is the mixture of a $\text{Ga}(n, \lambda)$ distribution with respect to $\lambda \sim \text{Ga}(\alpha, \beta)$.

Normal/IGa: $(x, w) \sim \text{NIGa}(\lambda, \nu, a, b)$, $x \in \mathbb{R}$, $w > 0$

$f(x, w) = f(x \mid w) f(w)$ with $x \mid w \sim N(\lambda, w/\nu)$ and $w \sim \text{IGa}(a, b)$, $\lambda \in \mathbb{R}$, $\nu > 0$, $a > 0$, $b > 0$.

Note: Marginally, $x \sim t(\lambda, \delta, \nu)$ is Student t with $\delta = b/(a\nu)$, $\nu = 2a$.

Pareto: $x \sim \mathrm{Pa}(a, b)$, $x \geq b$;

$f(x) = ab^a/x^{a+1}$, $a > 0$, $b > 0$,

$\mu = ab/(a-1)$, $a > 1$ and $\sigma^2 = b^2 a/[(a-1)^2(a-2)]$, $a > 2$.

Fisher–Snedecor: $x \sim F_{(\alpha,\beta)}$, $x > 0$

$$f(x) = \frac{\alpha^{\alpha/2}\beta^{\beta/2}}{B\,(\alpha/2, \beta/2)}\, x^{\alpha/2-1}(\alpha x + \beta)^{-(\alpha+\beta)/2},\ \ \alpha > 0,\ \beta > 0;$$

$\mu = \beta/(\beta - 2)$, $\beta > 2$, and $\sigma^2 = 2\beta^2(\alpha + \beta - 2)/[\alpha(\beta-2)^2(\beta-4)]$, $\beta > 4$.

Note: $x \sim F_{(\alpha,\beta)}$ can be derived as the distribution of
1. $x = (x_1/\alpha)/(x_2/\beta)$, where $x_1 \sim \chi^2_{(\alpha)}$ independently of $x_2 \sim \chi^2_{(\beta)}$; or,
2. $x = \beta y/[\alpha(1-y)]$ where $y \sim Be(\alpha/2, \beta/2)$.

Multivariate Distributions

Dirichlet: $\theta \sim \mathrm{D}_c(a)$, $\theta \in S_c$,

$$f(\theta) = \frac{\Gamma(a_\bullet)}{\prod_{i=1}^{c+1}\Gamma(a_i)}\ \prod_{i=1}^{c+1}\theta_i^{a_i-1},\ \ a_i \in \mathbb{R}^+, i = 1, \dots, c+1;\ \theta_{c+1} = 1 - \theta_\bullet,$$

$\mu_i = a/a_\bullet$, $\sigma_i^2 = \mu_i(1 - \mu_i)/(a_\bullet + 1)$ and $\sigma_{ij} = -\mu_i\mu_j/(a_\bullet + 1)$, $i \neq j$.

Multinomial: $x \sim M_c(n, \theta)$, $x = (x_1, \dots, x_{c+1})$, $x_i \in \mathbb{N}_0$, $\sum_{i=1}^c x_i \leq n$ and $x_{c+1} = n - \sum_{i=1}^c x_i$

$$f(x) = \frac{n!}{\prod_{i=1}^{c+1}x_i!}\ \prod_{i=1}^{c+1}\theta_i^{x_i},\ \theta \in S_c,\ \theta_{c+1} = 1 - \theta_\bullet$$

$\mu = n\theta$ and $\Sigma = n(\mathrm{diag}(\theta_1, \dots, \theta_c) - \theta\theta')$.

Multinomial-Dirichlet: $x \sim \mathrm{MD}_k(n, \alpha)$ for $x = (x_1, \dots, x_k)$, with $x_i \in \{0, 1, 2, \dots, n\}$, $\sum_{i=1}^k x_i \leq n$, $x_{k+1} = n - \sum_{i=1}^k x_i$

$$f(x) = \frac{n!}{\prod_{i=1}^{k+1}x_i!}\,\frac{B(\{\alpha_i + x_i\})}{B(\alpha)},\ \alpha = (\alpha_1, \dots, \alpha_k, \alpha_{k+1}),\ \alpha_i > 0,\ n \in \mathbb{N}$$

$\mu_i = nm_i$, $\sigma_i^2 = nm_i(1 - m_i)\frac{\alpha_\bullet + n}{\alpha_\bullet + 1}$ and $\sigma_{ij} = -nm_im_j\frac{\alpha_\bullet + n}{\alpha_\bullet + 1}$, where $m_j = \alpha_j/\alpha_\bullet$.

Note: An $\mathrm{MD}_k(n, \alpha)$ distribution is the mixture of an $M_k(n, \theta)$ distribution with respect to $\theta \sim \mathrm{D}_k(\alpha)$.

Multivariate normal: $x \sim N_k(m, V)$ for $x \in \mathbb{R}^k$

$$f(x) = (2\pi)^{-k/2}|V|^{-1/2}e^{-\frac{1}{2}(x-m)'V^{-1}(x-m)},\ m \in \mathbb{R}^k,$$

V is a positive definite $k \times k$ matrix;
$\mu = m$ and $\Sigma = V$.

Wishart: $X \sim W(s, A)$, X a $(k \times k)$ non-negative definite matrix, and $s > k + 1$, with

$$f(X) = c|A|^s \, |X|^{s-(k+1)/2} e^{-tr(AX)}, \quad c = \frac{\pi^{-k(k-1)/4}}{\Pi_{j=1}^{k} \Gamma\left(\frac{2s+1-j}{2}\right)}$$

$\mu = sA^{-1}$ and $\text{Var}(X_{ij}) = s(v_{ij}^2 + v_{ii}v_{jj})$ with $V = [v_{ij}] = A^{-1}$.

Multivariate Student t: $x \sim t_k(m, V; \nu)$ for $x \in \mathbb{R}^k$

$$f(x) = \frac{\Gamma((\nu + k)/2)}{\Gamma(\nu/2) \, [\Gamma(1/2)]^k} \, \nu^{-k/2} |V|^{-1/2} \left[1 + \frac{1}{\nu}(x - m)'V^{-1}(x - m)\right]^{-\frac{\nu+k}{2}},$$

with $m \in \mathbb{R}^k$, V a positive definite $k \times k$ matrix;

$\mu = m$, $\nu > 1$, and $\Sigma = \frac{\nu}{\nu-2} V$ $\nu > 2$.

Note: A $t_k(m, V; \nu)$ distribution is the mixture of an $N_k(m, wV)$ distribution with respect to $w \sim \text{IGa}(\nu/2, \nu/2)$.

Multivariate normal/Wishart: $(x, W) \sim \text{NWi}_k(m, v, \alpha, \Omega)$ for $x \in \mathbb{R}^k$ and W a positive definite $k \times k$ matrix,
$f(x, W) = f(x \mid W) f(W)$ with $x \mid W \sim N_k(m, W/v))$, $W \sim \text{Wi}_k(\alpha, A)$, $\alpha > \frac{k-1}{2}$, A positive definite $k \times k$ matrix.

Note: Marginally $x \sim t_k(\mu, \alpha A^{-1}/v, 2\alpha)$.

Appendix B

Programming Notes

Several of the problems in Chapter 6 and elsewhere require some programming, in particular the implementation of general univariate and bivariate random variate generation when a p.d.f. can be evaluated pointwise, and the implementation of iterative simulation in an MCMC simulation. For reference, we include brief R code fragments of possible implementations.

Random Variate Generation

Let X denote a random variable with univariate p.d.f. $f(x)$. Assuming that $\ln f(x)$ can be evaluated pointwise, the following function implements random variate generation. Evaluation up to a constant factor (or offset on the logarithmic scale) suffices. Let `lpdf(x)` denote a function that evaluates the log p.d.f. The function below assumes that `lpdf(x)` is vectorized, that is, for a vector x it returns a vector of $\ln f(x)$ values.

```
############################################################
# simulating from a univariate distribution


sim.x <- function(n=1, xgrid=NULL, lpdf, other=NULL)
{ ## simulates x ~ p(x) with
  ## lpdf  = log p(x) (a function)
  ##          need not be standardized
  ##          must evaluate p(x) for a vector of x values
  ## n     = number of r.v. generations
  ## K     = grid size
  ## xgrid = grid (equally spaced)
  ## other = (optional) additional parameters to be
  ##          used in the call to p(x), i.e., r
  if (is.null(xgrid)){
      cat("\n *** Error: need to specify xgrid for sim.x().\n")
      exit(-1)
  }
  delta <- xgrid[2]-xgrid[1] # grid size..

  if (is.null(other)) # no optional additional arguments
      lp <- lpdf(xgrid)
  else
      lp <- lpdf(xgrid,other)
```

```
pmf <- exp(lp-max(lp))
x <- sample(xgrid,n,replace=T,prob=pmf) +
    runif(n,min=-delta/2,max=+delta/2) # smear out x

return(x)
}
```

Bivariate Random Variate Generation

Let $X = (X_1, X_2)$ denote a bivariate random vector with p.d.f. $f(x_1, x_2)$. Assuming that $\ln f(x_1, x_2)$ can be evaluated pointwise, the following function implements random variate generation. As before, evaluation up to a constant suffices. Assume the function lpdf(x) evaluates the log p.d.f. for a bivariate vector x.

```
####################################################
# simulating from a bivariate distribution
sim.xy <- function(n=1, xgrid=NULL, ygrid=NULL, lpdf)
{ ## simulates (x,y) ~ p(x,y) with
  ## lpdf   = log p(x,y) (a function)
  ##          need not be standardized
  ## n      = number of r.v. generations
  ## K      = grid size
  ## xgrid  = grid (equally spaced)
  ## ygrid  = grid (equally spaced)
  if ( is.null(xgrid) | is.null(ygrid) ){
      cat("\n *** Error: need to specify xgrid for sim.x().\n")
      exit(-1)
  }
  dx <- xgrid[2]-xgrid[1]
  dy <- ygrid[2]-ygrid[1]

  xy <- cbind(sort(rep(xgrid,K)), rep(ygrid,K))
  ## a (K*K x 2) matrix with one row for each 2-dim grid point.
  lp <- apply(xy,1,lpdf)
  pmf <- exp(lp-max(lp))
  idx <- sample((1:nrow(xy)), n,replace=T,prob=pmf)
  dx <- runif(n, min=-dx/2, max=+dx/2) # smear out x
  dy <- runif(n, min=-dy/2, max=+dy/2) # smear out y
  XY <- xy[idx,] + cbind(dx,dy)
  return(XY)
}
```

MCMC Simulation

The last code fragment shows a typical Gibbs sampler implementation. The main function gibbs() implements the iteration over the steps of the MCMC simulation. The code implements a Gibbs sampler with two transition probabilities, generating parameters b and s^2 from the respective complete conditional posterior distributions.

```
init <- function()
  { # initialize par values
    fit <- lsfit(x, dta$Z)   # fits a least squares regr
    b <- fit$coef
    s2 <- var(fit$resid)
    th <- c(b,s2)
    return(th=list(b=b,s2=s2))
  }

gibbs <- function(niter=100)
  {
    th <- init()
    thlist <- NULL
    for(iter in 1:niter){
      th$b  <- sample.b(th)
      th$s2 <- sample.s2(th)
      thlist <- rbind(thlist,c(th$b,th$s2))
    }
    return(thlist)
  }

sample.b <- function(th)
  {# replace b by a draw from p(b | s2,y) = N(m,V)
    ## m = (X'X)^-1 X'y = least squares fit
    ## V^-1 = (X'X)*tau + S0^-1
    ## m    = V * (tau* X'y)
    tau <- 1/th$s2
    Vinv <- H*tau + S0inv
    V <- solve(Vinv)
    m <- V %*% (tau*t(W)%*%dta$Z)
    R <- chol(V)             # V = t(R) %*% R
    b <- rnorm(2,m=m) %*% R # b ~ N(m, V) as desired :-)
    return(b)
  }

sample.s2 <- function(th)
  { ## replace s2 by a draw from p(s2 | b,y)
    ## let tau=1/s2, then p(tau | b,y) = IG(a/2, b/2)
    ##     with a=n and b=S2=sum(Z[i]-Zhat[i])^2
    ## also, when v ~ IG(a,b) <=> 1/v ~ G(a,b), shape=a, rate=b
    b <- th$b
    n <- nrow(dta)
    Zhat <- W %*% c(b)       # need c(b) to make sure it's a col vector
    S2 <- sum((dta$Z-Zhat)^2)
    a1 <- a0+n
    b1 <- b0+S2
    tau <- rgamma(1,shape=a1/2, rate=b1/2)
    s2 <- 1/tau
    return(s2)
  }
```

References

Amaral Turkman, M. A. 1980. *Applications of predictive distributions*. PhD thesis, University of Sheffield. (Cited on page 13.)

Andrieu, C., Doucet, A., and Robert, C. P. 2004. Computational advances for and from Bayesian analysis. *Statistical Science*, **19**(1), 118–127. (Cited on page 129.)

Basu, D., and Pereira, C. A. B. 1982. On the Bayesian analysis of categorical data: the problem of nonresponse. *Journal of Statistical Planning and Inference*, **6**(4), 345–362. (Cited on page 40.)

Belitz, C., Brezger, A., Kneib, T., Lang, S., and Umlauf, N. 2013. *BayesX: Software for Bayesian Inference in Structured Additive Regression Models*. Version 2.1. (Cited on page 172.)

Berger, J. O. 1984. The robust Bayesian viewpoint (with discussion). Pages 63–144 of: Kadane, J. B. (ed.), *Robustness of Bayesian Analyses*. North-Holland. (Cited on page 1.)

Bernardo, J., and Smith, A. F. M. 2000. *Bayesian Theory*. Wiley. (Cited on pages 26 and 88.)

Best, N., Cowles, M., and Vines, S. 1995. *CODA Manual Version 0.30*. (Cited on pages 116 and 201.)

Bhattacharya, A., Pati, D., Pillai, N. S., and Dunson, D. B. 2015. Dirichlet–Laplace priors for optimal shrinkage. *Journal of the American Statistical Association*, **110**(512), 1479–1490. (Cited on page 134.)

Blangiardo, M., and Cameletti, M. 2015. *Spatial and Spatio-Temporal Bayesian Models with R-INLA*. Wiley. (Cited on pages 150 and 172.)

Blangiardo, M., Cameletti, M., Baio, G., and Rue, H. 2013. Spatial and spatio-temporal models with r-inla. *Spatial and Spatio-Temporal Epidemiology*, **4**(Supplement C), 33–49. (Cited on page 163.)

Blei, D. M., and Jordan, M. I. 2006. Variational inference for Dirichlet process mixtures. *Bayesian Analysis*, **1**(1), 121–143. (Cited on page 168.)

Blei, D. M., Kucukelbir, A., and McAuliffe, J. D. 2017. Variational inference: a review for statisticians. *Journal of the American Statistical Association*, **112**(518), 859–877. (Cited on pages 164, 165, and 171.)

Box, G. 1980. Sampling and Bayes inference in scientific modelling and robustness. *Journal of the Royal Statistical Society, A*, **143**, 383–430. (Cited on page 70.)

Box, G. 1983. An apology for ecumenism in statistics. Pages 51–84 of: Box, G., Leonard, T., and Wu, C.-F. (eds.), *Scientific Inference, Data Analysis, and Robustness*. Academic Press. (Cited on page 70.)

Brezger, A., Kneib, T., and Lang, S. 2005. BayesX: analyzing Bayesian structural additive regression models. *Journal of Statistical Software, Articles*, **14**(11), 1–22. (Cited on pages 172, 192, and 193.)

Burnham, K. P., and Anderson, D. R. 2002. *Model Selection and Multimodel Inference: A Practical Information-Theoretic Approach*. 2nd edn. Springer.

Carlin, B. P., and Chib, S. 1995. Bayesian model choice via Markov chain Monte Carlo. *Journal of the Royal Statistical Society, B*, **57**(3), 473–484. (Cited on page 136.)

Carlin, B. P., and Gelfand, A. E. 1991. An iterative Monte Carlo method for non-conjugate Bayesian analysis. *Statistics and Computing*, **1**(2), 119–128. (Cited on page 65.)

Carlin, B. P., and Louis, T. A. 2009. *Bayesian Methods for Data Analysis*. CRC Press. (Cited on pages viii and 78.)

Carpenter, B., Gelman, A., Hoffman, M., et al. 2017. Stan: a probabilistic programming language. *Journal of Statistical Software, Articles*, **76**(1), 1–32. (Cited on pages 172 and 186.)

Carvalho, C. M., Polson, N. G., and Scott, J. G. 2010. The horseshoe estimator for sparse signals. *Biometrika*, **97**(2), 465–480. (Cited on page 134.)

Celeux, G., Forbes, F., Robert, C. P., and Titterington, D. M. 2006. Deviance information criteria for missing data models. *Bayesian Analysis*, **1**(4), 651–673. (Cited on page 79.)

Chen, M.-H. 1994. Importance-weighted marginal Bayesian posterior density estimation. *Journal of the American Statistical Association*, **89**, 818–824. (Cited on page 58.)

Chen, M.-H., and Shao, Q. 1999. Monte Carlo estimation of Bayesian credible and HPD intervals. *Journal of Computational and Graphical Statistics*, **8**, 69–92. (Cited on page 47.)

Chen, M.-H., Shao, Q., and Ibrahim, J. G. 2000. *Monte Carlo Methods in Bayesian Computation*. Springer. (Cited on pages 54, 57, and 129.)

Chib, S. 1995. Marginal likelihood from the Gibbs output. *Journal of the American Statistical Association*, **90**(432), 1313–1321. (Cited on pages 129 and 130.)

Chib, S., and Jeliazkov, I. 2001. Marginal likelihood from the Metropolis–Hastings output. *Journal of the American Statistical Association*, **96**(453), 270–281. (Cited on pages 129 and 131.)

Christensen, R., Johnson, W., Hanson, T., and Branscum, A. 2011. *Bayesian Ideas and Data Analysis: An Introduction for Scientists and Statisticians*. CRC Press. (Cited on page viii.)

Cowles, M. K. 1994. *Practical issues in Gibbs sampler implementation with application to Bayesian hierarchical modelling of clinical trial data*. PhD thesis, University of Minnesota. (Cited on page 201.)

Cowles, M. K., and Carlin, B. P. 1996. Markov chain Monte Carlo convergence diagnostics: a comparative review. *Journal of the American Statistical Association*, **91**, 883–904. (Cited on pages 116 and 199.)

Damien, P., Wakefield, J., and Walker, S. 1999. Gibbs sampling for Bayesian non-conjugate and hierarchical models by using auxiliary variables. *Journal of the Royal Statistical Society, B*, **61**(2), 331–344. (Cited on page 106.)

Dawid, A. P. 1985. The impossibility of inductive inference. (invited discussion of

'Self-calibrating priors do not exist', by D. Oakes.). *Journal of the American Statistical Association*, **80**, 340–341. (Cited on page 14.)

Dellaportas, P., and Papageorgiou, I. 2006. Multivariate mixtures of normals with unknown number of components. *Statistics and Computing*, **16**(1), 57–68. (Cited on page 148.)

Dellaportas, P., Forster, J. J., and Ntzoufras, I. 2002. On Bayesian model and variable selection using MCMC. *Statistics and Computing*, **12**(1), 27–36. (Cited on pages 132, 137, and 138.)

Dempster, A. P., Laird, N. M., and Rubin, D. B. 1977. Maximum likelihood from incomplete data via the EM algorithm. *Journal of the Royal Statistical Society, B*, **39**(1), 1–38. (Cited on page 144.)

de Valpine, P., Turek, D., Paciorek, C. J., et al. 2017. Programming with models: Writing statistical algorithms for general model structures with NIMBLE. *Journal of Computational and Graphical Statistics*, **26**(2), 403–413. (Cited on page 172.)

Devroye, L. 1986. *Non-Uniform Random Variate Generation*. Springer. (Cited on page 43.)

Doucet, A., and Lee, A. 2018. Sequential Monte Carlo methods. Pages 165–190 of: Drton, M., Lauritzen, S. L., Maathuis, M., and Wainwright, M. (eds.), *Handbook of Graphical Models*. CRC. (Cited on page 60.)

Doucet, A., Freitas, N. D., and Gordon, N. 2001. *Sequential Monte Carlo Methods in Practice*. Springer. (Cited on page 60.)

Fahrmeir, L., and Tutz, G. 2001. *Multivariate Statistical Modeling Based on Generalized Linear Models*. Springer. (Cited on page 161.)

Gelfand, A. E. 1996. Model determination using sampling-based methods. Pages 145–161 of: Gilks, W. R., Richardson, S., and Spiegelhalter, D. J. (eds.), *Markov Chain Monte Carlo in Practice*. Chapman & Hall. (Cited on pages 70, 73, 75, and 85.)

Gelfand, A. E., and Dey, D. K. 1994. Bayesian model choice: asymptotics and exact calculations. *Journal of the Royal Statistical Society, B*, **56**, 501–514. (Cited on page 87.)

Gelfand, A. E., and Smith, A. F. M. 1990. Sampling-based approaches to calculating marginal densities. *Journal of the American Statistical Association*, **85**, 398–409. (Cited on pages 49, 57, 58, and 174.)

Gelfand, A. E., Hills, S., Racine-Poon, A., and Smith, A. F. M. 1990. Illustration of Bayesian inference in normal data models using Gibbs sampling. *Journal of the American Statistical Association*, **85**(412), 972–985. (Cited on page 166.)

Gelfand, A. E., Smith, A. F. M., and Lee, T. 1992. Bayesian analysis of constrained parameter and truncated data problems using Gibbs sampling. *Journal of the American Statistical Association*, **87**, 523–531.

Gelman, A., and Hill, J. 2006. *Data Analysis Using Regression and Multilevel/Hierarchical Models*. Cambridge University Press. (Cited on page 185.)

Gelman, A., and Meng, X. L. 1996. Model checking and model improvement. Pages 189–202 of: Gilks, W. R., Richardson, S., and Spiegelhalter, D. J. (eds.), *Markov Chain Monte Carlo in Practice*. Chapman & Hall. (Cited on page 73.)

Gelman, A., and Rubin, D. B. 1992. Inference from iterative simulation using multiple sequences. *Statistical Science*, **7**, 457–72. (Cited on page 199.)

Gelman, A., Carlin, J. B., Stern, H. S., et al. 2014a. *Bayesian Data Analysis*. Vol. 3. Chapman and &/CRC Press. (Cited on page viii.)

Gelman, A., Hwang, J., and Vehtari, A. 2014b. Understanding predictive information criterion for Bayesian models. *Statistics and Computing*, **24**, 997–1016.

Geman, S., and Geman, D. 1984. Stochastic relaxation, Gibbs distribution and the Bayesian restoration of images. *IEEE Transactions on Pattern Analysis and Machine Intelligence*, **6**, 721–741. (Cited on pages 90 and 98.)

Gentle, J. E. 2004. *Random Number Generation and Monte Carlo Methods*. 2nd edn. Springer. (Cited on page 43.)

Genz, A., and Kass, R. E. 1997. Subregion adaptative integration of functions having a dominant peak. *Journal of Computational and Graphical Statistics*, **6**, 92–111. (Cited on page 53.)

George, E. I., and McCulloch, R. 1997. Approaches for Bayesian variable selection. *Statistica Sinica*, **7**, 339–373. (Cited on pages 131, 132, and 133.)

George, E. I., and McCulloch, R. E. 1993. Variable selection via Gibbs sampling. *Journal of the American Statistical Association*, **88**(423), 881–889. (Cited on pages 131 and 132.)

Geweke, J. 1989. Bayesian inference in econometric models using Monte Carlo integration. *Econometrica*, **57**(02), 1317–39. (Cited on pages 52 and 68.)

Geweke, J. 1992. Evaluating the accuracy of sampling-based approaches to calculating posterior moments. In: *Bayesian Statistics 4*. Clarendon Press. (Cited on page 199.)

Geweke, J. 2004. Getting it right. *Journal of the American Statistical Association*, **99**(467), 799–804. (Cited on pages 127 and 128.)

Geyer, C. J. 1992. Practical Markov chain Monte Carlo (with discussion). *Statistical Science*, **7**, 473–511. (Cited on page 115.)

Gillies, D. 2001. Bayesianism and the fixity of the theoretical framework. Pages 363–379 of: Corfield, J., and Williamson, J. (eds.), *Foundations of Bayesianism*. Kluwer Academic Publishers. (Cited on page 12.)

Givens, G. H., and Hoeting, J. A. 2005. *Computational Statistics*. Wiley. (Cited on page 97.)

Gradshteyn, I., and Ryzhik, I. 2007. *Table of Integrals, Series, and Products*, Jeffrey, A., and Zwillinger, D. (eds.). Academic Press.

Green, P. J. 1995. Reversible jump Markov chain Monte Carlo computation and Bayesian model determination. *Biometrika*, **82**, 711–732. (Cited on page 138.)

Hastings, W. K. 1970. Monte Carlo sampling methods using Markov chains and their applications. *Biometrika*, **57**, 97–109. (Cited on page 90.)

Heidelberger, P., and Welch, P. 1983. Simulation run length control in the presence of an initial transient. *Operations Research*, **31**, 1109–1144. (Cited on page 199.)

Henderson, H. V., and Velleman, P. F. 1981. Building multiple regression models interactively. *Biometrics*, **37**, 391–411. (Cited on page 73.)

Hoff, P. D. 2009. *A First Course in Bayesian Statistical Methods*. Springer. (Cited on page viii.)

Hoffman, M. D., and Gelman, A. 2014. The No-U-Turn sampler: Adaptively setting path lengths in Hamiltonian Monte Carlo. *Journal of Machine Learning Research*, **15**(1), 1593–1623. (Cited on page 186.)

Jaynes, E. T. 1968. Prior probabilities. *IEEE Transactions on Systems, Science and Cybernetics*, **4**, 227–291. (Cited on page 22.)

Jaynes, E. T. 2003. *Probability Theory: The Logic of Science*. Cambridge University Press. (Cited on pages 13 and 21.)

Jordan, M. I., Ghahramani, Z., Jaakkola, T. S., and Saul, L. K. 1999. An introduction to variational methods for graphical models. *Machine Learning*, **37**(2), 183–233. (Cited on page 164.)

Karabatsos, G. 2015. A menu-driven software package for Bayesian regression analysis. *The ISBA Bulletin*, **22**, 13–16. (Cited on page 172.)

Kass, R. E., and Raftery, A. E. 1995. Bayes factors. *Journal of the American Statistical Association*, **90**, 773–795. (Cited on page 85.)

Kass, R. E., and Wasserman, L. 1996. The selection of prior distributions by formal rules. *Journal of the American Statistical Association*, **91**, 1343–1370. (Cited on page 17.)

Kempthorn, O., and Folks, L. 1971. *Probability, Statistics and Data Analysis*. Iowa State University Press. (Cited on page 7.)

Kneib, T., Heinzl, F., Brezger, A., Bove, D., and Klein, N. 2014. *BayesX: R Utilities Accompanying the Software Package BayesX*. R package version 0.2-9. (Cited on page 193.)

Korner-Nievergelt, F., von Felten, S., Roth, T., et al. 2015. *Bayesian Data Analysis in Ecology Using Linear Models with R, BUGS, and Stan*. Academic Press. (Cited on page 172.)

Kruschke, J. 2011. *Doing Bayesian Data Analysis: A Tutorial with R and BUGS*. Academic Press/Elsevier. (Cited on page 172.)

Kruschke, J. 2014. *Doing Bayesian Data Analysis: A Tutorial with R, JAGS and Stan*. Academic Press/Elsevier. (Cited on page 172.)

Kucukelbir, A., Tran, D., Ranganath, R., Gelman, A., and Blei, D. M. 2017. Automatic differentiation variational inference. *Journal of Machine Learning Research*, **18**(1), 430–474. (Cited on page 168.)

Kuhn, T. S. 1962. *The Structure of Scientific Revolutions*. University of Chicago Press. (Cited on page 5.)

Kuo, L., and Mallick, B. 1998. Variable selection for regression models. *Sankhya: The Indian Journal of Statistics, Series B*, **60**(1), 65–81. (Cited on page 132.)

Lauritzen, S. L., and Spiegelhalter, D. J. 1988. Local computations with probabilities on graphical structures and their application to expert systems. *Journal of the Royal Statistical Society, B*, **50**(2), 157–224. (Cited on page 174.)

Lin, D. 2013. Online learning of nonparametric mixture models via sequential variational approximation. Pages 395–403 of: *Proceedings of the 26th International Conference on Neural Information Processing Systems*. USA: Curran Associates Inc. (Cited on page 168.)

Lindgren, F., and Rue, H. 2015. Bayesian spatial modelling with R-INLA. *Journal of Statistical Software, Articles*, **63**(19), 1–25. (Cited on page 214.)

Lindgren, F., Rue, H., and Lindstrom, J. 2011. An explicit link between Gaussian fields and Gaussian Markov random fields: the stochastic partial differential equation approach. *Journal of the Royal Statistical Society, B*, **73**(4), 423–498. (Cited on page 214.)

Lindley, D. V. 1990. The 1988 Wald memorial lectures: the present position in Bayesian statistics. *Statistical Science*, **5**, 44–89. (Cited on page 10.)

Liu, J., and West, M. 2001. Combined parameter and state estimation in simulation-based filtering. Pages 197–223 of: Doucet, A., de Freitas, N., and Gordon, N. (eds.), *Sequential Monte Carlo Methods in Practice*. Springer. (Cited on page 64.)

Lunn, D., Spiegelhalter, D., Thomas, A., and Best, N. 2009. The BUGS project: Evolution, critique and future directions. *Statistics in Medicine*, **28**(25), 3049–3067. (Cited on page 174.)

MacEachern, S., and Berliner, L. 1994. Subsampling the Gibbs sampler. *The American Statistician*, **48**, 188–190.

Madigan, D., and York, J. 1995. Bayesian graphical models for discrete data. *International Statistical Review*, **63**, 215–232. (Cited on page 133.)

Marin, J.-M., Pudlo, P., Robert, C. P., and Ryder, R. J. 2012. Approximate Bayesian computational methods. *Statistics and Computing*, **22**(6), 1167–1180. (Cited on page 126.)

Mayo, D., and Kruse, M. 2001. Principles of inference and their consequences. Pages 381–403 of: Corfield, J., and Williamson, J. (eds.), *Foundations of Bayesianism*. Kluwer Academic Publishers. (Cited on page 9.)

Metropolis, N., Rosenbluth, A. W., Rosenbluth, M. N., Teller, A. H., and Teller, E. 1953. Equation of state calculations by fast computing machines. *J. Chem. Phys*, **21**, 1087–1092. (Cited on pages 90 and 97.)

Morris, J. S., Baggerly, K. A., and Coombes, K. R. 2003. Bayesian shrinkage estimation of the relative abundance of mRNA transcripts using SAGE. *Biometrics*, **59**, 476–486. (Cited on page 122.)

Neal, R. M. 1997. *Markov Chain Monte Carlo methods based on "slicing" the density function*. Technical Report. University of Toronto. (Cited on page 106.)

Neal, R. M. 2003. Slice sampling (with discussion). *Annals of Statistics*, **31**, 705–767. (Cited on page 106.)

Neal, R. M. 2011. MCMC using Hamiltonian dynamics. Chap. 5 of: Brooks, S., Gelman, A., Jones, G., and Meng, X.-L. (eds.), *Handbook of Markov Chain Monte Carlo*. Chapman & Hall / CRC Press. (Cited on pages 107 and 185.)

Neuenschwander, B., Branson, M., and Gsponer, T. 2008. Critical aspects of the Bayesian approach to phase I cancer trials. *Statistics in Medicine*, **27**, 2420–2439. (Cited on page 53.)

Newton, M. A., and Raftery, A. E. 1994. Approximate Bayesian inference by the weighted likelihood bootstrap (with discussion). *Journal of the Royal Statistical Society, B*, **56**, 1–48. (Cited on page 86.)

Ntzoufras, I. 2009. *Bayesian Modeling Using WinBUGS*. (Cited on page 172.)

O'Hagan, A. 2010. *Bayesian Inference, Vol. 2B*. 3rd edn. Arnold. (Cited on pages 1, 9, 14, and 17.)

O'Quigley, J., Pepe, M., and Fisher, L. 1990. Continual reassessment method: A practical design for phase 1 clinical trials in cancer. *Biometrics*, **46**(1), 33–48. (Cited on page 45.)

Park, T., and Casella, G. 2008. The bayesian lasso. *Journal of the American Statistical Association*, **103**(482), 681–686. (Cited on page 134.)

Patil, V. H. 1964. The Behrens–Fisher problem and its Bayesian solution. *Journal of the Indian Statistical Association*, **2**, 21. (Cited on page 33.)

Paulino, C. D., and Singer, J. M. 2006. *Análise de Dados Categorizados*. Editora Edgard Blücher.

Paulino, C. D., Soares, P., and Neuhaus, J. 2003. Binomial regression with misclassification. *Biometrics*, **59**, 670–675. (Cited on page 17.)

Paulino, C. D., Amaral Turkman, M. A., Murteira, B., and Silva, G. 2018. *Estatística Bayesiana*. 2nd edn. Fundacão Calouste Gulbenkian. (Cited on pages 17, 38, 54, 57, 84, 93, 158, and 199.)

Pitt, M. K., and Shephard, N. 1999. Filtering via simulation: Auxiliary particle filters. *Journal of the American Statistical Association*, **94**(446), 590–599. (Cited on pages 61, 62, and 63.)

Plummer, M. 2003. JAGS: a program for analysis of Bayesian graphical models using Gibbs sampling. In: Hornik, K., Leisch, F., and Zeileis, A. (eds.), *3rd International Workshop on Distributed Statistical Computing (DSC 2003)*. (Cited on page 172.)

Plummer, M. 2012. *JAGS Version 3.3.0 User Manual*. http://mcmc-jags.sourceforge.net, accessed on July 22, 2018. (Cited on page 181.)

Plummer, M., Best, N. G., Cowles, M. K., and Vines, S. K. 2006. CODA: Convergence diagnostics and output analysis for MCMC. *R News*, **6**(1), 7–11. (Cited on pages 116, 198, and 201.)

Polson, N. G., Stroud, J. R., and Müller, P. 2008. Practical filtering with sequential parameter learning. *Journal of the Royal Statistical Society, B*, **70**(2), 413–428. (Cited on page 64.)

Prado, R., and West, M. 2010. *Time Series: Modeling, Computation, and Inference*. Chapman & Hall/CRC Press. (Cited on page 64.)

Raftery, A. L., and Lewis, S. 1992. How many iterations in the Gibbs sampler? Pages 763–74 of: Bernardo, J., Berger, J., Dawid, A., and Smith, A. (eds.), *Bayesian Statistics IV*. Oxford University Press. (Cited on page 199.)

Raftery, A. E., Madigan, D., and Hoeting, J. A. 1997. Bayesian model averaging for linear regression models. *Journal of the American Statistical Association*, **92**(437), 179–191. (Cited on page 133.)

Richardson, S., and Green, P. J. 1997. On Bayesian analysis of mixtures with an unknown number of components (with discussion). *Journal of the Royal Statistical Society, B*, **59**(4), 731–792. (Cited on page 141.)

Rickert, J. 2018. A first look at NIMBLE. Blog: https://rviews.rstudio.com/2018/07/05/a-first-look-at-nimble/, accessed on July 16, 2018. (Cited on page 172.)

Ripley, B. D. 1987. *Stochastic Simulation*. Wiley. (Cited on pages 43 and 44.)

Robert, C. P. 1994. *The Bayesian Choice*. Springer. (Cited on pages 27 and 157.)

Robert, C. R., and Casella, G. 2004. *Monte Carlo Statistical Methods*. 2nd edn. New York: Springer. (Cited on pages 44 and 96.)

Rosner, B. 1999. *Fundamentals of Biostatistics*. Duxbury. (Cited on page 222.)

Ross, S. M. 2014. *Introduction to Probability Models*, 11th ed. Academic Press. (Cited on page 91.)

Rossi, P. E., Allenby, G. M., and McCulloch, R. 2005. *Bayesian Statistics and Marketing*. Wiley. (Cited on page 172.)

Ročková, V., and George, E. I. 2014. EMVS: The EM approach to Bayesian variable selection. *Journal of the American Statistical Association*, **109**(506), 828–846. (Cited on page 143.)

Rubinstein, R. Y. 1981. *Simulation and the Monte Carlo Method*. 1st edn. Wiley. (Cited on page 44.)

Rue, H., and Held, L. 2005. *Gaussian Markov Random Fields: Theory and Applications*. Chapman & Hall. (Cited on page 159.)

Rue, H., Martino, S., and Chopin, N. 2009. Approximate Bayesian inference for latent Gaussian models by using integrated nested Laplace approximations. *Journal of the Royal Statistical Society, B*, **71**(2), 319–392. (Cited on pages 150, 162, 163, 169, 214, and 217.)

Schofield, M. R., Barker, R. J., Gelman, A., Cook, E. R., and Briffa, K. 2016. A model-based approach to climate reconstruction using tree-ring data. *Journal of the American Statistical Association*, **2016**, 93–106. (Cited on page 185.)

Schwarz, G. 1978. Estimating the dimension of a model. *Annals of Statistics*, **6**, 461–466. (Cited on pages 77 and 83.)

Scott, S., Blocker, A., Bonassi, F., et al. 2016. Bayes and big data: the consensus Monte Carlo algorithm. *International Journal of Management Science and Engineering Management*, **11**(2), 78–88. (Cited on page 68.)

Shaw, J. E. H. 1988. Aspects of numerical integration and summarization. Pages 625–631 of: Bernardo, J. M., DeGroot, M. H., Lindley, D. V., and Smith, A. F. M. (eds.), *Bayesian Statistics 3*. Oxford: University Press. (Cited on page 52.)

Silverman, B. W. 1986. *Density Estimation for Statistics and Data Analysis*. London: Chapman and Hall.

Smith, A. F. M. 1991. Bayesian computation methods. *Phil. Trans. R. Soc. Lond. A*, **337**, 369–386.

Smith, A. F. M., and Gelfand, A. E. 1992. Bayesian statistics without tears. *The American Statistician*, **46**, 84–88. (Cited on page 58.)

Smith, B. 2007. BOA: An R package for MCMC output convergence assessment and posterior inference. *Journal of Statistical Software*, **21**, 1–37. (Cited on pages 116, 198, and 202.)

Spiegelhalter, D. J. 1986. Probabilistic prediction in patient management and clinical trials. *Statistics in Medicine*, **5**(5), 421–433. (Cited on page 174.)

Spiegelhalter, D. J., Best, N. G., Carlin, B. P., and van der Linde, A. 2002. Bayesian measures of model complexity and fit (with discussion). *Journal of the Royal Statistical Society, B*, **64**, 583–639. (Cited on pages 78 and 79.)

Stan Development Team. 2014. *RStan: The R Interface to Stan, Version 2.5.0*. (Cited on page 186.)

Sturtz, S., Ligges, U., and Gelman, A. 2005. R2WinBUGS: a package for running WinBUGS from R. *Journal of Statistical Software*, **12**(3), 1–16. (Cited on page 175.)

Tanner, M. A. 1996. *Tools for Statistical Inference*. 3rd edn. New York: Springer Verlag. (Cited on page 157.)

Tanner, M. A., and Wong, W. H. 1987. The calculation of posterior distributions by data augmentation. *Journal of the American Statistical Association*, **82**(398), 528–540. (Cited on page 105.)

Thall, P. F., Millikan, R. E., Müller, P., and Lee, S.-J. 2003. Dose-finding with two agents in phase i oncology trials. *Biometrics*, **59**(3), 487–496. (Cited on pages 126 and 127.)

Thomas, A., O'Hara, B., Ligges, U., and Sturtz, S. 2006. Making BUGS open. *R News*, **6**(01), 12–17. (Cited on page 172.)

Tibshirani, R. 1996. Regression shrinkage and selection via the Lasso. *Journal of the Royal Statistical Society, B*, **58**(1), 267–288. (Cited on page 134.)

Tierney, L. 1994. Markov chains for exploring posterior distributions. *Annals of Statistics*, **22**, 1701–1728. (Cited on page 96.)

Tierney, L. 1996. Introduction to general state-space Markov chain theory. Pages 61–74 of: Gilks, W., Richardson, S., and Spiegelhalter, D. (eds.), *In Markov Chain Monte Carlo in Practice*. Chapman. (Cited on page 91.)

Tierney, L., and Kadane, J. 1986. Accurate approximations for posterior moments and marginal densities. *Journal of The American Statistical Association*, **81**(03), 82–86. (Cited on pages 154 and 162.)

Tierney, L., Kass, R., and Kadane, J. 1989. Fully exponential laplace approximations to expectations and variances of nonpositive functions. *Journal of the American Statistical Association*, **84**(407), 710–716. (Cited on pages 156 and 157.)

Umlauf, N., Adler, D., Kneib, T., Lang, S., and Zeileis, A. 2015. Structured additive regression models: An r interface to BayesX. *Journal of Statistical Software, Articles*, **63**(21), 1–46. (Cited on pages 193, 194, and 195.)

Vehtari, A., and Ojanen, J. 2012. A survey of Bayesian predictive methods for model assessment, selection and comparison. *Statist. Surv.*, **6**, 142–228.

Vehtari, A., Gelman, A., and Gabry, J. 2017. Practical Bayesian model evaluation using leave-one-out cross-validation and WAIC. *Statistics and Computing*, **27**(5), 1413–1432. (Cited on pages 188 and 191.)

Walker, A. M. 1969. On the asymptotic behaviour of posterior distributions. *Journal of the Royal Statistical Society, B*, **31**(1), 80–88. (Cited on page 151.)

Wasserman, L. 2004. *All of Statistics*. Springer-Verlag. (Cited on page 14.)

Watanabe, S. 2010. Asymptotic equivalence of Bayes cross validation and widely applicable information criterion in singular learning theory. *Journal of Machine Learning Research*, **11**(Dec.), 3571–3594. (Cited on page 80.)

Welling, M., and Teh, Y. W. 2011. Bayesian learning via stochastic gradient Langevin dynamics. Pages 681–688 of: *Proceedings of the 28th International Conference on International Conference on Machine Learning*. Omnipress. (Cited on page 112.)

Zhang, Z., Chan, K. L., Wu, Y., and Chen, C. 2004. Learning a multivariate Gaussian mixture model with the reversible jump MCMC algorithm. *Statistics and Computing*, **14**(4), 343–355. (Cited on page 146.)

Index